THE UNCROWNED
KING OF IRELAND

THE UNCROWNED KING OF IRELAND

CHARLES STEWART PARNELL

HIS LOVE STORY AND POLITICAL LIFE

Katherine O' Shea

(MRS CHARLES STEWART PARNELL)

NONSUCH

First published in 1914
Copyright © in this edition 2005
Nonsuch Publishing Limited
The Mill, Brimscombe Port,
Stroud, Gloucestershire, GL5 2QG
www.nonsuch-publishing.com

© Katharine O' Shea 2005

The right of Katharine O' Shea to be identified as the Author
of this work has been asserted in accordance with the
Copyrights, Designs and Patents Act 1988.

A catalogue record for this book is available from the National Library.

ISBN 1 84588 534 1

Typesetting and origination by Nonsuch Publishing Limited
Printed in Great Britain

'No common soul was his; for good or ill
There was a mighty power'
HAWKSHAW – Sonnet IX

DEDICATED TO LOVE
'Had the whole rich world been in my power,
I should have singled out thee, only thee,
From the whole world's collected treasury.'
Moore

'No common soul was his; for good or ill
There was a mighty power'
HAWKSHAW

CONTENTS

Introduction	9
Preface	13
1 My Early Life	17
2. Family I At Rivenhall	21
3. Visitors At Rivenhall	25
4. Private Theatricals	31
5. A Memory Of Brighton	35
6. My Father's Death	39
7. My Marriage	43
8. Life In Madrid	47
9. Our Home At Bennington	53
10. A Day On The Downs	59
11. Beaufort Gardens	63
12. More Financial Difficulties	67
13. Captain O' Shea Enters Political Life	71
14. Mr Parnell And The Irish Party	79
15. The First Meeting With Mr Parnell	83
16. Early Correspondence	89
17. At Eltham	93
18. The Land League Trials	99
19. Parliamentary Associations	105
20. Hobbies And A Challenge	109
21. Astronomy And 'Sedition'	115
22. The Arrest Of Parnell	121
23. Kilmainham Days	125
24. More Kilmainham Letters	135
25. The 'Kilmainham Treaty'	145

26. The Phoenix Park Murders And After   151
27. Envoy To Gladstone   157
28. The Dawn Of Home Rule   165
29. The First Home Rule Bill   173
30. Mr Parnell In Danger – Founding Of The National League   177
31. A Winter Of Memories   185
32. Horses And Dogs   193
33. Captain O' Shea's Parliamentary Difficulties   197
34. Seaside Holidays   209
35. London Remembrances   215
36. The Parnell Commission   219
37. Brighton Haunts   227
38. The Divorce Case   233
39. A King At Bay   241
40. Captain O' Shea's Letters   249
41. Parnell As I Knew Him   271
42. Marriage, Illness And Death   277
Endnotes   288

INTRODUCTION

K ATHARINE O' SHEA, OR MRS Charles Stewart Parnell, as she preferred to be called after her short-lived marriage in 1891, is a completely underestimated woman.

The illicit sexual liaison of a great political leader, revealed in late 1890 by her husband Willie O' Shea's uncontested divorce suit, scandalised Victorian Britain and the non-conformist conscience and caused a deep split in Catholic and Nationalist opinion in Ireland and in the hitherto popular Irish Parliamentary Party.

Irish politics were traumatized for a generation by the fall of Parnell and the tragedy of his death in October 1891, as he fought a losing battle to retain his leadership.Some of the consequences of these events were even more long lasting – it frustrated hopes of Home Rule, which were not properly revived again for 20 years and, despite Gladstone's final effort, a second Home Rule bill was easily defeated in the House of Lords in 1894. Katharine, or 'Kitty' O' Shea as she was derisively called by the press and Parnell's opponents, served as the scapegoat. Never was the expression 'cherchez la femme' more aptly applied. Her many positive qualities and her real ability as a political aide and go-between were completely overshadowed.

In the decades after Parnell's death, some of his colleagues in the Irish Parliamentary Party published their reminiscences. To them, Parnell was often a distant and somewhat mysterious figure who, though admired by large numbers, allowed no one to come too close. His achievement, with the Land League and the Fenians, had been to galvanise and unite disparate Irish political forces behind a campaign to transform the system of land tenure by peaceful revolution in Ireland in order to achieve full internal self-government. This was a demand which Gladstone – and those in the Liberal Party prepared to follow him – were willing to concede in a hung parliament in 1886, but it split the Liberals three ways in the process. Both the Whigs round Lord Hartington and the Radicals round Joseph Chamberlain defected, eventually via the Liberal Unionists to the Conservative and Unionist Party. Nevertheless, Ireland up to 1890 seemed on the threshold of Home Rule – until scandal struck, the party was split, with the Liberals remaining in the political wilderness for 20 years, excepting a brief interval between 1892 and 1895.

The singular exception to Parnell's lack of intimacy with others was his relationship with the love of his life, Katharine O' Shea. She was a handsome and independent-minded woman, who was married in 1867 at the age of 22 to Willie O' Shea. From the beginning, even on honeymoon, she was bored, in later years left alone a lot and had a husband who continually incurred sizeable debts and was dependent on her relations (especially her aunt Mrs Ben Wood) to stay financially afloat. O' Shea, after various not very successful careers in the army, banking and stud-farming, became an Irish MP in 1880 while always refusing to take the party pledge.

In 1880, Mrs O' Shea was a politically very well connected hostess in London society – an mp's wife, niece of a liberal Lord Chancellor, and sister of a future field-marshal. After one or two rebuffs to her invitations, she made it her business to meet in person the young bachelor leader of the Irish Parliamentary Party in 1880, who was then at the height of his powers and much the same age as herself. They were immediately taken with each other. The relationship rapidly developed and within a few months he was writing letters to her as 'my own love' and 'dearest wifie'.

The two volumes, amounting in the original edition to some 500 pages of text, were then entitled *Charles Stewart Parnell: His Love Story and Political Life*. In many ways, however, they are more a personal memoir of Katharine O' Shea – first of her early life and marriage to Willie O' Shea, then her initial meeting with Parnell and their subsequent life together, including the substantial part she played in his political life. Very little is drawn from sources outside her memory and the letters and documents that were in her personal possession.

This book is essentially is three volumes rolled into one – a personal autobiography (up to Parnell's death) including highly romantic passages almost worthy of *Wuthering Heights,* the account of a close political collaborator and, finally, selected letters and speeches of Charles Stewart Parnell. It is not a biography of Parnell in any real sense, as it does not deal in any detail with the matters or aspects of his career in which she had no personal involvement. Nor does she say anything at all about her subsequent life. However, it is one of the most valuable and indispensable primary sources for historians and biographers. Katharine O' Shea is one of many spouses of famous people whose later writing and editorial work helped to keep their memories alive and to add greatly to the interest of what was known about them, even, in this case, at the risk of causing some mild further scandal.

The mood that dominates the book is that of romantic imagination. At her very first meeting in July 1880, there is a touch of romanctic chivalry echoing the courtly conventions of mediaeval literature: 'In leaning forward in the cab to say goodbye, a rose I was wearing in my bodice fell out on to my skirt. He picked it up and, touching it lightly with his lips, placed it in his buttonhole'. She later found it amongst his most private papers and when he died, she laid it upon his heart. Parnell was for her a man for whom it was worth breaking all the rules.

Their romance was fed by regular separation, by some months' imprisonment, the tragedy of the death of an infant child of theirs, by the clandestine nature of the relationship and by walks in wild conditions. Pacing up and down in the snow and moonlight, she told Parnell at her home in Eltham 'that the cloud shadows that flitted over the glistening whiteness were the phantoms of the hunters of King John's time, who used to hunt over this ground, renewing their sport in the moonlight'. She commented that Parnell loved to hear 'these little imaginations'.

On another occasion, they walked on a wild stormy day to the end of a pier and were tempted to throw themselves in and be free forever. 'As you will, my only love, but the children?' was her only remark, which brought him back to reality.

Towards the end, as his health finally broke, she looked into his 'deep, smouldering eyes' and knew that 'in the depth of those eyes was more than even my love could fathom, that in the martyrdom of our love was to be our reparation'.

There was a second persona, the 'dear Mrs O' Shea', to whom Parnell wrote letters setting out his political position, to be shown to Gladstone and others. No doubt, for many political reasons on both sides, Gladstone and Parnell had few direct meetings. Katharine O' Shea, with strong liberal connections of her own, acted as messenger and advocate with the Prime Minister and with the Liberal Chief Whip Lord Richard Grosvenor. She did this with considerable skill, tact and diplomacy. She also drafted letters and dealt with a lot of Parnell's affairs in his absence, though she had no contact with the Irish Parliamentary Party.

All this raised the question in the context of the divorce of 'who knew?' To know is one of the slipperiest terms in the English language, especially in a political context. Does one only know something if it is officially conveyed in a form that is signed and sealed so as to speak? Does one 'know' something, if it is only common knowledge or only fairly well established? Does one 'know' something, if one has only heard it as a rumour, or surmised in one's head that it may very possibly be so? Many denials of knowledge are in effect only denials of formal knowledge.

The Parnells were indignant at how Gladstone turned on them and sought to terminate Parnell's leadership in order to prolong Gladstone's own political career. His career eventually spanned almost 60 years and he did fulfil his hopes of becoming Prime Minister for a fourth and last time. Gladstone's ruthlessness in the name of morality, previously evident in the early 1880s, apparently had the power to shock a second time.

Historians have also discussed what Willie O' Shea knew. Again, the distinction between formal knowledge and reasonable deduction has to be borne in mind. It is pretty evident from O' Shea's letters that he harboured a burning anger against both his wife and Parnell – he was financially dependent on the one and for a time politically dependent on the other. After the forged letters in the *Times* had failed to unseat Parnell (indeed they assisted him to triumph), O' Shea, with the encouragement of his friend Joseph Chamberlain, sprung the surprise of a divorce suit. This was soon after the death of 'Aunt Ben' and done in the hopes of an office from Chamberlain, which of course never came. Because Parnell wanted to marry Katharine, he refused to defend the suit. The implication of Katharine's account is that O' Shea had his own affairs, which were a matter of total indifference to her.

The final element of the book is a lot of documentation, not only of the love affair, but of the politics and the negotiations. At her son Gerard O' Shea's insistence, a chapter containing his father's letters showing his efforts to act as an intermediary were published as well.

Despite playing an extraordinary role in the course of Irish history, Katharine was never able to accompany Parnell to Ireland. Nevertheless, she had no difficulty empathising with the Irish cause, nor did she take umbrage at the fact that Parnell was strongly anti-English. Though the desire never to be too long away from her influenced Parnell, especially in relation to the Kilmainham Treaty of 1882 which released him from jail, there is no evidence that she tried to influence him in a more conciliatory pro-British direction, as can at least be speculated about in the course of the friendship a generation later between Michael Collins and Hazel Lavery.

Katharine did not attempt to take Parnell away from Ireland, nor did she discourage him from fighting his last heroic battles. Curiously, she did see him as English, because he was of English descent. There is no evidence Parnell saw himself in that light, but her view may also have been coloured by the way in which most of Ireland repudiated Parnell. Indeed, among his patriot ancestors, he may have been particularly influenced by his maternal grandfather Admiral Charles Stewart, after whom he was named, an American hero of the war of 1812. Parnell at the end of his life believed he had brought matters to the point where self-government had become an inevitability, simply only a matter of time. He wanted to use his stepping down from the leadership as a bargaining-counter to secure more definite assurances from the Liberals on Home Rule.

The memoir contains no evidence that Katharine was upset by the vitriol thrown at her at a distance by public opinion in Ireland, the bishops and above all Tim Healy. Healy, though he became the first Governor-General of the Irish Free State, never lived down his misogynistic opportunism and purple rhetoric of that time. A significant – though much reduced – following remained with Parnell, both inside and outside of the party, including many of the most advanced nationalists. Both sides damaged themselves, but to have remained a Parnellite after all the hysteria had subsided was subsequently viewed as being a badge of honour. A myth built up of the lost or betrayed leader and many eventually turned away from parliamentary politics.

Modern Ireland has experienced sharper and more lethal conflicts. The vision of a self-governing Ireland has long since come to pass, to a fuller extent than even seemed possible then. It is suntil not clear how Parnell and Gladstone would have negotiated the passage of Home Rule round the House of Lords veto without the type of constitutional confrontation that took place in 1909-10.

Today, divorce has been introduced, allowing people in Parnell's and Katharine O' Shea's situation to marry or re-marry without necessarily having to point the finger. Parnell still has his critics, but not on the subject of morality. But in any case, what was done cannot be undone. Jane Jordan has recently written a biography entitled *Kitty O' Shea – An Irish Affair* (Sutton Publishing, 2005) which is largely based on Katharine's memoirs which are, as I have argued, disguised as biography.

Katharine O' Shea was attracted to and joined her life to a vigorous man of destiny. This book which she wrote and which was published in 1914, seven years before her death, is both her story and their story. She was a woman whose real character and ability deserve to be recognised, as well as her services to the leader of the Irish cause.

Martin Mansergh,
6 October 2005

PREFACE

O N OCTOBER 6TH, 1891, NEARLY twenty-three years ago, Charles Stewart Parnell died
in the arms of his wife; nearly twenty-three years ago the whole of the civilised world
awoke to laud – or to condemn – the dead chief. It ranked him with the greatest heroes, or
with the vilest sinners, of the world, because he had found and kept the haven of her arms
with absolute disregard of that world's praise or blame till death, the only power greater
than the love that held him there tore him from them.

And then the hate that followed him to the grave turned to the woman he had loved
to vent upon her its baffled spleen; not considering that such a man as he would keep the
heart of his wife as closely in death as he had kept it in life; so closely that none could come
near it; so secretly that none could find the way to plant therein a sting. And so for these
more than twenty-two years, I, his wife, have lived upon memories so happy and so precious
that, after time had brought back some meaning to my life, I took a certain pleasure in
reading all men had to say of him whom they so little knew. I have found many things in
these books that made me smile or made me sad. There were the writers who looked at
him obliquely and wrote that he was crooked, or from below and exclaimed on his want
of perspective, or from any and every point of view but that of an honest directness which
is, after all, the only point of view whence ordinary men can truly observe a great one. Yet,
never in all the 'lives', 'articles', or 'appreciations' that I have read has there been one that
could say – or one that desired to say – that Parnell was not a man who stands out sharp
and clear from other men for good or ill.

But now, after all these years, one of Parnell's erstwhile followers has arisen to explain
to another generation that Parnell was not really such a man as this, that he was one of
Ireland's eternal failures. One who held her dear indeed, but one who balanced her welfare
against the clutches of a light o' love with all the foolishness of callow degeneracy, so fondly
imagined chivalry by the weak. Not a man who gave his country his whole life and found
the peace and courage of that life in the heart of the woman he loved. No, that is how
a man lives and loves, whether in secret or before the whole world. That is how Parnell
lived and loved and now after these long years I break my silence lest the unmanly echo of
excuse given forth by Mr O' Brien in an age that loves excuse may cling about the name of
the man I loved. It is a very poignant pain to me to give to the world any account of the

sacred happiness of eleven years of my life and of the agony of sorrow that once seemed too great to bear; but I have borne it and I am so near him now that I fear to leave near the name of that proud spirit the taint of excuse that he loathed.

Parnell never posed as 'rather the victim than the destroyer of a happy home', as Mr O' Brien suggested in the Cork Free Press of last year and he maintained to the last day of his life that he suffered no 'dishonour and discredit' in making the woman he loved his own.

And because Parnell contravened certain social laws, not regarding them as binding him in any way and because I joined him in this contravention since his love made all else of no account to me, we did not shrink at the clamour of the upholders of those outraged laws, nor resent the pressing of the consequences that were inevitable and always foreseen. The freedom of choice we had ourselves claimed we acknowledged for others and were wise enough to smile if, in some instances, the greatness of our offence was loudly proclaimed by those who he knew lived in a freedom of love more varied than our own. For the hypocrisy of those statesmen and politicians who, knowing for ten years that Parnell was my lover, had with the readiest tact and utmost courtesy accepted the fact as making a sure and safe channel of communication with him; whom they knew as a force to be placated; those who, when the time came to stand by him, in order to give Ireland the benefits they had promised him for her, repudiated him, from under the cloak of the religion they thereby forswore; he and I with him, felt a contempt unspeakable. Twenty-four years ago, as I write this, I said to Parnell: 'You are fighting for Ireland's freedom, but she hugs her chains'. And still she hugs her chains and will hug them, for she killed the subtle brain and steadfast heart that alone could free her. For Parnell knew the Irish people, knew how to support their instability, how to guide their fervent patriotism, how to lead the uplifting of a spirit long cowed but never subdued.

And, as he knew them, so he loved them and had he lived one dreams that Ireland might, long years ago, have come into her own, the honoured mother of her nobler sons, who, no longer sent forth to toil for other nations, should spend themselves in her service to earn for her a name that should no longer be a byword and a sneer among the Nations.

In this book I am giving to the public letters so sacred to my lover and myself that no eyes other than our own should ever have seen them, but that my son was jealous for his father's honour and that I would not my lover's life should seem in these softer days a lesser thing, beset with fears and indecisions that he did not know. I have lived in those eleven years of Parnell's love so constantly that nothing has been lost to me of them and the few details of them that I give will show a little of what manner of man he was, while still I keep for my own heart so much that none shall ever know but he and I.

That part of the book dealing with the earlier stages of my life I had no idea of writing till it was suggested and urged upon me by my children. This chronicle of uneventful years was easy to me, for I have told it as I used to tell it to Parnell when he wished to rest from political talk and consideration. It will be of little interest to the general public except as showing the finger of Fate pointing down the path that led me to him. In regard to the political aspect of the book those who know the Irish history of those days will understand. My lover was the leader of a nation in revolt and, as I could, I helped him as 'King's Messenger' to the Government in office. It has been erroneously said by some of the Irish Party that I 'inspired' certain measures of his and biased him in various ways politically. Those who have said so did not know the man, for Parnell was before all a statesman; absolutely convinced of his policy and of his ability to carry that policy to its logical conclusion. Self-reliant and far-seeing, the master of his own mind.

I was never a 'political lady' and, apart from him, I have never felt the slightest interest in politics, either Irish or English and I can honestly say that except for urging him to make terms with the Government in order to obtain his liberation from prison, I did not once throughout those eleven years attempt to use my influence over him to 'bias' his public life or politics; nor, being convinced that his opinions and measures were the only ones worth consideration, was I even tempted to do so. In my many interviews with Mr Gladstone I was Parnell's messenger and in all other work I did for him it was understood on both sides that I worked for Parnell alone.

KATHARINE PARNELL
Brighton, April, 1914.

The following letter appeared in *The Times* of Sept 10, 1913:

SIR, –

As the only son of the late Captain William Henry O' Shea, I must protest against the scandalous insinuations contained in statements made by a Mr William O' Brien to the Cork Free Press and which were reproduced by you in your issue of Monday last. I had never heard of Mr William O' Brien until I saw the paragraph of which I complain. Mr O' Brien's claim to speak with authority upon the O' Shea v. Parnell case, about which he has no inside knowledge, appears to rest upon his assertion that he received two short notes from the late Mr Parnell.

The deduction drawn by Mr William O' Brien, 'The Irish leader would have been shown to be rather a victim than a destroyer of a happy home and the divorce would never have taken place', is a slander upon my late father and my mother and absolutely without foundation.

I have written to my mother (now the widow of the late Mr C.S. Parnell) upon the subject and she replies: – 'William O' Brien, of whom you ask, was a member of the Irish Party under Mr Parnell's leadership. I quite agree with you as to the insult to myself, your father's memory and, above all, to my late husband, Mr Parnell, that is contained in the unwarrantable interpretation Mr O' Brien has put upon the letter of my husband's he has published and I now propose, with your consent, to publish as soon as possible my self the letters of my late husband, which, as you know, I had left directions should be published after my death.'

I may say that the letters to which my mother refers constitute an absolute refutation of the allegations published by Mr William O' Brien.

I have instructed my solicitors, Messrs Henry Hilbery and Son, to write to Mr William O' Brien, care of the Cork Free Press.

I am, Sir, your obedient servant,
Hotel Metropole, Brighton,
Sept. 9, 1913.
GERARD H.W. O' SHEA.

CHAPTER I

MY EARLY LIFE

'Go forth; and if it be o'er stoney way
Old Joy can lend what newer grief must borrow,
And it was sweet and that was yesterday,
And sweet is sweet, though purchased with sorrow.' – F. THOMPSON

A S A CHILD I USED to waken to the dawn growing slowly into day, when the mist was rising from the lake and floating in soft clouds through the trees which overhung the water. I heard the faint, uncertain call of the wild duck as they alighted and the flapping of the wings of the half-awakened swans. Then came the soft swishing of the cart horses, as they stood in the water to drink before beginning the day's work and I listened with delicious fear in the gloom, wondering if it would be safe to creep downstairs without waking anyone and out under the great trees where the sun was beginning to tip the golden leaves; then on over the bridge to the other side of the lake to feed the swans. I was over the bridge before I had ceased wondering. On I would go in the spirit of glorious adventure, as fast as my little fat legs could carry me through the white gate into the cornfields and beyond the yellow corn stacked into sheaves. Then I used to fill the skirt of my short red frock with ears of wheat and take it to two old friends of mine who were too feeble to glean for themselves. They lived in tiny cottages at the top of the hill and always rewarded my labours with ripe bullaces from their little garden.

These old people and the farmer were great friends of mine and the latter always promised them that all 'Miss Katie' could glean should be sent by him to the miller to grind for them.

My life was always very full as a little girl and the days passed very quickly.

As I was a delicate child I was kept out of doors as much as possible and as soon as I was old enough to carry them I was allowed to go to fetch, the letters before breakfast from the little post office half a mile away. The Rivenhall curate was a great friend of mine and I used to insist upon collecting his letters also and turning in for a chat with him – should I find him in his garden. The reproach of my waiting elders on my return used to puzzle me till my father explained that while he and I liked our breakfast better than our letters, grown-up ladies wanted their letters much more than their breakfast.

My father was my dear companion and friend always and to him I took all my little troubles and griefs and all my joys. Long before I could do more than just hold the two reins he used to let me drive him to and from his church at Cressing, where the clerk stood ready to lift me down and pat old Prince for having trotted so quickly in my charge.

Those were .the days of high pews and while my father went to the vestry I used to amuse myself in peeping over the top to watch the people coming in and the old dame who kept the village school sorting out the children as they clambered and clattered up into the gallery. This old lady was a quaint figure, in an enormous poke bonnet and voluminous cloak. She wore her hair tightly banded each side of her gaunt face and on Sundays was always armed with a long cane, with which she 'settled' the school children into their places by administering a sharp tap to each one as he or she subsided into a seat – and decorum.

Then the organ emitted a wheezy gasp as my father came in and a jerky voluntary was played, while old Jim K., the clerk, marked the places in the books in the pulpit and in his own book. This functionary always sat at a desk just under the pulpit and said 'Amen' at intervals. I always thought it so clever of him to know the right times and felt great respect for his, to me, extraordinary perspicacity and also for the fact that he wore a surplice, or, as I thought, an outside shirt, like my father's, only 'littler' but then, of course, he was a 'littler' man.

I used to get very bored during the litany and had to relieve my weariness in speculations on the carved stone figures lying side by side, of a former lord of the manor and his dame, representing to after ages the devotion of their lives together, but to my childish mind merely suggesting a vague wonder that the stiff frilled collars they wore had not killed them before they had grown so old and dilapidated.

Meanwhile my wandering thoughts were jerked back to the business in hand by my father's sonorous 'Let us pray'. Jim stuck his head into his book, my father's sank into the pulpit and I collapsed on to the seat and meditated on the probable number of bull's-eyes the penny I was clasping so tightly in my hot hand might procure from the old body in the village who kept a few sweets in her window and had no objection to trading on Sunday.

My father had an excellent rule that twenty minutes was the utmost length of time anyone should be expected to listen to a sermon, but, as I had little idea of time, I used to listen anxiously for the rise and fall of his voice from the opening sentences; for I had early learnt that his voice would fall as he neared the final exhortation. There was a reverent hush for the blessing and then, while the people clustered together outside to 'pass the time of day' with Sir John, I would run as hard as I could to capture my sweets before I was lifted into the high four-wheeled dogcart to drive my father home.

My brothers and sisters were all so much older than myself – most of them married, with children of their own – and my mother was so absorbed in her brilliant boy Evelyn, the affairs of her elder daughters and her own literary work, that had it not been for my father I should have been a very lonely child.

My father, Sir John Page Wood, was descended from the Woods of Tiverton and was the eldest of the three sons of Sir Matthew Wood, Baronet, of Hatherley House, Gloucestershire. He was educated at Winchester and at Trinity College, Cambridge and after entering into holy orders, before he was twenty-four years of age, was appointed private chaplain and secretary to Queen Caroline, performing the last offices for her at her death in 1820 and attending her body to its final resting-place in Brunswick. He then became chaplain to the Duke of Sussex and in 1824 was appointed by the Corporation of London to the rectory of St Peter's, Cornhill.

In 1820 my father married Emma Caroline, the youngest of the three daughters of Admiral Michell (and my father's uncle, Benjamin Wood, MP for Southwark at the time, married the second daughter Maria, the 'Aunt Ben' of this book). My mother was born in

Lisbon, her father being Admiral of the Portuguese Navy. Of her two brothers one became Admiral (Sir Frederick Michell, K.C.B.) in the British Navy and the other, Charles Michell, became Colonel of the Royal Engineers.

She was married at the age of eighteen to my father, who was still at Cambridge and the improvident young pair found it extremely difficult to live on the very small allowance that was considered sufficient for my father at college. They appear to have been very happy notwithstanding their difficulties, which were augmented a year later by the birth of a son; and while my father became 'coach' to young men of slower wit, my mother, who was extremely talented with her brush, cheerfully turned her beautiful miniature painting to account for the benefit of her young husband and son. She soon became an exhibitor of larger works in London and the brothers Finden engraved several of her pictures.

She and my father seem to have idolised their first child, 'Little John' and his early death, at about four years old, was their first real sorrow. The boy was too precocious and when he was three years old his proud young parents were writing 'he can read well now and is getting on splendidly with his Latin!'

Constable, the artist, was a friend of my mother's, who thought highly of her work and gave her much encouragement and the young people seem to have had no lack of friends in the world of art and letters. Of my mother, Charles Sheridan said he 'delighted in her sparkling sallies' and the young Edwin Land- Seer was 'mothered' by her to his 'exceeding comfort'.

My mother was appointed bedchamber woman to Queen Caroline and became very fond of her. The consort of George IV appears to have taken the greatest interest in 'Little John' and I had until a short time ago – when it was stolen – a little work- box containing a half-finished sock the Queen was knitting for the little boy when her fatal illness began.

My parents then lived in London for some years while my father did duty at St. Peter's. In 1882, my father became vicar of Cressing, in Essex and he took my mother and their (I think three) children there, leaving a curate in charge of St Peter's. Thirteen children in all were born to my parents (of whom I was the thirteenth) and of my brothers and sisters there were seven living at the time of my birth.

There was little room for all these young people in the vicarage at Cressing and it was so extremely damp as to be unhealthy; so my parents moved to Glazenwood, a charming house with the most beautiful gardens I have ever seen in a place of moderate size. I think my brother Fred died here; but my first memories are of Rivenhall, where my parents moved soon after my birth. Rivenhall Place belonged to a friend of my father's, Sir Thomas Sutton Weston, of Felix Hall. The beautiful old place was a paradise for growing children and the space and beauty of this home of my youth left me with a sad distaste for the little houses of many conveniences that it has been my lot to inhabit for the greater part of my life.

My father was a tall, handsome old man with merry blue eyes and a ready smile. He had a cheery word for all, a gentle wit that never found pleasure in another's discomfiture and a natural dignity that kept him his friends and made no enemies. He troubled himself not at all about the differences between religious parties. Highly cultivated as he was, he possessed the unquestioning piety of a child and the simplicity of faith that 'thinketh no evil' and loveth all good.

In politics he was a thoroughgoing Whig and as he was an able and fluent speaker and absolutely fearless in his utterances, he became a great influence in the county during election times. I remember, when he was to speak at a political meeting, how he laughed as he tied me up in enormous orange ribbons and made me drive him there and how immensely proud of him I was (though, of course, I could not under stand a word of it all) as he spoke so persuasively that howls and ribald cries turned to cheers for 'Sir John's man'.

When he went to London to 'take duty' at St. Peter's, Cornhill, he and I used to stay at the Green Dragon, Bishopsgate Street. There was a beautiful old courtyard to this hotel with a balcony, overhung with creepers, running all round the upper rooms. I loved this place and when I was too young to care much for the long service and sermons, I was quite content that my father should tuck me up safely in bed before going to evensong at St. Peter's.

Sometimes I was not well enough to go to London with him and on these occasions comforted myself as much as possible with a compensating interest in the habits of the Rev. Thomas Grosse, who took my father's place at Cressing.

The Rev. Thomas Grosse was tall and the possessor of an enormous 'presence'; he had black curling hair and tiny, black, beady eyes. He was a very intellectual man, but did not understand a village congregation and many were the complaints to me of 'Miss Katie, when's our Sir John a-coming home to we? Us don' unnerstand a word parson says'. I used to point out to them that he had a lovely way of turning round. Of an enormous weight, he used to pirouette round on one foot as lightly as a girl. But this never seemed to appeal to the villagers as it did to me. He was, however, very good and kind to me and in the summer evenings, when he knew I was missing my father, he would take me out to look for glow-worms and show me the stars, teaching me the names of the planets. Years afterwards the knowledge I thus gained became a great happiness to me, as I taught Mr Parnell all I knew of astronomy and opened up to him a new world of absorbing interest.

About this time I was threatened with delicacy of heart and lungs and, much to my joy, I was ordered 'horse exercise'. A pony was bought for me and I rode daily – sitting alternately on the left and right side to counteract any tendency to weakness of the spine. I was intensely happy in my long rides alone on 'Eugenie'. Before 'Eugenie' I had a pony named 'Tom Tit', but he was considered too much for me to ride alone.

Friends of my brother Evelyn frequently stayed at Rivenhall and one of them, a colonel of Light Dragoons, was engaged to one of my elder sisters. This gentleman appealed to my youthful mind as being all that a hero should be and I used to stick a red fez on my golden curls and gallop my pony past the dining-room windows so that be might see and admire the intrepid maiden, as the prince in my fairy book did!

This gentleman gave me my first 'grown-up' book, 'Vanity Fair'. It was a first edition, illustrated, which I then prized very greatly and which I still have.

I loved the winter evenings at Rivenhall when my brothers were not at home. My father used to sit by the fire reading his Times, with his great white cat on his knee, while I made his tea and hot buttered toast and my mother and sister Anna read or sketched. I used to write the plots of tragic little stories which my 'Pip' (Sir John) used to read and call 'blood-stained bandits', owing to the violent action and the disregard of convention shown by all the characters concerned.

However, these childish efforts of mine led to greater results, as one evening my mother and sister laughingly offered to buy my 'plot' in order to 'write it up' into a novel. I was, of course, very proud to sell my idea and thenceforth both my mother and sister wrote many successful novels, published by Chapman and Hail and, I believe, at prices that are rarely realised by present-day novelists.

I was thus the unwitting means of greatly relieving my parents' anxiety of how to meet, with their not very large income, the heavy expense of educating and maintaining my brothers and the responsibilities of their position.

CHAPTER II

FAMILY LIFE AT RIVENHALL

'Children know,
Instinctive taught, the friend or foe.' – SCOTT

AMONG MY BROTHER'S FRIENDS I have happy recollections of the late Sir William Peel and I remember going into the great hall in a large new hat that had been greatly admired by my flattering old nurse to say good-bye to him when he was leaving after a visit. Sir William remarked cheerfully that I was wonderfully like a mushroom and to hide my mortification I brought my largest cat (I had thirteen of them!) to show him. 'Oh, what an ugly' – then, seeing my face of reproach, he hastily continued – 'but very fine cat'! Even in such little matters his sensitive kindness showed itself. To this day when members of the family wish to make excuses for any inexcellence they remark hopefully, 'but very fine cat'!

My brothers loved to tease me and, as I was so much younger than they, I never understood if they were really serious or only laughing at me. Evelyn was specially adroit in bewildering me and used to curb my rebellion, when I was reluctant to fetch and carry for him, by drawing a harrowing picture of my remorse should he be killed 'in the next war'. The horror of this thought kept me a ready slave for years, 'till one day, in a gust of temper, I burst out with 'I shan't be sorry at all when you're killed in a war 'cos I didn't find your silly things and I wish you'd go away and be a dead hero now, so there!' I remember the horrified pause of my mother and sister and then the howl of laughter and applause from Evelyn and Charlie. Evelyn was very good to me after this and considered, more, that even little girls have their feelings.

As a matter of fact, my mother was so entirely wrapped up in Evelyn that I think I was jealous, even though I had my father so much to myself. My mother was most affectionate to all her children, but Evelyn was her idol and from the time when, as a mere lad, he was wounded in the Crimean War, to the day of her death, be was first in all her thoughts.

During his long absences from home – and he went into the navy at fourteen – she wrote to him daily till her death and often I remember my father urging her to come in from the cold, damp air as she stood out on the avenue listening for his coming. Evelyn fully reciprocated the devotion of his mother and never fell short of her expectations. It was in his nature to work hard at the thing in hand; but for her sake the thought of failure became impossible and her intrepid spirit had the immense happiness of seeing her soldier son win honour after honour.

In the large hail of Rivenhall logs burnt in the great open fireplaces. Out of this hail opened a smaller one from which the broad shallow oak stairs led to the upper rooms. It was a breathless affair, when I was small, to leave the long dining-room and cross these halls, in the flickering light of the log fire, to my father's study, where I used to hammer wildly on the door – too sure that the long shadows were 'Something' about to catch me to turn the door-handle in the ordinary way. Safely arrived, I would sit happily on the floor reading books quite beyond my years and comprehension but, except for gently substituting Scott for a less edifying author, my father let me, read what I liked.

The drawing-room was hung with my mother's paintings and, though I was too young to appreciate them, I used to like to wander round the room looking at the pictures and specially considering the one of my father as a young man in hunting dress.

This picture rather worried me, as he had given up hunting and said it was because he was so old! His friends liked to tell me stories of his hard riding and of his erstwhile curate, who would hunt if his vicar did and who was no sooner on a horse than he was off again. 'A brave little man, my Pippin, but no sportsman', said my father and I understood later that, with nine children to educate and start out in life, my 'sporting parson' had to grow 'too old' very early in life.

Of my brothers and sisters I really knew only four at all well. Clarissa had died at seventeen and Fred when I was very young; Frank was away with his regiments my sister Poflie was married and away in India before I was born and my sister Emma married Sir Thomas Barrett-Lennard while I was still very young. She was always very kind to me and I used to love going to visit her at her house in Brighton. Visiting Sir Thomas Barrett-Lennard's country seat, Belhus, I did not like so much, because, though Belhus is very beautiful, I loved Rivenhall better.

There was a very old and large cedar tree on the lawn outside our drawing-room window, with a long, low swing where I used to sway gently backwards and forwards reading my mother's and Anna's manuscript. My mother and sister Anna used to let me read and criticise, at which I felt greatly honoured.

A solitary peacock called 'Jackhawks' used to haunt this spot and he had a startling habit of suddenly springing into the air with a wild cry and pecking savagely at the eyes of the person sitting in the swing. My mother was very fond of him and one day, finding him with a broken leg, sent a frantic message to the local doctor to come and mend it. He arrived thinking that a member of the family – with whom he was not on good terms – was the sufferer, but when my mother imperiously escorted him to the patient his indignation was swallowed up in amusement.

My mother was a fine musician and, as I grew older, I began to long to play as she did. There was a beautiful grand piano in the drawing-room and I used to try to pick out tunes upon it. My mother had spent much money on her eldest daughter's – Maria's (Pollie) – musical education. At the end of this Pollie said she detested it and would never play a note again if she could help it. When I asked that I might be taught to play my mother said, 'No. There is the piano, go and play it if you really want to learn.' In time I could play very well by ear and began to compose a little and seek for wider knowledge. A few miles away was Witham and there I found a teacher in the organist of the church. He was quite blind, but a wonderful musician. He taught me a good deal about music and also taught me to play the organ.

I began as I grew up to have a good singing voice and later on had lessons from Mme. Lemmens-Sherrington, but my father would have none of the songs and French operatic music my mother liked me to sing to her. Nothing but Handel might I sing to him and, unaware as I was of the difficulties of the composition, I used to sing 'God is for us', 'Comfort ye' and 'How beautiful are the feet' very creditably.

My father loved this music and it suited my voice better than light operatic music.

My love of music at this time led me to try composition and I used to set to music any verses that took my fancy. Among these I was much pleased with Longfellow's 'Weariness' and was so encouraged by my mother's praise of the setting that I sent the poet a copy. I was a very happy girl when he wrote to thank me, saying that mine was the best setting of his poem he had ever heard.

Armed with the manuscript of this music and some others, the next time I went to London with my father I went to Boosey's, the musical publishers and asked their representative to publish them.

'Quite impossible my dear young lady', he answered at once. 'We never take beginners' work!'

I plaintively remarked that even Mozart was a 'beginner' once and could not understand why he laughed. Still, with a smile, he consented to look at the manuscript and to my joy he ceased to laugh at me and tried some of it over, finally agreeing, much to my joy, to publish 'Weariness' and a couple of other songs.

I remember my father's pleasure and the merry twinkle in his eye as he gravely assented to my suggestion that we were a very gifted family!

While my brother Frank (who was in the 17th Foot) was stationed at Aldershot he invited my sister Anna and myself down to see a review. He was married and we stayed with him and his wife and children in the married officers' quarters, which appeared to us to be very gay and amusing.

I greatly enjoyed seeing the cavalry, with all the officers and men in full dress.

Many of the officers came over to call after the review and among them was Willie O' Shea, who was then a cornet in the 18th Hussars. There was a small drama acted by the officers in the evening which my brother's wife took us to see and there were many of the 18th Hussars, who paid us much attention, though, personally, I found the elderly and hawk- eyed colonel of the regiment far more interesting than the younger men.

I sadly wanted someone young enough to play games with me and the boy who was kept at Rivenhall for 'boots and knives' was my chosen companion for cricket. I thought this youth a marvellous player and when on one occasion I won the game I threw a stump into the air in my joy. My triumph was short-lived, for it came down on my head and cut it very badly.

My stammering companion dragged me to the house after wildly dabbing at the fast-flowing blood with my pinafore What with the boy's assurances that I was 'bleedin' to def' and the cry of my nurse at the sight of my blood-soaked pinafore, I was thoroughly frightened and slid out of the difficulties of explanations and the commotion by fainting This little episode led to the banishment of my chosen ally, the boot-boy and I was thrown more than ever on my own resources.

Regular lessons were forbidden, but my father used to teach me in a desultory way and had never-ending patience in answering questions. Looking far back to my childhood I can now see how he used to direct my reading, without my being in the least aware of it and how he drew me on to questions of countries, places and men that led continually to further interest and desire for knowledge which he never failed to supply.

He, Sir John, was for twenty-five years chairman of the Board of Guardians, for twenty-two years chairman of the Witham Bench and also visiting magistrate to the Chelmsford Gaol He was extremely popular and I was very proud that I might always drive with him to the court and to various meetings. I remember that I used to experience a great awe on the days when he visited the prison and I noticed that he was a little sad and silent as we drove home.

He was in great request throughout the county for dinner parties, which were in those days the chief form of social intercourse in Essex. To these he could not take me, but I used to lie awake till he came to 'tuck me up' and gently whisper 'God bless you, my Blessing', to which I would respond 'God bless you, Pip', in return.

My happiest days were when we took long walks and hunted for wild flowers together. My father knew a good deal about botany and taught me the names of the flowers I collected, their old English names and the derivations of them. I have still the books he gave me, that I might learn more of the flowers which grow without cultivation and the power of observation he awoke in me then has been a great solace to me through life.

My father's sister, Mrs Maddy, lived at Hill House, Messing and had, I believe, a very good collection of pictures, among them being an original Greuze, 'Girl with a Pitcher', which my mother copied exquisitely. I was too young to appreciate these beautiful pictures and my only memory of my visits to this art collection is of the torture I suffered in being made to eat minced mutton!

CHAPTER III

VISITORS AT RIVENHALL

'A chiel's a you takin' notes
And, faith, he'll prent it!' – BURNS

AMONG OTHER VISITORS TO RIVENHALL was Lieut.-Colonel Steele, of the Lancers, a dark, handsome man, who married my sister Anna.

I remember looking at Anna consideringly when I was told this was to be, for, as children do, I had hitherto merely regarded Anna as a sister too 'grown-up' to play with on equal terms and yet not as a person sufficiently interesting to be married to one of the magnificent beings who, like Evelyn's friends, wore such beautiful uniforms and jingly spurs. But my sister had soft, brown hair and a lovely skin, blue eyes that were mocking, gay, or tender in response to many moods and a very pretty figure. And I solemnly decided that she was really pretty and quite 'grown-up' enough to be loved by the 'beautiful ones'.

Anthony Trollope was a great friend of my father and mother and used to stay with us a good deal for hunting. He was a very hard rider to hounds and was a cause of great anxiety to my mother, for my sister Anna loved an intrepid 'lead' out hunting and delighted in following Trollope, who stuck at nothing. I used to rejoice in his 'The Small House at Allington' and go about fitting the characters in the book to the people about me – a mode of amusement that palled considerably on the victims.

The Reverend John Bellew was a well-known churchman and preacher in those days. He was much admired by my people, but I do not remember much of him, except that he had a very venerable appearance and that I felt very small and good when he was staying at Rivenhall.

I was very fond of figs when I was a tiny little child and it was in an excess of this feeling of virtue inspired by Mr Bellew, that, when a surprised parent asked me why I was unwilling to go and get something that was required from the dining-room, I replied with a shower of tears, 'Dem figs bodder me so!' – the figs of my temptation having been left nestling in a plate of cool green leaves in the dining-room.

The hounds used frequently to meet at Rivenhall and the Master, Mr Honeywood and I were great friends, though we should not have been so if he had known how I used to wander quietly off during the hunt breakfast, away to the covers they intended to draw and tramp about as much as possible to spoil the scent. I would wait till the 'quarry' got away and give wild 'view holloa' in the wrong direction, to save my furry friends.

I often used to see the hares feeding in the evening and could get very close to them as they nibbled the grass, watching me with their bright eyes and, seemingly, unconcerned at my presence. Of course, I never confessed my unsporting behaviour to any of the household, as my brothers always hunted when at home and my sister also and they and the Master would not have forgiven it. I did not mind the fox- hunting, but, the hares seemed so very much my friends.

I was always glad when our young cousin George (afterwards Sir George) Farwell (Lord Justice Farwell) came to see us. A dear lad, who quite won my childish admiration with his courtly manners and kind, considerate ways.

The Hon. Grantley-Barkley (who was seventy, I believe) was a dear old man who was very fond of me – as I was of him. I was but a child when he informed my parents that he wished to marry me when I was old enough! He was a dear friend of my father's, but, though the latter would not consider the matter seriously my mother, who was an extraordinarily sympathetic woman, encouraged the idea.

Grantley-Barkley was always called the 'Deerslayer' by his friends. A fine old sportsman, his house, 'The Hut', at Poole, Dorset, was a veritable museum of slain beasts and I used to shudder secretly at the idea of becoming mistress of so many heads and horns.

The dear old man used to write long letters to me before I could answer them in anything but laborious print and he wrote sheets to my mother inquiring of my welfare and the direction of my education. I still have many of the verses he composed in my honour and though the last line of the verse that I insert worries me now as much as it did when I received it, so many years ago, I still think it very pretty sentiment:

Then the Bird that above me is singing
Shall chase the thought that is drear,
When the soul to her side it is winging
The limbs must be lingering near!

This little one-sided romance died a natural death as I grew up; my old friend continuing to take the kindest interest in me, but accepting the fact that I was no exception to the law of youth, that calls to youth in mating.

My brother Frank suggested to my brother-in-law, Sir Thomas Barrett-Lennard, that Willie O' Shea, who was a first-class steeplechase rider, would no doubt, if asked, ride the horse Honesty that Tom was going to run in the Brentwood Steeplechase. He had already ridden and won many races. Willie readily agreed to ride and came to stay at Belhus for the race.

I was staying there at the time and though I was considered too young to be really 'out', as a rule I had my share in any festivities that were going on. I remember my brother-in-law saying casually to my sister Emma, who was giving a dinner party that evening: 'Who is Katie to go in with, milady?' and she answered promptly, 'Oh, she shall go in with O' Shea'. A mild witticism that rather ruffled my youthful sense of importance.

My first sight of Willie then, as a grown-up, was on this evening, when I came rather late into the ball before dressing for dinner. He was standing near the fire, talking with the eagerness that was not in those days bad form in young men of the steeplechase he had ridden and won on Early Bird.

I had been so much the companion of older men than he that I was pleased with his youthful looks and vivacity. His dress pleased me also and, though it would appear a terrible affair in the eyes of a modern young man, it was perfectly correct then for a young officer in the 18th Hussars and extremely becoming to Willie: a brown velvet coat, cut rather fully, seal-skin waistcoat, black check trousers and an enormous carbuncle and diamond pin in his curiously folded scarf.

When introduced to me he was most condescending and nettled me so much by his kindly patronage of my youthfulness that I promptly plunged into such a discussion of literary complexities, absorbed from my elders and utterly undigested, that he soon subsided into a bewildered and shocked silence.

However, in the few days of that visit we became very good friends and I was immensely pleased when, on parting, Willie presented me with a really charming little poem written about my 'golden hair and witsome speech'.

Of course, as usual, I flew to show my father, who, reading, sighed, 'Ah, too young for such nonsense. I want my Pippin for myself for years to come'.

Willie's family, the O' Sheas of Limerick, were a collateral branch of the O' Sheas of County Kerry. Willie's grandfather William O' Shea (of Rich Hill, Limerick), had three sons – Henry, John and Thaddeus. Thaddeus appears to have been the black sheep of the family, wasting his substance in gambling and in breeding unlikely horses to win impossible races. I always thought he sounded rather interesting and Willie was always a little regretful that he had never been allowed to know much of Uncle Thaddeus.

John went early to Spain, where – and in France – a branch of the family had been settled (the Ducs de Sanlucas) since the rebellion of 1641 in Ireland. Here John married Señora Dona Ysabel Hurtado de Corcuera, founded a bank and prospered exceedingly, firmly refusing all offers from Thaddeus of a share in the improbable glories – and certain expenses – of his racing stables.

Henry, Willie's father, was of a different build. As level-headed as John and far more generous, at the death of his father, he, the eldest of the three, took the family affairs in hand; and finding the estates mortgaged up to the utmost limit and the home of his childhood mocking its name (Rich Hill) in its hopeless ruin, he bound himself to a solicitor in Dublin, worked hard and in due course became himself a fully-qualified solicitor. He did extremely well and, developing a perfect genius for pulling together estates that appeared to be hopelessly bankrupt, business flowed in to him and he became a very wealthy man. He, equally with John, refused to participate in the ambitions of Thaddeus to establish a record-breaking racing stable, but he was by no means, deaf to frequent appeals for 'temporary' help till the latest wonder of Thaddeus's stable had shown his 'worth' at Punchestown.

Henry O' Shea married Catherine (a Comtesse of Rome), daughter of Edward Quinlan, of Tipperary. Two children were born to them – Mary (afterwards Lady of the Royal Order of Theresa of Bavaria) and William Henry, whom I married.

Henry O' Shea lived for his children and contentedly toiled in Dublin for their benefit, while they were being given the most thorough education his mind could devise for them. They alternated between France, England and Spain and certainly they became perfect linguists. Willie had no natural taste for learning, but he did fairly well at Oscott, very well in France and' Spain and finished up but languidly at Trinity College, Dublin, before he went into the 18th Hussar in which regiment his father purchased a commission for him.

He was sent into this regiment with these instructions from his father 'First become a smart officer; secondly, do what the other men do and send the bill in to me!' He was given an excellent allowance and be followed his father's instructions to the letter.

He was keen about his work in the regiment and took an honest interest in all that pertained to it. He also 'did what the other men did' and greatly enjoyed himself, sending 'the bill' in to his father, according to instructions.

He was a handsome lad, gay, somewhat irresponsible, generous and of a ready – if rather barbed – sense of humour. His cosmopolitan education had given him an ease of manner and self that made him popular with his contemporaries, even if it proved somewhat exasperating to his seniors in the regiment.

The 18th was a sporting regiment and Willie O' Shea, who had a perfect seat and hands, was much in request to ride in the various regimental races in which the 18th were so successful. Young, happy and healthy, perhaps he took his father's instructions as to 'sending in the bill' too literally, for in a few years' time the hard-working Dublin solicitor was vigorously protesting at the enormous cost of keeping his son in the 18th. Willie, contrite and hurt, promised to remember that even the parental purse had its limits, but very pertinently pointed out that he had been told to enjoy himself. As soon as it was possible his father bought his captaincy for him (practically all promotion in those days was purchased, at any rate in times of peace), thinking that the superior rank would bring some greater sense of responsibility to his most affectionate, but rather spendthrift son; but another few years brought 'the bill' in again to the extent of some £15,000. Henry O' Shea paid it without cavilling at the amount, but pointed out that Willie's mother and sister would be the sufferers if he paid any further debts, so that it was obvious to him that Willie would not ask him to do so and would in future make his ample allowance suffice for his needs, even if it necessitated his leaving the regiment. Willie at once agreed that he could, of course, expect nothing further and eventually did leave the regiment, just before I married him.

Henry O' Shea died in London before Willie and I married; he was the very kindest of fathers and Willie was devoted to him. He was clever, just and honourable in all his dealings and had the most charming manners and a merrier wit than all the rest of the O' Sheas put together. I think his only fault was that in giving his children so foreign an education they lost somewhat of the Irish charm which he possessed so strongly himself. He spoke with a brogue that was music in the ear and the contrast of this with his son's clear, clipped English and his daughter's (unaffected) French accent was distinctly amusing when the three were together.

Of the Comtesse O' Shea there is little to say but that, to me, she appeared to be a bundle of negations wrapped in a shawl – always in a very beautiful shawl. Even when I first knew her she and her daughter were evidently convinced that she was very old and feeble, although she could not have been much more than middle-aged and if there had been no daughter to lean upon I do not think she would have desired to lean. She was destitute of any sense of humour and highly educated, always, I think, an unhappy combination and her only definite characteristics were her assiduous practice of her religion and her profound sense of my undesirability as a daughter-in-law.

Willie's sister, Mary O' Shea, on the other hand, erred, if at all, on the side of definiteness. Had her health been better she would have been extremely pretty but rheumatic fever had twice worked havoc on her lovely skin and rendered her widely opened blue eyes pain-marked and heavy lidded. She also was sadly deficient in humour and wore herself and her friends out in her endeavours to make bad Catholics out of indifferent Protestants. She had naturally a very quick temper and had acquired a painfully acute and uncompromising conscience, which gave its possessor far more pain than any outbreak of the temper could cause to others; to whom indeed it came rather as a relief from a too even and conventional nature. She had taken conscientious a of her meticulously thorough education, was a human library of dry and solid information and was as ignorant – and as innocent – of the world at twenty-eight as she must have been at eight.

Her education had left her French in all her modes of thought and speech and she had a certain air and finish that were entirely so. Mary and I had a certain liking for one another and I think that, had she not shared her mother's conviction as to my 'undesirability', I might have become fond of her. She was betrothed to an Italian of old family and of the blackest of the black Roman society. I believe she was devoted to him in her quiet, methodical way, but after her third attack of acute rheumatic fever, leaving behind it the legacy of heart disease, shortly before they were to be wedded, she decided that her state of health would render her but a drag upon her prospective husband and that she would ask him to release her from her promise. Her quiet heroism was none the less because she took the stately way of going to his house in Paris, in company with several elderly ladies and a prince of the Church (a Cardinal) to do so. She died a few years later in much suffering but perfect happiness.

CHAPTER IV

PRIVATE THEATRICALS

'Ah, well, we're mummers all!'

ONE HAPPY DAY, WHEN MY brothers were at home, someone suggested that we should have some theatricals at Rivenhall.

We had several people staying with us at the time and promptly formed ourselves into parties to beat up the 'county' to come and help. My sister, Lady Barrett-Lennard came from Belhus, bringing Sir Thomas with her (protesting violently, though he eventually became more enthusiastic than any of us) and my sister Anna, who was now Mrs Steele.

Our devoted mother, who was wonderfully clever with her brush, left her beloved pictures and novel writing and set to work to paint the scenery for our play. She spent days perched up on the top of a pair of tall steps, painting away for dear life and at the same time listening intelligently to the various members of her family and her guests declaiming their parts below her and appealing for her approval.

'Lady Wood knew a man could not help looking a perfect ass, spouting it all in cold blood' and 'Dear Lady Wood quite understands how essential it is that I should enter left, the profile is *everything!*'

She never grew impatient, but painted serenely on, coaching us, greeting her guests gaily from her elevated position and pairing off men and maidens with an unerring intuition that stilled the bickerings that naturally arose in the scramble for the best parts.

My mother was still a very attractive woman with large grey eyes and the jet-black hair that she kept to the end of her days – a woman scorning throughout her life all the cosmetic adjuncts to feminine beauty, she was rewarded by nature with the preservation of her good looks in old age.

The scenery was most successful and the drop curtain a dream of realistic landscape where one could in imagination wander away into a veritable fairyland of distance.

After much discussion the burlesque of *Amy Robsart*, to be preceded by *Betsy Baker*, was selected. We were each one of us probably convinced that he or she alone was capable of taking the chief parts, but, after much discussion and a firm reminder from Frank that some of us must be content to fill the honourable office of audience, the parts were awarded.

My sister Anna was to act Betsy Baker, while I, to my great joy, was selected for the part of Amy Robsart. The other parts were filled by (the late) Sir Charles DuCane (afterwards

Governor of Tasmania), his cousin, Percy DuCane (of the Scots Greys), my sister, Lady Barrett-Lennard, Sir Thomas and my brother Charlie. I remember the latter made an extremely handsome Earl of Leicester. Sir Charles DuCane was 'Crummy', Sir Thomas 'Mouser' in *Betsy Baker* and Willie O' Shea was Queen Elizabeth.

O' Shea was a name not very well known amongst us in those days and during Queen Elizabeth's appearance on the stage some merry brother officers of Willie's began to sing in an undertone: ' O she's a jolly good fellow'. That was enough to set the whole 'house' off and a shout of laughter went up as Willie, who was then (and always) very sensitive to foolish puns upon his name, glowered at them from under his red Elizabethan wig. In one moment we had all caught the infection and the old house rang with 'O she's a jolly good fellow' and good Queen Bess, with a look of withering scorn, picked up his skirts and stalked off 'left' with as much dignity as he could muster.

Having been once bitten with the theatrical mania, we were restless and anxious for more and soon we were rehearsing for another comedy, to be enacted this time at Belhus, the home of my brother-in-law Tom and my sister Emma. I have forgotten what the play was, but Mr Spaulding (of the Foreign Office), Christopher Weguelin and Mr (afterwards Sir) Charles Hall were great acquisitions as they were fine amateur actors and had a 'finish' that our first performance perhaps lacked. We were properly coached for the series of plays we then began by the late Mrs Keeley, Mrs Stirling and Mr J. Clarke.

After the success of the Belhus theatricals we soared much higher and acted at Chelmsford, the theatre at Colchester and even in London. My mother was always most sympathetic, taking the greatest interest in our efforts and sitting in the wings to prompt and encourage us This was a great comfort to me, as I was nervous and my legs at Rivenhall used to shake and my lips tremble so much that it was the sometimes only her whispered encouragement that enabled me to sing, or to begin my part at all.

Willie O' Shea used to present me with most beautiful bouquets during these efforts and, in the pretty fashion of those days, bees and butterflies were so mounted as to appear hovering over the rare exotics.

The rehearsals in amateur theatricals are really the most amusing part of the entertainment and the learning and hearing one another's parts led to endless laughter, quarrels and fun.

My sister, Lady Barrett-Lennard, looked so lovely in the powder and patches worn in the old-world plays we so much affected that we often persuaded her to wear powder in the evening when there were house parties in Belhus. She was *petite* and possessed large, soft eyes and delicate features and in her diamonds and powder looked as though she had stepped down from one of Sir Thomas's ancestral pictures hung above her in the dining-room.

I was now given a little sitting-room of my own, where I could be undisturbed and receive my friends and our one outdoor servant; Tim Bobbin, put down a carpet and hung white curtains for me, afterwards filling the window seats with the best flowers he could get. Then my dear sister-in-law (my brother Charlie's wife) drove over to see us and spent a morning in lining my curtains with pink; and the little room glowed with colour.

My brother Charlie's wife has always been a 'Minna of sweet memories' to me and while my home was at Rivenhall I always looked forward with pleasure to the days on which she drove over, with her two children, from her home a few miles away.

Charlie, then the second surviving son of my parents, had always been delicate and in order to keep him constantly in the open air my father had had parents, had always been delicate and in order to keep him constantly in the open air my father had had him taught farming and when he married he bought a farm near Rivenhall.

Speaking of Tim Bobbin reminds me of the amusement of my family when I received, amongst innumerable other valentines, a gorgeous one from Tim. It was a wonderful affair of satin, paper-lace and orrisroot scent and had a magnificent representation of two hearts transfixed by a golden arrow. 'I would thou wert my bride, love', twirled gracefully round the hearts and the 'Respectful duty of your humble servant Tim Bobbin' was partly scrawled and mostly printed on the back.

I had many valentines. St Valentine's Day was still eagerly looked for in those days, but I gave this the place of honour, in spite of heading from Charlie, that my humble admirer, on being rallied on his own valentine, exclaimed stoutly 'Eh, Mr Charles, gi'en, a man had two thousan' a year an' Miss Katie to wife he med ask for naught better!'

In the summer I went to stay at Belhus once more and again met Willie, who was now a very welcome guest with all my people.

Unconsciously we seemed to drift together in the long summer days as we wandered through the park, seeking shelter from the heat in the avenue of great limes, where the air was heavy with scented bloom and the hum of bees. The rest of the household seemed intent on their own affairs and we were content to be left together to explore the cool depths of the glades, where the fallow deer ran before us, or the kitchen garden, where the high walls were covered with rose-coloured peaches, warm with the sun as we leant ate them. What we talked about I cannot remember but it was nothing very wise I should imagine.

Back to the house to tea with the others in the south drawing-room, where the scent of tuberoses and jasmine added to the sweetness of the summer evening and then Willie and I would pace the avenue in dreamy silence, while the shadows lengthened and the moon rose and the haze of the summer night drove the deer to higher ground towards the house.

Week after week went by in our trance of contentment. I did not look forward, but was content to exist in the languorous summer heat – dreaming through the sunny days with Willie by my side and thinking not at all of the future. I suppose my elders were content with the situation, as they must have known that such propinquity could have but one ending.

There was a man by whom I was attracted and who had paid me considerable attention– E. S., stationed at Purfleet. He was a fine athlete and used to fill me with admiration by jumping over my pony's back without touching him at all. I sometimes thought idly of him during these days with Willie, but was content to drift along, until one day my sister asked me to drive over with a note of invitation to dinner for the officers at Purfleet.

In the cool of the evening I set out, with Willie, of course, in attendance. Willie, on arrival, sprang out of the pony cart to deliver the note and as he was jumping in again glanced up at the window above us, where it happened E.S. and another officer were standing. Without a moment's hesitation Willie forward and kissed me full on the lips. Furious and crimson with the knowledge that the men at the the window had seen him kiss me, I hustled my poor little pony home, vowing I would never speak to Willie again; but his apologies and explanation that he had only just wanted 'to show those fellows that they must not make asses of themselves 'seemed so funny and in keeping with the dreamy sense I had of belonging to Willie that I soon forgave him, though I felt a little stab of regret when I found that E. S. declined the invitation to dinner. He never came again.

Willie had to join his regiment and in the evening before his going, as I was leaving the drawing-room, he stopped to offer me a rose, kissing me on the face and hair as he did so.

A few mornings after I was sleeping the dreamless sleep of healthy girlhood when I was awakened by feeling a thick letter laid on my cheek and my mother leaning over me singing 'Kathleen Mavourneen' in her rich contralto voice. I am afraid I was decidedly cross at having been awakened so suddenly and clasping my letter unopened, again sided into slumber.

So far nearly all my personal communication with Willie when he was away had been carried on by telegraph and I had not quite arrived at knowing what to reply to the sheets of poetic prose which flowed from his pen. Very frequently he came down just for a few

33

hours to Rivenhall and I drove to meet him at the station with my pony-chaise. Then we used to pass long hours at the lake fishing for pike, or talking to my father, who was always cheered by his society

At this time Colonel Clive, of the Grenadier Guards, was a frequent visitor. I was really fond of him and he pleased me by his pleasure in hearing me sing to my own accompaniment. I spent some happy hours in doing so for him when staying at Claridge's Hotel with my sister and I remember that when I knew he was coming I used to twist a blue ribbon in my hair to please him.

Once, when staying at Claridge's, my sister and I went to his rooms to see sketches of a friend of my brother Evelyn's, Mr Hozier and father of Mr Churchill. The drawings were, I believe, very clever and I know the tea was delicious.

It was some time after this that the 18th Hussars were stationed at Brighton. The 18th were great sportsmen and Willie a 'crack' steeplechase rider. He used to school young horses on the Downs above Brighton, both his own and those of other men, for his 'way with a horse' and his good hands were generally appreciated among his brother officers. Willie loved these early mornings and on one occasion, he rode off soon after daybreak on his steeplechaser, Early Bird, for a gallop on the race-course. At the early parade that morning Willie was missing and, as inquiries were being made as to his whereabouts, a trooper reported that Early Bird had just been brought in dead lame and bleeding profusely from a gash in the chest.

He had been found limping his way down the hill from the race-course. Willie's brother officers immediately set out to look for him and found him lying unconscious some twenty yards from a chain across the course which was covered with blood and evidently the cause of the mishap. They got him down to the barracks on a stretcher and there he lay with broken ribs and concussion of the brain.

He told us afterwards that he was going a hard gallops and neither he nor Early Bird had seen the chain till they were right on it, too late to jump. There had never been a chain up before and he had galloped over the same course on the previous morning.

I was at Rivenhall when I heard of the accident to Willie and for six unhappy weeks I did little else than watch for news of him. My sister, Lady Barrett-Lennard and Sir Thomas had gone to Preston Barracks to nurse him and as soon as it was possible they moved him to their own house in Brighton. For six weeks he lay unconscious and then at last the good news came that he was better and that they were going to take him to Belhus to convalesce.

A great friend of Willie's, also in the 18th – Robert Cunninghame Graham – was invited down to keep him amused and my sister, Mrs Steele and I met them in London and went down to Belhus with them. Willie was looking very ill and was tenderly cared for by his friend Graham. He was too weak to speak, but while driving to Belhus, he slipped a ring from his finger on to mine and pressed my hand under cover of the rugs.

Robert Cunninghame Graham, uncle of Rontine Cunninghame Graham, the Socialist writer and traveller, walked straight into our hearts, so gay, so careful of Willie was he and so utterly *bon camarade*, that we seemed to have known him for years. In a few days Anna and I left Belhus and Willie's father came over from Ireland to stay with him till he was completely recovered.

Before Willie left I was back at Belhus on the occasion of a dinner party and was shyly glad to meet him again and at his desire to talk to me only.

While the others were all occupied singing and talking after dinner we sat on the yellow damask sofa and he slipped a gold and turquoise locket on a long gold and blue enamel chain round my neck. It was a lovely thing and I was very happy to know how much Willie cared for me.

CHAPTER V

A MEMORY OF BRIGHTON

'But, oh! The fresh winds of the sea,
That rush'd and roar'd o'er the scudding tide;
And oh! For these hours so wildly free
When we stood there side by side.' – A.C. STEELE

MY SISTER ANNA AND I went down to Brighton for change of air to our sister, Lady Lennard's house. She and Sir Thomas were away and we were in proud possession of a great, tall house and an old caretaker, who was to look after us.

We were very happy by the sea all day and in the evening well-amused by Mr Cunninghame Graham, who was now back at Preston Barracks, having left Willie in his father's care at Belhus.

Cunningham Graham was solemnly invited to come to 'dinner' whenever he liked and my sister and I were interested observers of his expression when he first came. Anna and I had decided that we loved breakfast and hated dinner, so, having no one to please but ourselves, we 'dined' as we breakfasted, on bacon and eggs and such sort of early morning food.

Mr Graham was, after first shock, good enough to say he liked our late breakfast and certainly he at our simple feast very frequently. Looking back, I think he was very greatly attracted by my sister Anna, though as she was a ready married, his suit was hopeless.

In the evening we used to walk in the Lewes Crescent Gardens, where the scent of the wallflowers and drowsy swash of the sea lulled us into desire for sleep.

One evening when my sister and I were preparing for bed there was a sound of something falling on the balcony. Half laughing and half frightened we peeped out and there espied two lovely bouquets of flowers. They had evidently been flung up from the road below.

After a breathless consultation we cautiously peered over the balcony and saw two young men - apparently gentlemen – gazing up to see the effect of their floral bombardment. We hastily fled back into the drawing-room and bolted the window, with some vague idea that such adventurous spirits might turn into twin Romeos.

We must have looked very funny sitting up in bed that night, clasping our bouquets and bubbling in bed with laughter at our unsought conquest.

The next evening, each trying her best to appear unconcerned, we hung about before going to bed, listening for the gentle thud of flowers on the balcony. Again two bouquets were flung on the balcony and we snatched them in, slamming and bolting the window and shaking with laughter.

This became a nightly experience for a week or more and Anna's curiosity could bear it no longer. We dressed her up as a maid with cap and my apron and muffled her face p to 'keep her toothache from the wind.' The flowers used to arrive in boxes no and were taken out of these and flung up to the balcony by the same young men nightly

At a signal from me, when I spied the two cavaliers rounding the corner of the street, the 'maid' opened the front door and went stiffly along, as an elderly maid should, to 'post some letters'. As we had hoped the two men fell at once into the trap and besought the maid to take the flowers in to her young ladies.

She was properly shocked at such a suggestion and said it was as much as her place was worth if it got to 'My Lady's' ears. They assured her that the flowers were acceptable to the young ladies and that her lady's ears need not be assailed by the knowledge that the flowers had been taken in every evening and that it would be made worth her while to do them such a little service. She exclaimed at the deceitfulness of the young ladies – 'their ma away and all' – wavered and capitulated, staggering into the door armed with two enormous bouquets, a handsome tip and a whole packet of verses.

I hastily shut the door behind her and she fell into my arms helpless with laughter. I was half cross at having been out of the fun, but soon we were both rocking with laughter over the 'poetry' and planning to restore the 'tip' without getting into further mischief.

The men's cards were in the bouquets and from these we learned that they were brothers, belonged to a good London club and meant to pursue us to the end. We met them frequently out of doors in the daytime, but never by word or sign recognised them, nor allowed them to show their desire to salute us.

Anna and I were young and light-hearted in those days, but would have been horrified at the idea of allowing these young men to make our acquaintance in such a way.

When I contrast the girls of my youth with those of the present day I think we were more modest and decidedly more attractive!

When we told our mother (Lady Wood) about the bouquets and the rest she was much shocked at the thought of the expense the bouquets must have been and when the young fellows were discovered in the grounds at Rivenhall, waiting again with messages for the 'maid', she had them sternly warned off and yet, with her characteristic dislike of our being under any obligation to anyone, sent each amorous one a present.

Our mother tried to show us the indiscretion of our behaviour, but I would only demurely describe the gallant appearance of the 'tall one', who admired me most, while Anna would chuckle out 'as much as my place is worth if it comes to M'lady's ears.'

Soon Anna and I were startled out of our girlish nonsense at Brighton by receiving a telegram giving news of our mother being dangerously ill. The message came long after the last train had gone to London and in an agony of suspense, we decided to walk to the station in the early morning and try to get to London by a workman's train.

When we got to the station we found that there were no means of getting to town until much later. We were in despair, as our mother was said to be dying and as there was a goods train on the point of departure Anna and I boldly climbed on to the cab engine and begged the driver and stoker to let us go up with them. Of course, they refused, but so halfheartedly, when explained and they saw my tear-stained face, that we persisted. Still saying that he could not possibly do it the driver started the train and the stoker found us a couple of sacks to sit upon and kindly served us with their own hot coffee. It was very early morning in late Autumn, long before it was light and as we sat huddled together on the floor of the cab of the engine the weird journey, the rush through the dark night with only the flare of the engine's the to light us, lessened the tension of our anxiety about our mother.

On arriving in London we caught a fast train to Rivenhall and to our great relief found her better.

My mother and I went to Brighton again before the 18th Hussars left Preston Barracks. She hired a horse from the livery stable for me, so that Willie and I had long rides over the Downs together.

One day Evelyn came down and brought his beautiful chestnut mare down with him. He let me ride her and as we were getting on to the Downs he exclaimed, 'You ought to be able to ride well by this time' and gave the already excited mare a flick with his whip. She galloped away with me and I clung helplessly to her until, to my relief, she eventually found her way to her stables in the town.

My father soon wrote to say how dull he was without us and we went home. I had become tired of the life at Brighton and was glad to get home again.

Willie's father died in London early in the next year and we did not meet for some time afterwards. I think I saw him next at a small dance I was taken to by some friends and I did not recognise him at first, as, following the ugly fashion of the day, he had grown whiskers. He monopolised me the whole evening and called at the house to see me the next day.

I had now known Willie very well for three years, but I was very young and a curious distaste for my 'love affair' had grown up within me. I felt a desire to be left free and untrammelled by any serious thoughts of marriage; and, though I had not grown to dislike Willie, I wished him away when he looked fondly at me and half-consciously I longed to get back to the days when men were little more to me than persons to be avoided, as generally wanting something to be fetched or carried. I fancy my mother understood me better than anyone, for the day after the dance she interviewed Willie when he came; and I only remember a feeling of relief as he merely said good-bye to me in passing down the stairs, where I was childishly sitting, yawning violently to attain to the mistiness of outlook that I felt was expected of me!

With all the unreasonableness of girlhood I felt a sudden sense of regretful vanity that Willie's last glimpse of me then was while I was wearing a most unbecoming black silk jacket, much too large for me. It would have been so much more romantic to send him away with an aching remembrance of my fresh young loveliness, perfectly gowned!

Willie, I heard, went to Valencia and we saw nothing of him for a long time, though these pretty verses came to me from him:

FAREWELL

1.

In lightly turning o'er this page, may pause
A woman's hand awhile, which mine hath prest
In more than common clasp; for here I was
More than a common guest.

2.

Here, at the casement whence, 'mid song and laughter
We watch'd the buds whose bloom should deck thy hair,
Too wise to cast a more defined thereafter
Throughout a spring so fair.

8.
Alone, I write farewell within this book.
The summer sun is streaming o'er the park,
Oh, for the sunshine of a last fond look
Over a heart so dark

4.
Farewell to I know not if a merry meeting
For such a parting e'er shall make amend.
Harsh words have stung me; is their venom fleeting
Or hurtful to the end?

W.H. O' Shea

CHAPTER VI

My Father's Death

'And the peace of God, which passeth all understanding.'

THE FOLLOWING AUTUMN MY FATHER, mother and I went to stay at Belhus on a long visit, my father going to Cressing each week for the Sunday duty and returning to us on Monday morning.

We all enjoyed spending Christmas at Belhus. My mother and my sister Emma were devoted to one another and loved being together. We were a much larger party also at Belhus and there were so many visitors coming and going that I felt it was all more cheerful than being at home.

Among other visitors that winter, I well remember Mr John Morley – now Lord Morley – as he was told off to me to entertain during the day. He was a very brilliant young man and my elders explained to me that his tense intellect kept them at too great a strain for pleasurable conversation. 'You, dear Katie, don't matter, as no one expects you to know anything!' remarked my sister with cheerful kindness. So I calmly invited John Morley to walk with me and, as we paced through the park from one lodge to the other, my companion talked to me so easily and readily that I forgot my role of 'fool of the family' and responded most intelligently to a really very interesting conversation. With the ready tact of the really clever, he could already adapt himself to great or small and finding me simply to be interested, was most interesting and I returned to my family happily conscious that I could now afford to ignore my brother Evelyn's advice to 'look lovely and keep your mouth shut!'

John Morley, so far as I remember him then, was a very slight young man with a hard, keen face, the features strongly marked and fair hair. I had (to me) a kindly manner and did not consider it beneath him to talk seriously to a girl so young in knowledge, so excessively and shyly conscious of his superiority and so much awed by my mission of keeping him amused and interested while my elders rested from his somewhat oppressive intellectuality. I remember wondering, in some alarm, as to what topic I should start if he suddenly stopped talking. But my fear was entirely groundless; he passed so easily from one thing interesting to me to another that I forgot to be self-conscious and we discussed horses and dogs, books and their writers – agreeing that authors were, of all men, the most disappointing in appearance – my father, soldiers and 'going to London', with the greatest pleasure and mutual self-confidence. And I think that, after that enlightening talk, had I been told that in after years this suave, clever young man was to become – as Gladstone's lieutenant – one of my bitterest foes, I should perhaps have been interested, but utterly unalarmed, for I had in this little episode lost all awe of cleverness as such.

My father much enjoyed his stroll about the park and his quiet hours of rest in the soft light of the drawing-room at Belhus while we waited for dinner. When Sir John was with him his kindly son-in-law always advanced the late hour he liked to dine to an earlier one more suited to my father's health and the memory of never-failing kindly courtesies such as this were a comfort to remember, trivial as they may seem, as they soothed the everyday life of one who, unknown to ourselves, was slowly leaving us for ever. Soon my father had to give up his weekly visits to Cressing and gradually we noticed that he became more feeble every day with the continued recurrence of low fever, which left him weakened to combat the sleepless, feverish nights. Then came a time when he could not bear to let me go out of his sight and for a fortnight I did not leave him for a moment. He lay so still and quiet, with his finely chiselled face and white hair and looked so grand and far above all the little things we prized for his comfort's sake.

At night I lay on a sofa at the foot of his great bed – one that Queen Elizabeth slept in when on her way from Tilbury to London. One morning he called me to bring some writing paper and write down what he dictated and I did so. It was a letter to Mr Gurdon Rebow about the forthcoming election, in which my father had taken a great interest. The next day I hoped that he was better and he asked me for a hand-glass. I hesitated, as the look of approaching death was so evident to me and I feared it would shock him to see how much his face had altered. He insisted and I was obliged to comply lest he should understand why I feared to give it to him. He held the glass in his now feeble hand and gazed long and earnestly t his face, then gave it back to me with a sigh.

He sank swiftly and the days, which in other times might have appeared to pass slowly, when the serenity of such a peaceful life might have been monotonous, now passed all too soon.

Towards the end, Uncle William – afterwards Lord Hatherley (my father's brother)– came and prayed by my father's side. Kneeling by the bedside, holding my father's hand and mine in his, he whispered to me to say the Lord's Prayer with him. We said it together, my father, only just conscious, trying to follow. When we came to 'Thy will be done' I was too choked with sobs to repeat, or to feel it, but my uncle was insistent and a faint smile passed over my father's face as he tried to press his fingers in my hand. We waited by the bedside for some time, my uncle continuing to pray. Then my father's hand gently relaxed from mine in his last breath. I sank upon the bed by his side and the doctor came in from the next room and carried me out. A sedative was poured down my throat and I slept heavily, not moving again till I opened my eyes to see Willie and my sister bending over my bed.

Willie smiled at me and pulled out of his pocket, the loveliest little King Charles spaniel I had ever seen and put it on the bed to distract me. I was too much worn out and miserable to wonder at the presence of Willie, whom I believed to be in Madrid, but contented myself with curling round in bed with my new treasure. Later I heard that Willie had been telegraphed for by my mother and sister to come, as they feared that, after my long attendance on my father, I should fall ill when he died.

Willie had to return to Spain almost at once; and we were a very sad house party – my mother white and thin and terribly broken down by my father's death. I used to sit at the piano hour after hour playing to her and the day before my father was buried I sat extemporising at the piano to prevent her hearing the tramping of the men who were taking my father's coffin up the stairs to the room where he lay. My brother-in-law had the coffin made from an old oak tree out of the Belhus park.

Some weeks later I went home to Rivenhall by my mother's request to look for some things she wanted out of m father's library and to destroy his papers and sermons, as I had promised him before he died. I felt some difficulty in this, as I feared to set light to the old house in burning the papers. At last I took them down to the lake in the cold winter evening and watched them as they slowly sank, heavily weighted with stones, but only to come to the surface again in distant and darker shadows. The moorhens and wild fowl rose with weird cries as they found their shelter molested. This occupied me far into the night and I re turned heart-sick to the house where my father's cheery smile and genial presence would greet me no more. The hail was only lit by the fire of the dying logs and the large house seemed cold and desolate. The shadows of the spreading branches of the cedar outside the drawing-room, trailing their long length across the lawn and over the window, the smell of the thickly-falling spikes giving place to new and telling of half-awakened spring filled me with pain and loneliness.

The loss of my father was my first real sorrow and I wandered miserably round his study, where everything was as he had left it, including the things he had so lately touched – the letter-weight, pressed down on the answered letters and those now never be answered; his sermon case; his surplice folded on his table ready for the next services at the Church, now him never to take place. I felt that I could not bear the sadness and longing for him and as soon I could I returned to the warmer glow of the family circle at Belhus. There I found that the vexed question of ways and means - always a vexed question in clergyman's household when the head of the house dies – pressing heavily on my mother, who was left almost penniless by my father's death.

My mother and sisters were still discussing what was best to be done and my mother was speaking sadly as I went into her room. 'We must sell the cow and, of course, the pig', my eldest sister (Emma) replied in her sweet, cheerful voice, which produced a little laugh, though a rather dismal one and our sorrow was chased away for the moment.

My mother's sister, Mrs Benjamin Wood, on hearing of her troubles, settled a yearly income on her, thus saving her from all future anxiety, most of her children being provided for under our grandfather's – Sir Matthew Wood's – will.

CHAPTER VII

MY MARRIAGE

'Fair shine the day on the house with open door;
Birds come and cry there and twitter in the chimney,
But I go for ever and come again no more.' – STEVENSON

MY FATHER DIED IN FEBRUARY, 1866 and during that year we lived chiefly at Rivenhall. It was a. very quiet, sad year, but we had a few pleasant visitors. Sir George Dasent, of the *Times* and also Mr Dallas, who wrote leading articles for the same paper, were frequent visitors and Mr Chapman (of Chapman and Hall, publishers), with pretty Mrs Chapman, Mr Lewes and many other literary people were very welcome guests. My mother and sister Anna (Mrs Steele) were writing books and much interested in all things literary. At the end of the year we joined my eldest sister and her husband at Brighton and soon after this Willie returned from Spain and called on us at once, with the ever-faithful Cunninghame Graham. I now yielded to Willie's protest at being kept waiting longer and we were married very quietly at Brighton on January 25, 1867. I narrowly escaped being married to Mr Cunninghame Graham by mistake, as Willie and he – the 'best man' – had got into wrong positions. It was only Mr Graham's horrified 'No, no, no', when asked whether he would have 'this woman' to be his wife, that saved us from many complications.

My mother, brothers and sisters gave me beautiful presents and my dear sister Emma gave me my trousseau, while Willie himself gave me a gold-mounted dressing-bag. My old Aunt H. sent me a gold and turquoise bracelet. Willie saw this after I had shown him what my sister Mrs Steele had given me – carbuncle locket with diamond centre. Aunt was a very wealthy woman, my sister not at all, though in any case her present would have been much more to me than that of Aunt H. However, Willie merely remarked of Anna's gift: 'That is lovely darling and this', taking up Aunt H.'s bracelet, 'this, for the dog', snapped it round my little Prince.

Long afterwards he and I went to call on Aunt H. and as usual I had Prince under my arm. I noticed Aunt H. break off in a sentence and fix a surprised indignant eye on my dog. I had forgotten all about Prince's, collar being Aunt H.'s bracelet and only thought she did not like my bringing the dog to call, till I caught Willie's eye. He had at once taken in the situation and became so convulsed with laughter that I hastily made my adieu and hustled him off.

Sir Seymour Fitzgerald lent us Holbrook Hall for our honeymoon, a kindness that proved unkind, as the pomp and ceremony entailed by a large retinue of servants for our two selves were very wearisome to me. There was little or no occupation for us, as weather was too bad to get out much; our kind host had naturally not lent us his hunters and we were, or Willie was, too much in awe of the conventions to ask anyone to come and relieve our ennui. Indeed, I think that no two young people were ever more rejoiced than we were when we could return to the life of the sane without comment.

Willie had sold out of the army just before his marriage and his Uncle John, who had married a Spanish lady and settled in Madrid, offered Willie a partnership in his bank, O' Shea and Co., if he would put the £4,000 he received for his commission, into it. This was too good an offer to be refused, so I said good-bye to my people and bought some little presents for the servants at home, including a rich silk dress for my old nurse Lucy, who had been in my mother's service since the age of sixteen and who was much upset that her youngest and dearest nursling should be taken away to such 'heathenish, far-off places'.

Before leaving England Willie and I stayed for a few days in London and his mother and sister Mary called on us. They had not attended the marriage, as they would not lend their countenance to a 'mixed' marriage, though once accomplished they accepted the situation. They were very nice and kind and so gently superior that at once I became politely antagonistic. They brought me some beautiful Irish poplins which were made into gowns to wear in Madrid to impress the Spanish cousins and a magnificent emerald bracelet, besides £200 worth of lovely Irish house-linen. My mother-in-law and sister-in-law were most generous indeed and I then and always, acknowledged them to be thoroughly good, kind-hearted women, but so hidebound with what was, to me, bigotry, with conventionality and tactlessness, that it was really a pain tome to be near them. They admired me and very plainly disapproved of me; I admired them for their Parisian finish – (for want of a better term) – and for their undoubted goodness, but, though I was rather fond of 'Mary, they wearied me to death.

That week we crossed over to Boulogne and there we had to stay for a few days, as I was too ill from the crossing to go farther. Then we went to Paris and the second morning, Willie, seeing I was better, wanted to go out to *déjeuner* and told me to lie still and he would tell them to send a maid with my food, as he knew that I, not being used to French customs would not like a waiter to bring it. To make sure of my not being disturbed he locked the door. To my horror half an hour after he had gone there was a tap at the door and a manservant opened it with his key and marched in, despite my agitated protests in very home-made French. Once in, however, he made me so comfortable by his deft arrangement of' a most tempting meal and paternal desire that 'Madame should eat and recover herself', that I was able to laugh at Willie's annoyance on his return, to find the waiter once more in possession and removing the tray.

We then went to Paris to stay with my mother-in law and Mary for a few days, while they found me a French maid and showed me the sights. I had a great quantity of very long hair in those days and Willie insisted on my having it very elaborately dressed – to my annoyance – in the latest French fashion I did not consider becoming to me. My maid was also much occupied in making the toilet of my little dog. He was a lovely little creature and Caroline would tie an enormous pale blue bow on him as a reward for the painful business of combing him. From the time Willie gave me this little dog to the day it died, about six years afterwards, it went everywhere with me. He was as good and quiet as possible when with me, but if I ever left him for a moment the shrill little howls would ring out till the nearest person to him would snatch him up and fly to restore him to his affectionate, though long-suffering, mistress.

At Paris there was trouble with my mother-in-law and Mary at once because of him. They took me to see Notre Dame and as a matter of course Prince was in my arm under my cloak. As we came out I let my little dog down to run and the Comtesse nearly fainted. 'You took the dog into the church! 'Oh, Katie, how wrong, how could you! Mary! What shall we do? Do you not think——?' and turning a reproachful glance on me, Mary responded, 'Come, mother' and, leaving me amazed and indignant on the steps, they passed into Notre Dame again. With some curiosity I peeped in after them and beheld them kneeling at prayer just inside the door. They came out almost at once and the old Comtesse looked happier. 'You did not understand, dear', said Mary kindly, 'it is better not to take the little dog into a church.' I was young enough to resent being told I did not understand and promptly returned, 'I understand, Mary, that you and the Comtesse consider it wicked to take Prince into Notre Dame. Well, I don't and you must excuse me if I remind you that God made the dog and I seem to remember something about a Child that was born in a stable with a lot of nice friendly beasts about, so you need not have gone back to pray about me and Prince, I think!' And, scooping up Prince, I stalked off with a dignity that was rather spoilt by my not having sufficient French to find my own way home and having to wait at the carriage for them. We drove home with much stiffness and only thawed sufficiently to assure Willie how much we had enjoyed ourselves!

While I was abroad I often used to get away by myself to spend many happy hours in the beautiful churches with Prince tucked under my arm and often a friendly old priest would give us a smile as he passed on his way about the church, so it was apparently not a very deadly sin to take him with me.

Willie's mother and Mary became more reconciled to the little dog when they found how much admired he was in Paris. An old Frenchman, after seeing him one evening as Willie and I were leaving table d'hote, made inquiries as to where we were staying and called on Willie to offer £100 for 'madame's pet' if at any time she wished to sell him. Willie was too wise to approach me with the offer and assured monsieur that madame would consider the offer an insult only to be wiped out in monsieur's blood!

Happy in the knowledge that I looked extremely pretty in the gift – and peace offering – of my sister-in-law, a Parisian bonnet, exactly the size and shape of a cheese plate, made of white lace, wreathed with pink roses and tied under my chin with pale blue ribbon (the very latest fashion of the moment), we said good-bye to the Comtesse, Mary and their friends and went on to Biarritz. Our bedroom and sitting- room here looked out over the sea and my delight was great when I found that the great waves were breaking on the rocks just under the French windows of my bedroom. My pleasure in this was much intensified a few days after arrival, as I developed whooping cough and had to lie in bed for weeks with that and pneumonia. The English doctor had some difficulty in patching me up, but all through I was conscious of the roar of the waves as they hurled themselves against the beach and covered my window with spray. The sound of the sea soothed me to sleep when opiates could not and in the restless dawn I was wakened by the jingle of the bells on the donkeys as they were driven in to the hotel yard to be milked. These donkeys were driven in from Bayonne, as asses' milk was the only nourishment I could take then.

While I was getting better a chambermaid of the hotel, a Basque girl, who was my devoted nurse through out my illness, would talk to me in her native patois of her hopes and fears and of what she and her lover meant to do when they could marry. I used to love her pretty, kind face and her well-brushed brown hair, in which was twisted a bright coloured handkerchief, in the fashion of her country.

My convalescence was a pleasant time and I could have lived on the great red cherries my kindly nurse brought in such quantities. We parted with real regret and I gave the girl a beautiful ring off my finger, greatly pleasing her kind heart thereby.

Willie, on the long walks he took during my illness, made some really good sketches of the places around Biarritz and when I was able to go out we took long drives in the neighbourhood through winding wooded roads, the sea showing its boundless grandeur through the tall trees on the broken cliff.

The Duc de San Luca, a cousin of Willie's, used to come evening to play to me. He was a fine musician and his beautiful touch used to make even the not too good piano of the hotel sing with greater sweetness and power than it could have known before.

The Duc de San Luca was at that time a handsome man, with clear-cut features and curly white hair. He had great charm of manner and, like so many of the O'Sheas, had much of the elaborate courtesy of the foreigner combined with the charming friendliness of the Irishman. Though no longer young, he was a noted athlete and showed me with some pride wherever he had swum from headland to headland, tossed in the rough Atlantic sea. It was a feat of great endurance and one that no other man had succeeded in till then.

Our journey to Madrid the scenery interested greatly, the lank fir trees with cups tied on them to catch the exudations of resin, the vineyards with their profusion of promises with the glorious sunrise and the curious 'halt' of sunset were wonderful to untravelled mind.

As the train neared Hendaye I awakened to the most exquisite sunrise I have ever seen, vivid hues of crimson-purple, blue and orange-grey bathing the town, with its distant fringe of trees, in a flood of light and crowning the shadowed mountains in glory.

CHAPTER VIII

LIFE IN MADRID

*'Lending the colour of romance
To every trivial circumstance.'*

OUR ARRIVAL AT MADRID IN the evening we were met, to my annoyance, by many of my new Spanish relations. I was very tired, having been in the train for two days and nights and felt dusty and untidy in an old lace bonnet with a red rose stuck rakishly on one side. Prince, my little dog, was also very tired and disinclined to respond with any cheerfulness to the Spanish tongue which assailed us on every side.

Willie's aunt, Isabella O' Shea, a handsome, stout woman with large dark eyes and a kindly manner and her two daughters were there. They, of course, were cool and fresh and their pretty lace mantillas contrasted well with my dusty train-worn headgear.

They embraced me affectionately and promptly introduced a tall, regular-featured Spaniard as the great doctor of Madrid. I supposed he must be another cousin and, looked at Willie for enlightenment. He, however, only looked annoyed and suggested making a start for our hotel.

On arrival my aunt told me, through Willie, that, as she was sure I should be very tired, she had asked Dr ---- to come to meet us and to see me after I was in bed. I fear our interview must have proved unsatisfactory, as he could only speak Spanish and I was too cross and tired even to try to remember the little that Willie had taught me. Willie at last came to the rescue and drove him off, letting in the aunt and cousins, who all kissed me again. They were the last straw and I said, with a polite smile to Willie: 'if you don't take all these people away at once I shall howl'. He frantically told his aunt that he was hungry and with little cries and guttural sounds of concern they took him away to feed him and left me in peace.

When all was quiet in the hotel and street and Willie, back again, was sleeping peacefully, I crept into our sitting-room, glad to look about in the bright moonlight now I was free from the presence of so many strangers I opened the balcony window and the noise I made, though very slight, was sufficient to startle the wild dogs in the street feeding on the refuse flung out from the houses. They looked so starved and miserable as they gazed up and snarling and showing their very white teeth, that I thought they must be wolves from the mountains rather than dogs. At daylight they stole off to their hiding places and never approached anyone, or suffered themselves to be touched.

The next morning I was up early, anxious to see the city where all was new to me. Willie told me that – as was the custom in Madrid in the hot weather – our relatives would not be visible till the evening. He tried to curb my ardour by quoting a Spanish proverb, 'Only the English and dogs go out in the day', but it did not depress me and I insisted that I would join the 'dogs' at once. He pointed out that he did not want to get up and that Spanish girls did not go out unchaperoned. By the time I had assured him that marriage made a difference and that anyhow I was English, not Spanish, he was asleep again and I slipped out to explore.

Downstairs I found a man with melancholy eyes, to whom I let off a sentence that Willie had taught me, as being always likely to produce a sufficiency of food if I was alone and hungry in Spain. The melancholy one bowed profoundly and I waited with some nervousness to see what would happen in the way of food. Another waiter came, bowed and said some thing which sounded reproachful, though polite, but I firmly repeated my sentence and, after another bow and a helpless rolling of the eyes, he also disappeared. In a few moments a delicious meal arrived –hot coffee, eggs, poached with a peculiar cage pattern over them and French rolls. So I had a very good meal, quite undisturbed by the quiet peeps and guttural whispers of the servants, who passed constantly by the door to see the mad English señora who insisted on making a good breakfast.

Then, after a long wandering, from the radiance of the Puerta del Sol to the Carrera de San Jerónimo leading to light and open spaces, I found the streets, that had been so full of life when we drove from the station the evening before, absolutely deserted, except for a few men, chiefly gaily-dressed peasants in from the mountains, lying asleep in the shadow of the door ways.

The pavements seemed to burn my feet, though did not feel so breathless to me as on a hot day at home and I eventually found shelter in the Prado Gallery. The fashionable time for walking in the Prado was from midnight onwards and Willie had joined his relations the night before, so I knew I could count on a long morning to myself among the pictures.

That evening, after Willie had expressed satisfaction at my attire of bright blue poplin and of the diamond star in my hair, we strolled up to the Puerta del Sol to the cousins' house and found the porter and his wife taking their evening meal, consisting apparently of little, else than garlic, in their stone room at the entrance of the house. They eagerly welcomed me as the new relation of the Señor and Senora whom they served and then allowed us to proceed upstairs, ringing a bell to announce our coming, On our arrival upstairs a large door was flung open and I was presented to those of the cousins I had not seen before and a crowd of their friends..

It was a very large party invited to honour me and they were all most warm in their greetings, the ladies kissing me on the cheek and the men my hand. I was pleased and excited at my reception but rather bored at the amount of embracing I had to go through. These cousins of his were very fond of Willie and I was naturally gratified at their very obvious admiration of his bride. The strangeness of the scene made me feel gay and animated and enabled me to throw off the shyness which would otherwise have overcome me in being the centre of interest to all these strangers whose language I did not understand.

The two daughters were very graceful girls and the eyes of the elder, Margharita, were a perfect glow in her face. She was very lovely and wholly Spanish in appearance, though without that touch of heaviness in the lower part of the face that so many Spanish women have. The younger sister, Pepita, was more facile in expression, but, though pretty, did not possess the striking beauty of Margharita. She was much more lively than her sister, who was in a state of dreamy happiness at the presence of the young, Spaniard to whom she was about to be betrothed.

Of all the boy cousins who were present – the eldest, Guielmo, being away with his regiment–I was particularly charmed by Enrico, a dark, handsome lad, who came forward and offered me a crimson carnation, to the delighted approval of his family. He, like the rest, could only speak Spanish, but, he did not even do that, only with the most charming air of homage presented the flower and, though flushing rather hotly at the noisy approval of his relations, retired gracefully and unabashed.

Willie interpreted, but they were all so kind it was easy to make myself understood. The only one of the family who reminded me of their Irish blood was a younger boy, Juan, I think, who had very fair hair and skin and very blue eyes.

John O' Shea, the father, was a typical Irishman, with curly brown-grey hair and Irish blue eyes, a good-looking man of quick wit and attractive smile. He was an inveterate gambler and his card-playing heavy stakes was a perpetual distress to his Spanish and all the family, though he was an extra-ordinarily good player and his luck proverbial. His fear of cholera was an obsession with him and Willie had told me not to mention the word in his presence. A necessary warning, as rumours of cholera were as prevalent in that year as those of the expected revolution and made an easy topic of conversation.

I created quite a sensation in a mild way at dinner by asking for salt, as I was quite unconscious that at that time the tax on it in Spain was so great that salt was portioned out with the greatest care, even in the wealthiest families.

I remember I spoke with horror to Willie, that night, of the table manners of his relations and he was much annoyed with me that the sanitary toothpick and of washing out the mouth were a national custom both for men and women. During my stay in Spain I found it was so, but I never became reconciled to it.

Earlier in the evening of next day, in mantillas armed with fans, my aunt and cousins took me see the various places of interest Willie showed, where Queen Isabella still reigned and here, much to my astonishment, weeds were growing up between the flagstones of the courtyard and we waited to see Her Majesty as she drove out with beautifully strong, well-groomed mules in their richly coloured harness. The trappings 'of the old usage were always popular and raised enthusiasm whenever the Queen drove, her people willing with, externals as long as they could.

I much admired the grace of the women and the dark, animated beauty of their eyes and the flash of white teeth as they smiled in greeting. The men did not appeal to me so much and compared to disadvantage, in my eyes, with Englishmen and Irish men; but the women fascinated me.

My poor little dog hated these walks, as the Spaniards walk so slowly and Prince would have been ruthlessly trodden upon if I had not carried him in the crowd. He had been so spoilt in France and suffered from the lack of appreciation he met with from the Spanish.

I was introduced to Robert Owens, another cousin of Willie's. He was altogether Irish and looked it and, though a charming acquaintance, was only note-worthy as being the only man, Willie said, who would drink beer – and much beer – in Spain. The air, so pure and rarefied, seems to take away all desire for strong drink and I remember that. I never saw anyone in the slightest degree the worse for it during my stay in Spain. Willie, who knew Madrid – and most of Spain – as well as he knew London, told me that he had only once seen a drunken man in Spain and he was an Irishman.

The political horizon was very black in Madrid at this time and there was constant unrest among the people. Even the mere discussion of politics led to interesting little mock revolutions in cabarets, at street corners, in the regiments and in the schools; and more than once, while we were walking quietly in the Prado, shots and wild cries rang out and in sudden panic the gay promenaders would fly in all directions.

One evening a volley of bullets fell among us and catching up Prince and seizing my hand, made run hard up queer little side streets to our hotel.

As we were passing up to our rooms we were told two ministerial buildings had been attacked and there was much galloping of soldiers through the streets, while the Prime

Minister went past at the head of a troop. Willie went out only to find all was quiet and this slight outbreak of the Republicans over. These little disturbances became very frequent before we left Spain, but they did not cause me much alarm, as. I was sufficiently young to consider it picturesque and interesting.

About this time Margharita O' Shea was formally betrothed to her husband and Willie and I attended the ceremony. There was a very large gathering of relations and friends. She looked very lovely, but pale as usual and the crimson carnations I pinned into her hair made the contrast needed to render her strikingly beautiful. The ceremony was very simple, the bride and bridegroom-elect plighting their troth and after the festivities, returning to their parents' homes.

My walk was to the Retiro, where the gardens were very large and beautiful and the acacia trees in full bloom filling the air with delicious scent. These gardens were wilder and the air purer, I thought, than in the rest of Madrid, being nearer the desert and the mountain of the Guadarrama. Pretty, slight, dark-eyed children used to play there; and Willie, who was fond of children, used to wish he might have many, though I was too young to find them interesting.

On the eve of Ash Wednesday (Shrove Tuesday) we went to the Prado, where pancakes were being fried under the trees. The oil was of the rankest and the smell horrible, but I managed to eat a pancake to please my Catholic friends. It was a very interesting scene, the well-dressed people and the peasants all mingled together eating the greasy pancakes that they would not have touched at their own table. Beautiful women in their soft draperies and white and black lace mantillas, the waving fans and the hand- some dress of the peasants made an animated picture I have never forgotten.

Only very occasionally in those days did the French bonnet obtrude itself and the beautiful dress of the country was not spoilt by any attempt to graft French fashions on to it. I was delighted with the mantilla and found so many Spanish women were as fair as I that I could easily pass, in my mantilla, for a Spaniard. The then belle of society in Madrid was very fair, with golden hair and glorious dark eyes.

Now occurred my first real quarrel with Willie, though, on looking back upon the incident, I can see that a little more humour on my part and sympathy on his would have saved much bitterness.

An elderly Spaniard had paid me much attention for some time and, being very unsophisticated in those days, I thought that his compliments and gifts of flowers were merely the usual kindnesses of a fussy old man. In fact, I regarded him as a tiresome, though kind, old bore and was as shocked as astonished when, one evening in the Prado, he proposed, in a wealth of compliment of which I could not comprehend the half, that I should tie a long blue ribbon to my balcony next day when Willie was out, as a signal for him to come to my rooms. I was furiously angry and of course, forgot every word of Spanish that I knew. Willie came past at that moment, walking with one her ladies of our party and I unceremoniously took his arm and said I must go home at once. Of Willie took me home, but he was annoyed at the suddenness of my action and when I burst out that I had been grossly insulted by his old friend he laughed and told me not to be so imaginative. Recriminations followed and a had quarrel was the finish to what had been a very pleasant day.

I was angry and did not sleep well and when I rose late in the afternoon of the following day I found that Willie had gone out I was looking rather mournfully out of my window when I saw the flutter of a blue ribbon on the opposite balcony. For a moment I drew back in disgust, then a happy thought occurred to me and, dashing into my bedroom, I pulled out several yards of pale blue ribbon which I cut into long lengths. Stepping out on to the balcony, I looked carefully and ostentatiously up and down the street before tying each ribbon to one of the ornamental heads of the balcony. This done to my satisfaction, I threw on my mantilla and ran downstairs, stopping only to leave a message with the porter to the effect that if the Señor called he was to be told that Señor O' Shea awaited his visit with pleasure and yards of ribbon on a stick. Then I fled along to the cousins and inveigled them into spending a happy evening among my beloved owls on the way to the Manzanares.

I never knew what happened between the Señor and Willie, but when I was escorted back to the hotel by my friends Willie was home, very amiable and the ribbons had gone from the balcony. I did see the elderly Don Juan again, but he had become absolutely blind so far as seeing either myself or Willie was concerned.

When we had been in Spain for nearly a year there was some dispute about the business arrangements of Willie's partnership in his uncle's bank and Willie withdrew altogether from the affair. We then decided to return to England.

Though glad to go home, I parted from the Spanish relations with regret and have always since my visit to them thought that the admixture of Irish and Spanish blood is most charming in result.

CHAPTER IX

OUR HOME AT BENNINGTON

'How hard their lot who
Neither won nor lost.' – J. BEATTIE

ON OUR RETURN TO ENGLAND we lived in Clarges Street London, for some time, while Willie was looking for a place in the country where he could start a stud farm. Willie was very fond of horses and understood them well and I was delighted at the idea of his getting really good brood mares and breeding racehorses; we knowing, of course, nothing of the enormous expense and many losses such an undertaking was certain to entail.

At last we decided to take Bennington Park, Hertfordshire and on going there Willie bought some good blood stock, among the pick of which were Alice Maud, Scent and Apricot.

Bennington was a pretty place, with, two fine avenues of trees in a small park leading up to a comfortable house and when we arrived the park was a carpet of snowdrops. A lovely rose-walk led to the glasshouses and kitchen gardens. On one side of the house were the stables and after them the long rows of loose boxes, the groom's and gardener's cottages. The paddocks opened on and adjoined the park and the pasture was well suited to young stock.

Soon we had all the boxes tenanted and I spent many happy hours petting the lovely thoroughbred mares with their small velvety noses and intelligent eyes. .

When the foals began to arrive I spent most of my time in the paddocks with these dainty ladies, who led a life of luxury sauntering about the meadows – their funny and ungainly, though beautifully made foals running by their sides, or trotting merrily in front to impede the progress of the mares. I used to give the foals bowls of warm milk and they would come with their uncertain, clumsy young gallop to meet me directly I appeared.

We had great hope of a foal of Alice Maud's and Willie would talk with the utmost confidence of the racing victories that would be ours with Harpalyce, the son of Gladiator, a confidence that proved sadly misplaced.

My little pony was sent from Rivenhall and I found her very useful trotting through the Hertfordshire lanes to return the calls of the county people, as the mare Brunette which Willie gave me to drive in the T-cart was not considered safe for me to drive alone and I found it irksome to have a servant always with me.

By now I had my old nurse Lucy from Rivenhall to live with me and she was so glad to be with me once more that I promised her that she should never leave me again. She did not, till she died at a great age, years afterwards. Lucy was a splendid type of the old-fashioned and most faithful servant. Absolutely devoted to me, respecting Willie as belonging to me, she loathed my French maid from the bottom of her jealous old heart. Caroline had a tolerant shrug of the shoulders and an 'O, la, la', kept expressly for Lucy's benefit and this seemingly harmless expression used to make the old lady shake with anger that she was far too gentle to express. I used to take Lucy with me in the pony-cart, much to her pride, though she was sure that it would end in a violent death for us both. This dear old soul was generous to her fingertips and when Willie and. I came upon hard times he came to me one day and said: 'That dear fool came and poured her stockingful of savings out on my table and ran away before I could catch her! I have met with the greatest devotion and my life from my servants, but Lucy was the dearest them all.

Willie was much away from home, at races, etc., but having a first-rate stud-groom and twenty 'lads', the livestock was very carefully tended. I had to walk round every day when Willie was away and report on their condition to him. There was a stallion named Blue Mantle, who was subject to 'moods' occasionally and would vent his temper on his attendant with vicious teeth and sudden wicked 'down-cuts' of his forefeet and on these occasions Selby, the head man, would ask me to come and soothe the beautiful brute, who was as gentle as a lamb with me.

Willie's sporting friends often came home with him and most of the sporting world of that day were welcome visitors to Bennington. One young man, Sir William Call, was a particularly welcome friend and among others I have a warm remembrance of Sir Charles Nugent and Mr Reginald Herbert and his wife, the latter a very sporting little lady, who was an inveterate smoker, a habit unusual among women at that time. Captain Douglas-Lane gave me a beautiful white cat, 'Haymaker', which spent a happy life sleeping upon the back of any horse that happened to be at home.

The Rowlands, who used to train at Epsom, kept some mares with us; they were particularly charming people, with whom we sometimes stayed for the Epsom race meetings. I remember getting into trouble with some of the local ladies by spending several evenings in playing chess with. a fellow-visitor there–a famous tenor who, after singing his song of courtesy due, would retire into gloomy silence, guarding his precious voice in a corner until I took pity on his loneliness (for an artiste is rather out of his element in a sporting house party) and played many games of chess with him.

I never knew how Signor Campibello (plain Mr Campbell to his friends) got there, but I know he was most grateful for the quiet evenings of chess– and so was I.

The chief form of social intercourse in the county was the giving of long, heavy and most boring dinners. People thought nothing of driving eight or even ten miles (and there were no motor-cars then) to eat their dinner in each other's houses and this form of entertainment used to produce such an absolutely painful boredom in me that I frequently hid the invitations from Willie, who liked to 'keep up with the county'.

I did not mind giving the dinners so much, for I used to 'mix people horribly', as Willie said and it was rather amusing to send a stiff and extremely conventional 'county' madame, blazing with diamonds and uninspiring of conversation, in to dinner with a cheery sporting man of no particular lineage and a fund of racy anecdote. I think, too, that this sort of thing must have been good for both.

It also used to make me happy give some accompanying daughters a good time among the 'ineligible' men we had about. Men, mostly, without two sixpences to rub together', but nevertheless very gay-hearted and pleasant companions; a change for the dear prim girls, whose brothers made such a point of being 'away', except in the shooting seasons, that the girls – and so many girls – had no natural companionship with young men at all. The mothers fussed and Willie besought me to be more careful but the girls enjoyed themselves and that any reasonable human being should enjoy a 'county' dinner party is an achievement of which any young hostess may be proud.

On looking back I think that Willie and I must have been of great interest to all these dull people. The horses were, of course, a perpetual interest and we were, I think, sought after socially from my very disinclination to conform to the generally accepted modes of amusement.

Willie and I were a good-looking young couple and people liked to have us about. Willie, too, was a good conversationalist and had a ready wit that made him welcome, since an Irishman and wit are synonymous to the conventional mind. That his witticisms pertained rather to the France of his education than the Ireland of his birth was unrecognised, because unexpected.

I was – rather, I fear, to Willie's annoyance – labelled 'delightfully unusual' soon after our going to Bennington, the cause being that I received my guests one evening with my then abundant hair hanging loosely to below my waist, twisted through with a wide blue ribbon. To Willie's scandalised glance I replied with a hasty whisper, 'The very latest from Paris' and was rewarded with the mollified though puzzled expression very properly awarded by all men to the 'latest fashion' of their womenkind.

I put off the queries of the ladies after dinner in the same way and was rewarded by them by the general admission that it was a fashion for the few – who had the hair. Never did I admit that I had been out with the horses so late that I had had just time for Caroline to hurry me into a gown and shake down my hair, as my first guest arrived. So little do we deserve the fame forced upon us.

Sometimes Willie was delayed at a race meeting and did not get home in time for the dinner party he had insisted on my giving and the awkwardness resulting – greatly exaggerated in the estimation of those conventional folk – caused much irritation between us. It was far easier for these good people to believe that 'it was very odd' that Captain O' Shea should not be at home to receive his guests than that he had really missed a train.

My annoyance was even more acute when I had to go without him to a dinner miles away, in the unhappy knowledge that my hostess's gaze would wander beyond me, in greeting, seeking for the man w ho was not there to complete her table.

Our county member's family were among some of most agreeable of. the people living an where and I remember the two very pretty daughters as great friends of mine, as also were Lady Susan Smith and her husband. The former was a very handsome woman, curiously stiff in manner and very warm in heart, to whom, in spite of our utter unlikeness in I became extremely attached.

I think I must have been a rather a clever young woman. Once when Willie had gone away for a few days, leaving orders that his smoking-room was to be repapered, he telegraphed the same evening to returning the next day with several friends for the races near by. The room was, of course, not done and the men said they could not do it in the time so I drove over to Hertford, returning in triumph with rolls of paper, which I calmly proceeded to paste and put up myself, much to the disgust of our butler, who told my old nurse I was 'bad for trade'. I made him hold the steps for me – hence his discontent.

Bennington was eight miles from the nearest town and when Willie was away and I had no guests he wished me to have our great retriever, Ben, who was a splendid guard, in the house at night. One evening a tramp came to the pony stable when I was there alone with Ben and directly he spoke to me Ben leapt straight at his throat and I had a horrible ten minutes getting him off the man. At last I got the dog under control and made the man roll into the coachhouse – Ben would not let him rise. After I had praised Ben for his good guard of me and shut him up I had to go and attend to the poor tramp, whose injuries were sufficiently severe and the whole affair worried me so much that I decided that my King Charles spaniel was quite as much guard as I could bear to have about me. Willie could not see my point, but, as the men's cottages were far from the house and the butler by no means an adequate protection for anyone, he stipulated that I should at any rate keep his gun loaded in my bedroom at night when he was away. This I did, but the knowledge of having a loaded gun in my room rather got on my nerves, until I hit on the happy expedient of getting out of bed and discharging it (in the air) through my always open window the first time I woke in the night. I am sure this had an excellent effect in keeping off wanderers of evil intent and I heard, to my joy and Willie's, that a gardener courting one of the maids, found 'the Missis a perfect terror with that gun.'

Our Gladiator foal, of whom Willie had had such golden hope, became lame and after a time it was found that she (Harpalyce) had a disease of the joint. She was a great pet of mine and I was her chief nurse during the long illness she had before we were in mercy obliged to have her shot. She suffered badly and had to be slung and I sat up many nights with her trying to soothe the pain and tempt her appetite with little delicacies. She used to look at me with those large pathetic eyes, so pitiful in suffering animals (and none more so than in horses) and gently rub her velvet muzzle against my cheek.

We had some splendid horses to keep for other people and, among others, there was Blue Mantle belonging to a friend of Willie's – Captain Douglas – one of the most beautiful horses I have ever seen. He was very bad-tempered and unless his own groom was there he had to have his feed put in from the loft. This curious savageness of temper was not extended to me, as he would allow me to go into his box at anytime and pat and fondle him as much as I liked.

One evening when Willie was away, the stud groom rushed to the house to say that one of the horses, a very valuable stallion named Orestes, belonging to Mr Porter, the trainer, of Alfriston, Sussex had slipped in his box while being groomed and broken his leg. I sent frantically for several vetinary surgeons, but there was nothing to be done and I had to give the order to have the horse shot to end his sufferings. I then sat, horribly frightened, awaiting Willie's return, for the stud groom's gloomy reiteration of: 'It's your responsibility, ma'am; your responsibility', was not reassuring. However, Willie, while much upset at the accident and the necessity for shooting the horse, quite agreed that I had done the only thing possible in the circumstances, as did the owner – Mr Porter.

Porter had two very pretty daughters, whom I had to stay with me at Bennington. They were quiet little ladies and as far apart from the generally accepted idea of a trainer's daughters, 'fast, horsy and noisy', as could possibly be. Quiet, well-educated and charming girls, they were welcome visitors and very popular.

I used to send in a large consignment of fruit, vegetables and butter to the Hertford market every week, as we produced so much more of everything of the sort than we could consume. The grapes from our vineries were very fine – and I was much disgusted when the head gardener remarked to me that they had much improved since the foal and horse had been buried near the vines.

Our expenses were so heavy, both in the house and stables, that I was very glad to get the ready money for our market produce from garden and farm every week and, as time went on, the only veto I put upon the sale of produce was on behalf of my pigeons. I had a cloud of beautiful birds that used to settle on me whenever I appeared, cooing and pulling my hair and a few of these, special favourites, I allowed in my own sitting-room, where they would sit on my table and cause me much inconvenience while I wrote letters. I think Willie must have given orders that they were not to increase, as, though many families were hatched, they never, so far as I could see, reached maturity.

Willie was never good at dunning friends for money owed and as we had many brood mares, not our own, left with us for months at a time and the stable expenses, both for forage and wages, became appallingly large. It was always difficult to get the accounts in and while Willie did not like to worry the owners even for the amount for the bare keep of the animals, he was himself perpetually worried by forage contractors, the shoeing smith and the weekly wage bill, besides innumerable extra expenses pertaining to a large stable.

As I urged against the sale of the mares, which he so often threatened, their happy, peaceful maternity in the long lush grass and shade of trees by day, their comfortable boxes at night and their fondness of me, he used to stare gloomily at me and swear gently as he wished there were more profit than peace in their maternity and my sentimentality. But he could forget his worries in the pleasure of schooling the yearlings and we agreed always to hold on as long as possible to a life we both found so interesting and with the facile hope of youth we thought to get the better of our expenses in time.

In this year (1869) my eldest (surviving) brother, Frank became very ill and Willie and I went to Rivenhall see him He wanted me to nurse him on in my old home while Willie returned to Beninngton.

Frank had consumption and very badly; he suffered intensely and I think I have never longed for the presence of a doctor with more anxiety than I did for Dr Gimson's at that time. My perpetual fear was that the effect of the opiate he gave to deaden poor Frank's pain would wear off before he came again. When it grew dusk Frank desired me to put candles in every window, that he might not see the shadows – the terrifying shadows which delirium and continual doses of morphia never fail to produce.

Frank's very dear friend, Captain Hawley Smart, the novelist, came to Rivenhall in the hope that he could cheer poor Frank's last hours; but he was too ill to know or care and Hawley Smart could, like the rest of us, only await the pitying release of death.

From my position by the side of Frank's bed I could see the bridge over the lake and the white gate leading towards Witham and I watched with feverish anxiety for the sight of the doctor's cart – longing for his coming to relieve the tortured brain that was so filled with the horror of indefinable terrors; and the pain of my watching was increased by the knowledge that the morphia, even while it allayed the agony he was suffering, always added to the after horror of the awakening.

Dr Gimson was justly a hero in Essex. At one time, when unable to get anyone to help him, he strove alone to stem an outbreak of diphtheria in an Essex village some miles from his own practice and acted both as doctor and nurse when the supply of the latter failed. Single-handed, he worked night and day among the poor people: nursing, healing and cheering, for life or death, until the awful epidemic abated. To this day his memory is there venerated as that of a saint.

After Frank's death I returned to Bennington, taking his ex-soldier servant with me. The latter was a useless encumbrance, as it turned out, but it relieved my mother of his presence at Rivenhall.

We went on at Bennington in very much the same way until the end of that year. Willie had been betting very heavily in the hope of relieving the ever-increasing difficulty of meeting our heavy expenses and now, added to his losses in racing and the heavy expenses attendant on keeping up such a large stud, the kind-hearted bank manager insisted that the large overdraft on his bank must be cleared.

Hitherto, whenever he had become very pressing, Willie had sent him 'something on account' and we had given a breakfast for his hunt, as Willie said such a good fellow 'could not eat and ask at the same me'. Now, however, Mr Cheshire sorrowfully declined to eat and maintained that his duty to his firm necessitated his insisting upon the clearing of the overdraft. After consultation with him and another friend Willie decided that there was nothing to be done but send all our mares up to Tattersal's for sale. It was a heavy blow to us, but Willie had never had sufficient capital to carry on an undertaking requiring such enormous expenditure and his experience had been dearly bought.

As the long string of thoroughbred mares was led away to the station and I kissed their muzzles for the last time I cried bitterly. Poor Willie watched them go with a miserable face, which became even more so when a sympathetic old groom explained pitifully: 'Ah, dear ma'am, maybe you'll cry more when they all comes back'. And come back they did, escorted by Tommie, the pony, for not a bid of any importance was made for any of them. Though I was glad to see my favourites again, it of course meant more trouble in the immediate future, our affairs getting into a worse state every day till bankruptcy became imminent.

My brother-in-law, Sir Thomas Barrett-Lennard paid Willie £500 for the mares and Willie sent them to Belhus, where Sir Thomas had them turned into the park.

After this we managed to pay off all the servants and I arranged to go to Brighton with my old Lucy and our faithful Selby, the stud-groom, who desired to stay on with us until we could arrange our plans, as did also my maid Caroline.

When Willie was made bankrupt Mr Hobson – a gentleman living near us with his very charming wife, who afterwards became Mrs A. Yates – very kindly took my little old pony across the fields at night to his own place and kept him there so that he should not go into the sale of our goods. This defrauded no one, as the pony (my own) was beyond work, being my childhood's pet.

CHAPTER X

A Day on the Downs

'A son to clasp my finger tight.' – NORMAN GALE.

I WAS NOW NEARING MY first confinement and my aunt, Mrs Benjamin Wood, took a house for me at Brighton close to my sister's, Lady Barrett-Lennard. There my son Gerard was born.

I was very ill for some time after this and my mother, Lady Wood, stayed with me, employing her time in making a lovely water-colour sketch for me.

Willie's affairs were now settled and I had to give up all hope of returning to my dearly loved country home and all my pets; but I had the consolation of my beautiful babe and I forgot my sorrow in my greater possession. He was very healthy, so I had no trouble on that score.

A young solicitor who took Willie's affairs in hand, Mr Charles Lane (of Lane and Monroe), very kindly took upon himself to call on my Uncle William, who was then Chancellor of England and ask him to assist us our financial difficulties. Uncle William was much astonished at the application of this, obviously nervous, solicitor, who with the courage born of despair on to suggest that Lord Hatherley might give Willie a lucrative appointment.

Strangely enough it had never occurred to me to apply to Uncle William for anything and when Mr Lane called on us and solemnly presented me with a substantial cheque and a kind message from my uncle, Willie and I were as surprised as we were pleased, even though Mr Lane explained that 'the Lord Chancellor had no post suitable' for Willie's energies.

We then moved into a house on the Marine Parade, as the one we were in was very expensive and though I was glad to be next door to my sister, I felt it was not fair to my aunt, Mrs Wood, who was paying the rent for us.

As soon as we moved to the new house an old friend and noted steeplechase rider, came to stay with us for a few days with his wife. He became very ill at dinner and in a few hours was raving in delirium tremens, while his poor wife hid sobbing in my bedroom, as she was so much afraid of his violence. He was a big man and our doctor a little one, but after the first encounter, when the doctor was knocked down flat on entering the room, the doctor was absolutely master of the very dangerous situation. I have always had a great admiration for the medical profession.

Someone now gave me a magnificent prize-bred mastiff dog and this dog developed distemper so badly that I had to nurse him for weeks–with the help of Mr Mannington, the veterinary surgeon (who was known then as the best patcher-up of broken-down race-horses in existence). Poor Bismarck became paralysed in the hind-quarters, but, with unceasing care, we pulled him through and he grew into such a magnificent specimen that we had many good offers for him. At last, as we were unable to keep him properly exercised and Willie was offered a very large sum for him from a Frenchman, we let him go to France.

The Franco-Prussian War having broken out, Brighton was thronged with French people The women looked very handsome with the massive braids of hair worn by old and young, low on the neck and tied with ribbon, or hanging in loops wound round with silver cord. This French fashion was, of course, eagerly copied by English ladies and though I had a wealth of hair I found it was not nearly heavy enough when braided like this and Willie insisted on my buying additional braids, as indeed was necessary in all cases while this foolish French fashion lasted.

My faithful French maid Caroline stuck to us all through our fallen fortunes, as also did our stud-groom and though we could no longer pay them the high wages they had always had, they refused to leave us.

Caroline, whose hardest task had been to dress my hair and wash my little dog, now with the utmost cheerfulness took to cooking, scrubbing, cleaning and being literally a maid-of-all-work, while Selby, who had had more than twenty underlings to do his bidding and who had never even cleaned the horse he rode at Bennington, now did anything that needed doing, helping in the house, valeting his master. Finally, when Mr Hobson sent my old pony down, Selby installed himself as stable-boy as a matter of course and as though he had always been in the habit of receiving ten shillings a week for doing a great deal, instead of £200 a year for doing practically nothing.

Both Selby and Caroline considered it their first duty to keep Gerard, my little son, amused, so, in spite of our troubles, Willie and I were very comfortable, thanks to these faithful friends.

My aunt, Mrs Wood, now took a cottage for me at Patcham, just out of Brighton and I was able to have my pony there. The house at Patcham was a dear, little, old-fashioned place right against the Downs and there I used to walk for miles in the early morning, the springy turf almost forcing one foot after the other, while the song of the larks and scent of the close-growing, many-tinted herbage in the clear bright air filled me with joyous exhilaration.

Willie went to town and often was away for days, on various businesses and I was very lonely at home – even though I daily drove the old pony in to Brighton that I might see my sister.

I had a cousin of Willie's, Mrs Vaughan, to stay with me for some time, but she was perpetually wondering what Willie was doing that kept him so much away and this added irritation to loneliness. I had had such a busy life at Bennington that I suffered much from the want of companionship and the loss of the many interests of my life there. I felt that I must make some friends here and, attracted by a dark, handsome woman whom I used to meet riding when I walked on to the Downs, I made her acquaintance and found in her a very congenial companion. Quiet and rather tragic in expression, she thawed to me and we were becoming warmly attached to one another when Willie, in one of his now flying visits, heard me speak of my new friend. On hearing her name – it was one that a few years before had brought shame and sudden death into one of the oldest of the 'great' families of England – he professed himself to be absolutely scandalised and with an assumption of authority that at once angered me, forbade me to have any more to do with her. He met my protests with a maddening superiority and would not tell me why she was 'beyond the pale'. I explained to him my own opinion of many of the women he liked me to know and almost all the men, for I had not then learnt the hard lesson of social life and that the one commandment still rigorously observed by social hypocrisy was, 'Thou shalt not be found out'.

When I met Mrs — again she soothed my indignation on her behalf and as we sat there, high on a spur of a hill, watching the distant sea, she smiled a little sadly as she said to me:

'Little fool, I have gambled in love and have won and those who win must pay as well as those who lose. Never gamble, you very young thing, if you can help it; but if you do be sure that the stake is the only thing in the world to you, for only that will make it worth the winning and the paying.'

It was nearly ten years afterwards that I, feeling restless and unhappy, had such a sudden longing for the sea, that one morning I left my home (at Eltham) very early and went down to Brighton for the day. I was alone and wished to be alone; so I got out of the train at Preston, for fear I should meet any of my relations at Brighton station. A fancy then seized me to drive out to Patcham, about a mile farther on, to see if my former little house was occupied. Having decided that it was I dismissed my fly and walked up the bridle path beyond the house out on to the Downs, where, turning south, towards the sea, I walked steadily over the scented turf, forcing out of my heart all but the joy of movement in the sea wind, with the song of the skylarks in my ears.

The exhilaration of the down-lands filled my whole being as it had always done, but now my spirits rose with a quick sense of happiness that I did not understand. I sang as I walked, looking towards the golden light and sullen blue of the sea, where a storm was beating up with the west wind. Presently I realised that I was very tired and I sat down to rest upon a little hilltop where I could see over the whole of Brighton. It was now afternoon and I was tired and hungry. I idly wondered if I should go down presently and claim the hospitality that I knew my sister, Lady Barrett-Lennard, would so gladly offer me. But my gay spirits had suddenly deserted me and, though the larks were still singing in the sunshine where I sat, the wind seemed colder and the dark line of the stormy sea had grown very wide.

Presently the wind brought up the rain and I rose and began to descend the hill towards Brighton. I wondered apathetically if my sister was in Brighton or if they were all at Belhus still. Anyhow, I knew there would be someone at her house who would give me something to eat. Then I turned round and began deliberately to climb up the hill on to the Downs again. After all, I thought, I had come here to be alone and did not want to see my sister particularly. The family might all be there and anyhow I did not want to see anybody who loved me and could bias my mind. I had come down to get away from Willie for a little while – or rather from the thought of him, for it was rarely enough I saw him. If I went down to see Emma rand Tom they would ask how Willie was and really I did not know and then how were the children. Well, I could thankfully answer that the children were always well. Why should I be supposed to have no other interests than Willie and my children? Willie was not; as a matter of fact, at all interesting to me. As to my children, I loved them very dearly, but they were not old enough, or young enough, to engross my whole mind. Then there was dear old Aunt Ben, who was so old that she would not tolerate any topic of conversation of more recent date than the marriage of Queen Victoria. What a curiously narrow life mine was, I thought; narrow, narrow, narrow and so deadly dull. It was better even to be up there on the Downs in the drifting rain–though I was soaked to the skin and so desperately tired and hungry. I paused for shelter behind a shepherd's hut as I saw the lithe spare form of my brother-in-law, Sir Thomas, dash past, head down and eyes half closed against the rain. He did not see me and I watched him running like a boy through the driving mist till he disappeared. He had come over from Lewes, I supposed. He was a J.P. and had perhaps been over to the court; he never rode where he could walk – or rather run.

I waited, sheltering now from the rain and through the mist there presently came a girl riding. On seeing me she pulled up to ask the quick way to Brighton, as the mist had confused her. As I answered her I was struck by a certain resemblance, in the dark eyes and proud tilt of the chin, to my friend of many years ago whose battles I had fought with Willie and who had told me something of her life while we sat very near this place. The girl now before me was young and life had not yet written any bitterness upon her face; but as she thanked me and, riding away, laughingly urged me to give up the attempt to 'keep dry' and to fly home before I dissolved altogether, I had the voice of my old-time friend in my ears and I answered aloud, 'I am afraid; I tell you, I am afraid.'. But she was dead, I knew and could not answer me and I smiled angrily at my folly as I turned down the track to Preston, while I thought more quietly how the daughter whose loss had caused such bitter pain to my dear friend, when she had left all for love, had grown to happy womanhood in spite of all.

I was now feeling very faint from my long day of hard exercise without food, but there was a train about to start for London and I would not miss it.

On the platform for Eltham, at Charing Cross, stood Mr Parnell, waiting, watching the people as they passed the barriers. As our eyes met he turned and walked by my side. He did not speak and I was too tired to do so, or to wonder at his being there. He helped me into the train and sat down opposite me and I was too exhausted to care that he saw me wet and dishevelled. There were others in the carriage. I leant back and closed my eyes and could have slept but that the little flames deep down in Parnell's eyes kept flickering before mine, though they were closed. I was very cold; and I felt that he took off his coat and tucked it round me, but I would not open my eyes to look at him. He crossed over to the seat next to mine and, leaning over me to fold the coat more closely round my knees, he whispered, 'I love you, I love you. Oh, my dear, how I love you.' And I slipped my hand into his and knew I was not afraid.

CHAPTER XI

BEAUFORT GARDEN

'Nor to thyself the task shall be
Without reward; for thou shalt learn
The wisdom early to discern
True beauty in utility.'

W ILLIE WAS AWAY MORE THAN ever after this and I became so bored and lonely that I told him that I must join him in London if he meant to be there so much. He then proposed to give up the Patcham house and move the small household to Harrow Road, London, temporarily, till we had time to find something less depressing.

In going we also hoped to shake off an acquaintance who haunted us at Brighton and Patcham, a Mr D., but he soon found us out and, realising that I was determined to be 'not at home' to him, he took to leaving gifts of beautiful Spanish lace at the door, directed to me and only the words 'from Romeo' inside.

This man had lived most of his life in Spain and was a remarkably good judge of Spanish lace and I must confess I was tempted to keep the rich creamy-white stuff that arrived anonymously. This 'Romeo' was more than middle-aged and, when he wrote that for 'safety's sake' he would address messages to me through the 'agony' column of the newspapers, Willie's wrath was unbounded.

He wrote to poor 'Romeo' in sarcastic vein, alluding to his age and figure, his insolence in addressing 'a young and beautiful 'woman with his 'pestilent' twaddle. He told him, too, that he withdrew from all business transactions with him and would have much pleasure in kicking 'Romeo' if he dared call to the house again I was almost sorry for the foolish old man; but that was wasted on him, for he continued, undeterred by Willie's anger, to address 'Juliet' in prose and verse in the daily papers As he said, the 'Daily Press was open to all and the Captain could not stop that!' I used to laugh helplessly as Willie opened the morning paper at breakfast and, first, gravely turning to the 'agony' column, would read the latest message to 'Juliet' from her devoted 'Romeo', becoming so angry that breakfast was spoiled to him. The sudden cessation of our acquaintance prevented our making that of Mme. Adelina Patti as 'Romeo' had arranged a dinner in order that I should meet her.

A few weeks after we arrived in Harrow Road Willie began to complain of feeling ill and a swelling that had formed on his neck became very painful. He was confined to bed and after great suffering for weeks, Mr Edgar Barker, who was constantly in attendance, said he must operate to save Willie's life. I had no nurse, as at this time we were in such financial straits that I really did not know which to turn and Willie was too ill to be asked about anything. Mr Barker said to me, 'You must hold his head perfectly still and not faint'. So he operated and all went well, in spite of my inexperience in surgical nursing. Mr Barker, for whose kindness at this time I can never be sufficiently grateful, helped me in every way and would not allow even Willie's mother and sister to do so, as their presence irritated the patient so intensely.

During this time of trouble a Mr Calasher, a money lender, called to have some acceptances of Willie's met. I left Willie's bedside for a few minutes to see him and he was kindness itself, agreeing to a renewal on my signature alone and most kindly sending in some little delicacies that he thought Willie might fancy. When Willie had recovered and went to see Mr Calasher about the bills, it being then more than ever impossible to meet them, he (Mr Calasher) would not consent to a further renewal, but tore the bills across and gave them back to Willie, saying, 'Don't worry yourself, Captain O' Shea, but pay me when you can and add six per cent interest if you are able.' I am glad to say we did this within the year. His courtesy about these bills was a great relief to me, as Willie was far too ill to be spoken to about business and I was at my wits' end for money to meet every day expenses. The accommodating Jew who lends the indiscreet Christian his money – naturally with a business-like determination to increase it – has so much said against him that I am glad to be able to speak my little word of gratitude of one who was considerate and chivalrous to Willie as well as myself, much to his own detriment.

As Willie got better, my uncle – Lord Hatherley – and my aunt sent us various good things to make Willie strong and my days of nursing were lightened, since he was now able to amuse himself with our little boy. This young man, when only just able to toddle, took the opportunity presented by my being in close attendance on his father to lock me in the conservatory and, thus freed from supervision, to take his headlong way down the steep stairs. I had to thrust my hand through the glass panel of the door to unlock it and catch my baby just in time to prevent the dive he had set his heart on – into the hall two floors below. His temper was distinctly gusty in those days and once, during a walk with myself and my old Lucy, my small son flung himself down in the midst of the traffic in the Bayswater Road with tight-shut eyes and crimson face, working up the howl of rage that never struck terror to our hearts under ordinary conditions. I summoned up sufficient presence of mind, however, to whisk him up from under the very feet of a cab-horse.

The quickly-gathered crowd was very indignant with me and said it was 'a shame, poor little darling', but, since I was always addicted to such unreasonableness myself on seeing children and animals coerced into safety, I was not so indignant as was my old nurse.

Mr 'Romeo', still faithful, in spite of all rebuffs, sent me long letters of congratulation at Willie's recovery. One in particular I remember caused an indignant snort and sardonic chuckle from Willie when I gave it to him to amuse him. It said that in Willie's place he would have 'lain to kiss my feet for the rest of his life' had he been nursed as I had nursed Willie! Willie said he was glad that Romeo of the ample girth had not suffered this discomfort of gratitude.

Better circumstances arising on Willie's recovery of health, we were anxious to get away from the depressions of Harrow Road, with its constant processions of hearses and mourners on the way to Kensal Green Cemetery.

After a weary hunt we finally d upon a house in Beaufort Gardens. Willie insisted upon the extravagance of having a paper of silver and blue specially made in Paris for the drawing-room. This very beautiful paper showed up the extreme ugliness of our furniture to great disadvantage. However, it was all very comfortable and the change from Harrow Road agreeable.

My French maid rejoiced in returning to her light duties as lady's maid and reigned over a staff of maids in unison with the butler.

Selby, at last convinced that race-horses were out of the question with us, left us, with mutual expressions of esteem, to seek more congenial surroundings.

We went to Beaufort Gardens in 1872 and Willie insisted upon my making many new acquaintances. We soon found ourselves in a social swirl of visits, visitors and entertainments. I had always disliked society, as such and this appeared to me to be almost as bad as the Bennington dinner-party days, without the compensating circumstances. Willie, however, thoroughly enjoyed this life and as he was always worrying me to dress in the latest fashion and would have a Frenchman in to dress my hair before every party, I became very rebellious.

Here my eldest daughter was born and I was glad of the rest from parties and balls – even though so many people I did not care to see came 'to cheer me up!'

As soon as I was about again the life I found so wearisome recommenced. After escorting me home from a dance or reception that I had not wanted to go to, Willie would go off again to 'finish up the night' and one night, when in terror I was seeking for burglars, I found a policeman sitting on the stairs. He explained genially that the door was open and he thought it better to come inside and guard the door for the Captain's return!

Of the many small items of Willie's wishes that I loathed was having my hair dressed in the prevailing French style. One evening, when we were going to some stupid function, Cunninghame Graham came in, looked at my hair and cried aghast, 'Do take it down, Youngest. You look awful'. As my own conviction was similar I lost no time in doing so and afterwards used Cunninghame's opinion in defence of my own personality.

We gave dinner-parties to various people of note at that time, especially to the great world of Paris in London, or visiting London, for Willie's family had greatly intermarried in France and his mother and sister lived chiefly in Paris, while Willie was very popular at the French and Spanish Embassies. I remember on one dreary occasion the butler informed me confidentially that the cook was so desperately drunk that he 'had a misgiving' as to the 'success' of dinner. An agitated descent to the kitchen proved to me that the cook, already asleep under the table, affectionately embracing a bottle, was beyond any misgiving; and I sternly ordered her unsympathetic fellow-labourers to remove her, while I cooked the dinner myself. As regards the dinner this solution of the difficulty was absolutely successful, but a good cook makes a heated and absent-minded hostess.

Alfred Austin – not then Poet Laureate – was a great friend and constant visitor of ours at that time. He had been at school – at Oscott – with Willie and he was, I remember, extremely sensitive to criticism.

'Owen Meredith', Lord Lytton, was also a frequent visitor, especially when my sister Anna was with us – she being sympathetic to his genius.

I was always glad to see Willie's Spanish relations who came over to England, especially Guielmo, the eldest son of Willie's uncle, John O' Shea. Guielmo was devoted to my children and his coming was the signal for wild games with 'Cousin Giraffe', as they called him. Guielmo had a most charming little romance which he confided to me. He had, when very young, fallen in love with a beautiful young Spanish girl, the sister of a friend of his. She was absolutely blind and his parents and friends urged him to look elsewhere for a wife. But his was a faithful soul and after some years of determined waiting the elders gave way and a very happy and successful marriage was the result.

CHAPTER XII

MORE FINANCIAL DIFFICULTIES

Thus while Thy several mercies plot
And work on me, now cold, now hot,
The work goes on and slacketh not.' – VAUGHAN.

I THINK WILLIE AND I were beginning to jar upon one another a good deal now and I loved to get away for long walks by myself through the parks of London. Kensington Gardens was a great solace to me in all seasons and weathers and I spent much of my time there. I often turned into the Brompton Oratory on my way home for a few minutes' peace and rest of body and soul and these quiet times were a comfort to me when suffering from the fret and worry of my domestic life. The kneeling figures waiting for Benediction, the prevailing sense of harmony which seems to embrace one in the Catholic churches, soothed and rested me. The great comfort I have always found in the Catholic churches, both at home and abroad, is that one is allowed to rest in peace, to acquire knowledge if one will, but unforced, unretarded by spiritual busybodies, who are so anxious to help the Almighty that they hinder Him with their fussy, impertinent attentions to the souls to whom He is perhaps trying to speak.

I first made my way to the Oratory when my daughter Norah was baptised and some little time afterwards one of the Fathers called on me. Finally Father —— undertook to call regularly to instruct me in the Catholic religion. He and the other priests lent me any books I wanted – 'The Threshold of the Catholic Faith' and one other I have now. That I never got beyond the 'Threshold' was no fault of these good Fathers, who taught me with endless patience and uncompromising directness. But I had before me two types of Catholic in Willie and his mother and sister and both were to me stumbling-blocks. The former was, as I knew, what they call a 'careless Catholic' and I thought that if he who had been born in that faith that means so much, made so little of it, perhaps it was more of a beautiful dream than a reality of life. Yet when I turned and considered those 'good Catholics', his mother and sister, I found such a fierce bigotry and deadly dullness of outlook, such an immense piety and so small a charity, that my whole being revolted against such a belittling of God-given life. Now, I know that Mary and the Comtesse disliked me personally and also that my temperament was antagonistic to theirs, as indeed to Willie's, though the affection he and I had for one another eased the friction between us; but youth judges so much by results and my excursion into the Catholic religion ended in abrupt revolt against all forms and creeds. This feeling was intensified when my second little girl, Carmen, was born and christened at the Oratory. I would not go in, but stood waiting in the porch, where I had so often marked tired men and women passing in to pray after their hard and joyless day of toil and I felt that my children were taken from me and that I was very lonely.

My Uncle William, Lord Hatherly was Lord High Chancellor at this time and we were a good deal at his house, both at 'functions' and privately. His great friend, Dean Stanley, was very kind to me; Dean Hook came, too and many other Churchmen were continually in and out in their train. My cousin, William Stephens, who afterwards became Dean of Winchester, was then a very good-looking and agreeable young man, he followed my uncle about like a shadow and my uncle and Aunt Charlotte were devoted to him. But my uncle gathered other society than that of Churchmen about him and it amused me to watch for the pick of the intellectual world of the day as they swarmed up and down the stairs at the receptions, with the necessary make-weight of people who follow and pose in the wake of the great.

Willie insisted upon his wife being perfectly gowned on these occasions and as he so often got out of going to those functions and insisted on my going alone, certain other relations of Lord Hatherley's would hover round me with their spiteful remarks of: 'Dear Katie, alone again! Poor dear girl, where does he go? How odd that you are so often alone – how little you know!' I was fond of my old uncle and he of me, but these little amenities did not make me like these social functions better, especially as his wife, my Aunt Charlotte, had a most irritating habit of shutting her eyes when greeting me and, with her head slightly to one side, saying, 'Poor dear! Poor lovely lamb!'

Uncle William's failing eyesight finally led to his resignation and, though he felt that he needed his well-earned rest, it was a hard trial to him to resign the Chancellorship, to which he had worked his way, absolutely without aid or influence, from the lowest rung of the ladder of law. But in his days of rest he had the comfort of knowing that what he had worked for he had attained and, as was said of him by one who knew him so well – Dean Stanley – he had kept his 'heart and fingers clean'.

My Uncle William and his wife always deplored that they were childless and it was in an access of bitterness that he once exclaimed: 'God withholds sons, but the devil sends nephews!' in allusion to one who had given him considerable trouble.

My Aunt Charlotte led a very busy, fussy life and, when pressed for time, often sent her carriage for me, so that I should leave cards and where necessary, write her name in the visitors' book of the great or Royal houses where she and my uncle went as guests. They were the most devoted married people I have ever seen and, if there be such a state in married life, theirs was a perfect union.

My sister, Lady Barrett-Lennard, had a house in Whitehall Gardens for that season in order to 'bring out' her eldest daughter and, as my other sister, Mrs Steele, came up to town occasionally, I saw a good deal of them and was happier and more amused than I had been for some time. I had become fond of London, all my children were strong and healthy there and I was very proud of the gold, curly heads and fair skins as they went off to the park in the morning. I once accompanied a lady who was staying with us to her French dressmaker, Madame ——, who tried hard to persuade me to order some gowns, but who was delighted and did not worry me further, when I said, 'My children are my clothes!' She considered the sentiment so pretty!

My only son, Gerard, was now a beautiful golden-haired boy of four years, with a dazzlingly fair skin and dancing eyes of Irish blue. We wished to have his portrait painted by a lady who exhibited at the Royal Academy, but he was as naughty as he was beautiful and neither bribes nor threats could keep him still for a moment. We were in despair until I remembered his ambition to be left alone on the top of the housemaid's steps. There he was allowed to perch till a not very successful portrait was completed and he brought the sittings to a close with the confidently expected dive, head-first to the floor, causing the uncanny silence characteristic of this boy when hurt, a silence that always seemed to stop my heart while it rejoiced his father's The little boy would howl the house down in the ungovernable rages he at times indulged in, but when hurt he would shut his mouth tightly and no anxious inquiries could get more than a stifled 'I'm thinkin'' out of him.

This winter, following the birth of my second girl, was bitterly cold and my health, which had not been good for some time before her birth, caused much anxiety. After a consultation between Sir William Gull, Sir William Jenner and my usual doctor, it was decided that we should go to Niton, Isle of Wight, as I was too weak to travel far. My dear old aunt, Mrs Benjamin Wood, sent her own doctor to me and he recommended me to inject opium–an expression of opinion that horrified Sir William Jenner into saying, 'That man's mad, or wants to get rid of you!'

I had heard from Willie's Spanish cousins that smallpox was raging in Madrid and the doctors could not get enough vaccine to vaccinate their patients. This was in the summer and I bought as many tubes as I could get and sent them to Madrid. My apparently charitable act had made my own doctor so angry that he would not come near me this winter till he heard that I was really very ill. It appeared that I had upset some extraordinary red-tape etiquette of the medical profession. I showed him the letters of heart-felt gratitude that I had received from the Spanish doctors and they mollified him somewhat – even though he could not read them!

Our pecuniary affairs were again causing us considerable anxiety, but my dear aunt played the fairy godmother once more and sent Willie a cheque so that we could go to Niton without worry or anxiety and stop there until my health should be re-established. So we said good-bye to our friends and, among others, to the good priests of the Oratory, who begged me to pray for the faith to see what they had failed to convince me of.

We were delighted with the summer warmth of the sun at Niton and spent a happy Christmas basking in it. Since the hotel was very expensive, Willie established me in lodgings with the children and nurses in Ventnor and, finding the place decidedly dull, returned to London.

The children and I wandered about out of doors all day, but I was kept awake night after night by the foghorns and sometimes by signals of distress from Blackgang Chine. The proprietress of the house used to come to me at night and tell me how her husband had been called out to help in the lifeboat. Two terrible wrecks occurred there. We watched until morning for the boat while the storm was beating against the house and the waves were raging against the rocks and making sport of the human lives they were battering to death.

The local doctor at Ventnor, who had been put in charge of my shattered health, was not satisfied that it was in any way improving and, finding one day that I was in the habit of taking sleeping draughts, he snorted angrily off to the chemist and returned with a large tin of meat extract, with which he presented me, adding the intimation that it was worth a dozen bottles of my draught – which happened to be a powder – and that my London doctors were bereft of intelligence. I was too tired to argue the point and contented myself with the observation that all doctors save the one in attendance were fellows in unintelligence –a sentiment he considered suspiciously for some moments before snorting away like the amiable little steam engine he was. His specific for sleeplessness was much more wholesome than drugs and I have always found it so since then.

CHAPTER XIII

CAPTAIN O' SHEA ENTERS POLITICAL LIFE

D'un coeur qui t'aime,
Mon Dieu, qui peut troubler la tranquille paix,
Il cherche, en tout, ta volonté suprème.
Et ne se cherche jamais,
Sur la terre, dans le ciel même
Est il, d'autre bonheur que la tranquille paix
D'un coeur qui t'aime.' – RACINE.

WILLIE WAS TOO BUSY TO come down to Ventnor again and I became so depressed by the relaxing air and by the sight of the many poor, consumptive people I met at every turn, veritable signposts in their different stages of disease, of the road I had been warned that I was on, that I decided to go nearer home. My doctor suggested Hastings and there I went, taking my small family under the kindly escort of one of my nephews. When this young man had settled me with the children and maids at St Leonards, with most careful consideration for our comfort, he informed his Uncle Willie of the whereabouts of his family.

Willie soon came down and, as my health improved rapidly, we stayed on for some time, making frequent visits to my Aunt 'Ben' at Eltham, who was making our stay at the seaside possible. This was practically my first introduction to my aunt, as my former visits were when, as a little child, I was only allowed to sit by her side in the 'tapestry room' trying to do some needlework under her supervision and assisting her in the consumption of the luscious peaches she always had on the table. In those days I would have been wild with terror at the idea of being left alone with this aunt, who always wore the fashions of her early Victorian youth and who would not tolerate the slightest noise in the house. I now found her of fascinating interest and even the painful sense of 'hush' in her house, the noiseless stepping of the servants and the careful seclusion of sunlight had attractions for me. My uncle, Benjamin Wood, had died very many years before and my aunt never alluded to him. She herself had never left Eltham since his death and had only once been in a railway train, living in complete seclusion in her fine old Georgian house, only 'taking the air' in the grounds adjoining or emerging forth in her chariot to drive for an hour daily.

Her curious old-world mode of speech and what she termed 'deportment', together with her outlook on life across half a century ignored, lent a piquancy to her conversation that was delightful. She lived in the intellectual world of the Greek poets and of Addison, Swift and Racine; and there was a leisure and a scholarly atmosphere about her life that seemed to banish the hurry and turmoil of the modern world at her gate; She was extremely generous in subscribing to what she termed 'Organisations for the better conduct of charitable relief' and, though of no particular religious belief, she subscribed to the various objects of local charity when asked to do so by the clergyman of the parish. The latter gentleman once made the mistake of offering to read the Scriptures to her on the occasion of an illness and I well remember his face of consternation when she replied: 'I thank you, Mr —, but I am still well able to read and the Scriptures do not interest me'. Yet during the many years I spent in constant companionship with her the quiet peace which reigned by her side gave me the most restful and soothing hours of my life.

On these visits of ours, from St. Leonards, Willie and I only went for the day, since my old aunt objected to 'gentlemen visitors' staying in the house, declaring that it 'perturbed' the routine of her 'domestic staff.' After we had paid her several visits in this way she informed me that she had ascertained that I was much alone, that she was very tenderly attached to me and would wish to provide for me and my children if I would come to live near her so that I could be her constant companion. She added that she considered that this arrangement would be more 'seemly' for me, as Willie was obliged to be away from home so much.

After consultation with the (county court) judge, Gordon Whitbread, her nephew and my cousin, who always transacted her business for her, she bought a house for me at the other side of her park and arranged to settle a regular income on me and to educate my children. In return she asked that her 'Swan' – as she always called me – should be her daily companion. This I was until her death, at the age of ninety-four, about fifteen years later.

My aunt lived a life of great seclusion and, with the exception of George Meredith (the author) and the Rev ---- Wilkinson, who each came down once a week to read to her, her oculist and great friend, Dr Bader and two old ladies, friends of her youth She rarely saw anyone.

My aunt was very fond of me and I was with her nearly the whole of the day – reading to her, writing for her, wheeling her up and down the great tapestry room, or walking quietly in he grounds. Chislehurst is near Eltham and on the drives we took in the great old-fashioned 'chariot' (which had the motion of a ship nearing the shore) we sometimes met a beautiful woman driving herself, with one servant behind her. I remember on one occasion my aunt, who was very short-sighted, observed that her servants touched their hats as this lady went by. She said nothing at the time, but when we returned home and she stood on the steps of the house leaning on my arm, she turned and said to her coachman: 'Frost, I observed that you and Henry saluted a lady during our airing'

'Yes, ma'am, the Empress Eugénie, ma'am.'

'Never do that again, Frost. I forbid my servants to salute that lady.'

As I helped her up the steps she murmured indignantly to herself – for she was of the old regime and an ardent Legitimist.

I was generally with my aunt from the first thing in the morning, returning to my children at lunch time and in the afternoon I got home for dinner, should Willie happen to return. These quiet years with my aunt were a liberal education to me, as she was a good Latin and French scholar and so proficient in Greek that up to the last week of her life she translated Greek verse. She used to explain to me, when I asked why she was so particular in sending her servants to church, that, although she professed no belief herself, she had observed it was 'beneficial to others' and that her father – Admiral Samson Michell, of the

Portuguese Navy – had very carefully instructed his daughters – my mother and aunts – 'in the Christian religion; to his great solace'.

To the maids she particularly commended religious observance as being productive of 'propriety of conduct'. She always encouraged any religious feeling she observed in me and made me read Nelson's 'Festivals and Fasts' and Jeremy Taylor to her on Sundays; unless Willie came down from London and read French to her. Willie was an excellent linguist and his French had the perfect accent she delighted in.

Sunday evenings used to be rather a trial to me, as my aunt would order all her servants up to her sitting-room, so that they should repeat the verses she had given them to learn by heart, or the collects for the day, so that she might know that they had used their leisure hours during the week in a 'rational' manner. The servants hated these excursions into culture and, from the man-servant, whose 'piece' always lacked aspirates, to the kitchen maid, round, crimson and uncomfortable, whose 'portion' always halted despairingly in the middle, they kept their resentful gaze fixed upon me, who held the book – and the thankless office of prompter.

My aunt's house – 'The Lodge', Eltham – was fine old Georgian, spoilt inside by the erection of mock pillars in the hall. Years before I joined my aunt at Eltham, my mother, being of a curious disposition, took off some of the blue paper on a wall that appeared to move when the wind was strong. She thus discovered that the walls were hung with beautiful old tapestry depicting scriptural and mythological scenes

My aunt had all the papers removed by experts and the result disclosed a most wonderful collection of tapestry. It was Crown property and she was rewarded for the expense of restoring the beauty of the house by an application from the authorities to have it – the tapestry – delivered over to them. As it was found that to move it would be to ruin it, she was allowed to retain it in her possession and I believe it still hangs in the house, which has now been turned into the Eltham Golf Club.

I have heard that the late King Edward went over the house some years after my aunt's death and had one of the beautiful chimney-pieces removed to one of his own houses. I have a very fond memory of the old red house shadowed by great beech trees and of the very old elm trees in the 'little park', where a sudden crash in heavy summer weather would warn us that another of these dangerous old giants had fallen under the weight of years and foliage.

My aunt was very particular that no one should tread. upon .the highly polished floors of her house and, as the two large halls had only rugs laid about on the shining surface, one had either to make many 'tacks' to reach the desired door or seat, or take a short cut on tiptoe and risk her 'displeasure'.

It was amusing to watch George Meredith on his excursion from the front door to the dressing-room at the foot of the stairs, where my aunt kept three pairs of slippers for the use of her 'gentlemen readers' lest their boots should soil the carpets. To reach this little room he had – if in a good mood and conforming to his old friend's regulations – to walk straight ahead past the room and make a detour round a pillar of (imitation) green marble and a table, back to the door. On days of rebellion against these forms and ceremonies he would hesitate for a moment just inside the door and, with a reckless uplifting of his head, begin a hasty stride across the sacred places; a stride which became an agitated tiptoeing under the scandalised gaze of the footman. Before he began to read to my aunt the following dialogue invariably took place:–

'Now, my dear lady, I will read you something of my own.'

'Indeed, my dear Mr Meredith, I cannot comprehend your works.'

'I will explain my meaning, dear Mrs Wood.'

'You are prodigiously kind, dear Mr Meredith, but I should prefer Molière today.'

While Willie and I were still living in London we went down one day to see a furnished house we wished to rent for a few weeks and, remembering my Aunt Ben's injunction to convey her 'felicitations to her dear Mr Meredith', we called on him.

I had not before met George Meredith and had only read one of his works – and that 'behind the door' when I was very young, owing to some belated scruple of my elders. I remember as we neared the house, asking Willie the names of Meredith's other works, so that I might be ready primed with intelligent interest and Willie's sarcastic little smile as he mentioned one or two, adding, 'You need not worry yourself, Meredith will soon enlighten us as to his books. They say it's the one thing he ever talks about.' But we spent a delightful afternoon with Mr Meredith, who showed us all his literary treasures and the little house at the end of the garden where he wrote. While we sat in the lovely little garden drinking tea our host descanted on the exquisite haze of heat that threw soft shadows about the house and gave the great trees in the background the appearance of an enchanted forest. George Meredith was 'reader' to Chapman and Hall in those days and he spoke to me appreciatively of the work of my mother and sister, who published with Chapman and Hall.

In these days at Eltham I learnt to know George Meredith very well, as I saw him almost every week when he came down to read to my aunt. The old lady did not like triangular conversation, so as soon as they were fairly launched in reading or conversation, I would gladly slip away to my own occupations. To Aunt Ben, Meredith appeared to be a very young man indeed and in her gentle, high-bred way she loved to tease him about his very great appreciation of his own work – and person. Meredith took her gentle raillery absolutely in good part and would hold forth upon what the literary world 'of all time' owed him in his books and also upon what Lady This-or-That had said in admiration of his good looks at such-and-such a gathering. My aunt used to delight in these tales, which were delivered in the mock serious manner of a boy telling his mother of his prowess, real or imagined; and after a time of listening to him, with only her gently modulated little bursts of laughter to encourage him, she would say, 'Oh, my dear Mr Meredith, your conceit is as wonderful as your genius!' – bringing forth from him the protest, 'My dear lady, no! But it is a pleasure to you to hear of my successes and to me to tell you of them.' And so I would leave them to their playful badinage and reading.

Meredith was very fond of his old friend and always treated her with the chivalrous and rather elaborate courtesy that he well knew she delighted in. His weekly visits were a great pleasure to her and although she would not allow him to read anything modern and never anything of his own work, I think he must have enjoyed his reading and talk with this clever old lady, for often the stipulated two hours of the 'classics and their discussion' lengthened into the three or four that caused him to miss all the most convenient trains home.

One evening as I was going into the house I saw him standing on the terrace gazing after the retreating form of my little girl Carmen, then about six years old. As I came up he pointed at the stiff little back and said, "She was flying along like a fairy Atalanta when I caught her and said, 'What is your name?', 'Miss Nothin'-at-all' she replied, with such fierce dignity that I dropped her in alarm."

I called the child to come back and speak politely to Mr Meredith, but, to his amusement, was only rewarded by an airy wave of the hand as she fled down a by-path.

As I sometimes chatted to Mr Meredith on his way through the grounds to the station he would tell me of 'that blessed woman', as he used to call his (second) wife, already then dead and of how he missed her kind and always sympathetic presence on his return home and in his work Sometimes the handsome head would droop and I thought he looked careworn and sad as he spoke of her and in doing so he lost for the moment all the mannerism and 'effectiveness' which were sometimes rather wearisome in him. As my aunt grew very old she – in the last few years of her life – became unequal to listening and talking to her 'gentlemen readers' and to me she deputed the task of telling them so. In the case of George Meredith it was rather painful to me, as I feared the loss of the £300 a year my aunt had so long paid him for his weekly visits might be a serious one to him. But he, too, had aged in all these years and perhaps his visits to his old friend were becoming rather irksome to him in their regularity. Curiously enough, I shared my aunt's inability to enjoy his work and to the last I met his mocking inquiry as to my 'progress in literature' (i.e. his novels) by a deprecating "Only 'Richard Feverel'".

The house my aunt bought for me was just across her park and she had a gate made in the park fence so that I might go backwards and forwards to her house more quickly. My house was a comfortable villa with the usual little 'front garden' and larger one in the rear. There were excellent stables at the end of this garden. The house, 'Wonersh Lodge', had the usual dining-room and drawing-room, with two other sitting-rooms opening severally into the garden and a large conservatory, which I afterwards made over to Mr Parnell for his own use. My aunt furnished the house and we were most comfortable, while my children rejoiced in having the run of the park and grounds after the restraint of town life.

Willie was very much in London now and occupied himself in getting up a company to develop some mining business in Spain. He always drew up a prospectus excellently; on reading it one could hardly help believing – as he invariably did – that here at last was the golden opportunity of speculators and some influential men became keenly interested in these mining schemes of his.

A couple of years after having settled at Eltham my eldest little girl became dangerously ill with scarlet fever and diphtheria, owing to defective drainage. I sent my boy and my other little girl to Paris, to their O' Shea grandmother and aunt, to keep them from infection and nursed my daughter myself until I got diphtheria also and then we lay in bed together, isolated, in charge of a nurse and faithful maid. My little girl used to whisper huskily that it was 'lovely to be ill-in-a-bed wif mummy if only our necks didn't hurt so drefful much'. We were both very ill and I think that it was only the skilled and constant attention of Dr Barker that pulled us through. My aunt was very disconsolate at my long absence from her and was so shocked that the drains should have proved dangerous in the house she had bought for me that she had them entirely relaid by a London expert.

When my daughter developed scarlet fever I asked Willie to stay in London altogether until the infectious stages were past. This he did, but was at once laid up with measles on his own account. He was peculiarly subject to this complaint and, while I knew him, he caught the disease no fewer than four times.

When my little girl had recovered sufficiently to travel I took her down to Folkestone for change of air.

Our old friend, Hobson, brought down a beautiful collie dog, who became the fast friend and constant delight of my children until she died, of old age years afterwards, when she was laid in the honourable grave which the three moist-eyed young mourners procured by the removal of my best rose trees in the middle of the lawn.

At Folkestone I met my boy and girl returning from their grandmother in Paris. The two children had been away from me for some months and I hastened on to the steamer to greet them. I laughed as I caught sight of the very formal little Frenchman into which they had turned my sturdy young son and ignoring his polite lifting of his hat in greeting, had in two minutes rumpled him into the noisy, rough little sinner whom I loved. My little Carmen was more difficult. She looked like a little fairy in her French frills and laces and bitter weeping was the result of my trying to take her from her nurse. This exquisite little mortal did not thaw to me for some days, but with the help of Elfie, the collie, I gradually won her affections from the Paris of her baby-heart.

I was very glad to get back to my aunt again – someone who wanted me always. The children were necessarily much with their nurses and governess and Willie's Spanish business, had now grown into a company, some acute business friends of his thinking so highly of it that they put into it sums varying from £1,000 to £10,000. Our old friend Christopher Weguelin took great interest in it and eventually Willie was offered the post of manager, at La Mines, at a good salary. It was a very acceptable post to Willie, as he loved the life in foreign countries. There was a very good house and he had it planted round with eucalyptus trees to keep off the fever so prevalent there and from which the men working the mines suffered greatly.

Willie was, however, immune to fever and never had it. He was away in Spain for over eighteen months this time and did not come home at all during the period.

I had to pay frequent visits to London when samples of the sulphur were sent home for testing purposes, to see Mr Weguelin and to place the constant demands for new machinery in as ingratiating a way as possible before various members of the 'board'. It seemed impossible to get the English firms to do their business thoroughly and no sooner had Willie reported the arrival of the new machinery than he cabled that parts were missing. All there unbusinesslike methods caused him acute irritation, as he had the miners there on his hands, idle, perpetually awaiting something from England; and to relieve his feelings, he would write his reports in hot language to me that I might show them in the proper quarter, an irregularity which did not please the directors.

A machine for crushing the ore was sent out, but, though a success, the colour of the sulphur was not right. Then Willie invented and patented a very good machine for extracting the sulphur from the ore and I drew up a report from his instructions on this and had it verified by the engineers to the company. But it was too late and, though I was invited to the dinner, given by members of the board, at the house of the analyst who was to make the last test of the sulphur, the report was not satisfactory in view of the enormous amount of money already expended. Mr C. took me to the dinner and afterwards I went with my host to the testing-room, where the, report he made of the sulphur he tested was very good.

I remember the uncomfortable sensation I experienced, all during this experiment, from the rich beautiful voice of one of the guests of the evening, who was singing in the adjoining room. My companion was far too much absorbed in his work to notice it, but there was a mad, exultant ring in the voice that blended uncannily with the wild song and the blue flame and the most foul smell made by my host with his test-tubes. On our return to my fellow-guests I noticed that the other men looked uneasily at the singer as he got up from the piano. This poor friend of mine became hopelessly insane a few months afterwards and that horrible, wild song rang perpetually through the rooms he occupied in the Maison de Sante of his retirement.

On the basis of this last report Mr C. did what he could with the directors of the company, but it was of no use and they declined to sanction further expenditure. Mr C., whose kindness to me was that of an elder brother, said in his whimsical way, 'Make us one of your ripping pies and I'll have one more try at it with the two ——': two of the most influential directors. So I made the gorgeous beefsteak pie, for which I had been famous among my. friends since childhood, but C. came to me afterwards with a gloomy face and said, 'No use, the pigs wolfed that scrumptious pie and then, though I said you'd made it, declared that old Father William was to be ordered home at once and the mines closed.' I could not help laughing at the thought of a pie being expected to turn the decision of a body of hard-headed businessmen, but he was so hurt at my levity that I stopped to sympathise with him. He did not seem to regard his own position of discomfort at having introduced the affair to his company – a dead loss of many thousands of pounds.

My son now, at eight years old, proved too much for his French governess, so we arranged for him to go to a school at Blackheath, though he was two years younger than the age generally accepted there.

The little girls were started afresh with a German governess and on Willie's return from Spain he stayed at Eltham for a time.

We were pleased to see one another again, but once more the wearing friction caused by our totally dissimilar temperaments began to make us feel that close companionship was impossible and we mutually agreed that he should have rooms in London, visiting Eltham to see myself and the children at weekends. After a while the regularity of his weekend visits became very much broken, but he still arrived fairly regularly to take the children to Mass at Chislehurst on Sunday mornings and he would often get me up to town to do hostess when he wished to give a dinner-party. I had all my life been well known at Thomas's Hotel, Berkeley Square, as my parents and family had always stayed there when in London. So here I used to help Willie with his parties and to suffer the boredom incidental to this form of entertainment. He never seemed to have anyone at all amusing – with the exception of one or two old friends – Sir George and Lady O'Donnell, Major Whiteside and Graham and I liked these much better at Eltham, where one had more time to talk, than at those dinners.

On one occasion Willie, who always said that even if only for the sake of our children I ought not to 'drop out of everything', worried me into accepting invitations to a ball given by the Countess ----, whom I did not know and for this I came up to town late in the afternoon, dined quietly at the hotel by myself and dressed for the ball, ready for Willie to fetch me as he had promised after his dinner with some friends. I was ready at half-past eleven as had been arranged and the carriage came round for me at a quarter to twelve. At twelve the manageress, a friend from my childhood, came to see if she could 'do anything for me' as Captain O'Shea was so late. At 12.30 the head waiter, who used to lift me into my chair at table on our first acquaintance, came to know if 'Miss Katie' was anxious about 'the Captain' and got snubbed by the manageress for his pains. At one o'clock, white with anger and trembling with mortification, I tore off my beautiful frock and got into bed. At nine o'clock the next morning Willie called, having only just remembered my existence and the ball to which he was to have taken me.

Little Major Whiteside was, I think, at that time the smallest man in the British army and, in spite of the fact that they could see little else than busby when he was on horseback, his men trembled at his slightest roar, for he was a terrible little martinet. He and his two pretty sisters, who over-topped him so that if they stood each side of him he was invisible, had been very dear friends of ours for years. Although this valiant little warrior had the well-earned reputation in the army of being absolutely fearless, he could not stand the sudden and uproarious cawing of rooks aroused from slumber and on my taking him a short cut to the station through my aunt's rookery, after a visit to us at Eltham, I was astounded at the bound of terror and volley of language that came from the little major when our disturbing feet roused the rooks. Willie used to say that he was a V.C. hero, but only in patches.

Willie was now longing for some definite occupation and he knew many political people. While he was on a visit to Ireland early in 1880 he was constantly urged by his friends, the O'Donnells and others, to try for a seat in the next Parliament. A dissolution seemed imminent. I had often talked of becoming a member for some Irish constituency and now, on again meeting The O'Gorman Mahon in Ireland, he was very easily persuaded to stand in with him for County Clare. He wrote home to me to know what I thought of the idea, saying that he feared that, much as he should like it, the expenses would be almost too heavy for us to manage. I wrote back strongly encouraging him to stand, for I knew it would give him occupation he liked and keep us apart – and therefore good friends. Up to this time Willie had not met Mr Parnell.

CHAPTER XIV

MR PARNELL AND THE IRISH PARTY

'I loved those hapless ones – the Irish Poor – All my life long.
Little did I for them in outward deed
And yet be unto them of praise the meed
For the stiff fight I urged 'gainst lust and greed: I learnt it there.'
SIR WILLIAM BUTLER.

'THE INTRODUCTION OF THE ARMS Bill has interfered with Mr Parnell's further stay in France and it is probable he will be in his place in the House of Commons by the time this is printed.'

This paragraph appeared in the *Nation* early in 1880. On the 8th March of that year, the Disraeli Parliament dissolved and on the 29th April Mr Gladstone formed his Ministry.

In the Disraeli Parliament Mr Parnell was the actual, though Mr Shaw had been the nominal, leader of the Irish Parliamentary Party since the death of Mr Isaac Butt in 1879. Shaw continued the Butt tradition of moderation and conciliation which had made the Irish Party an unconsidered fraction in British politics. Parnell represented the new attitude of uncompromising hostility to all British parties and of unceasing opposition to all their measures until the grievances of Ireland were redressed. He carried the majority of his Party with him and in Ireland he was already the people's hero.

Born in June, 1846, Parnell was still a young man. He came of a fine race, he was a member of the same family as the famous poet, Thomas Parnell, as Lord Congleton, Radical reformer and statesman and, above all, Sir John Parnell, who sat and worked with Grattan in Ireland's Great Parliament and shared with him the bitter fight against the Union. On his mother's side he was the grandson of the famous Commodore Charles Stewart, of the American Navy, whose bravery and success in the War of Independence are well known. It was natural that a man of such ancestry should become a champion of the rights of his native land

Yet, though in 1879 he was the virtual chief of the Irish Party, eight years before he was an Irish country gentleman, living quietly on his estates at Avondale in County Wicklow.

It is a mistake to say that his mother 'planted his hatred of England' in him, as she so seldom saw him as a boy. He was sent to school in England at six years old and he used to tell me how his father–who died when he (Charles S. Parnell) was twelve years old – would send for him to come to Ireland to see him. His mother, Mrs Delia Parnell, lived chiefly in America, going over to Avondale that her children might be born in Ireland and returning as soon as possible to America. After her husband's death she only visited the place occasionally and altogether saw very little of her son Charles. He often told me how well he remembered being sent for in his father's last illness to go to him at Dublin and the last journey with his dying father back to Avondale. His father had made him his heir and a ward of Court.

In reality Parnell's hatred of England arose when he began to study the records of England's misgovernment in Ireland and of the barbarities that were inflicted upon her peasantry in the name of England's authority.

For years before he left the seclusion of Avondale this hatred had been growing. He followed the Fenian movement with the liveliest interest and he often accompanied his sister Fanny when she took her verses to the offices of the Irish World. The sufferings of the Fenian prisoners, so courageously borne, stirred his blood and awakened his indignation. It can be imagined with what inward anger the young man heard of the detective raid on his mother's house in Temple Street, Dublin – when they found and impounded the sword he was privileged to wear as an officer of the Wicklow Militia.

But it was the Manchester affair of 1867 and the execution of Allen, Larkin and O' Brien which crystallised his hatred of England. From that moment he was only biding his time. Yet he was slow to move and loath to speak his mind and, until he went to America in 1871, he was better known for his cricketing and his autumn shooting than for his politics. When he returned to Avondale with his brother John in 1872 the Ballot Act had just been passed and it was the consciousness of the possibilities of the secret vote as a weapon against England that finally persuaded him to be a politician.

But, though he joined the newly formed Home Rule League, it was not until 1874 that he stood for Parliament in Dublin County. He came out at the bottom of the poll. The election cost him £2,000; the £300 which he had received from the Home Rule League lie handed back to them. In April, 1875, he stood for Meath and was placed at the top of the poll.

When he entered Parliament the Irish Party, as I have said, was of little account. The case for Ireland was argued by Isaac Butt with fine reasonableness and forensic skill, but it produced absolutely no effect. The English parties smiled and patted the Irish indulgently on the head. In Ireland all the more resolute and enthusiastic spirits had an utter contempt for their Parliamentary representatives; from the machine, nothing was to be hoped. It was the mission of Parnell to change all that, to unite all the warring elements of the Nationalist movements into one force to be hurled against England.

But still he waited and watched – learning the rules of the House, studying the strength and weaknesses of the machine he was to use and to attack. He found it more instructive to watch Biggar than Butt, for Biggar was employing those methods of obstruction which Parnell afterwards used with such perfect skill. From June, 1876, he took a hand in affairs. Side by side with Biggar, he began his relentless obstruction of Parliamentary business until the demands of Ireland should be considered. Already in 1877 he was fighting Butt for the direction of the Irish Party. On September 1st of that year Parnell became president of the Home Rule Confederation of Great Britain in place of Butt and the victory was really won. Thenceforward Parnell was the true leader of the Irish movement inside Parliament and out of it. He attracted the support of Fenians by his uncompromising tactics and his fearless utterances and when the New Departure was proclaimed by Michael Davitt (just out of prison) and John Devoy and the Land League was formed in 1879, Parnell was elected president.

The objects of the League were 'best to be attained by defending those who may be threatened with eviction for refusing to pay unjust rents; and by obtaining such reforms in the laws relating to land as will enable every tenant to become the owner of his holding by paying a fair rent for a limited number of years'. The League was meant by its founders, Davitt and Devoy, to work for the abolition of landlordism in Ireland, which, in turn, should pave the way for separation. Though Parnell was himself working for Home Rule, the League became a tremendous driving power behind his constitutional demands.

For some months Disraeli's Government did nothing, while the agitation spread like wildfire. Then in November three of the leaders were arrested, on December 5th a fourth – and in a few days released! Ireland laughed and the League grew. On December 21st Parnell and Dillon sailed for New York to appeal for funds to save the tenant farmers and to tighten the bond between the new movement and the revolutionary societies of America. His triumphal progress through the States and Canada, his reception by the Governors of States, members of Congress, judges and other representative men and finally his appearance before Congress to develop his views on the Irish situation, are well known. It was on this journey – at Toronto – that he was first hailed as the 'Uncrowned King'.

The unexpected news of the dissolution summoned him home. In going out Disraeli tried to make Home Rule the issue of the election, but Lord Hartington - who was then leading the Liberal Party – and Mr Gladstone refused to take up the challenge. All the English parties were united in hostility to Home Rule.

But the violent manifesto of Disraeli threw the Irish voting strength in England into the Liberal scale. The Liberals swept the country.

Curiously enough, even in Ireland the issue of the election was not Home Rule. There it was the land and nothing but the land. For the harvest of 1879 had been the worst since the great famine; evictions were in full swing and the Land League had began its work.

The demand was for a measure securing the 'three F's': Fixity of tenure, fair rents determined by a legal tribunal and free sale of the tenant's interest. But in many constituencies the demand was for the extinction of landlordism.

Parnell carried the election on his back. He was fighting not only the Liberals and the Tories, but the moderate Home Rule followers of Mr Shaw. His energy seemed inexhaustible; from one end of Ireland to the other he organised the campaign and addressed meetings. The result was a triumph for his policy and for the Land League. Of the 61 Home Rulers elected, 39 were Parnellites.

CHAPTER XV

THE FIRST MEETING WITH MR PARNELL

"One evening he asked the miller where the river went.
"'It goes down the valley', answered he, 'and turns a power of mills.'"
R. L. STEVENSON

WILLIE AND THE O' GORMAN Mahon had been returned at the General Election and many and varied were the stories The O' Gorman Mahon told me subsequently of their amusing experiences. How they kissed nearly every girl in Clare and drank with every man – and poor Willie loathed Irish whisky – how Willie's innate fastidiousness in dress brought gloom into the eyes of the peasantry till his unfeigned admiration of their babies and live stock, scrambling together about the cabins, 'lifted a smile to the lip'.

The O' Gorman Mahon was then a tall, handsome old man with a perfect snowstorm of white hair and eyes as merry and blue as those of a boy. He could look as fierce as an old eagle on occasion, however and had fought, in his day, more duels than he could re member. A fine specimen of the old type of Irishman.

When he came down to Eltham to see us, Willie and I took him over to Greenwich and gave him a fish dinner. We sat late into the night talking of Irish affairs and The O' Gorman Mahon said to me: 'If you meet Parnell, Mrs O' Shea, be good to him. His begging expedition to America has about finished him and I don't believe he'll last the session out.'

He went on to speak of Mr Parnell; how aloof and reserved he was and how he received any inquiries as to his obviously bad health with a freezing hostility that gave the inquirers a ruffled sense of tactlessness.

Willie broke in to say that he and I were going to give some political dinners in London and would ask Parnell, though he was sure he would not come. The O' Gorman Mahon paid some idle compliment, but I was not interested particularly in their stories of Parnell, though I mentally decided that if I gave any dinners to the Irish Party for Willie I would make a point of getting Parnell.

I was growing very tired and was longing for our guest to go and catch his train for London, but he made no move and Willie seemed to be lapsing into a gloomy trance when The O' Gorman Mahon electrified me by saying, 'Now, Willie, 'twill slip easier into her ear from you!'

Willie roused himself and said, 'You see, Katie, we...'

Then The O' Gorman Mahon took up the tale and the gist of it was that nearly all the expenses of the election had fallen to poor Willie's share, that The O' Gorman Mahon was almost penniless – this announced by him with the grand air of a conqueror – and that Willie, with more zeal than discretion, had guaranteed the whole of the expenses for both and where the amount, which they found totalled to about £2,000, was to come from they did not know.

Willie and The O' Gorman Mahon looked at me like disconsolate but hopeful schoolboys and I cheered them up by promising to do what I could to get my aunt to help, though I really did not in the least think she would do so. However, their sanguine spirits rose once more and at last The O' Gorman Mahon made the dash for his train that I was hoping for, first seizing my hands and kissing me on the cheek and telling Willie that I was much too good for him. Willie did not like these pleasantries as a rule, but The O' Gorman Mahon had such a courtly way with him that he could only smile assent.

On the 26th of April the members of the Irish Party met in Dublin to elect a chairman and the meeting was adjourned without coming to a decision, but in May Mr Parnell was chosen as leader of the Party. Willie voted for him, with twenty-two others and telegraphed to me to say that he had done so, but feared that Mr Parnell might be too 'advanced'. The fact was that many people admired steady-going William Shaw, the then chairman, as being very 'safe' and doubted whither their allegiance to Mr Parnell would lead them. Years after, when their politics had diverged, Mr Parnell said: 'I was right when I said in '80, as Willie got up on that platform at Ennis, dressed to kill, that he was just the man we did not want in the Party.'

After the meeting of Parliament Willie was insistent that I should give some dinner parties in London and, as his rooms were too small for this purpose, we arranged to have a couple of private rooms at Thomas's Hotel – my old haunt in Berkeley Square. There were no ladies' clubs in those days, but this hotel served me for many years as well as such a club could have done.

We gave several dinners and to each of them I asked Mr Parnell. Among the first to come were Mr Justin McCarthy (the elder), Colonel Colthurst, Richard Power, Colonel Nolan and several others; but – in spite of his acceptance of the invitation – Mr Parnell did not come. Someone alluded to the 'vacant chair' and laughingly defied me to fill it; the rest of our guests took up the tale and vied with each other in tales of the inaccessibility of Parnell, of how he ignored ever the invitations of the most important political hostesses in London and of his dislike of all social intercourse – though he had mixed freely in society in America and Paris before he became a politician for the sake of the Irish poor. I then became determined that I would get. Parnell to come and said, amid laughter and applause: 'The uncrowned King of Ireland shall sit in that chair at the next dinner I give!'

One bright sunny day when the House was sitting I drove, accompanied by my sister, Mrs Steele (who had a house in Buckingham Gate), to the House of Commons and sent in a card asking Mr Parnell to come out and speak to us in Palace Yard.

He came out, a tall, gaunt figure, thin and deadly pale. He looked straight at me smiling and his curiously burning eyes looked into mine with a wondering intentness that threw into my brain the sudden thought: 'This man is wonderful – and different.'

I asked him why he had not answered my last invitation to dinner and if nothing would induce him to come. He answered that he had not opened his letters for days, but if I would let him, he would come to dinner directly he returned from Paris, where he had to go for his sister's wedding.

In leaning forward in the cab to say good-bye a rose I was wearing in my bodice fell out onto my skirt. He picked it up and, touching it lightly with his lips, placed it in his button-hole.

This rose I found long years afterwards done up in an envelope, with my name and the date, among his most private papers and when he died I laid it upon his heart.

This is the first letter I had from Mr Parnell:–

LONDON,
July 17, 1880.

MY DEAR MRS O' SHEA,–We have all been in such a 'disturbed' condition lately that I have been quite unable to wander further from here than a radius of about one hundred *paces allons*. And this notwithstanding the powerful attractions which have been tending to seduce me from my duty towards my country in the direction of Thomas's Hotel.

I am going over to Paris on Monday evening or Tuesday morning to attend my sister's wedding and on my return will write you again and ask for an opportunity of seeing you.–

Yours very truly,
CHAS. PARNELL.

On his return from Paris Mr Parnell wrote to me and again we asked him to dinner, letting him name his own date. We thought he would like a quiet dinner and invited only my sister, Mrs Steele, my nephew, Sir Matthew Wood, Mr Justin McCarthy and a couple of others whose names I forget. On receiving his reply accepting the invitation for the following Friday, we engaged a box at the Gaiety Theatre – where Marion Hood was acting (for whom I had great admiration) – as we thought it would be a relief to the 'Leader' to get away from politics for once

On the day of the dinner I got this note:–

HOUSE OF COMMONS,
Friday

MY DEAR MRS O' SHEA,–I dined with the Blakes on Wednesday and by the time dinner was over it was too late to go to the meeting – the Post Office is all right here

I cannot imagine who originated the paragraph I have certainly made no arrangements up to the present to go either to Ireland or America or announced any intention to anybody.

Yours,
CHAS. S PARNELL

He arrived late, but apologetic and was looking painfully ill and white, the only lifelight in his face being given by the fathomless eyes of rich brown, varying to the brilliance of flame. The depth of expression and sudden fire of his eyes held me to the day of his death.

We had a pleasant dinner, talking of small nothings and, avoiding the controversial subject of politics, Mr Parnell directed most of his conversation to my sister during dinner. She could talk brilliantly and her quick, light handling of each subject as it came up kept him interested and amused. I was really anxious that he should have an agreeable evening and my relief was great he said that he was glad to go to the theatre with us, as the change of thought it gave was a good rest for him.

On arrival at the theatre he and I seemed to fall naturally into our places in the dark corner of the box facing the stage and screened from the sight of the audience, while my sister and the others sat in front.

After we had settled in our seats Mr Parnell began to talk to me. I had a feeling of complete sympathy and companionship with him, as though I had always known this strange, unusual man with the thin face and pinched nostrils, who sat by my side staring with that curious intent gaze at the stage and telling me in a low monotone of his American tour and of his broken health.

Then, turning more to me, he paused; and, as the light from the stage caught his eyes, they seemed like sudden flames. I leaned a little towards him, still with that odd feeling of his having always been there by my side; and his eyes smiled into mine as he broke off his theme and began to tell me of how he had met once more in America a lady to whom he had been practically engaged some few years before.

Her father would not dower her to go to Ireland and Parnell would not think of giving up the Irish cause and settling in America. The engagement therefore hung fire; but on this last visit to America he had sought her out and found himself cold and disillusioned.

She was a very pretty girl, he said, with golden hair, small features and blue eyes. One evening, on this last visit, he went to a ball with her and, as she was going up the stairs, she pressed into his hand a paper on which was written the following verse:

'Unless you can muse in a crowd all day
On the absent face that fixed you,
Unless you can dream that his faith is fast
Through behoving and unbehoving,
Unless you can die when the dream is past,
Oh, never call it loving.'

He asked me who had written the lines and I answered that it sounded like one of the Brownings (it is E.B. Browning's) and he said simply: 'Well I could not do all that, so I went home.'

I suggested that perhaps the lady had suffered in his desertion, but he said that he had seen her, that same evening, suddenly much attracted by young advocate named A——, who had just entered the room and decided in his own mind that his vacillation had lost him the young lady. The strenuous work he had then put his whole heart into had driven out all traces of regret.

After this dinner-party I met him frequently in 'the Ladies' Gallery of the House. I did not tell him when I was going; but, whenever I went, he came up for a few minutes; and, if the Wednesday sittings were not very important or required his presence, he would ask me to drive with him. We drove many miles this way in a hansom cab out into the country, to the river at Mortlake, or elsewhere. We chiefly discussed Willie's chances of being returned again for Clare, in case another election was sprung upon us. Both Willie and I were very anxious to secure Mr Parnell's promise about this, as The O' Gorman Mahon was old and we were desirous of making Willie's seat in Parliament secure.

While he sat by my side in the meadows by the river he promised he would do his best to keep Willie in Parliament and to secure County Clare for him should the occasion arise. Thus we would sit there through the summer afternoon, watching the gay traffic on the river, in talk, or in the silence of tried friendship, till the growing shadows warned us that it was time to drive back to London.

Soon after my first meeting with Mr Parnell, my sister, Mrs Steele, invited Mr Parnell, Mr McCarthy and myself to luncheon. We had a very pleasant little party at her house. During lunch Mr Parnell told us he was going to his place in Ireland for some shooting and Mr McCarthy and my sister chaffed him for leaving us for the lesser game of partridge shooting, but he observed gravely, 'I have the partridges there and here I cannot always have your society.'

I had to leave early, as I was anxious to return to see my aunt; and Mr Parnell said he would accompany me to the station. When we got to Charing Cross the train had already gone; and Mr Parnell picked out a good horse from the cab rank, saying it would be much pleasanter to drive down on such a beautiful afternoon. We did so, but I would not let him stay, as I was not sure what state of confusion the house might be in, left in my absence in the possession of the children and governess. I told him I had to hurry over the park to my aunt, as really was the case and he reluctantly returned to London.

On the next Wednesday evening Mr Parnell was to dine with me at Thomas's Hotel. He met me at Cannon Street Station as the train came in and asked me to have some tea with him at the hotel there and go on to Thomas's together. We went to the Cannon Street Hotel dining-rooms, but on looking in he saw some of the Irish members there and said it would be more comfortable for us in his private sitting-room. I was under the impression that he lived at Keppel Street, but he told me he had just taken rooms in the Cannon Street Hotel. We had tea in his sitting-room and he talked politics to me freely till I was interested and at ease and then lapsed into one of those long silences of his that I was already beginning to know were dangerous in the complete sympathy they evoked between us.

Presently, I said: 'Come! We shall be late!' and he rose without a word and followed me downstairs. There were some members of his Party still standing about in the hall, but, as he always did afterwards when I was with him, he ignored them absolutely and handed me into a waiting cab.

He and I dined at Thomas's Hotel, that evening and after dinner I returned home to Eltham. Mr Parnell left for Ireland by the morning mail.

From Dublin he wrote to me:

September 9, 1880.

MY DEAR MRS O' SHEA, – Just a line to say that I have arrived here and go on to Avondale, Rathdrum, this evening, where I hope to hear from you before very long.

I may tell you also in confidence that I don't feel quite so content at the prospect of ten days' absence from London amongst the hills and valleys of Wicklow as I should have done some three months since.

The cause is mysterious, but perhaps you will help me to find it, or her, on my return.

Yours always,

CHAS. S. PARNELL.

Then from his home: –

AVONDALE, RATHDRUM,
September 11, 1880.

MY DEAR MRS O' SHEA, – I take the opportunity which a few hours in Dublin gives me of letting you know that I am still in the land of the living, notwithstanding the real difficulty of either living or being, which every moment becomes more evident, in the absence of a certain kind and fair face.

Probably you will not hear from me again for a few days, as I am going into the mountains for some shooting, removed from post offices and such like consolations for broken-hearted politicians, but if, as I hope, a letter from you should reach me even there, I shall try and send you an answer.

Yours very sincerely,

CHAS. S. PARNELL.

CHAPTER XVI

EARLY CORRESPONDENCE

Whate'er the senses take or may refuse
The Mind's internal heaven shall shed her dews
Of inspiration on the humblest lay.' – WORDSWORTH.

WHENEVER I WENT TO TOWN, or elsewhere, I always returned at night to see that my children were all right and to be ready to go to my aunt as usual every morning. One day, on my return from a drive with my aunt, I found that my old nurse Lucy, who still lived with me, was very ill, having had a stroke of paralysis while I was away. It affected her speech and sight as well as the whole of one side and I was very unhappy lest the maid whom I kept expressly to wait on her had hurt her in some way – the doctor said she must have had a shock. The dear old woman lay still, continuously feeling my fingers for my rings that she might know that I was with her and evidently she wished to tell me something which her poor lips could not form. She lingered only a couple of days before she died and left a great void in my heart. My children missed their admiring old confidante sadly. She had always been devoted to me as the youngest of her 'own babies' as she called my mother's children and had shared in all my fortunes and misfortunes since I returned from Spain. She was always very proud and so fearful of becoming a burden to anyone, that she rented a room in her sister's house so that she should feel independent. So often, when 'times were bad' with us, she would press some of her savings into my hand and say that 'The Captain must want a little change, Dearie, going about as he does!'

In her earlier life she had had her romance and had spent some years in saving up to marry her 'sweet-heart', as she, called him; but shortly before the wedding her father's business failed and she immediately gave him all her little nest-egg, with the result that her lover refused to marry her. So then, at the great age of ninety, after her blameless life had been passed since the age of sixteen in unselfish devotion to us all, we laid her to rest by the side of my father and mother at Cressing, Willie taking her down to Essex and attending the funeral.

As she lay dying I got this note from Mr Parnell –

DUBLIN,
September 22, 1880.
MY DEAR MRS O' SHEA,–I cannot keep myself away from you any longer, so shall leave tonight for London.

Please wire me to 16 Keppel Street, Russell Square, if I may hope to see you tomorrow and where, after 4 p.m.

Yours always,
C. S. P.

Owing to the piteous clinging to my fingers of my old Lucy I was unable to go to London even for an hour to meet Mr Parnell, so I telegraphed to that effect and received the following letter:

EUSTON STATION,
Friday evening, September 24, 1880.
MY DEAR MRS O' SHEA, – On arriving at Keppel Street yesterday I found that your wire had just arrived and that the boy refused to leave it as I was not stopping there. Going at once to the district postal office I asked for and received the wire and today went to London Bridge Station at 12.15.

The train from Eltham had just left, so I came on to Charing Cross and sent a note by messenger to you at Thomas's with directions to bring it back if you were not there, which turned out to be the case. I am very much troubled at not having seen you, especially as I must return to Ireland tonight – I came on purpose for you and had no other business. I think it possible, on reflection, that the telegraph people may have wired you that they unable to deliver your message and, if so, I must reproach myself for not having written you last night.

Your very disappointed
C. S. P.

From Dublin he wrote me:

Saturday morning, September 25, 1880.
MY DEAR MRS O' SHEA, – My hurried note to you last night I had not time to sympathise with you in this troublesome time you have been going through recently; how I wish it might have been possible for me to have seen you even for a few minutes to tell you how very much I feel any trouble which comes to you.

I am just starting for New Ross, where there is a meeting tomorrow.

If you can spare time to write me to Avondale, the letters will reach me in due course.

Yours always,
C. S. P.

September 29, 1880.
MY DEAR MRS O' SHEA, – I have received your wire, but not the letter which you say you were writing me to Dublin Monday.

I suppose then you may have sent it to Rathdrum instead, whither I am going this evening and that I may soon have the happiness of reading a few words written by you.

I am due at Cork on Sunday, after which I propose to visit London again and renew my attempt to gain a glimpse of you. Shall probably arrive there on Tuesday if I hear from you in the meanwhile that you will see me.

On Friday evening I shall be at Morrison's on my way to Kilkenny for Saturday and shall be intensely delighted to have a wire from you to meet me there.

Yours always,
CHAS. S. PARNELL.

Meanwhile Willie was in communication with Mr Gladstone, Mr Tintern (one of the Liberal agents) and others, in reference to a meeting held by him.

Mr Tintern wrote from Tenby commenting with satisfaction on the report of Willie's successful meeting, on Willie's kind mention of the Government and on the good the meeting must do by promoting orderly progress and better feeling between one class and another. But he expressed surprise that Willie should think the Government had not treated him and West Clare well. He at least...! Mr Gladstone wrote from Downing Street on the 21st September about the meeting in much the same terms. He expressed himself as gratified to think that the important local proceedings with regard to the land question showed the union of people and pastors against the extremists.

Life at Eltham went on in the same routine. My aunt was well and would sit for long hours at the south door of her house – looking away up 'King John's Chase' – the ruins of King John's Palace were at Eltham and my aunt's park and grounds were part of the ancient Royal demesne. In these summer evenings she loved to sit at the top of the broad flight of shallow steps with me and tell my little girls stories of her life of long ago. In her day all girls, big and little, wore low-necked frocks with short sleeves and she was always distressed that her 'butterflies', as she called my two little girls, had long black legs instead of the white stockings and sandals of her youth.

She would repeat poetry to them by the hour, if I could get them to sit still long enough; and I sat by her side on these waning summer days, hearing her voice, but unheeding, dreaming in silence, as she talked to the children.

Sometimes her favourite Dr Bader would bring his zither down from London and play to us; or my aunt and I would sit in the great tapestry room with all of the seven windows open, listening to the song of the æolian harp as the soft breeze touched its strings and died away in harmony through the evening stillness. And my aunt would doze in her chair while I dropped the book I had been reading to her and drifted into unknown harmonies and colour of life; waiting in the stillness of the summer evening for the meaning of that intent considering gaze, with the thousand fires behind it, that was always subconsciously present with me now.

Sometimes, too, my aunt would sing in her soft, gentle old voice the songs of her youth, to the accompaniment of her guitar. 'We met, 'twas in a crowd' was a favourite old song of hers, half forgotten since she used to sing it to the music of her spinet seventy years before, but Dr Bader found the words in an old book and the dear old lady crooned it sentimentally to me as we sat waiting for the hooting of the owls which signalled to her maid the time for shutting her lady's windows.

And I was conscious of sudden gusts of unrest and revolt against these leisured, peaceful days where the chiming of the great clock in the hail was the only indication of the flight of time and the outside world of another age called to me with the manifold interests into which I had been so suddenly plunged with the power to help in the making and marring of a destiny.

CHAPTER XVII

AT ELTHAM

'But then – I supposed you to be a fellow guest?'
'Ah, no', he answered me in that cold unshaken voice, 'I have but come home.'
(The Bogman) – HONORA SHEE

IN THE AUTUMN OF 1880 Mr Parnell came to stay with us at Eltham, only going to Dublin as occasion required. Willie had invited him to come and I got in some flowers in pots and palms to make my drawing-room look pretty for him.

Mr Parnell, who was in very bad health at that time, a few days later complained of sore throat and looked, as I thought, mournfully at my indoor garden, 'which I industriously watered every day. It then dawned upon .me that he was accusing this of giving him sore throat and I taxed him with it. He evidently feared to vex me, but admitted that he did think it was so and 'wouldn't it do if they were not watered so often?' He was childishly touched when I at once had them all removed and he sank happily on to the sofa, saying that 'plants were such damp things!'

His throat became no better and he looked so terribly ill when – as he often did now – he fell asleep from sheer weakness on the sofa before the fire, that I became very uneasy about him. Once, on awaking from one of these sleeps of exhaustion, he told me abruptly that he believed it was the green in the carpet that gave him sore throat. There and then we cut a bit out and sent it to London to be analysed, but without result. It was quite a harmless carpet.

During this time I nursed him assiduously, making him take nourishment at regular intervals, seeing that these day sleeps of his were not disturbed and forcing him to take fresh air in long drives through the country around us. At length I had the satisfaction of seeing his strength gradually return sufficiently to enable him to take the exercise that finished the process of this building-up and he became stronger than he had been for some years. I do not think anyone but we who saw him then at Eltham, without the mask of reserve he always presented to the outside world, had any idea of how near death's door his exertions on behalf of the famine-stricken peasants of Ireland had brought him.

Once in that autumn, after he came to us, I took him for a long drive in an open carriage through the hop-growing district of Kent. I had not thought of the fact that hundreds of the poorest of the Irish came over for the hop-picking and might recognise him.

After driving over Chislehurst Common and round by the lovely Crays, we came right into a crowd of the Irish 'hoppers' – men, women and children. In a moment there was a wild surge towards the carriage, with cries of 'The Chief! The Chief!' and 'Parnell! Parnell! Parnell!' The coachman jerked the horses on to their haunches for fear of knocking down the enthusiastic men and women who were crowding up – trying to kiss Parnell's hand and calling for 'a few words.'

He lifted his cap with that grave, aloof smile of his and said no, he was not well enough to make the smallest of speeches, but he was glad to see them and would talk to them when they went home to Ireland. Then, bidding them to 'mind the little ones', who were scrambling about the horses' legs, to the manifest anxiety of the coachman, he waved them away and we drove off amid fervent 'God keep your honours!' and cheers.

These Irish hop-pickers were so inured to privation in their own country that they were very popular among the Kentish hop-farmers, as they did not grumble so much as did the English pickers at the scandalously inefficient accommodation provided them.

Often before Parnell became really strong I used to watch for hours beside him as he slept before the drawing-room fire, till I had to rouse him in time to go to the House. Once, when he was moving restlessly, I heard him murmur in his sleep, as I pulled the light rug better over him: 'Steer carefully of the harbour – there are breakers ahead'.

He now had all the parcels and letters he received sent on to me, so that I might open them and give him only those it was necessary for him to deal with. There were hundreds of letters to go through every week, though, as he calmly explained: 'If you get tired with them, leave them and they'll answer themselves'.

Often among the parcels there were comestibles and among these every week came a box of eggs without the name and address of the sender. I was glad to see these eggs as the winter came on and with it the usual reluctance of our hens to provide us with sufficient eggs, but Mr Parnell would not allow me to use them, for he said: 'They might be eggs, but then again they might not' and I had to send them a good distance down the garden and have them broken to make sure of their genuineness and then he would worry lest our dogs should find them and poison themselves.

On his visits to Ireland he wrote to me continually: –

DUBLIN,
Tuesday.

MY DEAR MRS O' SHEA,–I have just a moment on my return from Ennis to catch the late post and reply to your wire.

I received your two letters quite safely and you may write me even nicer ones with perfect confidence. I blame myself very much for not having written you on my way through Dublin on Saturday, as you were evidently anxious about your notes, but I hope you will forgive me as there were only a few minutes to spare.

I trust to see you in London on Tuesday next. Is it true that Captain O' Shea is in Paris and, if so, when do you expect his return? ... I have had no shooting, weather too wet, but shall try tomorrow, when you may expect some heather.

DUBLIN,
Friday evening, October 2, 1880.

Have just received your wire; somehow or other something from you seems a necessary part of my daily existence and if I have to go a day or two without even a telegram it seems dreadful.

I want to know how you intend to excuse yourself for telling me not to come on purpose if I must return. (To Ireland) Of course, I am going on purpose to see you; and it is also unhappily true that I cannot remain long.

Shall cross Monday evening and shall call at Morrison's for a message.

Please write or wire me in London to 16 Keppel Street, Russell Square, where I shall call on Tuesday.

DUBLIN,
Monday night, October 4, 1880.

Just arrived ... I write you on the only bit of paper to be found at this late hour (a scrap taken from one of your own notes), to say that I hope to reach London tomorrow (Tuesday) evening and to see you on Wednesday when and where you wish. Please write or wire me to Keppel Street. This envelope will present the appearance of having been tampered with, but it has not.

DUBLIN,
Tuesday evening, October 5, 1880.

A frightful gale has been blowing all day in Channel and still continues.

Under these circumstances shall postpone crossing till to morrow evening.

Can meet you in London at 9 tomorrow evening anywhere you say.

DUBLIN,
Monday evening, October 17, 1880.

MY OWN LOVE, – You cannot imagine how much you have occupied my thoughts all day and how very greatly the prospect of seeing you again very soon comforts me.

On Monday evening I think it will be necessary for me go to Avondale; afterwards I trust, if things are propitious on your side, to return to London on Tuesday or Wednesday.–

Yours always,
C.

AVONDALE, RATHDRUM,
October 22, 1880.

I was very much pleased to receive your wire this morning, forwarded from Dublin, that you had received my note of last Saturday. I was beginning to fear that it had gone wrong.

After I had finished at Roscommon and received your message in Dublin on Monday I decided upon coming here where I have been unexpectedly detained.

If all goes well you will see me in London on Monday evening next ... I send you enclosed one or two poor sprigs of heather, which I plucked for you three weeks ago, also my best love and hope you will believe that I always think of you as the one dear object whose presence has ever been a great happiness to me.

Meanwhile the Government had been temporising with the land question. They had brought in a very feeble Compensation for Disturbances Bill and they had allowed it to be further weakened by amendments. This Bill was rejected by the House of Lords, with the result that the number of evictions in Ireland grew hourly greater and the agitation of the Land League against them; outrages, too, were of common occurrence and increased in intensity.

Speaking at Ennis on September 19th Mr Parnell enunciated the principle which has since gone by the name of 'The Boycott'.

'What are you to do', he asked, 'to a tenant who bids for a farm from which another tenant has been evicted?'

Several voices cried 'Shoot him!'

'I think', went on Mr Parnell, 'I heard some body say "Shoot him!" I wish to point out to you a very much better way – a more Christian and charitable way, which will give the lost man an opportunity of repenting. When a man takes a farm from which another. has been unjustly evicted, you must shun him on the road when you meet him; you must shun him in the shop, you must shun him on the fair-green and in the market-place and even in the place of worship, by leaving him alone; by putting him into a sort of moral Coventry; by isolating him from the rest of the country, as if he were a leper of old – you must show him your detestation of the crime he has committed.'

Forster, the Irish Secretary, who had some amount of sympathy for the tenants, was, however, a Quaker and the outrages horrified him more than the evictions. Nor, strangely, was he able to connect the one with the other. Undoubtedly the evictions almost ceased, but, said he, they have ceased because of the outrages and the outrages were the work of the Land League; and he pressed for the arrest of its leaders. This was unwise, considering that it was Parnell who had advocated the abandonment of violence for the moral suasion of the boycott.

On November 3rd Forster decided to prosecute the leaders of the Land League and among them Parnell, Dillon, Biggar, Sexton and T. D. Sullivan. Two days later, in a speech at Dublin, Parnell expressed his regret that Forster was degenerating from a statesman to a tool of the landlords. Biggar when he heard the news exclaimed, 'Damned lawyers, sir, damned lawyers! Wasting the public money! Wasting the public money! Whigs damned rogues! Forster damned fool!'

DUBLIN,'
November 4, 1880.

MY DEAR MRS O' SHEA,–I take advantage of almost the first moment I have had to myself since leaving you to write a few hasty lines. And first I must again thank you for all your kindness, which made my stay at Eltham so happy and pleasant.

The thunderbolt, as you will have seen, has at last fallen and we are in the midst of loyal preparations of a most appalling character.

I do not suppose I shall have an opportunity of being in London again before next Thursday, but trust to be more fortunate in seeing Captain O' Shea then than the last time.

Yours very truly,
CHAS. S. PARNELL.

Saturday.

MY DEAR MRS O' SHEA,–I hope to arrive in London on Tuesday morning and trust to have the pleasure of seeing you before I leave. Do you think you shall be in town on Tuesday?

Kindly address 16 Keppel Street.

Yours very truly,
CHAS. S. PARNELL.

On November 5th that year the village was great on the subject of 'gunpowder, treason and plot' and during dinner that evening there was such a noise and shouting outside my house that I asked the maid who was waiting what all the excitement was about.

She answered breathlessly that 'the procession, ma'am, have got Miss Anna Parnell in a effigy 'long-side of the Pope and was waiting outside for us to see before they burnt 'em in the village'.

This electrifying intelligence was received with grave indifference by Mr Parnell till the disappointed maid left the room; then with a sudden bubble of laughter – 'Poor Anna! Her pride in being burnt, as menace to England, would he so drowned in horror at her company that it would put the fire out!'

The cheering and hooting went on for some time outside the house, but, finding we were not to be drawn, the crowd at last escorted the effigies down to the village and burnt them, though with less amusement than they had anticipated.

DUBLIN,[2]
November 6, 1880.

MY DEAR MRS O' SHEA, – You can have very little idea how dreadfully disappointed I felt on arriving here this evening not to find a letter from either you or Captain O' Shea. I send this in hope that it may induce you to write in reply to my last letter and telegram, which would appear not to have reached you.

Yours very sincerely,

CHAS. S. PARNELL.

AVONDALE,
Monday.

MY DEAR MRS O' SHEA, – I enclose keys, which I took away by mistake. Will you kindly hand enclosed letter to the proper person[3] and oblige.

Yours very truly,

CHAS. S. PARNELL.

DUBLIN,
Wednesday night, November 11, 1880.

MY DEAREST LOVE, – I have made all arrangements to be in London on Saturday morning and shall call at Keppel Street for a letter from you. It is quite impossible for me to tell you just how very much you have changed my life, what a small interest I take in what is going on about me and how I detest everything which has happened during the last few days to keep me away from you – I think of you always and you must never believe there is to be any 'fading'. By the way, you must not send me any more artificial letters. I want as much of your own self as you can transfer into written words, or else none at all.

Yours always,

C. S. P.

A telegram goes to you and one to W.[4], tomorrow, which are by no means strictly accurate.

DUBLIN,
December 2, 1880.

MY DEAR MRS O' SHEA, – I succeeded in getting the train at Euston with just ten minutes to spare and, arriving here this morning, found that my presence today was indispensable.

I need not tell you how much I regretted leaving Eltham so suddenly; but we cannot always do as we wish in this world.

My stay with you has been so pleasant and charming that I was almost beginning to forget my other duties; but Ireland seems to have gotten on very well without me in the interval.

Trusting to see you again next week on my way to Paris.

Yours very sincerely,

CHAS. S. PARNELL.

I have been exceedingly anxious all day at not receiving your promised telegram to hear how you got home.

CHAPTER XVIII

THE LAND LEAGUE TRIALS

'The surest way to prevent seditions is to take away the matter of them.' – LORD BACON.

THROUGH THE WHOLE OF 1880 Parnell was determinedly organising the Land League throughout Ireland and during the winter, doubtless encouraged by the enormous distress that prevailed over the whole country, the force and power of the League grew with a rapidity that surpassed even the expectations of Parnell and his party. All through the vacation Parnell and his followers held meetings in carefully calculated areas of Ireland and in his speeches Parnell explained the meaning and wide-reaching scope of the League's agitation, i.e. that tenant farmers were to trust in their own combination alone and 'should give no faith to the promises of the English Ministers'.

During the early session that year Parnell had introduced a Bill called 'Suspension of Ejectments Bill' and this first pressed upon the House the necessity of dealing with the Irish landlord troubles. Parnell's party urged this Bill with so united a front that Mr Gladstone was obliged to consider the main substance of it and he agreed to insert a clause in the 'Relief of Distress Bill' which would deal with impending evictions of Irish tenants. But the Speaker of the House held that the interpolation of such a clause would not be 'in order' and the Chief Secretary for Ireland (Mr Forster) then, by Mr Gladstone's direction, brought in his 'Disturbances Bill', which was to all practical purposes Parnell's Bill under another name.

In the course of the debate on this Bill Mr Gladstone himself said that 'in the circumstances of distress prevalent in Ireland (at that time) a sentence of eviction is the equivalent of a sentence of death'. These absolutely true words of Gladstone's were used by Parnell very many times during his Land League tours both in speeches and privately and many times he added – as so often he did to me at home – bitter comment upon the apathy of the English Government, upon the curious insensibility of the English law makers, who knew these things to be true in Ireland and yet were content to go on in their policy of drift, unless forced into action by those who saw the appalling reality of the distress among the Irish poor that was so comfortably deplored in London.

In this connection Parnell used to say that the fundamental failure in the English government of Ireland was: first, the complete inability of the Ministers in power to realise anything that was not before their eyes; and, secondly, their cast-iron conviction that

Ireland was the one country of the world that was to be understood and governed by those to whom she was little but a name.

In all this time of trouble and eviction Parnell went backwards and forwards between England (Eltham) and Ireland as occasion required and so successful were his efforts in spreading the agitation and linking up the League that the Government became uneasy as to the outcome of this new menace to landlordism. Finally, Parnell and fourteen of his followers were put on trial, charged with 'conspiracy to impoverish landlords'. Parnell, of course, went over to Ireland for these 'State trials', but he considered the whole thing such a farce, in that it was an impotent effort of the Government to intimidate him, that he could not take it seriously in any way. No jury (in Ireland) would agree to convict him he was well aware and he attended the trials chiefly, he said, for the 'look of the thing' and to give the support of his presence to his colleagues. Incidentally, he told me on one occasion that he had considerably hurried the jury when he was very anxious to catch a train in time for the night mail to England (Eltham) by ' willing' them to agree (to disagree) without the long discussion of local politics with which all self-respecting Irish jurors beguile the weary ways of law. He observed that here, in the question of how far an unconscious agent can be 'willed' into a desired action, he had discovered another and most entrancing study for us when we had more time to go into it thoroughly.

Talking of the Land League's procedure against the interests of the Irish landlords, I may, I think, here pertinently remind those who have, among so many other accusations, brought against Parnell the charge of self-seeking in regard to money matters, that Parnell himself was an Irish landlord and of very considerable estates and that this land campaign (really, of course, directed against eviction) meant, to all practical purposes, the loss of his rents and that not only for a time, as in other cases, but, with the very generous interpretation put upon his wishes by the 'Chief's' tenants, for all time – or rather for all his lifetime. Captain O' Shea also had certain estates in Ireland and naturally, not being in sympathy with Parnell's policy, but being at heart a thorough Whig and a strong advocate for Mr Shaw, the ex-leader of the Irish party, he was furious at the League's anti-landlord work and refused to have any hand in it. He considered that hapless as was the plight of those who had to pay in rent the money they did not possess, that of the landlord whose rent was his all was but little to be preferred.

During this period the stories of the evictions brought home to me by Parnell himself made my heart sick and often he sat far into the night at Eltham speaking in that low, broken monotone, that with him always betokened intense feeling strongly held in check, of the terrible cruelty of some of the things done in the name of justice in unhappy Ireland. How old people and sometimes those sick beyond recovery, women with the children they had borne but a few hours before, little children naked as they had come into the world, all thrust out from the little squalid cabins which were all they had for home, thrust out on the roadside to perish, or to live as they could. I in my English ignorance used to say: 'Why did they not go into the workhouse or to neighbours?' and Parnell would look wonderingly at me as he told me that for the most part such places were few and far between in Ireland and 'neighbours', good as they were to each other, were in the same trouble. There were instances where a wife would *beg and with none effect*, that the bailiffs and police should wait but the little half-hour that her dying husband drew his last breath; and where a husband carried his wife from her bed to the 'shelter' of the rainswept moor that their child might be born out of the sight of the soldiers deputed to guard the officials who had been sent to pull their home about their ears. And, remembering these and so many other tales of some of the 50,000 evictions that he afterwards calculated had taken place in Ireland, I have never wondered at the implacable hatred of England that can never really die out of the Irish heart.

On December 4th, 1880, he wrote to me from Dublin:

I was exceedingly pleased to receive your letters; to say the truth, I have been quite homesick since leaving Eltham and news from you seems like news from home.

The Court refused our application today for a postponement of the trial (of the Land League), but this we expected and it does not much signify, as it turns out that we need not necessarily attend the trial unless absolutely directed to do so by the Court.

You will also be pleased to hear that the special jury panel, of which we obtained a copy last night, is of such a character as in the opinion of competent judges to give us every chance of a disagreement by the jury in their verdict, but we cannot, of course, form an absolute conclusion until the jury has been sworn, when we shall be able to tell pretty certainly one way or the other.

Since writing Captain O' Shea it does not look as if I could get further away from Ireland than London, as Paris is inconvenient from its distance.

I have no letter from him yet in reply to mine.

And again on the 9th:

I returned from Waterford last night and shall probably get through all necessary work here by Saturday evening so as to enable me to start for London on Sunday morning. I do not know how long I can remain in London, but shall run down and see you on Monday and perhaps my plans will be more fixed by that time.

I have decided not to attend any more meetings until after the opening of Parliament, as everything now can go on without me.

Kindly inform Captain O' Shea that the meeting of Irish members will be in Dublin on the 4th January.

On December 12th of that year Mr Parnell wrote from Avondale to say that the jury panel was to be struck on the following Monday for the prosecution of the Land League.

...And it will be necessary for me to see it before giving final directions.

I have consequently postponed my departure till Monday evening.

I have come here to arrange my papers and find a number which I should not like to destroy and which I should not like the Government to get hold of in the event of their searching my house in the troublous times which appear before us. May I leave them at Eltham?

And the next day:

I have just received a note from Healy, who is to be tried at Cork on Thursday, saying that his counsel thinks it of the utmost importance I should be present.

This is very hard lines on me, as I had looked forward to a little rest in London before my own trial commences; but I do not see how it can be helped, as Healy's is the first of the State trials and it is of the utmost importance to secure an acquittal and not merely a disagreement. I shall leave Cork on Thursday night and arrive in London Friday evening and shall call to see you at Eltham Saturday. Your letters, one directed here and the others to Morrison's, reached me in due course and I hope to hear from you again very soon.

Parnell, now, always made my house his head quarters in England and on his return from Ireland after the trials came down at once as soon as he had ascertained that I was alone.

There were times when he wished to keep quiet and let no one know where he was; and, as it became known to the Government that Mr Parnell frequented my house a good deal, it was somewhat difficult to avoid the detectives who were employed to watch his comings and goings.

On one occasion in 1880 he was informed privately that his arrest for 'sedition' was being urged upon the Government and that it would be well to go abroad for a short time. I think his enigmatic reply, 'I will disappear for a few weeks', must have puzzled his informant. He came down to me at night and when I answered his signal at my sitting-room window and let him in, he told, me with a deprecating smile that I must hide him for a few weeks. As I sat watching him eat the supper I always had ready for him at 3 a.m. I felt rather hopeless, as he was a big man and I did not see how he could be hidden from the servants. He said the latter must not know he was there, as they would talk to the trades people and they to the Government men. He did not wish to be arrested until later on, when it might be more useful than not

Then he awaited suggestions and at length we decided that a little room opening out of my own must be utilised for him, as I always kept it locked and never allowed a servant into it – except very occasionally to 'turn it out'. It was a little boudoir dressing-room and had a sofa in it.

Mr Parnell was then still feeling ill and run down and enjoyed his fortnight's absolute rest in this room. None of the servants knew that he was there and I took all his food up at night, cooking little dainty dishes for him at the open fire, much to his pleasure and amusement. He spent the time very happily, resting, writing 'seditious' speeches for future use and reading *Alice in Wonderland*. This book was a favourite of his and I gave it to him with the solemnity that befitted his grave reading of it. I do not think he ever thought it in the least amusing, but he would read it earnestly from cover to cover and, without a smile, remark that it was a 'curious book.'

In all this fortnight no one had the least idea that he was in the house and the only comment I ever heard upon my prisoner's diet was that 'the mistress ate much more when she had her meals in her sitting-room'.

At the end of this fortnight he had arranged to go to Paris on some Land League business and wanted me to go to see him off. He had brought certain political correspondence from Avondale and London and placed it in my charge and this I kept in a box in this little private room, where I hid him. But there were two papers that he did not wish left even here and, fearing arrest, could not carry on him. For these he had a wide, hollow gold bracelet made in Paris and after inserting the papers he screwed the bracelet safely on my arm; there it remained for three years and was then unscrewed by him and the contents destroyed.

The winter of 1880 was terribly cold and as I let him out of the house in the bitterly cold morning. I wished he did not consider it necessary to go to Paris by such a roundabout route as he had chosen.

However, we drove off to Lewisham that morning, quite unobserved; from thence we went by train to New Cross and drove by cab to London Bridge. At Vauxhall we started for Lowestoft; for Mr Parnell had arranged to .go to Paris via Harwich. I was anxious about him, for the cold was intense and the deep snow over the large dreary waste of salt marshes seemed reflected in his pallor. Our train slowly passed through the dreary tract of country, feet deep in its white covering and we could see no sign of life but an occasional seagull vainly seeking for food and sending a weird call through the lonely silences.

I wrapped Parnell up in his rugs as he tried to sleep. I loathed the great white expanse that made him look so ill and I wished I had him at home again, where I could better fight the great fear that so often beset my heart: that I could not long keep off the death that hovered near him. A lady and gentleman in the carriage remarked to me – thinking he slept – that my husband looked terribly ill, could they do anything? And I noticed the little smile of content that flitted over his face as he heard me briskly reply that 'No, he had been ill, but was so much better and stronger that I was not at all uneasy.' It was the cold glare of the snow that made him look so delicate, but he was really quite strong. He hated to be thought ill and did not see the doubt in their faces at my reply.

Arrived at Lowestoft I insisted upon his resting and having a good meal, after which he felt so cheered up that he decided to return to London with me and go to Paris by the usual route the next day!

We had a new Irish cook at this time, from County Tipperary and her joy exceeded all bounds when she learnt that the Irish leader was really in the house and she was to cook for him. I had to ask Mr Parnell to see her for a moment, as she was too excited to settle to her cooking. Directly she got into the room Ellen fell down on her knees and kissed his hands, much to his horror, for, although used to such homage in Ireland, he disliked it extremely and he told me with some reproach that he had expected to be quite free from that sort of thing in my house.

At Christmas he tipped my servants generously and indeed Ellen and the parlour maid Mary vied with each other in their attention to his comfort. The enthusiasm of the cook was so great that she bought an enormous gold locket and, having inserted a portrait of Mr Parnell in it, wore it constantly. Mary, not to be outdone, thereupon bought a locket of identically the same design and wore it with an air of defiance, when bringing in tea, on New Year's Day.

This was against all regulations and I said laughingly to Mr Parnell that he was introducing lawlessness into my household. He answered, 'Leave it to me' and when Mary appeared again he said gently to her, 'Mary, that is a magnificent locket and I see you are kind enough to wear my portrait in it. Mrs O' Shea tells me that Ellen has bought one also, but I just want you and Ellen not to wear them outside like that, for Mrs O' Shea lets me come down here for a rest and if people know I'm here I shall be worried to death with politics and people calling.' So Mary promised faithfully and Ellen came running in to promise too and to threaten vengeance on 'the others' if absolute silence was not observed. The lockets went 'inside' and only a tiny bit of chain was allowed to show at the throat in evidence of homage continued, though hidden.

Meanwhile, events were fusing in Ireland. Parnell had gone over there immediately after Christmas. From Dublin he wrote:

DUBLIN
Monday evening, December 27, 1880.

MY DEAR MRS O' SHEA, – I have been exceedingly anxious all day at not receiving your promised telegram to hear how you got home; trust I may have something tomorrow morning that it is all is all right[5].

Yours in haste,
C. S. P.

MORRISON'S HOTEL,
Tuesday, December 28, 1880.

MY DEAREST WIFE, – You will be delighted to learn that everything is proceeding first-rate so far.

The jury sworn today cannot possibly convict us and there is a very fair chance of an acquittal. I do not think the Government will attempt to prevent me from being present at the opening of Parliament, though I am not quite sure yet whether it will be prudent for me to leave until Wednesday evening. So far as I can see there is no necessity for the presence of any of the Traversers; one of them, Gordon, who has broken his leg, has not appeared at all and his absence has not been even mentioned or noticed.

I was immensely relieved by your letter this morning. You must take great care of yourself for my sake and your and my future.

Yours always,
C. S. P.

I have wired and written to Madrid[6] explaining situation lest my observations at yesterday's meeting as to doubt of my being in Parliament, intended to throw dust in eyes of Government, might be literally interpreted.

DUBLIN,
Thursday, December 30, 1880.

MY DEAREST LOVE, – Your letters have reached me quite safely and you cannot tell how much pleasure they give me. I fear I was very foolish to allow you to come with me the day of my departure; I felt sure it would do much harm and until your first letter arrived I was in a continual panic lest some dreadful disaster had happened.

That my poor love should have suffered so much makes my heart very sore and she must take great care of herself for the sake of our future.

I enclose letter from W.[7]

Yours always affectionately,

C.S.P.

Will send you photo tomorrow.

DUBLIN,
January, 1881.

MY DEAREST WIFIE, – Was most delighted on return this morning from Avondale to find your three letters and telegrams. I think it would make you happy and more contented during my absence if you knew how I watched for your letters and how often I read and re-read them.

I felt very much tempted to run over and spend the New Year and Sunday with you, but feared you might not be alone.

It pains me very much that my own love was unhappy about that stupid thing in the Freeman on Thursday. An old and ugly woman with whom I was very slightly acquainted, but who wanted to put herself en evidence, perched herself just behind me and got a gentleman sitting next to her to hand me down a slip of paper, on which was written some message of congratulation. I only rewarded her with a stare, did not even bow or smile and certainly sent no communication of any kind in reply. That was all. I will ask my own dearest to believe in me while I am away and never again to feel unhappiness from want of confidence.

I have made all arrangements to leave by mail on Wednesday morning and shall be with my own wifie on Wednesday evening about eight.

Yours,

C. S. P.

Mr Parnell held the Party meeting in Dublin on January 4th and returned to me on January 5th, in time for the meeting of the House (on 6th January, 1881), not having thought it necessary to remain in Ireland till the termination of the trials – a circumstance which, curiously enough, was not publicly re marked upon. We spent some days together at Eltham and I took Mr Parnell to see my aunt, who was much charmed with him. His quiet manners and soft, clear voice pleased her greatly, as also did his personal appearance. She took his arm and paced up and down the tapestry room with him, while she told him how she was introduced to O' Connell in the old days, when her husband, Benjamin Wood, was MP for Southwark. She had met O' Connell at the House and heard what was said to have been one of his greatest speeches. She said, 'I much prefer your voice, Mr Parnell, for Daniel O' Connell's enunciation was startling to me'.

Though such a great age, my aunt had still a very pretty round arm and as she always wore the net sleeves of her youth, fastened with old-fashioned bracelets, Mr Parnell noticed this and commented upon the fact to me. The old lady was much gratified when I told her of this. She enlisted his sympathy by telling him that she had to pay £500 a year in order to keep her beautiful old grounds intact, as the Crown desired to sell the place for building lots and she was determined to die in the old house she had lived in for over fifty years.

The State trial ended on January 25th, 1881, the foreman of the jury stating: 'We are unanimous that we cannot agree', as Mr Parnell had assured me they would. He was in Court and loudly cheered as he hastened off to catch the boat to England.

CHAPTER XIX

PARLIAMENTARY ASSOCIATIONS

'Live today – past is registered – the future is unguessed – the instant ours.'
— MORTIMER COLLINS.

FORSTER'S COERCION BILL WAS INTRODUCED on January 24th, 1881 and on the 25th Mr Gladstone moved that it should have precedence of all other business before the House. Mr Parnell fiercely opposed this motion and kept his followers hard at work in Opposition– thus forcing the House to sit from 4 p.m. on Tuesday until 2 p.m. of the next day. The details of these sittings have been recounted *ad nauseam* and I need not repeat them here, but only record Parnell's fierce joy in these political fights and my pride in, him as I watched him from the Ladies' Gallery. Sometimes Willie would wish to give the seats he secured in the Ladies' Gallery to friends of his and on such occasions I always knew that Mr Parnell would ballot one for me. Of course, later on I could always secure a seat without ballot, if one was vacant, as I had to wait to receive messages from Mr Parnell and Mr Gladstone and it was made known to the attendants that on any important occasion I held priority of place.

On January 27th the debate was resumed and the House sat continuously for forty-one hours. Mr Parnell retired to the Westminster Palace Hotel for a few hours' rest during this sitting and after the little rest drove quickly to one of our meeting places to tell me of his plans before I went down to Eltham.

As a rule, after an all-night sitting he used to drive down to Eltham in order not to become well known on the Eltham railway and come through the conservatory into my sitting-room, where I would have supper ready for him before the fire, with his smoking-jacket and slippers ready to put on. He seldom spoke after his first greeting. He would take off his frock-coat and boots and, when I slipped on the others for him, he would eat his supper quite silently, thinking over the events of the night. I never worried him to talk. Supper finished, he would light a cigar and sit down in his own armchair, saying, 'Well, Queenie, the Old Man spoke tonight', or So-and-so spoke and then slowly tell me of all that had passed during the sitting and his opinion of the present and future, so far as politics were concerned.

Sometimes when he had spoken himself he would say: 'I did not speak well tonight' and sometimes it was: 'I lost that quotation you gave me and brought it out sideways and there it was all the time crushed up in my hand! Then I forgot the fellow's name and called him "the poet".'

'Well, Shakespeare can be called "the poet,"' I would return soothingly.

'Yes? Is that so? It seemed to worry some of the reporters; one came and asked me what I meant! You must make me learn it better next time.'

Once he began to talk he confided all his thoughts to unreservedly and the more freely that he had not been worried to talk when he came in cold or tired. He used to say that it was such a relief to get right away from the House when a sitting was over and he enjoyed the drive down to Eltham in a hansom cab every night or early morning. It was only an eight-miles drive, but part of it was then very pleas, ant, through country lanes and over a common. Now London has swallowed up most of these pretty bits.

After relieving his mind of all political affairs of the day he would talk of things that were of home interest to us – of his stone quarries at Arklow, his saw-mills, etc., of what Kerr, his Irish agent, was doing at Avondale; or of some of his hobbies at home. So we would talk till daylight sent pale gleams of light under the window curtains and he would say: 'I am really sleepy, Queenie; I'll go to bed' and as a rule he would sleep soundly until about four o'clock in the afternoon, when he would come down to breakfast in my sitting-room.

Parnell was always generous in letting any members of his Party speak when they had a chance of distinguishing themselves and he would at once give way when he thought any member could speak better on any subject than himself. This most of his Party, if not all, acknowledged at one time. I mention the characteristic because I have noticed in more than one of the so-called 'Lives' written by those strangely ignorant of the man's real character, that considerable stress is laid upon Parnell's jealousy.

He was jealous, abnormally so where his affections were concerned, but not in political life.

Gladstone once said that 'Parnell always knew what he wanted to say and said it', but he was not a ready speaker and his constitutional nervousness, hidden though it was under the iron mask of reserve he always wore in public, rendered public speaking very painful work to him. He was extremely modest about his own speeches and frequently would say to me that So-and-so 'would have put that much better to the House, but I could not have trusted him to say it and leave it'. He considered that most Irish men spoilt things by over-elaboration. Here also I may record a protest at the tales of gross discourtesies, spoken utterly without motive, recorded in some of these 'Lives'.

The Parnell I knew – and I may claim to have known him more intimately than anyone else on earth, both in public and private life – was incapable of such motiveless brusqueries. That Parnell could crush utterly and without remorse I know; that he could deal harshly, even brutally, with anyone or anything that stood against him in the path he meant to tread, I admit; but that he would ever go out of his way to say a grossly rude thing or make an unprovoked attack, whether upon the personal appearance, morals, or character of another man, I absolutely deny. Parnell was ruthless in all his dealings with those who thwarted his will, but – he was never petty.

Parnell had a most beautiful and harmonious voice when speaking in public. Very clear it was, even in moments of passion against his own and his country's foes – passion modulated and suppressed until I have seen, from the Ladies' Gallery, his hand clenched until the 'Orders of the Day' which he held were crushed into pulp and only that prevented his nails piercing his hand. Often I have taken the 'Orders' out of his pocket, twisted into shreds – a fate that also over-took the slips of notes and the occasional quotations he had got me to look out for him.

Sometimes when he was going to speak I could not leave my aunt long enough to be sure of getting to the Ladies' Gallery in time to hear him; or we might think it inexpedient that I should be seen to arrive so soon after him at the House. On these occasions, when I was able, I would arrive perhaps in the middle of his speech and look down upon him, saying in my heart, 'I have come!'; and invariably I would see the answering signal – the lift of the head and lingering touch of the white rose in his coat, which told me, 'I know, my Queen!'

This telepathy of the soul, intuition, or what you will, was so strong between us that, whatever the business before the House, whether Parnell was speaking or not, in spite of the absolute impossibility of distinguishing any face or form behind the grille of the Ladies' Gallery, Parnell was aware of my presence, even though often he did not expect me, as soon as I came in and answered my wordless message by the signal that I knew.

Sometimes he would wish to speak to me before I went home and would signal by certain manipulations of his handkerchief to me to go and await him at Charing Cross, or another of our meeting-places and there he would come to me to tell me how things were going, or to chat for a few minutes, or get from me the replies to messages sent through me to Mr Gladstone.

* * * * * * *

THE GROSVENOR HOTEL,
Wednesday morning, February 28, 1881.

MY DEAR MRS O' SHEA, – I am just leaving for Paris, where I shall remain for a few days.

The Cork and other meetings will be postponed, as Coercion Bill will not be passed by Sunday.

Please write me as before and send some addresses.

Yours always,

C. S. P.

DOVER,
Wednesday, February 23, 1881.

MY DEAR MRS O' SHEA, – Am just starting for Calais.

Kindly send on my portmanteau with my letters and other things in my room or in the wardrobe to me at Hotel Brighton, Rue de Rivoli, Paris.

Yours always,

C. S. P.

February 25, 1881.

MY DEAREST KATIE, – I have just received your three letters and am so delighted to read them hurriedly before sending you this line in time for post.

I never had the slightest doubt of my darling and cannot imagine why she should think so.

Did not know I was going when leaving here, but was induced to leave by private information, the nature of which I will send you in my next.

Am not yet sure whether I shall return, but shall manage to see you in any case.

Yours,

C.

PARIS,
Sunday, February 27, 1881.

Have received following telegram which do not understand:

'Motive actuating latest arrival worthy consideration – telegraph all right.'

Please explain who is latest arrival.

Yours very truly,

C. S.P.

Have no letter from you today.

HOTEL BRIGHTON, 218 RUE DE RIVOLI, PARIS,

Sunday evening, February 27, 1881.

MY DEAR MRS O' SHEA, – I cannot understand your telegram received today at all, although I have been thinking it over all the evening. I wired back as you appeared to request in it, 'All right'.

There was no letter for me from you at the usual address, so I enclose another; as I fear something may have gone wrong. You can write me freely in my own name under cover to this address: Thomas Adams and Co., Limited, 33 Rue d'Hauteville, Paris and they will forward the letters safely to me.

I have been warned from Dublin that there is some plot on foot against us which has been originated by information received from Cork and you will guess the original source.

I am expecting further information tomorrow in reference to it. I have received five letters in all from you since my arrival in Paris. Best not post your letters at Eltham.

I did not know when leaving you that I was going – my departure was influenced by information of reliable kind that my arrest was intended for passage in Clare speech and that bail would be refused and I should be left in jail until Habeas Corpus was suspended, when I could have been again arrested. I think, however, they have now abandoned this intention, but will make sure before I return.

This is my third letter to you since my arrival here.

Yours,

C.S.P.

HOTEL BRIGHTON, 218 RUE DE RIVOLI, PARIS,

Tuesday, March 1, 1881.

MY DEAREST LOVE, – Today I have received your four letters, the earliest of which was written on Saturday. You do not seem to have written on Friday, as there was nothing for me on Saturday or Sunday.

I propose returning, to London on Thursday morning, leaving here Wednesday evening, but it is just possible I may not leave till Thursday morning, in which case I shall not be able to see my Katie until Friday.

If I return Thursday morning, my Queen may expect to see me about one o'clock.

Your letters make me both happy and sad, happy to hear from my own, but sad when I see how troubled you are. –

Always yours,

CHARLES.

GLASGOW,

Tuesday, April 19, 1881.

DEAREST KATIE, – I send you authority for letters. They are in two forms, one authorising delivery to you and the other to bearer.

Tonight I leave by boat for Dublin, arriving tomorrow morning. I trust my own wifie has not permitted herself to be too unhappy and that she has not been worried. I am writing with her own beautiful face before me and have just kissed it.

Always, your husband.

Please write me to Morrison's.

CHAPTER XX

HOBBIES AND A CHALLENGE

'Admire, exult – despise – laugh, weep – for here
There is much matter for all feeling; Man!
Thou Pendulum betwixt a simile and tear.' – BYRON.

IN THE EARLY SUMMER OF 1881 my aunt had one of her old friends to stay with her and I seized the opportunity of freedom to take my children to Brighton for a month, after settling the old ladies together. I had gone down before the children to take rooms for them and was walking across Brighton Station when I was suddenly joined by a tall man whom I did not recognise for a moment until he said quietly, 'Don't you know me?' It was Mr Parnell, who had slipped into the train at Clapham Junction, knowing that I was going to Brighton and who had cut off his beard with his pocket scissors in the train in order to avoid being recognised at Brighton. He had wrapped a white muffler round his throat and pulled it as high as possible over the lower part of his face, with the result that the manageress of the hotel he stayed at was certain that he had an infectious illness of the throat and rather demurred at letting him in. It was only by the expedient of complaining loudly at being .kept waiting in the draught with his 'raging toothache' that 'Mr Stewart' was reluctantly admitted. I could not bear his appearance neither bearded nor shaven – so he went off soon after arrival, was properly shaved and relieved the hotel staff by discarding the muffler and assuring them that he was free from pain now his 'tooth' was out.

He went to Cork soon after this and to please me, was photographed without the beard and with the ring I had given him on his finger. We had had a little quarrel and were very unhappy until we had made it up again and he had this photograph done to remind me that he wore my ring. He also gave sittings to Henry O' Shea (no relation of Captain O' Shea) for a portrait (pencil) at this time and this was sent to him while he was in Kilmainham. He liked this sketch much and wrote to the paper for which it was done to this effect. When he left the prison he brought the sketch home to me and I have it now. It hung in our dining-room till he died and he always liked it, but I still think it a little hard and expressionless; the eyes are too large and empty. There was a painting done of Parnell years afterwards and here also the artist failed with the eyes. This latter portrait was not, I think, done from life, but from photographs, so there was reason for the failure in this respect, photographs making unsatisfactory studies. The artist who painted this last picture gave Parnell blue eyes; presumably following the idea that Parnell was an Irishman and must therefore have blue eyes, whereas the facts were that Parnell was not an Irishman, but the son of an Englishman resident in Ireland and his American wife and had brown eyes, not large, but with the smouldering fires in them that gave character to his cold, high-bred face.

Parnell had so many hobbies and interests in his home life that it is difficult to enumerate them all. He once said rather wearily that if he had not 'taken off his coat' in the Irish cause and for the Irish people he could have been always happy at home working at things so much more congenial to him.

At one time he took up all the intricacies of book-keeping in order that he might check his Irish agent's accounts and many weeks he sat immersed in double entry, estate accounts keeping, commercial booking, etc., in the evening, while I sat near him typing replies to his letters ready for his signature. He used to threaten me with lessons in book-keeping, so that I might be ready to help him with the estate management at Avondale when we went to live there; but I felt that my duties as his extra and most private secretary were sufficiently arduous and declined instruction in account-keeping.

Many hours were also spent in architectural drawings, which interested him greatly. At that time Brighton Station was being rebuilt and Parnell was intensely interested in getting the 'span' of the roof. He spent hours at odd times pacing the station, measuring distances, heights, depth of roof, etc. etc. and in drawing up plans in order that he might build a cattle shed on the same lines at Avondale. These plans he afterwards submitted to a well-known architect for his opinion on them and they were returned as absolutely correct in every detail. He then reduced the whole thing to scale and had the cattle shed made from these plans at Avondale.

I well remember his look of reproach at me when I laughed while reading him a letter from his agent at Avondale the following winter. The agent said that Mrs Delia Parnell (Parnell's mother) had arrived unexpectedly at Avondale and, after seeing the new cattle shed, had at once decided to give an entertainment in it. This she had done, having the cattle shifted from their comfortable quarters, the place boarded in and a temporary floor laid down.

Parnell did not see that this expensive and trouble some eviction of his cattle for so frivolous a reason was in the least funny and was very greatly annoyed at the whole proceeding. He was always most chivalrously kind to his mother, however and his protest on this occasion was very gentle, though coupled with firm insistence, on the instant restoration of the cattle-house to its tenants.

Another of his hobbies was the 'assaying' of small pieces of quartz from the stream at Wicklow and I used to help him for hours at this, keeping his blow-pipe constantly at work, while he, silent and absorbed, manipulated the crucibles. When we went to live at Brighton, after my aunt's death, he had a furnace fitted up in one of the rooms so that he could work on a larger scale. His endeavour to obtain gold from this quartz was rewarded to a certain extent; but the working was, of course, far too laborious and expensive to be profitable otherwise than as a hobby. However, Parnell for five years worked at it in various odd hours till he had extracted sufficient gold to line my wedding ring, even though his hope of getting enough for the whole ring was not fulfilled.

When working at these things Parnell was absolutely oblivious to the passing of time and it was with difficulty that I prevailed upon him to take sufficient exercise, or even to take his meals before they were spoiled by waiting. He would order his horse, 'President', to be taken to a certain place about a half-mile from the house, at the hour he wished to ride and then become so absorbed in the particular hobby of the moment that even I could get nothing from him but an abstracted smile and a gentle 'Is that so?' in answer to the intimation that his horse had been waiting some two hours or more for him.

Many a day I have let him work up to the last possible moment and then literally pulled off the old 'cardigan' jacket he worked in and forced him into his frock-coat for the House; and it happened more than once that he was due to attend a meeting in Ireland and when I had packed his things and had the carriage at the door ready for him he would throw himself into a chair and with his slow, grave smile say, 'You are in a hurry to get rid of me; I will not go yet. Sit down and let me look at you a bit, my Queen.' I would protest that he must go, that he would lose the mail train. 'Then I'll be no use at the meeting, for it will be over!' he would mockingly reply; and so, when the last possible chance of his being in time had vanished, he would sit opposite me through the evening talking of politics, Avondale, the assaying – of anything that came into his head – always watching me with that intent, considering gaze that was my bewilderment and my joy.

When he failed a meeting like this, where hundreds of people were waiting for him – or other appointments, private or public – I sometimes would want him to telegraph, or write, apologising or excusing his non-attendance, but this he would never do, saying, 'You do not learn the ethics of kingship, Queenie. Never explain, never apologise'; adding, with his rare laugh: 'I could never keep my rabble together if I were not above the human weakness of apology.'

When Parnell came home from Ireland after these meetings he would sit smoking and watching me as I went through the pockets of the coats he had worn while away. It was a most interesting game and he enjoyed it as much as I when I brought out a new trophy from the depths of the deepest and most obvious side-pocket. It was a point of honour that he should not 'feel or look' till he got home to me and I have a dear little collection of souvenirs now from these pockets – little medals with the images of various saints, scapulars and badges, slipped in by the deft, modest fingers of sweet-faced nuns, in the crowds, whose startled, deprecating blushes when he turned and caught the delinquent in the act always won a courteous bow and smile from the heretic 'Chief' whose conversion their patriotic hearts so ardently desired. I found also odds and ends pressed upon him by the hero-worshipping peasants, some gruesome scrap of the rope that had hanged some unknown scamp and hero, so 'aising to the bone-pains, an' his riv'rance not looking, a bit of a twisht roun' yer honour's arm!' or perhaps a flattened old bullet that, had gained some fancied power in its evil journey through a man's heart. Then there were the brand-new kerchiefs of most vivid green, most beautifully embroidered by the clever fingers of 'herself' and so many four-leaved and therefore 'lucky', shamrocks from the 'colleens', who went singing all the year if they thereby earned a smile from the Chief. Even the little children used to make sudden, shy offerings to their hero; a 'quare bit ave a stone', a 'farden me mither giv me', or some uneasy looking fragment of what might once have been a bird's egg. Of sticks, blackthorns and others, I once had an enormous collection brought back to me at various times by Parnell, but these, together with the two riding-whips I had myself given him, were stolen from me some ten years ago, when I was moving from one house to another. The two riding-whips I prized very highly, for Parnell was so pleased when I gave them to him. One was gold-mounted, the other silver-mounted and each had 'C.S.P.' engraved upon it.

Among my stick collection was one made of horn – a curious thing, carved and inlaid with ivory, sent him by some unknown American admirer. He used this stick on his last journey upstairs from the sitting- room to the bed where he died.

In January of 1881, Willie, who had rooms then in Charles Street, Haymarket, came down to Eltham suddenly, very angry indeed with me because he had seen some men watching his lodgings and imagined that I had engaged a detective to do so. As I had never had an idea of doing anything of the sort I was extremely annoyed and a violent quarrel was the result. As a matter of fact the men were watching the upper floor, where a friend of Willie's lived and this friend's wife afterwards divorced him.

All these months, since my first meeting with Mr Parnell, Willie knew at least that I frequently met him at the House. He had invited him to Eltham himself, though when the visit was first proposed I said my house was too shabby, the children would worry so nervous a man and we had better not break the routine of our (Willie's and my) life (which by then was tacitly accepted as a formal separation of a friendly sort), giving any and every excuse, because of the danger I knew I was not able to withstand.

But Willie was blind to the existence of the fierce, bewildering force that was rising within me in answer to the call of those passion-haunted eyes, that waking or sleeping never left me. Willie then, as always, was content that what was his, was his for good or ill. He knew that men, in our past life together, had admired me, even that some had loved me; but that was to their own undoing, an impertinence that had very properly recoiled upon their own heads. His wife could not love anyone but himself; perhaps unfortunately she did not even do that, but after all love was only a relative term – a little vulgar even, after girlhood had passed and the mild affection of his own feelings towards her were no doubt reciprocated, in spite of the unfortunate temperamental differences that made constant companionship impossible.

So Parnell came, having in his gentle, insistent way urged his invitation and from Willie. And now Willie and I were quarrelling because he, my lawful husband, had come down without the invitation that was now (for some years) understood as due to the courtesy of friends and because he had become vaguely suspicious. Flying rumours had perhaps reached his ears; and now it was too late, for he dared not formulate them, they were too vague; too late, for I had been swept into the avalanche of Parnell's love; too late, for I possessed the husband of my heart for all eternity.

I had fought against our love; but Parnell would not fight and I was alone. I had urged my children and his work; but he answered me: 'For good or ill, I am your husband, your lover, your children, your all. And I will give my life to Ireland, but to you I give my love, whether it be your heaven or your hell. It is destiny. When I first looked into your eyes I knew.'

When Willie arrived so suddenly at Eltham Mr Parnell was not there, but Willie went into his room and finding his portmanteau, sent it to London and left my house, declaring he would challenge Parnell to fight a duel and would shoot him.

'My dear Mrs O' Shea', wrote Parnell from London on the 7th of January, 'will you kindly ask Captain O' Shea where he left my luggage? I inquired at both parcel office, cloak-room and this hotel at Charing Cross today and they were not to be found.'

Willie later challenged Parnell, sending The O' Gorman Mahon to him as his second; but the duel was not fought. My sister, Mrs Steele, came down to see me and patched up a peace between myself and Willie; and Mr Parnell, while making arrangements to go abroad to meet Willie, explained to him that he (Parnell) must have a medium of communication between the Government and himself, that Mrs O' Shea had kindly undertaken the office for him and, as this would render negotiations possible and safe, he trusted that Willie would make no objection to his meeting her after the duel.

'I replied to Captain O' Shea's note yesterday', writes Parnell, 'and sent my reply by a careful messenger to the Salisbury Club; and it must be waiting him there.

'He has just written me a very insulting letter and I shall be obliged to send a friend to him if I do not have a satisfactory reply to a second note I have just sent him.'

Willie then thought he had been too hasty in his action and, knowing I had become immersed in the Irish cause, merely made the condition that Mr Parnell should not stay at Eltham.

From the date of this bitter quarrel Parnell and I were one, without further scruple, without fear and without remorse.

The following are 'cypher' letters of private messages to me bearing upon the matter of the threatened duel:

July 20, 1881.

MY DEAR MRS O' SHEA, – Just a line to say that I am very well and wondering when I shall see you again.

I hope that your cold is better.

Yours very truly,

CHAS. S. PARNELL.

HOUSE OF COMMONS,
Thursday night, July 22, 1881.

MY DEAR MRS O' SHEA, – I have received both your very kind letters quite safely and am looking forward to seeing you somewhere or somehow tomorrow.

I am very much troubled at everything you have to under go and trust that it will not last long.

Yours always,

CHAS. S. PARNELL.

I am still quite well. Thank you very much for enclosure.

WESTMINSTER PALACE HOTEL,
VICTORIA STREET, LONDON, S.W.,
Sunday evening, July 25, 1881.

MY DEAR MRS O' SHEA, – I write to ask you to send my travelling cap, if it is at Eltham, to me here, as I may have to go over to Paris or Boulogne some day this week.

I hope your eyes are quite well again and that you are enjoying these cool times.

I have been very lonely all today and yesterday. Have not seen anyone that I know.–

Yours always,

CHAS. S. PARNELL.

July 20, 1881.

MY DEAR MRS O' SHEA, – I am still staying at the same address and have postponed going to France, so you need not send my cap.

Yours always,

CHAS. S. PARNELL.

CHAPTER XXI

ASTRONOMY AND 'SEDITION'

'– and there is one stirring hour ... when a wakeful influence goes abroad over the sleeping
hemisphere ... Do the stars rain down an influence?'
– ROBERT LOUIS STEVENSON.

DURING HIS LEISURE MOMENTS AT Eltham Mr Parnell took up the study of astronomy
with the vigour that always characterised him when he was interested in a subject.
He had picked out from my bookshelf a book of stars – one of Sir Robert Ball's, I believe,
that I had bought at random one day and became at once interested. From the teaching
of an old friend of my father's I had a fairly good knowledge of astronomy and, though by
no means well up in the latest research and discoveries, I was able to tell him much of the
stellar systems that was new to him. Finding how he devoured the little book of Sir Robert
Ball's, I got several of the latter's interesting works for him, besides Herschel's.

Then Mr Parnell told me of a magnificent telescope he had at Avondale and sent for
it. When this arrived he sent for a few sacks of Portland cement, with which he made a
pedestal in my garden and himself mounted the telescope upon it. He made an ingenious
arrangement whereby the slightest touch would tilt the telescope to the desired angle and
we spent many nights, he and I, watching the stars and following the courses of the planets
till they faded in the dawn. Then he thought of how near to us was the Observatory at
Greenwich and got a permit to go over the Observatory. After that, on the days when my
aunt had her readers with her, I used to accompany him to the Observatory, where we
spent many hours.

He could always absorb very quickly any knowledge that appealed to him and he soon
had the pleasure of teaching me much about the latest discoveries and about a subject
intensely interesting to him – the wonderful way in which the telescopes used in the great
observatories of the world are made.

In time this study of the stars began to worry him too much and he reluctantly gave
up all serious work on the subject. He said it was all too immense and absorbing to think
about in a life that was primarily concerned with politics. But the pedestal remained and
still we occasionally mounted the telescope and kept vigil with the stars through the
summer night.

On April 7th, 1881, Mr Gladstone had introduced his Land Bill into the House of Commons. It was a better Bill than the Irish Party had reason to expect, but it had grave defects and the Irish had not been consulted; while the Government's policy of coercion and Forster's attitude towards Parnell and his followers made co-operation between the Liberals and the Irish impossible. Parnell's policy was to hold aloof and press for amendments. After being crippled in the House of Lords the Bill became law. At a Land League Convention held in Dublin on September 14th a resolution was adopted, on the suggestion of Parnell, that the Act should be tested by selected cases. 'Nothing', said Parnell 'could be more disastrous to our cause or our organisation and to your hopes of getting your rents reduced, than an indiscriminate rush of the tenantry into the Land Courts.'

A few days later Parnell was drawn in triumph through the streets of Dublin. The same day Forster wrote to Gladstone suggesting that Parnell should be arrested under the Coercion Act.

He suggested, moreover, that in his next speech at Leeds, on October 7th, Mr Gladstone should impeach Parnell and his policy. Gladstone obeyed. The people of Ireland, he cried, wished to use the Land Act and Parnell would not let them, but 'the resources of civilisation were not yet exhausted.'

Parnell retorted with passion and scorn in his famous Wexford speech delivered on October 9th.

'You have', he said, 'gained something by your exertions during the last twelve months, but I am here today to tell you that you have gained but a fraction of that to which you are justly entitled. And the Irishman who thinks that he can now throw away his arms, just as Grattan disbanded the volunteers in 1782, will find to his sorrow and destruction, when too late, that he has placed himself in the power of a perfidious, cruel, unrelenting English enemy.

'It is a good sign that this masquerading knight-errant, this pretended champion of the liberties of every other nation except those of the Irish nation should be obliged to throw off the mask today and to stand revealed as the man who, by his own utterances, is prepared to carry fire and sword into your homesteads unless you humble and abase yourselves before him and before the landlords of this country. But I have forgotten. I had said that he had maligned everybody. Oh, no; he has a good word for one or two people. He says that the late Mr Isaac Butt was a most amiable man and a true patriot. In the opinion of an English statesman no man is good in Ireland until he is buried and unable to strike a blow for Ireland and perhaps the day may come when I may get a good word from English statesmen as a moderate man when I am dead and buried.

'When people talk of public plunder they should first ask themselves and recall to mind who were the first public plunderers in Ireland. The land of Ireland has been confiscated three times over by the men whose descendants Mr Gladstone is supporting in the fruits of their plunder by his bayonets and buckshot. Oh, yes; but we can say a little more than that too; we can say, or at all events if we don't say it others will say it, that the doctrine of public plunder is only a question of degree. Who was it that first sanctioned this doctrine of public plunder? will be asked by some persons. I am proceeding in the demand that the improvements of the tenants – and their predecessors in title – shall be theirs, no matter how long ago they may have been made. I am proceeding upon the lines of an amendment in the Land Act of 1881, which was introduced by Mr Healy, framed by Mr Gladstone's Attorney-General for Ireland and sanctioned by Mr Gladstone, his whole Cabinet, the House of Commons and the House of Lords and I say that it is a question of degree if you extend that limit of twenty years, within which period the improvements of the tenants have been protected by the legislature, to that period, no matter how long, within which those improvements have been made.

'So that if we are to go into this question the utmost that Mr Gladstone and the Liberal Party will be able to make out of it will be to find that there are some persons very, much better entitled to call him a little robber than he is to call me a big one. But I was forgetting a point; he has a good word for Mr Shaw. He has discovered that there are only four or five honest Irishmen in the country and one of these is Mr Shaw. He blames me for not having disapproved of what he calls the dynamite policy. Well, I am not aware that Mr Shaw has repudiated the dynamite policy either; but I'll tell you what Mr Shaw said and you must bear in mind that, in addition to speaking well of him as an honest Irish man, Mr Gladstone also offered him a situation as one of the Land Commissioners. Mr Shaw did not repudiate the dynamite policy any more than I did; but I'll tell you what he did eighteen months ago in the county of Cork. He said that his blood boiled whenever he saw a process-server and that he never met one without feeling inclined to take the linchpin out of his car. Now, gentlemen, if I said that to you today Mr Gladstone would have me in Kilmainham before three weeks were out. Nay, more, if I had ever spoken anything like that Mr Gladstone would have had me in Kilmainham long ago.

****

'In one last despairing wail he says that when the Government is expected to preserve the peace it has no moral force behind it. The Government has no moral force behind it in Ireland. The whole Irish people are against them. They have to depend for their support on the self-interest of a very small minority of the people of this country and therefore they have no moral force behind them.

'Mr Gladstone, in those few short words, admits that the English Government has failed in Ireland; he admits the contention that Grattan and the volunteers of '82 fought for; he admits the contention that the men of '98 lost their lives for he admits the contention that O'Connell argued for; he admits the contention that the men of '48 staked their all for; he admits the contention that the men of '65, after a long period of depression and of apparent death of all national life, in Ireland, cheerfully faced the dungeon and the horrors of penal servitude for and admits the contention that today you in your over-powering multitudes have re-established and, please God, will bring to a successful and final issue, namely, that England's mission in Ireland has been a failure and that Irishmen have established their right to govern Ireland by laws made by themselves for themselves on Irish soil.

'I say it is not in his power to trample on the aspirations and the rights of the Irish people with no moral force behind him. These are very brave words that he uses, but it strikes me that they have a ring about them like the whistle of a schoolboy on his way through a churchyard at night to keep up his courage. He would have you to believe that he is not afraid of you because he has disarmed you, because he has attempted to disorganise you, because he knows that the Irish nation is today disarmed, so far as physical weapons go. But he does not hold this kind of language with the Boers...'

****

'Suppose they arrest you, Mr Parnell', asked an Irish member, who dined with the Leader on the evening of the speech, 'have you any instructions to give us? Who will take your place?' 'Ah!' he said, deliberately, looking through a glass of champagne which he had just raised to his lips. 'Ah, if I am arrested Captain Moonlight will take my place.' [8]

All through 1881 Parnell was constantly paying flying visits to Ireland and also to various parts of England, working up the 'League', addressing meetings and privately ascertaining for himself how far the temper of the 'reactionaries' could be trusted to do the work he wished without becoming too greatly involved in the tactics of the 'Invincibles' proper. He came home to me now always between the times of his journeyings up and down the country and if it was not certain that I should be alone he would write me a formal though friendly note or letter that anyone could have been shown, in which was given some word or sign that let me know a place or time of meeting him, either in London or nearer my home.

On some of these occasions my duties to my aunt would keep me, so that I might be an hour or more late in arriving at the place where he awaited me; but never once in all those years did he once fail me or leave the place of appointment before I came, even though it might be at the loss of the mail train to Ireland and leaving some thousands of people waiting in vain for the speech he was too far away to make. Sometimes I would become conscience-stricken on such an occasion, but he would only comment that one speech more or less was a little matter and what was lost by a speech not made was amply compensated for by the deepened impression of his mystery and power gained by the people. 'For it is the strange thing I found out early in political life', he would say, 'they think I'm much more wonderful when I do nothing than when I'm working hard.'

Saturday evening, August 1, 1881.

MY DEAR MRS O' SHEA, – I had arranged to go to a meeting at Durham today, but was unable to do so at the last moment.

I think you have some books of mine at Eltham, which I propose going down to look for on Monday, about eleven or twelve, unless I hear from you that you can find them for me.

Yours very truly,

CHAS. S. PARNELL.

Please reply to House of Commons, where I shall call for my letters on Monday morning.

August 17, 1881.

I have been rendered very anxious by not receiving any news from you today and trust that nothing has happened to you and that you are not ill.

I had a very satisfactory conversation yesterday and things look much straighter.

Yours truly,

C.

HOUSE OF COMMONS,
August 19, 1881.

I arrived home quite right and am very much pleased to learn this evening that you have good hopes.

Yours always,

C.

MORRISON'S HOTEL, DUBLIN,
September 10, 1881.

MY DEAR MRS O' SHEA, – Will you kindly address and post enclosed.

I am quite recovered from my attack and the doctor says that I shall be able to travel in a few days.

Yours very truly,

CHAS. S. PARNELL.

The enclosure was the following letter:

MORRISON'S HOTEL, DUBLIN,
September 10, 1881.

MY OWN WIFIE, – I know that you must have been much worried yesterday by my failure to send you a few words, but my Beauty will forgive her own husband.

Your wire has been put into my hand as I write and shall have an instant answer.

It gives me so much pleasure to know that your trouble has not returned since I left and that my wires give you pleasure. Your King thinks very very often of his dearest Queen and wishes her not to be sad, but to try and be happy for his sake. Everything is going on very well here and your King is much satisfied.

MORRISON'S HOTEL, DUBLIN,
September 25, 1881.

MY OWN LOVELIEST, – I send you these few words to assure Wifie that her husband always thinks of her and hopes that she is well and happy.
YOUR OWN KING.

October 4, 1881.

MY OWN WIFIE, – I have satisfied myself, by two separate tests today, that there is a good deal of silver in the dark stone of which there is so much in the old mine. In fact nearly the whole lode consists of this (the miners are working in it in the North Level). I cannot say how many ounces there will be to the ton until I get it assayed, but if there should be six or eight ounces to the ton it ought to pay to work.
YOUR OWN KING.

MORRISON'S HOTEL, DUBLIN,
October 7, 1881.

MY OWN WIFIE, – I called today to see him9 on my return from Dungarvan, but he was out and I waited for him three hours. Calling again at eleven tonight, he was again out, but returned just as I was writing to make an appointment for the morning. He says that he leaves tomorrow (Friday) evening and stops to shoot on Saturday in Wales and goes on Tuesday to Paris to see the Papal Nuncio, who he says has requested him to come. This, then, is the last letter I can send you for the present through Eltham, so I hope to have the other address from you tomorrow morning.

My dearest Katie must have been very lonely ever since. Did she get my three letters? Her husband has been so busy he has not even had time to sleep, but he has never been too busy to think of her.

I can go over to London early next week if I may see you. Should I remain in London or go down to you?

With numerous kisses to my beautiful Queenie.
C. S. P.

October 8, 1881.

MY DEAREST LITTLE WIFIE, – Your husband has been very good since he left you and is longing to see you again. He has kept his eyes, thought and love all for you and my sweetest love may be assured that he always will.

Tomorrow I go to Avondale, thence to Wexford on Sunday, whence I return Monday morning and hope to be with my Queenie on Tuesday or Wednesday at latest

Everything in Dublin has been settled up pretty satisfactorily and I trust only to have to make an occasional appearance in Ireland during the rest of the autumn and winter.
ALWAYS YOUR KING.

On October 11th, Forster crossed to England, having first arranged with Sir Thomas Steele, Commander-in-Chief in Ireland, that, should the Cabinet agree to arrest Parnell, Forster would wire the one word 'Proceed'.

The same day Parnell returned to Avondale and on the next night was back in Dublin.

MORRISON'S HOTEL,
October 11, 1881.

MY OWN KATIE, – I found two letters and two wires from your King's Queen here on my arrival an hour ago. Your telegram this morning took a great weight off my mind, as your silence made me almost panic-stricken lest you had been hurt by that ---- and had not been able to get to town.

Tomorrow I go to Kildare10 and shall try and start for London Friday morning; but I cannot be sure of this, as 'something'11 may turn up at the last moment and there is also a meeting of the Executive on Saturday, which they want me to stay for.

However, Wifie knows I will do the best I can and she will get a wire from me on Friday, soon after or as soon as she receives this, telling her what I have done. If I arrive London Friday night shall go to same hotel and shall wait for my darling.

Will she mind asking for my number?

ALWAYS YOUR OWN KING.

CHAPTER XXII

THE ARREST OF PARNELL

'Beyond the hills, beyond the sea,
O Love, my love, come back to me,
And bring me back yon summer's day.' – LADY LINDSAY.

ON OCTOBER 12TH, 1881, I was in London on Mr Parnell's business – to ascertain the movements of the Government. He, of course, was in Ireland and had warned me that it would be impossible for him to keep out of prison much longer and that any further effort to avoid arrest would be inexpedient on all counts. I was much depressed about this and urged him to put it off as long as possible.

My health was then delicate and I felt an unreasonable fear and loneliness when he was away from me. He was very tender and considerate to me, but pointed out that the turmoil and rebellion he had brought to a head in Ireland must be very carefully handled to be productive of ultimate good and that he could 'mark time' with the Land League better in Kilmainham than out, thus rendering this force more useful to the Home Rule campaign and less wanton in destruction. Parnell used, but never abused, the weapons of political strife he forged.

He desired immediate information of the decision of the Government to arrest him, that he might destroy any papers that, if found on him, might frustrate his plans and cause unnecessary difficulty to those working with him. So when on October 12th information was sent to me, at the house where I waited in London in the neighbourhood of Piccadilly, that a Cabinet Council had been hurriedly summoned, I wired in code to Parnell and directly after the Cabinet Council I was able to inform him that Forster had left for Ireland with the warrant for his arrest.

I could not bear the thought of his arrest and after writing to him under cover to a person in Ireland who would, I knew, get my letter to him, whether in or out of prison, I telegraphed to Parnell again to know if he could meet me at Holyhead if I started at once. I had so much of his business in hand now and he had expected to see me at least once more before the inevitable separation of his imprisonment. I felt almost unable to cope with the situation; I was not strong and I was full of anxiety as to the probable effects upon Parnell's health of life in Kilmainham Gaol. In addition to my anxiety, the deception I had to practise towards Captain O' Shea, seldom as I saw him, told upon my nerves just now. However, Parnell's message in reply, written in our private code, reassured me. While he still thought it better to suffer arrest at once, he would not go out of his way to meet it and would be careful when in Kilmainham so that his imprisonment should be of short duration. He would not allow me to go to the fatigue of a journey to Holyhead, nor would he go abroad to avoid arrest and I went home comforting myself as I could with his confident spirit and loving messages.

On October 13th there was a terrible gale through out the South of England and at Eltham, after a sleepless night, I was up early – far too early to disturb my old aunt – and wandered out through her park in the gale. The battling with the wind lifted a little the load of restlessness and anxiety as to what was happening in Ireland from my heart. The fierce wind blowing through my hair braced me and cleared the 'cobwebs' from my brain and, leaning against a tree for support, I watched the havoc of the storm as the crimson and russet leaves were swirled across the park from the rookery, rising in places like water-spouts into the air as they met the opposing current of wind in the open. The old trees bowed beneath the gale as though at last the weight of years was too much for them and a warning crash from the one against which I leant, made me stagger breathless into the wind again, as a large branch was torn from it close to the place where I had stood. In the slow-breaking day I fought my way as far as the old house and holding on to the railings that separated the lawns from the park I turned to look down the long elm avenue. I was a little frightened at the force of the gale, which now seemed to be screaming around me and as I looked towards the avenue, where leaves and small branches were flying before the wind, there was a terrific crash and the whole of one side of the avenue fell, ripping and tearing till I thought every tree in the place was coming down. Heavy with foliage, these old trees had given in to the fury of the storm and the falling of one upon another with all the weight of their huge branches had completed the ruin.

I was with my aunt as usual all that day and was glad of the quiet and rest. The old lady gazed out at the still raging storm and told me tales of her youth, while I listened to the voice I loved in the wind outside, saying to me again and again what he had said before he left me, 'Be brave, Queenie. I cannot stay outside while all these others are arrested and it is bound to be soon now.'

Towards evening, when the storm had cleared a little and my aunt had fallen asleep before the fire, I went home to get the evening papers I always had sent over from Blackheath before Willie came down from London to dinner, as he had written to say he would do. However, on my return home I found Willie already there, extremely pleased to be able to announce to me that Parnell had been arrested that morning. I knew his news directly I saw his face and as I was really prepared for it I did not flinch, but replied languidly that I had thought Parnell 'couldn't keep out of gaol much longer, didn't you?'

But Willie was so fiercely and openly joyful that my maids, who were ardent Parnellites, were much shocked and I, being terribly overwrought, laughed at their disgusted faces as I went to dress for dinner. It was really the laugh of tears, but that laugh of jangled nerves and misery did me good service with Willie and we got through dinner amicably enough, while he descanted upon the wickedness and folly of Parnell's policy and the way the Irish question should really be settled and would be if it could be left in his hands and those who thought with him. He observed me closely, as he criticised Parnell and his policy and reiterated his pleasure in knowing he was 'laid by the heels'.

I was now quite calm again and smiled at him as I reminded him that I was now as ardent a Parnellite as Parnell himself and had already done so much hard work for 'the cause' that my politics were far more reactionary than when he had introduced Parnell to me: unlike his (Willie's) own, which were less so. My heart being in Kilmainham Gaol with my lover, I was momentarily at peace and could ask Willie questions as to the mode of life and prison discipline of political prisoners. Willie, as are so many men, was never so happy as when giving information.

The next day I received my King's letter, written as he was arrested:–

MORRISON's HOTEL, DUBLIN,
October 13, 1881.

MY OWN QUEENIE, – I have just been arrested by two fine looking detectives and write these words to wifie to tell her that she must be a brave little woman and not fret after her husband.

The only thing that makes me worried and unhappy is that it may hurt you and our child.

You know, darling, that on this account it will be wicked of you to grieve, as I can never have any other wife but you and if anything happens to you I must die childless. Be good and brave, dear little wifie, then.

YOUR OWN HUSBAND.

Politically it is a fortunate thing for me that I have been arrested, as the movement is breaking fast and all will be quiet in a few months, when I shall be released.

Speaking at the Guildhall on the day of Parnell's arrest Mr Gladstone said: 'Within these few minutes I have been informed that towards the vindication of the law, of order, of the rights of property and the freedom of the land, of the first elements of political life and civilisation, the first step has been taken in the arrest of the man who has made himself pre-eminent in the attempt to destroy the authority of the law and substitute what would end in being nothing more than anarchical oppression exercised upon the people of Ireland.'

When he uttered the word 'arrest' he was stopped by the audience rising en masse and cheering frantically. 'Parnell's arrest' – I quote from the *Life of Forster* – 'was hailed almost as though it had been the news of a signal victory gained by England over a hated and formidable enemy.'

Sexton, O' Kelly, Dillon, O' Brien and J.P. Quinn, secretary of the League, were quickly arrested, while warrants were issued for Biggar, Healy and Arthur O' Connor. Healy was in England and Biggar and O' Connor managed to join him there.

CHAPTER XXIII

KILMAINHAM DAYS

'Love is not a flower that grows on the dull earth;
Springs by the calendar; must wait for the sun.
E'en while you look the peerless flower is up
Consummate in the birth.' – J.S. KNOWLES.

AT THE NEWS OF THE arrest a wave of indignation swept through Ireland. In Dublin there were riots. In many places shops were closed and towns and villages went into mourning as if for the death of a king.

Five days later the Land League countered the arrest by issuing the No Rent manifesto.

Parnell was really opposed to it, Dillon openly so, but the majority of the leaders then in Kilmainham Gaol approved of it and it was signed and published in United Ireland on October 17th. The signature is interesting, it runs thus: – 'Charles S. Parnell, President, Kilmainham Gaol; A.J. Kettle, Honorary Secretary, Kilmainham Gaol; Michael Davitt, Honorary Secretary, Portland Prison; Thomas Brennan, Honorary Secretary, Kilmainham Gaol; Thomas Geston, Head Organiser, Kilmainham Gaol; Patrick Egan, Treasurer, Paris.'

Meanwhile arrests and evictions went on all over Ireland and the Coercion Act was used mercilessly and unscrupulously on behalf of the landlords. The Ladies' Land League and its president, Miss Anna Parnell, became very busy.

* * * * * * *

From the time of Parnell's arrest onward until the birth of his child in the following February I lived a curiously subconscious existence; pursuing the usual routine of my life at home and with my aunt, but feeling that all that was of life in me had gone with my lover to prison and only came back to me in the letters that were my only mark of time. I had to be careful now; Willie became solicitous for my health and wished to come to Eltham more frequently than I would allow. He thought February would seal our reconciliation, whereas I knew it would cement the cold hatred I felt towards him and consummate the love I bore my child's father.

October 14, 1881.

MY OWN DEAREST WIFIE, – I have found a means of communicating with you and of your communicating in return.

Please put your letters into enclosed envelope, first putting them into an inner envelope, on the joining of which you can write your initials with a similar pencil to mine and they will reach me all right.

I am very comfortable here and have a beautiful room facing the sun - the best in the prison. There are three or four of the best of the men in adjoining rooms with whom I can associate all day long, so that time does not hang heavy nor do I feel lonely. My only fear is about my darling Queenie. I have been racked with torture all today, last night and yesterday, lest the shock may have hurt you or our child.

Oh, darling, write or wire me as soon as you get this that you are well and will try not to be unhappy until you see your husband again. You may wire me here.

I have your beautiful face with me here; it is such a comfort. I kiss it every morning.

Your KING.

KILMAINHAM,
October 17, 1881.

MY DEAR MRS O' SHEA, – I was very much pleased to receive your two letters, which reached me safely after having been duly perused by the Governor. I am also writing to Captain O' Shea's Paris address to acknowledge his.

The last letter which you directed to Morrison's also reached me.

If you have not done so already, please inquire in London about the messages you were expecting and about any others that may arrive in future and let me know in your next whether you have received them.

This prison is not at all damp, although the air on the north side is rather so, but I am on the south side and am so far exceedingly comfortable and not in the slightest degree dull. We are allowed to play ball and you will be glad to hear that I won my first game against one of the best and most practised players in the place, although I have not played for twenty years.

I have received the *Times, Engineer, Engineering, Mining Journal, Pall Mall Gazette, Universe*, from a London office, also the Engineer directed in your handwriting.

Shall be delighted to hear from you as often as you care to write.

Yours always,

C. S. P.

When you write again please let me know how you are. I have been very anxious for news on that point.

October 19, 1881.

MY OWN DARLING QUEENIE, – I have just received your charming little letter of Tuesday, which I have been anxiously expecting for the last week. It has taken an enormous load off my mind. I shall send you a long letter tomorrow or next day, but for the present you had better not come over, as there are five or six other men in rooms adjacent to mine who find out about everybody who visits me. Besides, you would not be permitted to see me except in presence of two warders and it might only make you more unhappy.

You must not be alarmed about rumours that the Government have evidence that we are involved in a treasonable conspiracy. There is absolutely no foundation whatever for such a statement and it is only made to defend their own proceedings.

Dearest little Queenie, keep up your spirits. I am very comfortable and very well and expect to see my darling before the New Year.

Don't put my name in inner envelope in future, as if opened it might implicate others.

October 21, 1881.

MY OWN DARLING WIFIE, – I wrote you a short note this afternoon, which I succeeded in getting off safely. Now after we have been all locked up safely for the night and when everything is quiet and I am alone, I am going to send my own Queenie some news. But first I must tell you that I sleep exceedingly well and am allowed to read the newspapers in bed in the morning and breakfast there also, if I wish.

I want, however, to give you a little history from the commencement of my stay here.

When I heard that the detectives were asking for me a terror – one which has often been present with me in anticipation – fell upon me, for I remembered that my darling had told me that she feared it would kill her; and I kept the men out of my room while I was writing you a few hasty words of comfort and of hope, for I knew the shock would be very terrible to my sweet love.

I feared that I could not post it, but they stopped the cab just before reaching the prison and allowed me to drop the letter into a pillar-box. My only torture during those first few days was the unhappiness of my queen. I wired Mrs S. to know how you were, but the wire was sent back with a note that it could not be delivered as she had gone to R. Finally your first letter came and then I knew for the first time that you were safe. You must not mind my being in the infirmary. I am only there because it is more comfortable than being in a cell and you have longer hours of association, from 8 a.m. to 8 p.m., instead of being locked up at 6 and obliged to eat by yourself. The infirmary is a collection of rooms and each has a room to himself – Dillon is in a cell, but he is allowed as a special privilege to come over and associate with us during the daytime. I am obliged to invent little maladies for my self from day to day in order to give Dr Kenny an excuse for keeping me in the infirmary, but I have never felt better in my life. Have quite forgotten that I am in prison and should very much miss the rattle of the keys and the slam of the doors. The latest discovery is heart affection.

The only thing I don't like is that the Government insist upon sending a lot of police into the gaol every night, two of whom sleep against my door and two more under my window. Just at present we are all in great disgrace on account of the manifesto and the poor warders have been most of them dismissed and fresh ones brought in. A very strict watch is kept and I have been obliged to exert my ingenuity to get letters out to you and to get yours in return. If Wife is very good and becomes strong and happy again I may let her come over and see me after a time, but for five days more I am not to be allowed to see any visitor, but I will write you again about your coming. They have let us off very easily. I fully expected that we should have been scattered in different gaols through the country as a punishment, but they evidently think no other place safe enough for me. Indeed, this place is not safe and I can get out whenever I like, but it is probably the best policy to wait to be released. And now good-night, my own dear little Wifie. Promise your husband that you will sleep well and look as beautiful when we meet again as the last time I pressed your sweet lips.

YOUR OWN HUSBAND.

October 26, 1881.

MY DEAR MRS O' SHEA, – Many thanks for your kind letter. I am anxiously waiting for another note from you to say that you have quite recovered from the indisposition you speak of.

I was in hopes that time would pass more slowly in prison than outside, but it seems to pass quite as quickly as anywhere else except those hours at Eltham.

Yours always,

C.S.P.

October 28, 1881.

MY DEAR MRS O' SHEA, – Not having heard from you this week, I write this to say that I hope you are better and that the absence of a letter from you is not to be attributed to any increase in the indisposition of which you spoke in your last.

I am glad to be able to tell you that I am exceedingly well. Health and spirits never better.

Yours very truly,

CHAS. S. PARNELL.

November 1, 1881.

MY DEAR MRS O' SHEA, – Thanks very much for your letters and telegram.

I was rather indisposed yesterday, but am very much better today. I am told that everybody gets a turn after they have been here for three or four weeks, but that they then become all right. I write you this lest you and other friends should be troubled by exaggerated reports in the newspapers.

My esteemed friend Mr Forster has become very disagreeable lately. He refuses to allow me to see my solicitor except in presence and hearing of two warders, so I have declined to see him at all. He also refuses to allow me to see visitors except in the cage, which I have also declined to do, but probably things may be relaxed again after a time.

Yours very truly,

C. S. P.

Parnell had a certain visitor who was permitted to see him in Kilmainham on his 'necessary and private' business, though not alone and this gentle man was able to take his letters out and bring them to him, unobserved and after putting them into another outer envelope address them to 'Mrs Carpenter' at an address in London, whence I fetched them. Or sometimes he would send a formal letter to me at Eltham enclosing one addressed to some political or other personage. If Willie were at Eltham I would show him this note asking me to post enclosure on a certain date. The enclosure was, of course, to me – sent thus to keep me from the fatigue of going to town so often. The Governor of Kilmainham for some reason became suspicious of Parnell's visitor and forbade his interview except in the close proximity of two warders selected by himself and Parnell refused to see him at all under these restrictions. He wrote me a friendly letter then, telling me this and other little news of his prison like, as to an ordinary acquaintance and addressed it direct to Eltham, sending it to be approved by the Governor and posted in the ordinary way. In this letter, that anyone might have seen, there was a message by a private sign to go to the house in town for a letter within a few days. On doing so I found my letter as usual, posted by a friendly warder and contained in it was a recipe for invisible ink and this ink could only be 'developed' by one particular formula, a combination known only to one chemist. We were saved an infinity of trouble and anxiety, as we could now write between the lines of an ordinary or typewritten letter without detection and it was no longer essential to get a third person to direct the envelopes. In time the Governor again became suspicious and the friendly warder was dismissed – or Parnell was told so. However, this was only a temporary inconvenience, as Parnell was able in a couple of days to reorganise his communications with me and this time they were not broken.

November 2, 1881.

I have just succeeded in having my communications, which were cut for a while, restored and have received your letter of Friday night. In writing me please always acknowledge receipt of my letters by their date. I have quite recovered. My illness did me good and I have a first-rate appetite.

You must not mind the reports about my health. In fact, our 'plots' have been completely disarranged by the necessity of writing and wiring my Queenie that there is nothing the matter with me.

I hope to be able to arrange to see you as soon as I hear that W. is firmly fixed

I look at my beautiful Queen's face every night before I go to bed and long for the time when I may be with you again. Only for that I should be happier here than anywhere else.

November 5, 1881.

MY DARLING WIFIE, – When I received your dear letter today I had just time to send you a few hasty lines in acknowledgment; now when everything is quiet and with your own sweet face before me I can give my thoughts up entirely to my Queen and talk to you almost as well as if you were in my arms. It seems to me a long, long time since our hasty good-bye, although the first three weeks of my present life – which term will have been completed tomorrow morning – has seemed only .a moment. I often feel very sad when I think of poor unhappy Katie waiting for her husband who does not come any longer as he used to come, but who will come again to her and will not again leave her.

I am trying to make arrangements that my own Queenie may come to me this time. I shall ask my ruler here if I may see my cousin, 'Mrs Bligh, who is coming from England to see me', in his office and with only himself present. After all, darling, the only way in which I could have escaped being here would have been by going to America and then I could not have seen you at all and I know I should not have been so happy or so comfortable in America as here and, besides, I should have been beset by so many dangers there.

I admire supremely my life of ease, laziness, absence of care and responsibility here. My only trouble is about your health and happiness and this has been my only trouble from the first. Queenie, then, will see that she also must try not to be so unhappy, especially as her husband's love is becoming stronger and more intense every hour and every day.

You will be anxious to know what my short illness was about. It was of a very unromantic kind – not the heart, but the stomach. I had not much appetite for some days and was tempted by a turkey to eat too much, thence very severe indigestion and considerable pain for about an hour. However, 'our doctor', by means of mustard and chlorodyne, got me all right again and my appetite is now as good as ever. In fact, I have gotten over very quickly the 'mal du prison' which comes on everybody sooner or later more or less severely.

One of the men in this quarter, who has been here for nearly nine months, poor fellow, looks after me as if he was my – brother, I was going to say, but I will substitute Mary my parlour-maid). He makes me a soda and lemon in the morning and then gives me my breakfast. At dinner he takes care that I get all the nicest bits and concocts the most perfect black coffee in 'Kaffee Kanne' out of berries, which he roasts and grinds fresh each day. Finally, in the evening, just before we are separated for the night, he brews me a steaming tumbler of hot whisky. He has marked all my clothes for me also, sees that the washerwoman does not rob me. Don't you begin to feel quite jealous?

I am going to ask Katie to put her proper initials upon the inner envelope of her next letter – thus, K. P. Your writing on the outside envelope of the one which came today will do splendidly.

I do not think there is the least probability of my being moved; this is the strongest place they have and they are daily trying to increase its strength according to their own notions, which are not very brilliant. My room is very warm and perfectly dry. They wanted me to go to another, which did not face the sun, but I refused, so they did not persist.

With a thousand kisses to my own Wifie and hoping soon to lay my head in its old place.

Good-night, my darling.

November 7, 1881.

I did not advertise in Standard.

MY DARLING QUEENIE, – Your two letters received and King is very much troubled about you.

I am very warm – have fire and gas in my room all night if I want it.

Dearest Wifie must try and get back her spirits and good looks for her own husband's sake.

C. S. P.

November 12, 1881.

MY DARLING WIFIE, – I have received my darling's letter of the 9th quite safely, also the enclosure in the previous one, which I will keep as you wish it; but I shall not want it, my own love.

The statement about the food was only to prepare the way to get up a collection in the country so as to save the American money for other purposes.

We think of announcing by and by that we have gone on Government food and then start the subscription, as there is no other way of getting money from the country. In any case, this could not affect me, as I am in the infirmary and should be entitled to get whatever Dr Kenny orders for me. Wifie may depend upon it that whatever happens we shall take good care of ourselves; at present we are living upon all the good things of the world – game, etc. The authorities have intimated to me twice that I may go out if I will say that I will go abroad, but I have replied that I am not in any hurry and that when I go out I shall go or stay where I please. In fact, I much prefer to wait here till the meeting of Parliament.

Will write Wifie a long letter tomorrow.

November 14, 1881.

MY OWN QUEENIE, – Your husband continues very well and very much contented with the position of things outside.

I am told the Government don't exactly know what to do with us now they have got us and will take the first decent excuse which presents itself of sending us about our business.

Queenie's letters give me great comfort, as I think I see by them she is not quite so unhappy as she was and has more hope of seeing her King soon again. I am in a continual state of alarm, however, lest something may hurt you.

ALWAYS YOUR KING.

Saturday.

MY OWN QUEENIE, – I hope my darling will not hurt herself going after those letters. I have got some paper to write direct to you and shall try one on Monday. I do not use for writing to anybody else, so that Queenie need not be afraid of that, but she should write very lightly and with a gold pen.

My own little Wifie, I so wish I could be with you to comfort and take care of you, but will you not try to care for yourself my darling, for my sake?

YOUR OWN LOVING KING.

MY DEAREST QUEENIE, I write hastily to say that I am receiving your darling letters all right, though the watch is very close and it is difficult to get them either out or in.

I am exceedingly well, sleep very well, go to bed at ten or eleven, or whenever I like, get up at nine, or whenever I like.

Do, beautiful Wifie, take care of yourself and your King's child.

November 18, 1881.

Use thinner letter paper in future, as envelopes are suspiciously bulky.

Your own King continues very well and has received your two letters safely.

Our mutual friend is waiting for me at present and probably has some more for me and will take this. I have, just heard on good authority that they intend to move me to Armagh the end of this week or beginning of next in order to give me an opportunity of escaping while there. However, they may change their mind and in any case it will make no difference to me personally. Armagh is healthier and nicer in every way, I am told by our Chief W., who comes from there. I am also told, on the same authority who in formed me of projected move to Armagh, that we shall be certainly all released before Christmas.

I am disposed to think I have got heavier, but shall know tomorrow when I weigh.

Best love to our child.

YOUR LOVING HUSBAND.

November 21, 1881.

MY OWN QUEENIE, – Yours of the 18th has reached me safely and though I am relieved to know that my darling is a little less miserable, yet I am still very much troubled and anxious about you. Has he left yet? (Captain O' Shea was staying at Eltham for some days) It is frightful that you should be exposed to such daily torture. My own Wifie must try and strengthen herself and get some sleep for her husband's sake and for our child's sake, who must be suffering much also.

I am convinced that if it had not been for the unfortunate result of Tyrone I should not be here. I hope that Stafford may be followed by another success in Deny and that it may open their eyes to the danger of their present proceedings. I can really honestly tell Wifie that my health is not only as good, but better than it has been at any time for the last twelve months.

I don't know who it was sent me the quilt; I am sending it to Wicklow, as it is green – a colour I detest. I don't want it here at all, as there are too many things on my bed as it is.

EVER YOUR OWN KING.

November 29, 1881.

The Woolwich or Charlton post offices will do very well when you recommence writing.

MY OWN QUEENIE, – I was very happy in receiving my darling's letter of yesterday today. My messenger was looking very frightened and fears his letters may be opened any day. So perhaps it will be safest for Wifie not to write again for a few days, until I see further, or until I can manage another address. I can manage, however, to write my Queenie two or three times a week. You must not be frightened if you see we have all gone on P. F (prison fare). It will not be so as far as we are concerned here and will only be for a week as regards the others, but Wifie must not tell anybody that I have not done so, as it would create discontent amongst the others. The man who has been taking care of me is going out tomorrow and will be a loss to me. He has been very ill during the last week from bad sore throat and was very nearly suffocated the night before last, so I sent O' Gorman Mahon to Forster about him, with the desired effect of getting his discharge. One of the others will supply his place to me, but not so well.

Have not been weighed yet, but will tomorrow. I think Wifie has my last weight. After eight at night I read books, newspapers and write until about twelve or one, when I go to bed. I also think a good deal of my own darling during that time when everything is quiet and wonder how soon I shall be with you again.

The time is passing rather more slowly this month than the first, but still it is not yet monotonous.

With best love.

Thursday.

MY OWN QUEENIE, – I have just received your two letters, one of Tuesday, the other 25th and am enormously relieved to find you are well. You can direct the next envelopes in a feigned hand; it is safer than sending you any more. The outside envelope of yours of the 25th appears to have been tampered with, but the inside one is all right. I am trying to arrange that you may see me as soon as he (Captain O' Shea) is gone to Madrid and you become quite strong and will write you more fully about it tomorrow.

ALWAYS YOUR KING.

Gum your inside envelopes well. There is no risk of my being moved.

December 3, 1881.

MY OWN QUEENIE, – Your letter of the 1st has just reached me.

You ought to have had a note by the 1st explaining about P. fare and suggesting caution until another means of communication can be found, as my messenger fears his letters may be opened any day.

I am exceedingly well and am not really on prison fare, as we can get anything we want here.

Am rejoiced to learn that Wifie hopes our child will be strong – I think it ought to have a good constitution.

All my pains and aches have quite disappeared and I have become quite acclimatised. I expect to be so fresh when I get out that even Wifie won't be able to hold, me, although her bonds are very strong and pleasant.

ALWAYS YOUR KING.

Tuesday, December 6, 1881.

MY QUEENIE, – I have not yet been able to arrange other means of communication for my own darling, but hope to do so shortly.

Her dear letter of the 1st has reached me quite safely but it would be a risk for her to write again to the same place. In any case I will send you in my next a prescription which will enable you to write ordinary letters with something added.

Your King never felt nearly so well in his life before. The strong exercise, ball-playing, which I have missed very much during the last few years of my life, is improving me immensely, as strong exercise always agreed with me.

YOUR OWN KING.

Wednesday, December 7, 1881.

MY OWN QUEENIE, – You will see a paragraph about my health in the Freeman of Friday which may worry you, so I write to say that it is very much exaggerated for the purpose of preventing a change in our rooms to some which are not in any way so nice.

I have caught a slight cold, which the doctor thinks will pass off in a day or two.

I will write you direct tomorrow with the secret ink of which the prescription is on the other side. No. 1 is for writing, No. 2 is for bringing it out. Wifie may write me with this to the same address as usual and in the same way, but she should write also with ordinary ink on the first page of the letter something as follows

DEAR SIR, – I have yours of ---- inst. and will pay attention to the directions given.

Yours truly,

R. CAMPBELL.

The secret handwriting should be with a clean quill pen and should be written lightly.

I feel much better this afternoon than I did this morning.

ALWAYS YOUR LOVING HUSBAND.

You had best test the No. 1 solution by attempting to bring it out with No. 2. If it does not come out well increase the strength of both solutions. Use unglazed rough paper. Do not be worried, darling and take good care of our child.

Friday, December 9, 1881.

MY OWN QUEENIE, – I wired you yesterday as I was dreadfully frightened about the effect the par in Freeman would have on you and hope you did not get into overmuch trouble about telegram.

The feverish cold quite passed away yesterday after one night and I am up today but keeping a poor mouth, so as to try and baulk a pretty scheme for moving us from our present rooms into others where they think we will be safer. You must not pay any attention to O' H.'s account, as it was carefully got up.

I don't eat bread, only for breakfast, but D. and I have each two raw chops smuggled in daily which we do for ourselves and we also make our own tea.

We also always have a cold ham in stock – Queenie must not think I am deceiving her about anything – I never felt as well in my life as when I wrote to tell her so the evening before I was taken ill and next morning I woke with a hot head.

At present I am getting all my food from the Governor's kitchen and it is excellent.

We hope by the row we are making to compel Government to make the food sufficiently good to satisfy the men and take expense of their keep off our resources.

In future you had best brush any letters I write you to E. with No. 2 solution, as, unless you desire me not to do so, I will write you for the future alternately to E. and W. Place so as to save you the trouble and fatigue of going to London so often.

ALWAYS YOUR OWN HUSBAND.

December 13, 1881.

MY OWN QUEENIE, – Your two letters have reached me quite safely and are all right.

I am quite well again now and could go out were it not that the weather is so cold that the doctor does not think it prudent.

I hope my darling is well and has not been hurt by the anxiety. My mind has been in the utmost distress about my Wifie and her child all the week and you do not know what a relief your telegram from London was.

December 14, 1881.

MY DARLING QUEENIE, – Your second letter reached me all right and I can read them perfectly. But, my darling, you frighten me dreadfully when you tell me that I am 'surely killing' you and our child.

I am quite well again now, my own and was out today for a short time and will take much better care of myself for the future. It was not the food, but a chill after over-heating myself at ball. But I do not intend to go back on prison fare, even nominally, again, as the announcement that we were on it has served the purpose of stimulating the subscription.

Rather than that my beautiful Wifie should run any risk I will resign my seat, leave politics and go away somewhere with my own Queenie, as soon as she wishes; will she come? Let me know, darling, in your next about this, whether it is safe for you that I should be kept here any longer.

YOUR OWN HUSBAND.

There can be no doubt we shall be released at opening of Parliament, but I think not sooner.

Dr K. was allowed to be with me at night while I was ill and we are not to be changed from our rooms.

December 15, 1881..

MY OWN DARLING QUEENIE, – Nothing in the world is worth the risk, of any harm or injury to you. How could I ever live without my own Katie? – And if you are in danger, my darling, I will go to you at once.

Dearest Wifie, your letter has frightened me more than I can tell you. Do write, my darling and tell me that you are better. I have had nothing from you for several days. I am quite well and strong again.

We have made arrangements so that everybody will be allowed to feed himself for the future, the poorer men getting so much a week.

YOUR OWN HUSBAND.

December 16, 1881.

MY OWN QUEENIE, – I think it will be best to make the change you suggest in yours of yesterday, but you need not trouble or fatigue yourself about it immediately.

I am going on all right, darling and expect to have another game of ball tomorrow, but shall take care not to heat myself.

I could not very well make any arrangement or enter into any undertaking with Government unless I retired altogether from politics.

Your letter has relieved me very much. I have been dreadfully frightened about you for the last week. Do take care of yourself, my own darling and I will also take good care of myself for the future.

We have both to live for each other for many happy years together.

You need not write near so heavily or use so much ink and it would be also better to have a softer paper, more like blotting paper.

YOUR OWN KING

December 21, 1881.

Your two letters of the 20th and that of the 19th duly received. Have not yet been able to read those of 20th, but will reply tomorrow.

I am very well and delighted to hear that Queenie is safe.

In haste,

YOUR OWN KING.

December 22, 1881.

Many happy returns of Christmas, my own darling.

Though your husband cannot be with you this time, he looks forward to very many happy returns with you.

I am very, very happy that my own Wifie is better and that she has been relieved from some of the intolerable annoyance for a time.

Your husband is quite well. We have succeeded in getting our new exercise ground.

ALWAYS YOUR LOVING KING.

Xmas Eve.

Letters of 22nd and 23rd arrived safely.

MY OWN QUEENIE, – Just as the coming day is approaching I send my own love what she has asked me for and trust that it will make her forget our squabble of last Xmas Day, as I had long since forgotten it.

My darling, you are and always will be everything to me and every day you become more and more, if possible, more than everything to me.

Queenie need not be in the least anxious about me. I have been getting my meals from the Governor's kitchen up to the present, but tomorrow we return to the old arrangement of being supplied from the outside. Nominally we are to get only one meal a day from the outside, but in reality they will permit those who wish and can afford it to get the other two meals as well from outside, at their own expense, of course and those who are with me in these quarters intend to do this. I do not receive any letters from any ladies I know, except one from Mrs S., shortly after I came here. She wrote to sympathise and said she had been ill. I replied after a time, asking how you were, but forgot to ask how she was and she has not written since. Am glad to say that none of my 'young women' have written.

Let me know as soon as he goes and I will write you home. .

Government are not likely to go out for a while, but they will scarcely go out without letting me out first.

YOUR OWN KING.

December 30, 1881.

MY OWN QUEENIE, – Your two letters just received but not read yet. I hope Wifie is sleeping better and getting stronger like her husband.

I am very nervous about the doctors and you should at all events tell one of them the right time, so that he may be on hand otherwise you may not have one at all. It will never do to run this risk. I will write Queenie a long letter tonight.

CHAPTER XXIV

MORE KILMAINHAM LETTERS

The soul of a philosopher will consider that it is the office of philosophy to set her free.'
– SOCRATES

January 3, 1882.

MY OWN DARLING QUEENIE, – Many happy New Years, my own love, with your husband to make you happy.

My Queenie must take great care of herself and must be sure to have at least one doctor in February. It will never do to let it trust to chance.

There is every prospect of my being able to see my darling soon, but it does not do to be too sure, as things change so much from day to day.

January 7, 1882.

MY OWN QUEENIE, – If Queenie could see her husband reading her letters over and over again every night she would have more faith in their readable quality and power for giving her husband happiness than she can have in looking at the blank paper as the result of her work. The paper of that of the 6th, which reached me today, is exactly suited; but Wifie, in sending two sheets, one of them quite blank, makes a bad conspirator, but I must forgive her, as the result is by no means blank to me.

I do feel very anxious about you, my darling and can not help it. You must tell the doctor and never mind about ----.

Could you not go to London or Brighton about the beginning of February? London would be best, if you could get him away on any pretext; but if you could not, Brighton would leave you most free from him.

It is perfectly dreadful that Wifie should be so worried at night. I had hoped that the doctor's orders would have prevented that.

I am being fed very well. Chops or grilled turkey or eggs and bacon for breakfast, soup and chops for luncheon and joint and vegetables, etc., for dinner and sometimes oysters. The 'one meal a day' is only a pretence. Each man gets £2 when arrested and 15s a week and can feed himself as he likes. Most of them pocket the money and make the Government feed them. You can understand the unwillingness of W.'s friend to leave under these circumstances. The Government food is much better now after the row about it, so most of the men can manage very well with it and send the 15s home or put it in bank. I expect the majority of the Irish people will be here after a time, the pay is so good and it is quite a safe place. I am very well, dearest Queenie and enjoying our new exercise yard very much.

YOUR OWN KING.

January 11, 1882.

MY OWN QUEENIE, – Yes, I will go to you, my love, immediately I am released. There is nothing in the world that I can do in Ireland, nor is it likely that I shall be able to do anything here for a long time to come. Certainly until the Coercion Act has expired I will not speak here again, so Queenie need not be afraid that when she gets me again she will lose me.

I am disposed to think that Government at present intend to release me shortly before opening of Parliament, but, of course, they may change their mind and hasten or postpone my release. Anyhow, let Queenie's mind be quite at rest, I am very well and am growing more vigorous every day, the air and exercise in the new yard suiting me exactly.

I long very, very much to be with my own Wifie again and wish I could take care of and comfort her in the time that is coming – Queenie has been very good and very loving to her husband to give him this child and to take such care of it during this long, sad interval, but she must remember that she is far more to me than all the world beside and that she must specially take care of herself, as her King cannot now live without her.

I had forgotten to tell you that the jacket and other things you gave me have been very useful and comfortable. During my illness I wore it all the time and wear it now in the mornings to read the newspapers. It has quite cured pain in shoulder.

I do trust you have been now relieved for a time by his departure and that you are getting a little sleep. It is enough to have killed you several times over, my own Queenie.

ALWAYS YOUR OWN HUSBAND.

January 17, 1882.

MY OWN QUEENIE, – The large paper is very good, the best for the purpose of any you have tried yet.

Your husband is so happy that you have at last been left free for a time.

Queenie may send her letters from any place about that she likes, but she had best not write direct, as there is a very sharp-eyed man over the letters.

Very much lighter writing will do and it might he written between the lines of the ordinary ink, but it is best not to risk anything just now.

I think Brighton will do very well if Wifie likes it and if it would be safe for her to be so far from London. Her King could be there quite well, as he intends to take a holiday when released and will not go to work at once.

Have just received formal and usual notice of further detention, first three months being up. 'The other two have also received theirs. This has no significance one way or the other, as nobody has ever been released at the end of the exact period. My own Wifie must try and keep herself well and strong. Does she feel so? I wish I could be with my poor darling.

It is really the only reason why I wish for a change and my Queenie's loneliness and weariness makes me very unhappy.

Yesterday and today as three of us were exercising in our yard the gates in adjoining yard leading into the outer world were opened twice to permit some carts to come in and go out. A low wall only separated the two yards, across which we could have easily sprung; there was no warder in our yard and only one in the next, with his back turned to us. So, you see, we can get out whenever we want to. Trying to escape is six months with hard labour, so we have nothing to gain by it, even if they keep us till end of Act in October, which they are not at all likely to do.

YOUR OWN LOVING HUSBAND.

January 21, 1882.

MY OWN QUEENIE, – On further consideration i think it would be much too risky for my darling to go to Brighton, as you would be too far from the doctor, so let it be London or home. I shall find means to see my Wifie wherever she is.

It looks like our release shortly.

Yours of 19th received.

January 23, 1882.

We have got an air-gun and practise every day.

MY OWN QUEENIE, – Your letter of the day before yesterday makes me very nervous about my own love again, as I fear from it that you are going to distress and worry your self about me again. I can assure you, my own, that I am exceedingly well and am likely to remain so.

Notwithstanding the newspapers, it is most unlikely they will keep us here till the commencement of session. D., indeed, will probably go out in a day or two on account of his health; but in any case my Queenie must not think of worrying about her husband, as he is very comfortable and happy where he is, if he might only see his own Wifie some times. I should feel quite lonely now in London without being able to see my darling and I should very much prefer to stay here than to be all alone in London while Wifie is suffering, except that I know it would comfort her to have me even so near her.

I hope you have received my letter saying that I think London or home the best for you and not Brighton; the latter would be much too far from the doctors. Does Wifie feel strong and well? I fear my poor Queenie has had a dreadful time of it and our poor little child also.

YOUR OWN LOVING KING.

January 28, 3,882.

MY OWN DEAREST QUEENIE, – I did not like to write direct, lest there should be any mistake, especially as my paper is not very suitable. It looks as if they were going to keep me here for a while longer, probably till a month or so after the opening of session, in order that they may get their new rules more easily.

I do not know what to say, my darling, about your going to Brighton, but Queenie will decide best for herself. I hope Wifie will not feel much worried about not seeing me so soon as she hoped. Her husband is very well indeed and in the best of spirits.

I do not like your going to London so often, it may hurt you. Is there any address you could get nearer home, so that you would not have to go so far?

My poor little Wifie, I wish I could be with you, but Queenie must be good and take care of herself. It looks today as if D. would go out soon; in that case it would facilitate our release.

YOUR OWN KING.

January 31, 1882.

Have received your two letters postmarked E. Be cautious about writing for a few days. I am very well and trust my darling is well.

Rumours about legal adviser being arrested, but will send you another address tomorrow.

February 2, 1882.

MY OWN QUEENIE, – Have just received your third letter with E. postmark – shall write you tomorrow direct so as to avoid for you the fatigue of going to London. The writing between the lines comes out perfectly and you need at no time write more heavily.

With best love and urgent request that my darling will take care of herself.

YOUR OWN KING.

February 3, 1882.

MY OWN QUEENIE, – You really must try and sleep properly at night and stop worrying yourself about me. I can assure my darling there is nothing to feel unhappy about so far as my health goes. I really cannot remember when I have ever felt so well in my life.

It is very very hard not to be able to see each other and that my poor Wifie should not have her husband with her now – I think after this letter I shall be able to write you a few lines occasionally home, so as to save Wifie going to London, but if she writes to me in the same way she must be very careful and write very lightly and between the lines. A gold pen is, I think, better than a quill.

The alarm about the legal adviser has blown over, so Queenie may direct as usual.

The Paris failures don't concern us in any way, as every thing is secure (an allusion to political funds banked in Paris).

Give my best love to our little child and take good care of yourself and it for my sake.

YOUR OWN HUSBAND.

February 10, 1882.

MY OWN QUEENIE, – I have received your note postmarked 7th, but have not had time to read it yet.

I hope my darling will take better care of herself; that journey to London in the fog was most dangerous for her.

I think that we shall probably be released by the middle of March, as it will be known then which way the tenants intend to go and we shall be able to decide whether it is worth our while remaining here any longer.

How does Queenie intend letting her husband know how she is?

YOUR OWN LOVING KING.

February 14.

MY OWN DARLING QUEENIE, – Today I have written you direct, sending a few words between the lines, just to see how it will answer. I find that rubbing with blotting paper after the words are dry takes away any glistening or appearance of letters. My own Wifie had best not try writing direct here, but send all her letters as usual and continue to do so.

The note I have just written goes out through a warder and I think I shall always be able to manage in that way, but in case Queenie should get a letter from me through the Governor she will see it marked with his initials on the top left-hand corner and in that case she might write me a commonplace letter direct here, but nothing between the lines.

Wifie is very good indeed to write her husband such beautiful letters; if she only knew what a pleasure and happiness every word from her is to her husband it might make her feel a little less unhappy. I am very much troubled about my darling having become so thin and fear that you have suffered a great deal more than you have ever told me and that you are not strong. I often reproach myself for having been so cruel to my own love in staying so long away from her that time, which has led to such a long, long separation. I was dragged into that Kildare engagement, otherwise I should have been safe with Wifie. Until then I had settled that I should leave Ireland after Wexford. It would, however, have been very difficult for me to have kept out of the country even if I had left then and on the whole I hope it will turn out all for the best. At least, I am very glad that the days of platform speeches have gone by and are not likely to return. I cannot describe to you the disgust I always felt with those meetings, knowing as I did how hollow and wanting in solidity everything connected with the movement was. When I was arrested I did not think the movement would have survived a month, but this wretched Government have such a fashion for doing things by halves that it has managed to keep, things going in several of the counties up till now. However, next month, when the seeding time comes, will probably see the end of all things and our speedy release.

I hope Wifie has got her house in London; I am exceedingly anxious about those long journeys to London for you, my own. Your husband is very well indeed and is, I think, actually beginning to grow fat!

I think Queenie ought to congratulate me at being away from the House instead of pitying me.

When I get out I hope to have a good long rest with my own little Wifie somewhere and to listen to the waves breaking as we used those mornings of spring last May.

YOUR OWN LOVING HUSBAND.

February 17, 1882.

MY OWN QUEENIE,–I had written my Queenie a nice long letter which she should have liked very much, but an alarm came before my messenger arrived that, we were all going to be searched and I was obliged to burn it.

I intend to try and send you a letter direct, written between the lines – I find that by rubbing the words after they are dry it removes all the glistening appearance.

Queenie had best not write me direct at any time, but she can send me a word in the usual way as soon as she is able to tell me how she is. Your King will wait very anxiously for that word. Oh, my Queenie, do take care of yourself and do not run any risk by remaining at E.

It is exceedingly likely that we shall all be released about the end of March, as then the lading time comes and the tenants will have to decide whether they will pay or not and as the majority have decided to pay already it is most likely the minority will then follow suit.

YOUR OWN KING.

February 17, 1882.

MY OWN DARLING QUEENIE, – I cannot describe to you what a relief your little note was that everything was quite right. Oh, my Wifie, when I had your two short messages of the 14th your poor husband burst into tears and could not hold up his head or think of anything until my darling's note arrived that everything was right.

My own, you must be very good and quiet until you are quite strong again and do not be in a hurry to get up.

I have only just a minute to close this as my Mercury is waiting.

YOUR OWN LOVING HUSBAND.

My baby was born on February 16th, 1882. I was very ill, but the joy of possessing Parnell's child carried me through my trouble. She was a beautiful baby, apparently strong and healthy – for the first few weeks – and with the brown eyes of her father. This child of tragedy rarely cried, but lay watching me with eyes thoughtful and searching beyond the possibility of her little life. I used to seek in hers for the fires always smouldering in the depths of her father's eyes, but could not get beyond that curious gravity and understanding in them, lightened only by the little smile she gave when I came near.

* * * * * * *

March 5, 1882.

MY DEAR MRS O' SHEA, – It is so long since I have heard from you that I sometimes wonder whether you have quite forgotten me.

In case you see any of my friends who may inquire after me, will you kindly tell them that I am very well and that there is no truth in the stupid rumour which appeared in some of the London papers about the seven days solitary confinement – I was merely prevented from receiving or sending letters for a week; the latter portion of the sentence did not trouble me much, as I am an even worse correspondent in here than when I was outside.

I think you will scarcely know me when you see me again, I have become so fat.

I have not heard from your sister for a great many months; in fact have only had one letter from her since I have been here.

Believe me, yours very truly,

CHAS. S. PARNELL.

March 16, 1882.

MY OWN DARLING QUEENIE, – You are very good to your husband in writing so often and so lovingly to your King, even when you must have been suffering terribly. I cannot describe to my little Wifie how hopeless and utterly miserable I felt until your little note came that all was quite right. I am very happy, my own, that our little daughter pleases you and that you are not too much disappointed and that she is strong and good-tempered. Does Queenie think she will be too big? I shall love her very much better than if it had been a son; indeed, my darling, I do love her very much already and feel very much like a father. What do you intend to call her?

Will you not give her papa's best love and innumerable kisses?

I have been arranging a little happiness, I hope, for Queenie, as soon as she is strong and well enough to come over here and can manage it. I have been training up Captain Barlow, the chairman of the Prisons Board, to allow me to see my married sisters in private. Today I got him to give me a private visit with one of them, Mrs Dickinson, for the first time and I did so with the intention of passing Queenie off as another married sister after a time. Wifie will then be able to come and see for herself how well her husband looks and how happy and comfortable he is. I don't know whether they intend to move me or not and do not like to guess, but wherever I go I shall be probably very well off. The dusting they got in the House the other night about treatment of the rank and file will do them good. I am told that all the police in the King's County were drafted into Tullamore and put into plain clothes to form an audience for Forster. Shall send Wifie my weight tomorrow with certificate of chief warder so that you may believe it.

Do you remember what it was the last time? I think Wifie has the ticket and that it was about twelve stone.

I hear from all over the country that the tenants are every where settling, so we shall be probably out in a couple of months, unless we are kept to make sure that they pay the next time.

I hope my own love will take good care of herself and not try to go to London too soon. I want Queenie when I see her to be an even younger little Wifie than when I gave her that last kiss.

The idea of nursing our little daughter was too preposterous. Do, my own darling, think of yourself and take great, great care of your husband's own little Wifie.

Good-night, my own darling Queenie.

YOUR LOVING HUSBAND.

March 28, 1882.

MY OWN DARLING WIFIE, – I have only just got an opportunity of sending my Queenie a few lines and will write a nice long letter tonight.

No letter came to me from you between that dated March 14 and the two of March 20. A reference to his (Captain O' Shea's) return from Paris makes me think that you may have sent me one between, informing me that he had gone, which I did not receive. If you think one has been intercepted write in future to Mr W. Kerr, Casino, Rathdrum and they will reach me safely, otherwise no change need be made.

The letter written between the lines, of which I spoke, was that refused by the warder and I did not send it.

Mrs S. has written me that she has 'seen you recently' and that you 'have not yet left your room', assuming that I know all about it. What am I to say to her?

I have not been weighed yet, but shall try today and send my own darling the true weight. It must be considerably more than 12–5.

My beautiful little Wifie must continue to take great care of herself and not go too often to town.

YOUR OWN LOVING KING.

March 24, 1882.

MY OWN QUEENIE, – Since writing you yesterday have received your letter dated 17th, which had accidentally gone astray, so if there is no other letter which I ought to have got you can send to the same address as usual.

YOUR OWN KING.

March 27, 1882.

MY OWN DARLING QUEENIE, – I am very anxious about our little daughter. Is it dangerous?

Was weighed yesterday – 12 st. 7 lb. Have certainly gained five or six pounds since I have been here; How did Wifie find out I had grown a beard?

YOUR OWN LOVING KING.

I don't think we shall be moved.

March 29, 1882.

MY OWN DARLING LITTLE WIFIE, – I am very much relieved to hear that our little child is better and is likely to be all right soon; but fear my poor Queenie must have been exhausted by all that hunting about for nurses. I cannot consent to Wifie turning nurse even when brown eyes do come. She is much too good and beautiful for anything of the kind.

Do you remember a small pair of scissors with fine points that Queenie once gave me in London? I have got them still and cut my cigar with them every morning.

Shall write Mrs ---- as you suggest and say am sorry to hear you had not yet left your room and that I had seen the event in the Times and hoped you would soon be quite well again. If my own can make an arrangement now for him (Captain O' Shea) to keep away, I think she ought to do so. It will be too intolerable having him about always. When I see Wifie again or am released, I can consider the situation, but until then, if you can you had best make some arrangement.

Wifie must not be frightened at the vapourings of the Government yesterday; they amount to nothing and they know perfectly well that neither I nor any of my friends outside have sanctioned in any way certain recent deplorable occurrences. They are simply the result of leaving the people without guidance and appear to be quite spontaneous. In any case the country is likely to quiet down as the days get longer and the crops commence to spring up. D. is to be released immediately the House adjourns for Easter and after a time, when they find nothing happening as a consequence of his release, they will probably take courage and let me out also. Anyhow this Government are going down the hill very fast and are not likely to last more than another session and we will take care that if they once go out they shall not come in again very quickly. My own loveliest Wifie, I do not think they intend moving me.

YOUR LOVING HUSBAND.

March 30 – The London correspondent of Freeman is very ignorant.

March 80, 1882.

MY OWN LITTLE WIFIE, – The letter posted at Bexley reached me all right after it had gone astray for two or three days. Queenie's of 28th has also reached me.

I suppose you did not address one to Casino, as I have had none from there. I wrote yesterday to say that I think you had best make some arrangement about him pending my release and when that takes place we can consider further.

I will let my darling see me any time as soon as she is quite strong again. We are going to have a weekly biography of doubtful Irish members in Irishman or rather United Ireland which will come out again shortly in such a form as to save it from seizure.

If Queenie sends me some of our daughter's hair I will put it in the locket I have with Wifie's. Would Sophie make a nice second name? It was the name of one of my sisters whom I was said to be most like of the family; but possibly it might make suspicions.

I am very anxious about my darling going to London so often, it must be very bad for you. You may try your next letter upon ordinary paper, unglazed and do not crowd what you write in ordinary ink into one little space in the middle of the sheet. After the solution has dried if you rub over the letters with an ink eraser it will remove all the glistening and appearance of letters. I wonder they have never opened any of them, but they may do it at any time. It would not hurt me in any way as I do not use it for any other purpose. Unless, indeed, they sent it to a certain person.

Queenie must not be alarmed about stupid rumours in the papers. You know what these liners are and the Freeman agent in London is singularly stupid and badly informed.

YOUR LOVING HUSBAND.

April 5, 1882.

MY OWN DEAREST WIFIE, – I think it very likely that some thing will be done by the Government shortly on the arrears question. If this be so, things will undoubtedly quiet down a great deal and it will give us an opportunity of coming to some arrangement. I do not in the least apprehend that any further steps will be taken against me in any case, though, of course, they would eagerly grasp at the slightest thing in order to try and throw discredit on me.

So far as I can judge, the number of outrages has diminished very materially during the last two or three weeks and is likely to continue decreasing.

My own Wifie must remember that I was only 12 st. 2 lb. when I came here, as I had fallen away very much after I left her and that I have got back 5 lb. since, notwithstanding my illness, which left me very thin indeed. Poor little Queenie must be greatly troubled and anxious at all the rumours she hears, but she need not regard any of them; she knows what newspaper men are.

Give my best love and ever so many kisses to our little daughter. I am very much troubled about her health and hope it will not make her permanently delicate.

I am longing very very much to see my own Wifie. I love you, my darling, more and more every day and I should feel quite reconciled to giving up politics for ever and living with my sweet Katie all by ourselves away from everybody and everything. I do not think anything will ever induce me to speak from a platform again. I always disliked it excessively, but I should loathe it now. Wifie must not, however, suppose that I am annoyed with the way things have gone. On the contrary, everything has succeeded remarkably and much better than anybody could have expected.

It is thought that D. (Dillon) will be released tomorrow. – Good night, my own Wifie.

YOUR LOVING HUSBAND.

April 7, 1882.

MY OWN DEAREST WIFIE, – I am so happy from receiving your letter of the 5th today, although part of what you say about our daughter makes me very anxious indeed.

I hope the poor little thing will soon get over it. Her hair is absolutely lovely. I am so glad it is more like Queenie's than mine, although there is enough of mine in it to spoil it somewhat and render it less beautiful than Wifie's. Still, there is a splendid golden tint in it which is quite exceptional.

Wifie need not feel at all anxious about me or anything which the Government are likely to do or be able to do. Although there have been one or two bad events things are getting much quieter every day. D. is going abroad and will not even appear in the House for a couple of months. My mother's health has, I fear, become very much broken latterly and after a time I think of applying to go over to see her, but I must try and get O' K. (O' Kelly) out first.

I am still keeping very well, although have missed the ball-playing very much for the last three weeks, as O' K., who used to play with me, has been ill. I think my weight is very good considering the hard exercise I have been taking and the good condition I am in. I hope my precious one is getting strong again and that she will have some good news to tell me of our little daughter when she writes next.

YOUR OWN LOVING HUSBAND.

I will not speak of my anguish when I found that the child of my love was slowly dying and that the doctors I called in could do nothing for her. Slowly she faded from me, daily gaining in that far-reaching expression of understanding that dying children have so strongly and my pain was the greater in that I feared her father would never see her now.

Willie was very good; I told him my baby was dying and I must be left alone. He had no suspicion of the truth and only stipulated that the child should be baptised at once – urged thereto, I think, by his mother and sister. I had no objection to this. Parnell and I had long before agreed that it would be safer to have the child christened as a Catholic and he had no feeling at all against the Catholic religion, considering, indeed, that, for those who required a religion it was an admirable one. I made an altar of flowers in my drawing-room, as the child was much too ill to be taken to church and there the priest, Father Hart, came and baptised Sophie Claude. Sophie, after Parnell's sister, Claude, after Lord Truro, an old friend of mine.

A few days before the death of my baby I had the unspeakable comfort of knowing that Parnell could come to me for a few hours and perhaps see his child while she lived. His nephew, son of his sister Delia (Mrs Thomson), had died in Paris and the authorities gave Parnell leave on 'parole' to attend the young man's funeral. A brilliant, handsome fellow, great sympathy was felt with the parents of this only son.

Spring was very early that year and in the April morning when the air was fragrant with the sweet freshness of the spring flowers and the very breath of life was in the wind, Parnell came to me and I put his dying child into his arms.

That evening he had to go on to Paris.

GRAND HOTEL,
12 BOULEVARD DES CAPUCINES, PARIS,
Thursday, April 13, 1882.

MY OWN QUEENIE, – I hope to leave Paris on Saturday morning. The doctor says the fever is not infectious, but I doubt it very much, as a great many people amongst the American colony are having it just now. I am staying here, but I am obliged to go to the house, which has been well disinfected, to see my sister, who is very much cut up. The risk to me is a minimum, as I had this fever very badly when I was young and they say people very rarely have it a second time and then only slightly.

At all events it is the ordinary typhoid, which doctors say is not catching.

I shall take a Turkish bath every day I am here and adopt other precautions.

YOUR OWN LOVING KING.

GRAND HOTEL,
12 BOULEVARD DES CAPUCINES, PARIS,
Saturday, April 15, 1882.

DEAR MRS O' SHEA, – I think of leaving Paris to spend a few days in the south or elsewhere on Monday morning. Had intended starting this evening, but caught a slight cold coming over, which the doctor, whom my sister insisted on seeing me, says is nothing, but think I had best not travel till Monday.

I am very glad that I came over, as my sister is in a very low state and my coming has picked her up very much.

Believe me, yours always truly,

CHARLES S. PARNELL.

GRAND HOTEL,
12 BOULEVARD DES CAPUCINES, PARIS,
Sunday, April 16, 1882.

MY DEAR MRS O' SHEA, – Having fallen into the hands of the doctor, he informed me today that he was coming again tomorrow morning and upon my saying that I wished to commence my journey to the country tomorrow he said he would let me go on Tuesday morning. Perhaps it is better so, as I might catch fresh cold if I started so soon as tomorrow.

I was out a good deal yesterday by the doctor's orders and dined with my sister in the evening. She is much better.

Today a north wind is blowing and I shall not go out much, although my cold is quite gone. I think I caught it from leaving off a flannel jacket which I used to wear when asleep in prison. It would have been a bad chest cold had I not taken two Turkish baths immediately I felt it coming on.

I am staying here under the name of Stewart and have not been found out yet.

Yours very sincerely,

CHARLES S. PARNELL.

After his nephew's funeral he returned to Eltham, having before telegraphed to Willie to say that he was coming. He wished to conciliate Willie as much as possible and believed that his politics might now prove useful.

All that night of the 21st April Parnell and Willie sat up in my dining-room discussing the Irish question and bit by bit working out the 'Kilmainham Treaty'. Willie wanted me to join them, but I would not leave my baby and when the daylight came and they went to lie down for a few hours rest before Parnell left for Ireland, my little one died as my lover stole in to kiss us both and say good-bye.

Overlooking the valley in the Catholic churchyard at Chislehurst is her little grave, headed by a granite cross and wreathed about with clematis and white roses; and often as we drove past on our way home through the summer evenings Parnell would go in to scatter the wild flowers he had gathered for me over little Sophie's resting-place.

The following letter from my sister-in-law, Mary O' Shea, I insert, as proving, I think very conclusively, that my little one's paternity was utterly unsuspected by the O' Sheas.

PARIS, AVENUE WAGRAM 137,
Sunday, May 21, 1882.

DEAREST KATIE, – We are very pleased to be able to hope that you are better. How is your dear aunt? We trust she is better. I cannot express our feelings of affectionate regard for her, nor can I say adequately how truly we desire her happiness here and for all eternity in Heaven. She has been so sweet a friend and so charming in all her ways towards your dear children, 'the butterflies', most attractive designation. Dear Lady O' Donnell wrote a rapturous description of the little creatures. She loved your dear little Claude and shared your grief at losing her, but, happy child, how glorious is her existence! What a contrast to ours, we who must struggle on, working out our salvation in fear and trembling! William (Caption O' Shea) will have told you of mamma's long and trying illness; she is getting on favourably and, as ever, patient and united to the will of God. I can scarcely leave her for an instant. Last Sunday I was not at Mass even. On the Feast of the Ascension I was able to go to St. Augustine and before doing so I made a call in company with a friend at a house where I had never been before and, of course, shall never be again12.

We have friends from Italy at present staying in Paris, but they perfectly understood that I cannot leave my dear mother and do not expect visits. I called only once upon them, but they came here Friday; mamma was for the first time able to sit up and Prince and Princess Emmanuel de Gonzaque came and met here the Bishop of Killaloe, who inquired most kindly for you and is always interested about William, to whom he wrote offering his tribute of sympathy, as well as with you, on the death of your dear baby. He had not since heard from any of us, as I could neither find time for letters nor for going out, but he received two newspapers a few days ago and perfectly understands the hurry of busy life at this season in London. I have had these last few days, that my dear and infinitely precious Malade has been better and somewhat independent of my constant attention, to seek for facilities in public libraries and other privileges for dear Comtesse de Greppis Abbé – I have partly succeeded. Mamma hopes the children are well. Is dear little Carmen strong? And her amiable and devoted sister – how is she? We hope their brother is in perfect health, no memory even of delicacy still. Doctors say the temperature has been variable all this month and that transition from heat to cold must be guarded against.

With mamma's love and kindest wishes for your health and comfort and praying that all blessings may be granted to you and to those you love, with her kindest feelings. I remain, dearest Katie, your affectionate
MARY O' SHEA.

CHAPTER XXV

THE 'KILMAINHAM TREATY'

'Shall I say stipulation, King?'
'No, Queenie, he prefers 'suggestions desirable to be entertained!'
– EXTRACT FROM AN OLD DIARY.

PARNELL, IN ACCORDANCE WITH HIS 'parole', returned to Kilmainham at the end of the term of leave and immediately formulated the conditions of the arrangement it was proposed to make with the Government. The draft of this historic document was as follows:

KILMAINHAM, April 25th, 1882.

'We think in the first place that no time should be lost in endeavouring to obtain a satisfactory settlement of the arrears question and that the solution proposed in the Bill standing for second reading to morrow – Wednesday – would provide a satisfactory solution, though the Church Fund would have to be supplemented by a grant from Imperial resources of probably a million or so.

'Next as regards the permanent amendment of the Land Act, we consider that the rent-fixing clauses should be amended to as great an extent as is possible, having in view the necessity of passing an Amending Bill through the House of Lords; that leaseholders who have taken leases either before or since the Act of 1870 should be permitted to apply to have a fair rent fixed and that the purchase clauses should be amended as suggested by the Bill, the second reading of which will be moved by Mr Redmond tomorrow.

'If the Government were to announce their intention of proposing a satisfactory settlement of the arrears difficulty as indicated above, we on our part would make it known that the No Rent manifesto was withdrawn and we should advise the tenants to settle with their landlords; we should also then be in a better position than we ever occupied before to make our exertions effective in putting a stop to the outrages which are unhappily of late so prevalent.

'If the result of the arrears settlement and the further ameliorative measures suggested above were the material diminution of outrages before the end of the session and the prospect of the return of the country after a time to something like a normal condition, we should hope that the Government would allow the Coercion Act to lapse and govern the country by the same laws as in England.'

Willie wrote to Gladstone on April 13th and two days after Gladstone replied promising to communicate with Forster. The rest of the letter was taken up with compliments to

Willie and some carefully worded phrases which really meant that Gladstone was prepared to go to very great lengths indeed to quiet Ireland and to keep her quiet.

Willie sent to Chamberlain a copy of his letter to Gladstone. Chamberlain was impressed and guarded. He welcomed negotiations, but pointed out that if the Government were going to smile on the Irish Party the Irish Party must smile on the Government. With some amount of exaggerated fervour he mooted the possibility of an anti-Irish movement comparable with the anti-Semitic movement abroad. That, he pointed out, would be bad for everybody and accordingly he welcomed the olive branch. In the sequel, of course, Chamberlain took a very active part in pressing for the release of Parnell.

While on 'parole' and after his return from Paris, Parnell entered into communication with Mr Justin McCarthy with regard to the proposed 'Treaty' and the following letter was written from Eltham:--

Saturday, April 2, 1882.

MY DEAR MCCARTHY, – I have arrived in England and will call to see you tomorrow afternoon some time. I cannot at present give you the exact hour, but would it be too much to ask you to remain at home after three o'clock? I trust you will have some news of result of Cabinet today.

Yours very truly,

C. S. P.

This letter was followed up by one from Kilmainham.

(Confidential.)
KILMAINHAM,
April 25, 1882.

MY DEAR MCCARTHY, – I send you a letter embodying our conversation and which, if you think it desirable, you might take the earliest opportunity of showing to Chamberlain.

Do not let it out of your hands, but if he wishes you might give him a copy of the body of it.

Yours very truly,

CHARLES S. PARNELL.

(Enclosure.)

The enclosure was identical with the draft treaty – apart from a few verbal alterations of which the chief was the substitution of 'an Amendment Bill' for an 'Amending Bill' in the second paragraph.

Tuesday, April 25, 1882.

MY OWN QUEENIE, – I enclose you a letter. What do you think I had best say to it13?

I told my friend in Jermyn Street what steps to take, so that the matter referred to in enclosed will probably go on all right without, or with, the further participation of the writer. I thought of writing him that I had received his note too late to reply for Wednesday, but that in any case my letter from Paris ought to be sufficient indication of confidence.

I missed nine train on Sunday and came on by twelve, sleeping at Crewe and getting on board mail boat before mail train arrived. Everything went off very nicely and quietly and I have not caught any cold this time. O' K. had aired my bed very carefully, etc. and they were all very glad to see me again, with the exception of the authorities.

I have been thinking all day of how desolate and lonely my Queenie must be in her great sorrow. I wish so much that I might have stayed to comfort her, but I have indeed every hope and confidence that our separation will not now last very long. It is too terrible to think that on this the saddest day of all others14 – and, let us hope, the saddest that we both shall ever see again – my Wifie should have nobody with her.

Good-bye, my own darling,

YOUR LOVING KING.

Mr Parnell wrote as follows to Captain O' Shea:–

April 28.

I was very sorry that you had left Albert Mansions before I reached London from Eltham, as I had wished to tell you that after our conversation I had made up my mind that it would be proper for me to put Mr McCarthy in possession of the views which I had previously communicated to you. I desire to impress upon you the absolute necessity of a settlement of the arrears question which will leave no recurring sore connected with it behind and which will enable us to show the smaller tenantry that they have been treated with justice and some generosity.

The proposal you have described to me as suggested in some quarters, of making a loan, over however many years the payment might be spread, should be absolutely rejected, for reasons which I have already fully explained to you. If the arrears question be settled upon the lines indicated by us, I have every confidence – a confidence shared by my colleagues – that the exertions which we should be able to make strenuously and unremittingly would be effective in stopping out rages and intimidation of all kinds.

As regards permanent legislation of an ameliorative character, I may say that, the views which you always shared with me as to the admission of leaseholders to the fair rent clauses of the Act are more confirmed than ever. So long as the flower of the Irish peasantry are kept outside the Act there cannot be any permanent settlement of the land question, which we all so much desire.

I should also strongly hope that some compromise might be arrived at this season with regard to the amendment of the tenure clauses. It is unnecessary for me to dwell upon the enormous advantages to be derived from the full extension of the purchase clauses, which now seem practically to have been adopted by all parties.

The accomplishment of the programme I have sketched would, in my judgment, be regarded by the country as a practical settlement of the land question and would, I feel sure, enable us to co-operate cordially for the future with the Liberal Party in forwarding Liberal principles; so that the Government, at the end of the session, would, from the state of the country, feel themselves thoroughly justified in dispensing with further coercive measures.

Yours very truly,
C.S. PARNELL.

Saturday, April 30, 1882.

MY OWN QUEENIE, – He (Captain O' Shea) came over to see me, so I thought it best to give him a letter, as he would have been dreadfully mortified if he had had nothing to show.

Everything is going very well and I hope will continue straight.

Received two letters from my own lovie yesterday.

Do, my own, keep up as much as you can.

YOUR OWN KING.

I had reason to know, from various sources of information kept open by me on Parnell's behalf during his imprisonment, that the Government would liberate him with considerable relief if given any surety of conciliatory policy on his part. Parnell at liberty was a disturbing force and the culminating embarrassment of English government in Ireland, but Parnell in prison had become merely a concentrated embarrassment in that there was now no governmental possibility of dealing with the reactionary spirit he had let loose in Ireland – a spirit that was at least better controllable as a weapon in Parnell's hand than as the scattered and absolutely irresponsible fulminations, unreasoning and motiveless, of lawless desperadoes.

With Parnell as her chief the Ireland he had roused might indeed be a scourge of whips to the British Government, but without him this Ireland was undoubtedly a scourge of scorpions.

So Parnell came out of Kilmainham on the treaty arranged at Eltham and as Willie was to be the official bearer of the olive branch to the Government, he went over to see Parnell on his return to Kilmainham and to get from him a letter for his own satisfaction, as he said Parnell was 'so shifty' he could not be trusted to carry out any agreement that was not in writing and the letter was to set forth the various modifications of his policy of obstruction that he would undertake to observe on his (immediate) liberation and assurance of future concessions to Ireland. This letter had in substance been written at Eltham, but Parnell had stipulated for a few days to consider the matter further and would not give Willie his final decision then. On the other side he had to consider that any treaty with the Government would place him in a very awkward position with the Land League and would certainly affect the financial aid to the Irish cause so generously contributed by America. It was also certain, he knew, that the Government would be obliged, in either case, to liberate him with the other Irish political prisoners at no distant period and this without his placing himself under any obligation at all to the Government. This would please the extreme party of his followers far better, even though it would keep open the way to further outrage and crime in Ireland.

I had never before ventured to influence Parnell in any way politically; but now I greatly dreaded for him this latter policy of the extremists and the perpetual strain of watchfulness and control it engendered – with the Coercion Laws such a policy must, in the long run, inevitably produce, unless, indeed, England was prepared to yield to force; an unthinkable proposition.

So now I threw the whole strength of my influence on the side of the treaty of conciliation and urged upon him the greater good for Ireland likely to accrue in the making by him of immediate peace. I was very anxious that he should 'reign' by constitutional means and had every hope of establishing such amicable communications between him and the Government as would lead to that end. But he had this great force now to reckon with – the force of centuries of cruelty, wrong and oppression that had bred an irresponsibility and callous disregard of suffering, nay, rather a vindictive madness and lust of destruction in Ireland. In his seeking for a weapon to use for the betterment of England's government of Ireland, Parnell had discovered this underlying force of hate and, using the influence of his personality, he strove to direct it into the service of the Ireland that he loved. But he afterwards stood appalled at the intensity of the passion of hate that he had loosed and no one but he – and I with him – knew the awful strength of that force of destruction that was only held in subservience by the sheer dominance of his will. He replied to my pleadings: 'Yes, I hold them now with my back to the wall, but if I turn to the Government I turn my back to them – and then...?'

But my great fear for him won his decision for peace and he wrote and signed the 'letter' that Willie wanted to take to the Government.

The Prime Minister had been prepared for its coming and made known that such a treaty of peace would be acceptable. Willie took this letter to Forster, who knew of no understanding with the Prime Minister and was absolutely against any such negotiations. He scoffed at the letter, at its terms and at Willie for bringing it, but the latter pointed out that the matter was one for the Prime Minister's consideration alone and Mr Forster was bound to submit it to him without delay. He of course did so, but with confidence as to its rejection and, on its immediate acceptance and the liberation of Parnell, resigned his office as Chief Secretary for Ireland.

Lord Cowper resigned with him. This was on the 2nd of May. On the 26th of April discussion on Mr Redmond's Land Bill was started in the House of Commons. This Bill, which had been drafted by Parnell in Kilmainham, proposed to amend the Land Act of 1881 in four main particulars: (1) Arrears of excessive rent; (2) admission of leaseholders to the benefit of the Land Court; (3) amendment of tenure clauses; (4) extension of purchase clauses by the advance from the State of the whole of the purchase money. Mr Gladstone applauded the Irish Party and opposed the Bill. He practically admitted that recent decisions of the Irish judges were nullifying the effect of the tenure clauses, but he did not want yet to reopen the question. He recognised, however, the necessity of dealing with 'Arrears'.

When, on May 2nd, he announced to the House the resignation of Lord Cowper and Mr Forster and the decision of the Cabinet to release the three Irish mp's who had been in Kilmainham since October, he definitely promised an Arrears Bill and stated that there was no present intention to renew the Coercion Act. So, with this public promise of Mr Gladstone and with the tacit understanding that Parnell would 'slow down the agitation', Parnell came out of gaol. 'It is an act', averred Mr Gladstone, 'done without any negotiation, promise, or engagement whatever'.

Two days later Forster denounced the action of the Cabinet. He believed that the unconditioned release of the Irish leaders would tend to the encouragement of crime. As he went on to justify the arrests, Parnell entered the House and took his seat. The Irish cheered wildly. Then Forster continued: 'The real reason why these gentlemen were arrested was because they were trying to carry out their will – 'their unwritten law' ... by working the ruin and the injury of the Queen's subjects by intimidation of one kind or another. If Mr Parnell had not been placed in Kilmainham he would very quickly have become in reality what he was called by many of his friends – the King of Ireland.' He did not say Parnell and his friends had directly incited, what they had done was far more dangerous. They had established a system of intimidation. ... They should have been released after a public promise had been given, or when Ireland was quiet, or fresh powers had been granted to the Government. 'A surrender is bad, a compromise or arrangement is worse. ... If all England cannot govern the Member for Cork then let us acknowledge he is the greatest power in Ireland today.'

Mr Gladstone, in reply, said he had no right to humiliate Parnell by demanding a penitential confession of guilt and once more he disclaimed that the release was the result of a bargain. Parnell following him, asserted – what was the truth – that no mention of his release was made by him in any written or oral communication with his friends.

The same night, May 4th, was announced the appointment of Lord Spencer as Lord-Lieutenant and Lord Frederick Cavendish as Chief Secretary. The post had first been offered to Sir Charles Duke, but he had refused the offer. It is stated that in certain quarters the name of Mr Chamberlain had been mentioned and that he had signified his willingness to accept the offer if it were made. Apparently it was not made. We cannot avoid speculating what would have happened had he gone to Ireland. He had taken a leading part in the release of Parnell; would that have saved him – since the Phoenix Park murderers did not intend to kill Lord Frederick? And if Mr Chamberlain had been killed in May, 1882, what other course might British politics have taken? Would Tariff Reform ever have been a Tory election cry? Would there have been no Boer War? Would the Tories not have enjoyed that long term of office which for years kept the question of Home Rule in abeyance? It were foolish to say yes or no to any of these questions, but at least we may say that the fact Mr Chamberlain was not asked to become Irish Secretary in 1882 is one of the most momentous in British politics.

While in Kilmainham Parnell had found it absolutely impossible to control in any way the incitements to crime and the wild expenditure of the Ladies' Land League. His sister, Anna Parnell, was at the head of this marvellous organisation which she spread in well-ordered ramifications throughout the country. Her generalship was magnificent and complete and there appeared to be no detail of this revolutionary army with which she was not completely familiar and completely determined to control. Parnell wrote to her again and again from prison, pointing out the crass folly of the criminality for which the Ladies' League, now, solely existed. He even urged the Governmental representations made to him for the suppression of this league of anarchy and the hopeless financial position it was creating – the estimated weekly expenditure of these ladies running into thousands of pounds; money contributed chiefly by America for the fighting policy of the Irish Party – but to no purpose.

The fanatic spirit in these ladies was extreme in Anna Parnell; it was abnormal and Parnell saw no way of saving her, or the country, from her folly but by fulfilling his threat of vetoing the payment of another penny to the Ladies' Land League. This he then did and thus automatically broke up this wild army of mercenaries. Anna Parnell never forgave her brother for this act and to the last day of his life refused to hold any communication with him again. Parnell had much family affection and many times made overtures of peace to his sister, of whom he was really fond and for whose strength of mind and will he had much respect. On two occasions he met her accidentally and tried to speak to her, but she resolutely turned from him and refused any reply to the letters he wrote her.

It may interest my readers to know that the keys of Kilmainham Gaol are still in my possession.

CHAPTER XXVI

THE PHOENIX PARK MURDERS AND AFTER

'The blood more stirs
To rouse a lion than to start a hare.'
– SHAKESPEARE

O N PARNELL'S RELEASE FROM KILMAINHAM he returned to me at Eltham and on May 6, 1882, went to Weymouth to welcome Michael Davitt, who came out of Portland prison on that day. He returned to Eltham that Saturday evening and the next morning, Sunday, I drove with him to Blackheath Station, as he had to go to London to see Davitt and others. At the station I asked him to get me a newspaper before he left and waited for it in the carriage.

From where I sat in the carriage I could see Parnell's back as he stood just inside the station door. I was watching him and he half turned and smiled at me as he opened the paper – the *Sunday Observer* – to glance at the news before he brought it to me. He told me afterwards that he wanted to see what was said about Michael Davitt. He had now come to the top of the steps and, as he suddenly stopped, I noticed a curious rigidity about his arms – raised in holding the newspaper open. He stood so absolutely still that I was suddenly frightened, horribly, sickeningly afraid – of I knew not what and, leaning forward, called out. 'King, what is it?' Then he came down the steps to me and, pointing to the headline, said, 'Look!' And I read, 'Murder of Lord Frederick Cavendish and Mr Burke!'

I heard the train coming in and tried to pull myself together, for the awful significance of the horrible thing to my lover, just released from Kilmainham on the Treaty, came home to me with a rush of pain. His face was ashen and he stared, frowning heavily, before him, unconsciously crushing the hand I had slipped into his until the rings I wore cut and bruised my fingers.

I said to him, 'Quick, you must catch this train. See Davitt and the others as arranged and as many more as you can find. Go, you will know what to do but you *must* meet them all at once.' He turned heavily away, saying, 'I shall resign' and I answered as I ran beside him to the platform, 'No, you are not a coward.'

Before I left Blackheath I wired to Willie to bring Parnell to dinner at Eltham if he could possibly manage it and spent one of the most terrible days of my life considering the effect this awful crime would probably have upon my lover's career.

Willie came down that evening, Parnell with him. They were both very gloomy and depressed and Parnell, after his greeting of me – as though this were our first meeting since he came out of prison – sat gazing stonily before him, only glancing across at Willie with the stormy flare in his eyes when the latter – who was really sorry for Parnell, as well as shocked at the murders – said something that jarred upon him. During dinner Willie told me of what had been done during the day, of the absolute horror and consternation of the Irish Party, of what Mr Chamberlain had said on hearing of the murders and of Parnell's continuous threat, throughout that awful day, of retiring from public life altogether.

Willie said to me: 'I wish you would urge Parnell not to talk so, Dick; he can't resign his seat now, the thing's impossible; he must show that it simply does not touch him politically in anyway.'

I turned to Parnell and said: 'I do absolutely agree with Willie about it, Mr Parnell. It would be throwing the whole country over and a reflection upon all who joined in that Treaty.'

Parnell at last roused himself and said: 'Well, I will write to the G.O.M. (Gladstone) and offer to resign and abide by his decision; the thing makes me feel hopeless of doing any good.'

On the wall of the dining-room where we sat hung a large engraving of the 'House' of 1880. All the members of that Parliament were in the picture and among them, of course, Mr Parnell and Captain O' Shea. As the maid turned to leave the room, after placing the coffee tray on a little side table, this picture, which hung immediately behind Parnell, fell to the floor with a crash that, in the state of nervous tension we were all in, brought us to our feet in alarm. Willie's chair overturned as he jumped up; but Parnell's was steady, held in a grip that showed his knuckles white as he held it slightly raised off the floor, while he stood, half turned, staring at the picture as it lay among the splintered glass.

Willie laughed and, coming to help the parlour maid to pick up the picture, exclaimed: 'There goes Home Rule, Parnell!' But he also had in him a slight dash of the superstition that was so highly developed in Parnell's fatalistic nature and his smile turned to gravity as he glanced at Parnell's tense expression and listened to my hasty explanation of the fall: 'Perhaps the wire was rotten, or the maid had shaken the picture as she passed!' Parnell took the loose end of the wire in both hands and tried to break it. He could not. Willie said: 'Mary (the parlour maid) was the other side of the room, so she could not have shaken it.' Parnell said nothing and we began to speak of other things.

Afterwards I said to him: 'You did not really mind about that picture, did you? It was only a rotten wire!' and he answered: 'It was an omen, I think, darling, but for whom? Willie or me?' and when I told him I wished he would not talk such nonsense and that I did not believe in omens or want any falling pictures to be 'omens' for either of them, he smiled and said no more.

The immediate consequence of the Phoenix Park murders was the introduction of a Crimes Bill by Sir William Harcourt on May 11th. Parnell was not approached on the subject. He was given no opportunity of criticising the proposals and of suggesting any more moderate measure which might have appealed to that great body of Irish Nationalists who viewed the murders with horror. The new Bill went roughshod over Irish opinion and the conciliatory effect of the Arrears Bill, introduced a few days later, was altogether marred.

On May 15th, 1882, there was a scene in the House about the Kilmainham Treaty. Mr Charles Lewis asked Mr Gladstone to produce the letters which were the evidence of the intentions of the recently released members. Mr Gladstone did not wish to produce these letters, but saw no reason why, if the writers and those to whom the letters were addressed did not object, the letters should not be produced. Parnell then rose and read the letter he had given to Captain O' Shea

Then Lord John Manners 'must ask' if this was the only letter received by the Government; to which the Premier returned that he had some information in addition to the letter (he did not say considerable information). Then Mr Forster had his little revenge in blandly asking if Mr Parnell had read the whole of the letter. Parnell replied that he had read the whole of the copy given him by Captain O' Shea, but the original had another paragraph which he had no objection to reading.

Then Captain O' Shea wanted to explain the whole circumstances. Mr Forster, still smarting under the snub to him of Parnell's release, would not play up to Mr Gladstone, but handed Willie the letter as it had been given to him to take to Mr Gladstone. Captain O' Shea ran his eye over it and handed it back to Mr Forster amid laughter from the Conservatives. Mr Forster declined to take back the letter and, after a moment's hesitation, Captain O' Shea read it through, including the paragraph in which Mr Parnell undertook that in the circumstances stated, he would with his party co-operate with the Liberals in forwarding their principles as far as he could.

Then a member wished to know if Mr Gladstone had had the letter in his possession at the time he stated that there was no compact between the Land Leaguers and the Liberal Party; to which the Premier replied that he certainly had and that he again and emphatically repeated the statement.

On May 16th Sir Stafford Northcote began to heckle the Government again upon the subject of the Kilmainham Treaty. He wanted to know many things and among others was anxious to hear if Michael Davitt was released as a condition of Mr Parnell's support of Liberal principles. Mr Gladstone was prepared to answer questions, but not to volunteer statements. No member of the Government had had interviews with Mr Parnell – to his knowledge – and there was no stipulation as to the release of Michael Davitt or on any other subject. Several other members then joined in the baiting of the Premier, but without other result than the ruffling of that old eagle's feathers.

Mr Gibson made a speech, during which there was the unusual scene of the Premier's rising to make a personal statement and Mr Gibson's refusing to give way.

The Premier sat down. The Speaker called Mr Gibson to order amid uproar and Mr Gibson at last gave way to let Mr Gladstone get his protest home.

Mr Gladstone declined to express any opinion on Mr Forster's conduct in bringing before the House a private communication received by him as a Cabinet Minister after he had left the Cabinet. Mr Gladstone was, he said, in no better position to pass judgement upon such conduct than was any other member of the House – a comment that was received with loud cheers. Mr Forster hastily explained that he would not have done so had it not been for the statement of Captain O' Shea. Captain O' Shea promptly rose to give battle, but was suppressed by the Speaker. Mr Gladstone wanted to know if a fair statement of the charge against the Government was, as Mr Balfour had set forth, that Mr Parnell was to obtain his release and to obtain legislation as to arrears, on condition that he would obtain peace for the Government in Ireland and give the Liberals support in the House with his party? He was answered by cheers from the Opposition and Mr Gladstone turned to the Speaker: 'May I say, sir, that there is not one word of truth in it from beginning to end?'

Sir William Harcourt made a speech pointing out the inability of Mr Balfour to make fair comment on the matter in hand. Branching oil, he then answered Mr Gibson's questions to his own satisfaction and was followed by Lord John Manners, who was loath to let the drop. Mr Forster again complained that it wasn't fair and that the other boy began it!

After other intervention Mr Chamberlain tried to soothe all sides by explaining that the sentence that was not in the copy letter read by Mr Parnell was not noticed by him when he first was shown the original by Captain O' Shea and, though the latter gentleman had asked to withdraw that sentence, it had seemed of so little importance that he (Mr Chamberlain) had really not noticed it was omitted when Mr Parnell read the letter.

Captain O' Shea here intervened with a very telling little speech, in which he made it quite clear that, although he was not well up in the etiquette of Cabinet Ministers, he had had a fairly long acquaintance with the usages of gentlemen and from the latter point of view the conduct of Mr Forster on the previous night was most extraordinary. He must characterise Mr Forster's conduct as 'disloyal to his old friends and malignant to his old enemies.'

The second reading of the Arrears Bill was moved by Mr Gladstone on May 22nd. In the course of his speech he said: 'Eviction in the exercise of a legal right may be to the prejudice of your neighbours, may involve the highest reprehension and may even imply deep moral guilt. There may be outrages which – all things considered, the persons and the facts – be less guilty in the sight of God than evictions.'

The Bill was bitterly opposed by the Tory Party.

I had written to Mr Gladstone expressing a wish that he should see Mr Parnell. He wrote in answer from Downing Street on May 25th, 1882, declining to do so in private, though in public he was more than ready to co-operate with Parnell.

I suggested in reply that we should meet and talk the matter over and it was arranged that he should come to see me at Thomas's Hotel on July 2nd. He arrived punctually at three o'clock. We had a long talk about Parnell and about politics – chiefly, of course, as referring to Ireland. He was extremely agreeable and courteous and I remember very well the great charm of manner he possessed, a charm that struck me afresh at each subsequent meeting. A natural charm and, no doubt, a natural insincerity, but one which is such an immense asset in the career of a great man: that of making others believe – or wish to believe – that they are on the same plane of intellect and diplomacy as himself! He was a very great old man, I thought, as his wonderful eagle's eyes showed just sufficient admiration in them to savour of homage without offence. And I may say here that, with all the perfect courtesy of which, when he chose, he was past master, he knew before the conclusion of our interview and allowed me to know that he knew, what I desired that he should know – that my personal interest in Parnell was my only interest in Irish politics.

Mr Gladstone having agreed that it would be of considerable convenience to the Government to be in private and amicable communication with Mr Parnell and that I, whose interests were inseparable from those of the Irish leader, would be confidently accepted as such intermediary by him, we parted satisfied, I think, on both sides with the afternoon's compact.

After this first interview with Mr Gladstone I had frequently to see him at Downing Street – taking him drafts, clauses and various proposed amendments (of Bills affecting Ireland) that Parnell proposed, altered and suggested privately to Gladstone before putting them before the House. Parnell, of course, always intent on the betterment of the law as affecting Ireland; Gladstone bargaining for the Irish vote, when without it he would have lost his majority.

Parnell would sometimes write the rough draft of what he wished Gladstone to know, or sometimes write what he had to say in the form of a letter (often dating it from my house!), but occasionally he would do neither, as, on more than one important occasion, he said: 'I don't trust that Grand Old Spider farther than I can see him. Sweetheart, learn this by heart and let it off at him yourself.' Then I had to take down in my own handwriting what he wished proposed to Gladstone and at the subsequent interview 'let it off' at him. Very often letters were sufficient and in this case I almost invariably wrote them, or, if the letter was in Parnell's handwriting addressed to me, under cover of my envelope, I would request its return and this was done; letters intended for Parnell by Gladstone being invariably addressed to me.

It was by my suggestion Mr Gladstone opened these private negotiations with Mr Parnell and I was myself much amused to find that both these great statesmen were of one mind as to the danger of such a trusting of one another as such negotiations necessitated. When I said to Parnell, 'Why not see Gladstone yourself privately and get what you can from him, in return for the Irish vote?' he at once replied that such a proceeding would be fatal to the 'cause' and when I said much the same thing to Gladstone at our first interview – which latter was a brilliant inspiration of Parnell's own – he replied that 'such a proceeding' would be fatal to his position, but, he added, 'it might be advantageous to the Irish leader and myself if you, Mrs O' Shea, would accept the thankless office of go-between, as you suggest. A safe and secret intermediary might well prove to be of the greatest assistance to us both in our efforts for the welfare of the country.' I have wondered since which country the G.O.M. had in his mind as he spoke.

On June 17th and 18th, 1882, Gladstone wrote to me. The letter of the 17th was little more than a formal acknowledgment, but in his note of the following day he referred me to something which had passed at our last interview. He had on that occasion directed my attention to the proposal to amend certain severe clauses of the Crimes Act.

Meanwhile the Irish were fighting the Crimes Bill inch by inch. It had been read a second time on May 25th after three nights' debate. The most drastic clause, from the legal point of view, was the suspension of' the right of trial by jury in all grave cases of agrarian crime, which (and the Government would decide when) would be tried by a Court of three judges, in such district as the Attorney-General might decide. Public meetings could be proclaimed and newspapers suppressed. The police were vested with power to search private houses and arrest night wanderers. Finally and against this the Irish Party especially protested – magistrates were empowered to convict summarily on charges of incitement, boycotting and membership of a secret society.

This was the iron heel with a vengeance; it took from the Irish the last vestige of citizen right. Parnell opposed, yet not violently, the remembrance of the Phoenix Park murders held him back. But the speeches of his followers were bitter in the extreme. 'What profit', cried Dillon, 'can you ever expect from governing a nation which nothing conciliates and nothing can subdue?' Of all the fifty Coercion Acts passed in the eighty-eight years since the Union this was: the worst.

The second reading was carried by 383 votes against 45.

Parnell expressed a desire that Gladstone should have his (Parnell's) views distinctly put before him by me – not in writing. This did not suit Gladstone. He had no intention of giving away his hand in regard to the Crimes Bill and, in the then temper of his own Party and of the Conservatives, was not at all desirious of making any further private concession that would certainly place him in a too favourable light (as regards this Bill) in the eyes of the Irishmen.

He was determined not to see me again with reference to the Crimes Bill and on June 23rd he wrote me to that effect. It was obvious from the tone of his letter that he was annoyed by the continued opposition of the Irish Party, which, from his point of view, only served to impede the progress of the Arrears Bill.

On one of my visits to Downing Street I told Gladstone of the inner working of the Ladies' Land League, about which he was curious. I mentioned to him the enormous sum these Lady Leaguers had expended and the great difficulty Parnell had had in suppressing them. On hearing the sum of their estimated weekly expenditure a grim smile flitted over his face. 'Very satisfactory', he remarked, 'as the ladies have evidently put these large sums beyond the power of – of the Land League's expenditure!

Gladstone would not sit still when he talked to me, but liked to pace up and down the long room with me. On my entry he would rise from his desk to greet me and, solemnly handing me a chair, would walk down the room to the door at the ends which was always open when I entered, close it firmly and, pacing back to the door of my entry, push it. These preparations always made me smile – a smile in which he joined as, coming up to me and offering me his arm, he said: 'Do you mind walking up and down the room, I talk better so.' So we paced up and down while I voiced Parnell's instructions and listened to the G.O.M.'s views, intentions and tentative suggestions, always on my part keeping to 'It is considered that, etc.', in giving Parnell's point and always receiving 'Your friend should, etc', or 'I am prepared to concede to your friend, etc., in return.'

He was so careful in this regard that one day I said: 'What is it you shut up in that room, Mir. Gladstone, when I come to see you?'

'Persons, or a person, you do not come to see, Mrs O' Shea. Only a secretary or so and occasionally, in these times of foolish panic, detectives. No', in answer to my look of inquiry, 'no one can over-hear a word we say when we pace up and down like this and, as you do not mind it, it refreshes me.'

Always as I stood face to face with this Grand Old Man on leaving and looked into his slate-coloured eyes, so like those of an eagle, I experienced a sudden uneasy feeling, in spite of his gracious courtesy, of how like to a beautiful bird of prey this old man was: with the piercing, cruel eyes belying the tender, courteous smile and how, relentless as an eagle, men like this had struck and torn their victims. But to me, personally, he always showed the marvellous charm of manner which sent me away feeling that I was at least a compelling force in the great game of politics and worthy of the place I held.

The political history of this time has been written many times and from various points of view and in this book I do not propose to repeat it, but only to record such point or detail as at the time affected my King in his home life.

CHAPTER XXVII

ENVOY TO GLADSTONE

*'Good Cinna, take this paper and look yon, lay it in the
praetor's chair, where Brutus may but find it!'*
– SHAKESPEARE (JULIUS CAESAR)

A S I HAVE RECORDED IN the concluding chapter of the first volume, negotiations
concerning the Crimes Bill were broken off, but before the end of June, 1882, I was
once more acting as envoy to Gladstone. The following is a characteristic memorandum
drafted by Parnell for transmission by me to the Prime Minister:–

Although the Coercion Bill as likely to pass into law is of such a character as to render it impossible for
him to take any further part. in the Irish Land movement, yet he trusts that the administration of the
Act by the Government will be of such a moderate character as to enable him to co-operate generally
with Mr G. in Parliament and in the English constituencies in carrying to a successful end that land
legislation the foundations of which were so broadly laid in the Act of last session and in gaining those
other measures of general reform for the benefit of the peoples of both England and Ireland which now
constitute the programme of the Liberal Party.

Since his (Parnell's) release he has taken steps to secure that no portion of the invested surplus of
the fund shall be drawn without his signature and he will endeavour to provide that future remittances
from the offices of the central organisation in America shall be added to this fund; the remittances
through the Irish World, however, he has no hopes of being able to control in any way.

The Coercion Bill to go through all its stages in six days – Supply to be facilitated.

Duration to be limited to three months after assembly of a new Parliament if present Parliament is
dissolved within three years – treason felony struck out on report.

Centres of disturbance are being rapidly created through out Ireland, owing to loss by tenants of
legal interest in their holdings through sale or expiry of period of redemption. The formation of the
new Landlord Corporation accompanied by a harsh administration of the Coercion Act will tend to
encourage landlords to resist reasonable concessions.

He has placed new clauses on the notice paper for the Arrears Bill which will go far to meet these
difficulties and will do what he can to facilitate Supply and the passage of that Bill, also to prevent
obstruction to other Government business.

These notes were submitted a second time to Mr Gladstone, with the addition of the following paragraphs:–

This danger might be met by insertion of clauses in Arrears Bill having compulsory retrospective effect as far back as June, 1880 and making provision for payment of costs.

It is most desirable that Parliament should reassemble after short holiday to make whatever permanent amendments the Government think necessary in the Land Act.

On June 29th Mr Gladstone wrote thanking me for my letter and returning 'the enclosure'. Reference was made by him to the murders of Mr Walter Bourke and Corporal Wallace in Galway; and though I have no doubt he did not suspect Parnell of the least shade of complicity, it was plain that he did not completely acquit the extremists of the Irish World. This was the enclosure he returned:–

MOUNT HOLYOKE MILLS, MASS., U.S.A.
CHARLES STEWART PARNELL, ESQ.

DEAR SIR, – In the present excited and doubting state of Irish opinions and feeling at home and abroad I write to you, though knowing well that such doubt and excitement will be all allayed ere this reaches you.

To those of us here who have made a life-long study of Irish history and English misrepresentation, the present efforts to drag you into any unpatriotic attitude of dickering with English Government seem just small enough for their worth. But because I myself ('si licet parvos componere magnis') have often, while of the League in this country, been strongly tempted to throw up in disgust my official connection with such dense ignorance and chronic growlings as frequently characterised many of our followers, so I fear more from the extent of your patience to forbear from properly suppressing such jerky followers than from your honest resolve to bear the worst from our National persecutors.

This week Ford, of the *Irish World*, editorially calls for a new deal, placing Davitt as leader of the agitation and leaving you as leader only of the Parliamentary Party to which the other should not be subordinate

Every other Irish-American paper deprecates strongly any thing like this. Every intelligent friend of Ireland here does the same. I wish to God all our people over there understood for once that the rational, organised, feelings of the Irish in America are voiced, not by the Irish World, but by the League Executive here, which comprises the bishops, priests and all other intelligent Irish-Americans supplemented by a goodly array of native American sympathisers.

In you alone centres the chief hope for success among all these. What you say and do is what we here have to support; were you now to withdraw from the leadership the injury to the cause would be incalculable. Though Davitt's and Dillon's names are sure to strike an enthusiastic chord in the hearts of the masses here, Parnell's alone combines enthusiasm, obedience and united confidence. You now occupy a grand and awfully responsible position, for you have touched the heart core of a whole nation and you've brought millions of persecuted people to the threshold of prosperity and made the whole Irish race all the world over look to you as their guide and leader to future prosperity and. freedom for their old cradle-land.

I only feebly – and doubtless boringly – put before you the result of the aggregate opinions gathered from our most intelligent clergy and people here. We care not for redressing the wretchedness and ignorance of the English farmers; our aims and hopes are for Ireland's progress and national independence. If the English Radicals help you, God bless them for it; but they must help you achieve Irish prosperity and self-government first ere they seek Irish support for their own cause. That is the feeling here.

Permit me here to suggest that if there were issued, in pamphlet form, a full exposure of the grand jury system, poor law guardian electoral law, public, cess and poor-rate tax, annotated by a brief, pithy explanation of their powers, privileges and extent of controlling popular suffrage, 'twould be a strong factor in moulding American sympathy for us.

Healy's pamphlet we had republished here and I was often, for weeks, engaged in mailing it to American readers, who were led to ask for it through the writings of Redpath and 'Nasby'. I wish you would get Healy to undertake to write up a pamphlet on the subjects above suggested. There is complete ignorance here – as in most rural districts at home – of the laws, customs and powers of such institutions as grand juries, poor law guardians, Parliamentary electors and tax gatherers.

I was chatting yesterday with our State Chief Magnate – Governor Long –who said that 'if Mr Healy were a representative type of Mr Parnell's co-workers, then Ireland had nothing to regret in her present staff of statesmen.'

I am in constant receipt of letters from Nationalists and Clan na Gaels, headed by John Devoy, all of whom promise unswerving aid and allegiance to whatever you will enjoin. This, too, in face of the energetic and persistent Opposition I made at Chicago to any amalgamation of L. L. and their forces, as Healy and O' Connor can tell you.

I would beg pardon here for wearying you by so long a letter, but I write it, only for what I believe Ireland's good, to Ireland's best friend.

I won't ask you to answer it unless you 'feel like' doing so yourself. Who and what I am matters not if what I say be to the point of practical work for our Common Cause.

When I was in office I forbore saying a great many things which I felt convinced should be said; I think Mr Egan thoroughly honest and patriotic, but not fully alive to the damage done Irish unity here by the action of Ford. The moneys sent through the Irish World would be sent by the honest contributors had Ford gone to limbo. Egan, David Brennan and young Quinn gave too much countenance to that editorial demagogue.

Don't fear the Nationalists here, quorum pars nulla sum; but the Nationalists at home, especially in the west, are toto Corde against Davitt and Brennan, though perfectly pleased with you. I know their 'county centres' there and often read their letters, while I am looked upon here as the most Conservative of Land Leaguers and the special 'favourite' of the clergy; yet all the Clan na Gaels place full confidence in me.

But I am too wearisome. God bless you and keep you firm in your good work of self-sacrificingly working for the amelioration of our ill-treated Fatherland, is the wish of

YOURS SINCERELY, ––-

This letter was from a notorious Invincible. Gladstone had expressed a wish to see one of his letters.

The progress of the Crimes Bill was more hotly contested than ever in the committee stage, which extended over twenty-four sittings of the House. Clauses were fought word by word, sentence by sentence. On the clause instituting a levy on the ratepayer of a district as compensation in cases of murder or maiming the committee sat continuously for thirty hours. Finally sixteen of the Irish members, among them Parnell, Dillon, McCarthy, Redmond, Sexton and Biggar and then nine others were named for obstruction and suspended. Thereafter the discussion was guillotined and the remaining clauses were rushed through almost without debate. The exiled Irish members met and passed a formal protest against the action of the House and expressed their determination to take no further interest in the progress of the Bill, which would therefore have no moral force in Ireland. In their absence a Government amendment limiting the power of police search to the daytime was defeated in spite of the vehement support of Mr Gladstone. The Bill was read a third time on July 8th and was passed by the Lords four days later, receiving, the Royal Assent on the following day. In less than a week 17 counties were proclaimed; and by the beginning of August 170 suspects were in custody.

An important division took place on July 6th, from which a large number of Irish members were absent. Mr Dillon distinguished himself on this occasion by speaking against Parnell's orders. The following day Gladstone wrote complaining of both of these circumstances and Parnell gave me the following note as the basis of a reply to the letter:– 'Write Mr G. that fifteen of the members had returned home to attend to their business, which had been neglected for the last two months. Mr P., however, believes that he can keep as many men in London for the remaining stages of the Arrears Bill as for the Coercion Bill and has sent telegrams to those absent urging their return. Dillon is curiously wilful at times, but his speech, though ill-judged, was ineffective.'

Further negotiations were then in progress and the following 'notes' for my guidance therein will show their trend:–

Mr P. fears events of Friday and Saturday will have injurious effect in Ireland and amongst Irish in English constituencies, also upon the temper of the Irish Party, many of whom are urging that the Arrears Bill and supply should be obstructed.

Centres of disturbance are being rapidly created all over Ireland owing to loss by tenants of legal interest in their holdings through sale or expiry of period of redemption.

This danger might be met by insertion of clauses in Arrears Bill having compulsory retrospective effect as far back as June, 1880 and making provision for payment of costs.

The formation of Landlords Corporation will tend to encourage landlords to resist reasonable concessions and it is most desirable that Parliament should reassemble after short holiday to make whatever permanent amendments the Government think necessary in the Land Act.

The Coercion Bill having been disposed of, he will do all he can to prevent obstruction to other Government business and to facilitate supply and the passage of Arrears Bill and trusts that he may be assisted by a moderate administration of the Coercion Act in Ireland and that his amendment with regard to the prison treatment of political prisoners may be favourably met by the Government.

He thinks he will be able to induce his friends to vote for the simple closure, but considerable management will be requisite and he does not wish it to be known at present that he favours anything more than an opposition to the two-thirds plan.

He still hopes that the administration of Coercion Act will be of such a character as to enable him to influence favourably opinion in the English and Scottish constituencies.

He has placed a sub-section on the Notice Paper of the Arrears Bill, making it obligatory on Court to stay proceedings in ejectment and recovery of rent where tenant pays or tenders a year's rent.

He considers this absolutely necessary to prevent many landlords defeating the Bill and so foiling its compulsory character.

If no other of his amendments are accepted, this certainly ought to be.

Arrears Bill through Committee before report of crime.

Clause in Arrears Bill dating judicial rent from gale day next after date of application to fix rent.

Oppose any amendment to closure resolution which would involve a proportionate majority, such as two-thirds.

Land question to be dealt with at Autumn Session. Outrages month previous to Treaty of Kilmainham – nearly 600. Ditto last month – only 165.

This enormous reduction has not at all been effected by provisions of Crimes Act, as, with exception of appointment of Special Commission in Dublin, the Act has been but little used and so far as it has been used its effect has been to increase popular excitement, to increase the distrust of the people in the administration of the law and to bring odium upon the Government in Ireland.

The partial conduct of the trials by Judge Lawson, the action of the Crown lawyers in directing almost every Catholic to stand aside from the juries for the trial of the capital cases will render it exceedingly difficult for the Irish Members to give any support to the Government when the Session re commences.

As the winter approaches evictions of tenants who have been sold out increase. It is to be feared that the party favourable to outrages and who receive their instructions from America, may resume their operations on a large scale and that it may not be possible to restrain them.

Some recognition ought to be extended to those who have done so much to restore peace in Ireland during the last few months and who are willing to do more if the Irish Government gives a chance by the suspension of proceedings which are alike irritating to the popular mind and destructive of that understanding between the Irish Members and the Liberal Party so necessary for the stability of the latter and for the carrying of measures of reform.

Have every confidence that if the Irish Government be checked as regards its objectionable proceeding, the condition of the country will continue to improve and remain satisfactory.

He (Parnell) is anxious to be in a position as soon as possible to inform Mr E. (Egan) that if he resigns the Treasurership and returns to Ireland, no proceedings against him under the new Act are contemplated by the Government.

There is a sum of £16,000 in America which will shortly arrive and which he is anxious to hand over to Mr E.'s successor, who, in the event of Mr E.'s resignation, will be his (Mr P.'s) own nominee.

A standing order of the House directing that Bills relating exclusively to Ireland, after second reading, shall be referred to a Grand Committee consisting of the Chief Secretary to the Lord Lieutenant, the Irish Law Officers of the Crown and those members of the House representing Irish constituencies and that unless the House should otherwise direct with regard to any particular Bill the Committee stage of such Bills in the whole House shall be dispensed with.

A Bill to amend the Land Act to be introduced next Session by the Irish members and read a second time on a Wednesday by help of the Closure and to confirm the following points:–

1st. That the judicial rent shall date from gale-day preceding the application to fix fair rent.

2nd. That pending decision of application to fix fair rent the Land Commission Court shall have power to stay proceedings in ejectment and for recovery of rent on such terms and conditions as it shall think fit.

3rd. The definition of the term 'improvement' as in Mr Redmond's Land Bill of last Session and the other amendments of 'Healy's clause' of the Land Act as provided by Mr R.'s Bill, except that instead of the presumption being in favour of the improvements having been executed by the tenant or his predecessor without limitation of time, that presumption shall only extend back for a period of thirty-five years from the passing of the Act of 1881.

4th. Power to the Land Commission to break leases on the application of either party, where, having regard to all the circumstances of the case and if it be shown by the party applying that he was not in a position at the time of contract to pay freely, the Court considers it just and reasonable to do so.

5th. An extension of the purchase clauses so as to enable the whole of the purchase money to be advanced and the period of repayment to be extended.

On July 21st the Arrears Bill passed the Commons by 169 to 98. Lord Eversley (Mr Shaw Lefevre) rightly observes that instead of appealing to justice, Mr Gladstone based his support of the Bill on expediency. For years tenants had been burdened with excessive rents on land which their efforts had raised from prairie value. The wiping out of the accumulated arrears of these unjust rents could hardly be termed a mere act of expediency.

On July 31st the Lords returned the Bill to the Commons cut to pieces. Certain minor concessions were made and the Bill was sent back otherwise in its original form. When next it appeared in the Lords, the Irish landlord peers revolted. The Bill promised them part payment of what they had looked upon as a bad debt; and so – not for the sake of justice, but for the sake of that bait of two years' rent – they supported the Bill, which was passed by the Lords on August 10th. On or about August 18th, when it became law, fifty suspects were released.

I had addressed an appeal to Mr Gladstone against the death sentence passed upon a young Irishman on very doubtful evidence. On September 14th he wrote saying that he would certainly bring the appeal under the notice of Lord Spencer.

I was in correspondence with Mr Gladstone throughout November of this year, but found it difficult to pin him to a definite statement. Parnell was particularly anxious to fix a period to the operation of the Crimes Act. But the time of the House was taken up largely in devising a scheme to prevent obstruction. This scheme was 'the Closure'. In a letter dated November 2th Lord Richard Grosvenor, writing on Mr Gladstone's behalf, stated that there had never been any stipulation with respect to Irish legislation.

At the opening of Parliament in the beginning of 1883 the Speech from the Throne referred in glowing terms to the decrease of crime in Ireland. But, nevertheless, apparently there was still need for coercion. I refer in another chapter to Forster's bitter attack on Parnell on this occasion.

Ireland did not figure largely in the Parliamentary legislation of 1883, though a number of minor Irish Bills, on tramways, fisheries and so forth, which received the support of Parnell, were carried. The Irish Party brought in a Bill to amend the Land Act of 1881 and on March 14th Parnell moved the second reading. The Bill proposed, among other things, (1) to date the judicial rent from the gale-day succeeding the application to the Land Court; (2) to bring leaseholders and others within the scope of the Act; (3) to amend the purchase clauses with a provision for the advance of the whole of the purchase money and for the extension of the term for repayment; and (4) the use and enjoyment by the tenant of his improvements not to be held as compensation. Mr Gladstone offered uncompromising opposition to the Bill, which, he contended, was virtually a reconstruction of the Land Act and it was rejected by 250 to 53.

Nearly all these concessions have since been made and most of them by the Tory Party.

This Liberal opposition to legitimate Irish demands helped, like Forster's attack on Parnell, to strengthen the latter's position in Ireland.

Although Gladstone and Parnell were fighting in Parliament, I was still acting as the intermediary in friendly negotiations between them.

Parnell's position in Ireland was impregnable, but the extremists in America were exasperated by his constitutional agitation. Early in 1883 Patrick Ford started a dynamite crusade against England in the *Irish World* and attempts were actually made to blow up public buildings in London, while a nitro-glycerine factory was discovered in Birmingham. Immediately an Explosives Bill of the most drastic character was introduced by Sir William Harcourt and rushed through the Commons in a single sitting. The Irish Party offered no opposition.

It is significant of the tactics of Mr Gladstone that he was secretly striving to influence the Vatican against Home Rule. A Mr Errington, an Irish Catholic, but a Whig Member of Parliament, had been sent to Rome with a letter of recommendation from Lord Granville. Mr Gladstone had also written about him through Cardinal Manning, who was opposed to the mission. His business was at first to work for a Papal reprimand of priests who engaged in Land League agitation. He succeeded finally in engineering a rescript, dated May 11th, 1883, calling upon bishops to restrain priests from taking part in the Parnell testimonial.

The following telegram will serve to show somewhat of the conditions under which the Liberal and Irish Parties were working in the late summer of 1883:—

August 6th, 1883.
From Mrs O' Shea, Eltham,

To Lord Richard Grosvenor, mp, House of Commons.

Most important Tramways Bill should be postponed. Please telegraph to me if it is possible to postpone it. If it does not come on at reasonable hour, if impossible to postpone it, can you see me for few minutes if I go up?

Mr Parnell wished the Bill postponed in order to have time to get the full voting strength of his Party together, if the full voting strength was required.

In a letter to me under date of August 25th, Lord R. Grosvenor assumed that I should be satisfied with the arrangements made for the Registration Bill. He seemed very much shocked by recent speeches of Irish members in the House and he alluded to the restraining influence of Parnell's presence; Parnell had been ill the previous Saturday and unable to attend the House. Lord Richard said some very kind things about Parnell's good intentions.

Here are some further 'notes' for consideration by Mr Gladstone for my use in the negotiations:–
The Irish Local Government Board should sanction the giving of outdoor relief in the Unions scheduled under the provisions of the Emigration Sections of the Arrears Act and more especially should this be done in the case of evicted families, hundreds of whom, owing to inability to pay costs, have been unable to obtain the benefit of Arrears Act and are living in extreme poverty.

* * * * * * *

He (Parnell) has been considering what useful measures for Ireland the Government might pass this session without the expenditure of much time or incurring any risk and he has selected the following as complying with these conditions
(1) The Registration Bill of the Chief Secretary with the amendments of Mr Dawson.
(2) The Labourers Bill.
(3) The Poor Law Guardians Election Bill, as read a second time and including the abolition of the proxy vote.
He also thinks that the Government should agree to define the expression 'undue influence' in the Corrupt Practices Bill in a manner satisfactory to the Irish members.
If he were assured of the passage of these measures and if the Registration Bill were passed or material progress made with it in the intervals of the stages of the Corrupt Practices Bill, he feels sure that he could influence his friends from time to time during the rest of the session so as to secure considerable facilities for Government business, except the Criminal Code Bill, which he must continue to oppose owing to certain objectionable provisions contained in it.
A suitable definition of 'undue influence' is of great importance, as it would enable him to afford his friends a fairly sufficient reason for withdrawing from further opposition to the Corrupt Practices Bill, since it is not desirable that he should take them into his confidence as regards the prospect or promise of the legislation for Ireland indicated above.

* * * * * * *

Leaseholders.
The lessee of any holding who at the expiration of any lease existing at the passing of the Land Law (Ireland) Act, 1881, would be deemed to be a tenant of a present ordinary tenancy from year to year, at the rent and subject to the conditions of the lease, shall from and after the passing of this Act and notwithstanding that such lease has not expired be deemed to be a tenant of a present tenancy at the rent mentioned in said lease and his holding shall be subject to all the provisions of the said Act of 1881 with regard to present tenancies. Provided that such lessee shall not be deemed to be a present tenant.
(a) Where substantial consideration has been given by such lessee for the said lease and such lessee objects to being deemed a present tenant.
(b) Where such lessee is not the immediate occupying tenant of such holding.
(c) Where the holding is of such a character as to come under any of the exceptions contained in the fifty-eighth section of the Land Law (Ireland) Act, 1881.
(From Arrears Act, s. 13).–Suspension of Proceedings.–
Where any proceedings for the recovery of the rent of a holding to which this Act applies, or for the recovery of such holding for non-payment of rent have been taken before or after an application under this Act in respect of such holding and are pending before such application is disposed of, the Court before which such proceedings are pending shall, on such terms and conditions as the Court may direct, postpone or suspend such proceedings until the application under this Act has been disposed of.
Revision of Rents.
(1) The landlord or tenant of any holding, subject to statutory conditions, or such landlord and the tenant jointly, at the expiration of three years from the commencement of the statutory term, may apply to the Court to revise the judicial rent of such holding.

(2) In making such provision, the. Court shall have regard to the prices of the principal articles of produce of such holding as compared with the prices when the judicial rent was fixed.

Date of Judgement.

In any application to the Court made within three months after the passing of this Act for the fixing or revision of a judicial rent the judgement of the Court shall date and have reflect as from the date of the gale-day coming next before the date of the passing of this Act.

Shall apply to any rent due on ordinary payable on the last gale-day of the present year.

Willie was very anxious that Mr O' Hart (O' Hart's Irish Pedigrees) should be granted a pension from the Civil List. Mr Gladstone had already declined to include him in the List of Beneficiaries. Now at Willie's urgent request I most reluctantly asked Mr Gladstone to reconsider his decision as to Mr O' Hart and on September 19th, 1884, received a snub for my pains. I had told Gladstone that Lord Spencer was credited with having expressed the opinion that Parnell had some connection with the Phoenix Park murders. Gladstone now said he was sure that Spencer did not really believe this.

In October, 1884, Mr Trevelyan ceased to be Irish Secretary and entered the Cabinet as Chancellor of the Duchy of Lancaster. The vacant post was offered to, Mr Shaw Lefevre, but on hearing that Lord Spencer intended to seek for the renewal of the Coercion Act when it expired in September, 1885, he refused the offer. Mr (afterwards Sir Henry) Campbell-Banner man became Chief Secretary on October 24th.

CHAPTER XXVIII

THE DAWN OF HOME RULE

'No one has the right to limit the aspirations of a people.'
– CHARLES STEWART PARNELL.

DURING 1884 PARNELL HAD KEPT quiet and my negotiations on his behalf with Gladstone were intermittent.

In the early part of the year, however, a document of tremendous import was submitted – none other than 'A Proposed Constitution for Ireland', drawn up by Parnell, which was as follows:–

An elected Chamber with power to make enactments regarding all the domestic concerns of Ireland, but without power to interfere in any Imperial matter.

The Chamber to consist of three hundred members.

Two hundred and six of the number to be elected under the present suffrage, by the present Irish constituencies, with special arrangements for securing to the Protestant minority a representation proportionate to their numbers; the remaining 94 members to be named in the Act constituting the Chamber.

The principle of nomination regarding this proportion of members to last necessarily only during the duration of the first Chamber.

The number of elected members, suffrage and boundaries of constituencies for election of succeeding Chamber to be capable of alteration by the preceding Chamber, excepting those special arrangements for securing to the Protestant minority a proportionate representation, which arrangements shall be fixed and immutable.

The first Chamber to last for three years, unless sooner dissolved by the Crown.

The Chamber shall have power to enact laws and make regulation regarding all the domestic and internal affairs of Ireland, including her sea fisheries.

The Chamber shall also have power to raise a revenue for any purpose over which it has jurisdiction, by direct taxation upon property, by Customs duties and by licences.

The Chamber shall have power to create departments for the transaction of all business connected with the affairs over which it has jurisdiction and to appoint and dismiss chief and subordinate officials for such departments, to fix the term of their office and to fix and pay their salaries; and to maintain a police force for the preservation of order and the enforcement of the law.

This power will include the constitution of Courts of Justice and the appointment or payment of all judges, magistrates and other officials of such Courts, provided that the appointment of judges and magistrates shall in each case be subject to the: assent of the Crown.

No enactment of the Chamber shall have the force of law until it shall have received the assent of the Crown.

A sum of one million pounds sterling per annum shall be paid by the Chamber to the Imperial Treasury in lieu of the right of the Crown to levy taxes in Ireland for Imperial purposes, which right would be held in suspense so long as punctual payment was made of the above annual sum.

The right of the Imperial Parliament to legislate regarding the domestic concerns and internal affairs of Ireland will also be held in suspense, only to be exercised for weighty and urgent cause.

The abolition of the office of Lord Lieutenant of Ireland and all other offices in Ireland under the Crown connected with the domestic affairs of that country.

The representation of Ireland in the Imperial Parliament might be retained or might be given up. If it be retained the Speaker might have the power of deciding what questions the Irish members might take part in as Imperial questions, if this limitation were thought desirable.

Such Naval and Military force as the Crown thought requisite from time to time would be maintained in Ireland out of the contribution of one million pounds per annum to the Imperial Treasury; any excess in the cost of these forces over such sum being provided for out of the Imperial Revenue (i.e. by Great Britain).

The Militia would also be levied, controlled and paid by the Crown and all forts, military barracks, posts and strong places of the country would be held and garrisoned by the Crown forces.

No volunteer force to be raised in Ireland without the consent of the Crown and enactment of the Imperial Parliament and, if raised, to be paid for and controlled by the Crown.

On May 11th, 1884, Lord Richard Grosvenor wrote a non-committal acknowledgment of the receipt of this memorandum.

The Government was then devoting its attention to the Franchise Bill and the Redistribution of Seats Bill and it had been decided to incorporate Ireland in the scheme. This Parnell considered to be of tremendous importance. Speaking in December, 1883, at the Dublin banquet held in his honour, he alluded to the force which had then been gained for Ireland. The change was, in fact, enormous. Instead of the franchise being confined practically to the farmers, it would now include the labourers and the cottier tenants and the number of voters in Ireland would go up from 200,000 to 600,000. How would those labourers and cottier tenants vote? Lord Randolph Churchill (who supported the Bill against his Party) and Mr Chamberlain thought, strangely enough, that their inclusion would help the landlord interest. Parnell knew better and when the Bill became law, in December, 1884, he leapt into action. This was the weapon for which he had been waiting. From December to March of the following year he went through Ireland organising for the imminent General Election.

In the early months of 1885 the Liberal Government was in a bad way. It had narrowly escaped defeat on the vote of censure for its failure to relieve Gordon at Khartoum. The Cabinet was divided against itself. Many of the Liberal members were inclined to rebel and the Irish were working with the Tory Opposition. Ireland was the rock upon which the Government was to come to a wreck. The majority of the Cabinet was in favour of continued coercion. Mr Chamberlain, Sir Charles Duke and Mr Shaw Lefevre were strongly opposed to it. But on the subject of local government for Ireland the difference of opinion was even more dangerous. Chamberlain submitted a scheme for an elective National Council in Dublin, with control over administrative Boards and Departments, but not over the police and the administration of the law. It had been ascertained indirectly that Parnell would accept this scheme and would not oppose a moderate Coercion Act. Gladstone was prepared to go a step farther and give the National Council control over the police. A vote was taken in the Cabinet. All the Peers, with the exception of Lord

Granville[15], were against and the Commoners, with the exception of Lord Hartington, were in favour of the scheme. Therefore 'for the present' the scheme was abandoned. This was in May. The battle over coercion remained to be fought. In less than four weeks the Government was out of office.

Gladstone had not been able to make up his mind to abandon coercion altogether, though he had endeavoured to sweeten the draught with the promise of a Land Purchase Bill and Parnell had been able to arrange privately with the Conservative Opposition that if they came into power coercion would be dropped.

On June 8th the Government was beaten on the second reading of the Budget. The ostensible question, which concerned nobody, was that of a tax on wine and beer. The whole of the thirty-nine Irish members voted for the Opposition and the Government was beaten by twelve. Thereupon Gladstone resigned and Lord Salisbury formed his first Ministry. Parnell held the key of the position. He had put the Tories into power; at his will he could put them out again.

Lord Carnarvon became Lord Lieutenant, Sir Michael Hicks-Beach Chief Secretary and the intention was expressed to govern Ireland by constitutional methods. Coercion for the time being was abandoned, Lord Carnarvon had thought much on Irish questions and his rule was in marked contrast to that of his immediate predecessors.

On July 14th Lord Richard Grosvenor suddenly remembered Parnell's draft Constitution for Ireland which I had submitted to Gladstone. Did it still hold good? To this letter I replied and on July 23rd Lord Richard wrote again asking for a plain answer. But this at the moment it was impossible to give, for the attitude the Tories would take up with regard to Home Rule was not yet certain Lord Carnarvon, the Lord Lieutenant, was believed to be very favourably disposed to the Irish demands and Lord Randolph Churchill seemed willing to go far. On July 28th Lord Richard wrote again, imploring us to show our hand. Evidently the Irish vote was worth securing.

It is interesting to note that on July 17th Mr Chamberlain, speaking at Holloway, urged that the pacification of Ireland depended on the concession to her of the right to govern herself in the matter of purely local business

At the end of July Parnell met Lord Carnarvon in London. The Lord Lieutenant had already been in communication with Sir Charles Gavan Duffy and Mr Justin McCarthy upon the subject of Home Rule and there can be little doubt he was in earnest in his agreement with the principle How far he was used by his Party as a catspaw to play for the Irish vote is another question. At least Lord Salisbury knew of the proceedings of his colleague and was perhaps not averse to using Lord Carnarvon's convictions to win Parnell's support at the forthcoming elections without giving a definite Party pledge. The conversation between Lord Carnarvon and Parnell led the latter to believe that the Tories were prepared to support a measure of local government for Ireland. But how far were the Liberals prepared to go?

On August 4th Mr Gladstone wrote to me further with reference to the proposed constitution for Ireland. Did this represent Parnell's views now? He was urgent in asking for an answer. In one of my notes I had spoken of the suggestion that a proposition of his son, Mr Herbert (now Lord) Gladstone, should be substituted for it. Mr Gladstone now assured me on the best authority that no such proposition had been made. I gathered, however, that his son had made some suggestions.

To this a long and comprehensive reply was sent – apparently too long and comprehensive. No doubt he wanted a definite and limited scheme to be set before him. I had referred in my letter to certain changes which had occurred since the draft was sent. I knew that Gladstone knew what those changes were, for the frantic appeals for a definite statement were precisely the counter-bidding against the heightened biddings of Lord

Randolph Churchill and the Conservative Party in which Gladstone declared he would not engage. He was obviously disinclined to make an offer until Parnell had pinned himself down to a final demand. If only he could know what the Home Rule Party wanted!

The following day Mr Gladstone set out on a yachting expedition (to Norway) and a few days later, on August 11th, Parliament was prorogued.

Parnell opened his campaign in Dublin on August 11th, when he announced that he and his Party would stand for an Irish Parliament and nothing else. There was no talk now of a National Council. Lord Hartington replied declaring Parnell's proposals to be fatal and mischievous and on September 9th Lord Richard wrote, on behalf of Mr Gladstone, who was back in England, pleading for details.

On October 7th Lord Salisbury, speaking at Newport (Mon.), made a diplomatic statement about Ireland which suggested much and promised nothing.

Later in the month I sent Mr Gladstone a paper containing the views of Mr Parnell and on November 3rd Lord Richard Grosvenor replied, referring me to the Government of the day, but thanking me for the information. There was some mention in the letter of Willie's prospects for Mid-Armagh. Apparently that affair was off, since Willie had himself written to such an effect. Willie was given a gentle rap on the fingers for having in Ireland talked over the plans for his election with another person.

On November 9th, at Edinburgh, Mr Gladstone made a speech which rivalled Lord Salisbury's in elusiveness. The constitutional demands of Ireland must not be disregarded, but it would be a vital danger if at such a time there was not a Party politically independent of the Irish vote.

Parnell desired precisely the contrary and on November 21st, the eve of the General Election, a manifesto was issued calling upon Irish voters in Great Britain to vote against the Liberal Party.

Before Parnell's interview with Lord Carnarvon I had sent Gladstone Parnell's suggestions for a new Home Rule Bill. Mr Gladstone wrote expressing satisfaction at the news of the intended interview, but he would not be drawn. Nevertheless Parnell made another attempt and on December 14th, 1885, addressed the following letter from my house at Eltham:

NORTH PARK, ELTRAM, KENT,
December 14th, 1885.

MY DEAR MRS O' SHEA, – It appeared to me from Mr Gladstone's utterances in Scotland that he would admit the justice of Ireland's claim for autonomy and also the expediency of soon endeavouring to satisfy it provided the result of the General Election went to show an overwhelming preponderance of the opinion of the, representatives of Ireland in favour of this claim. A very proper reservation was also made regarding the maintenance of the supremacy of the Crown in Ireland and all the authority of Parliament necessary for this supremacy.

We now know that more than five-sixths of the Irish members elected by household suffrage have been returned, mostly by very large majorities, as supporters of the institution of an Irish Parliament, that a clear majority, seventeen out of thirty-three, from the Ulster constituencies have been so returned and that only one county and one city in Ireland, Antrim and Belfast respectively, are without Nationalist representation.

Under these circumstances does it not seem that the question has now resolved itself firstly into a consideration of the details of the proposed settlement and secondly, as to the procedure to be adopted in obtaining the assent of Parliament and if needful of the British electorate to this settlement? As regards the first matter, the rough sketch, which I sent you some weeks back, appeared then and still appears to me, the smallest proposal which would be likely to find favour in Ireland if brought forward by an English Minister, but it is not one which I could undertake to suggest publicly myself, though if it were enacted I would work in Ireland to have it accepted bona fide as a final settlement and I believe it would prove to be one.

This proposal was carefully designed with a view to propitiate English prejudice and to afford those guarantees against hasty legislation, interference in extraneous matters and unfair action against particular classes, apprehended by many persons as a result of the establishment of an Irish Parliament. It did not involve a repeal of the Act of Union, an irrevocable step and the Imperial Parliament having conferred the privilege by statute would thus always be in a position to recall it by a similar method, if the privilege was abused.

It provided for a special proportionate representation for the large Protestant minority of Ireland. It also left to the Imperial Parliament the practical decision from time to time as to the matters which did or did not come within the province of the local legislature. These are all important concessions and guarantees and some opinion must surely have been formed by now upon these and other details.

As regards the question of procedure, I am desirous of knowing after a time whether the solution of the Irish question would be made the first and only business by a Liberal Government till the question was settled. The reform of procedure would probably be found not so necessary or pressing if the Imperial Parliament could get rid of its Irish work. It appeared to me that the best way to turn out the present Government would be by a general vote of censure without special reference to Ireland, or by a vote directed against some act of policy other than Irish, for which occasion may shortly arise. We might then either abstain or vote for the censure as might be deemed best. I have not seen Lord Carnarvon and shall probably not arrange to do so for a week or two, as I wish to know how the other side is disposed first. I have always felt Mr Gladstone is the only living statesman who has both the power and the will to carry a settlement it would be possible for me to accept and work with.

I doubt Lord C.'s power to do so, though I know him to be very well disposed. However, if neither party can offer a solution of the question I should prefer the Conservatives to remain in office, as under them we could at least work out gradually a solution of the Land question. You will see from this letter that I am very much in the dark, except as to my own mind and that of Ireland, that I want information as to whether Mr Gladstone has, as I suppose, accepted the principle of a Chamber for Ireland with power over her domestic and internal affairs and, if so, which, if any, of the details contained in sketch he objects to or is in doubt about. Further, it is important that I should be advised before the meeting of Parliament what procedure would, in his judgment, be best for bringing about that change of Government which would enable Mr Gladstone to deal authoritatively with the Irish question.

Yours very truly,
CHAS. S. PARNELL.

I sent this letter to Gladstone and on December 16th, three days before the completion of the General Election, he dispatched from Hawarden a long reply; but he said nothing more than he had already said in public at Midlothian and elsewhere and in private letters to me. Throughout this period the one fact apparent was that he would pledge the Liberal Party to nothing until he was in office and supported by the Irish Party. While there was a Tory Government in alliance with Parnell he would do nothing. Whether or not he was sincere in his advice to us to take Home Rule rather from the Tories than the Liberals if possible – because many Liberals would support a Tory Home Rule Bill, while all Tories would oppose a Liberal measure – this I cannot say. He offered it constantly, though he urged that a trafficking with both Parties for the purpose of getting the best terms possible, when, as in the end it must be, avowed, would injure a Tory measure and kill a Liberal one.

The result of the election was that the Tories in alliance with the Parnellites outnumbered the Liberals by four. The Liberals in alliance with Parnell would have outnumbered the Tories by 167. Parnell had swept the board in Ireland and in the House of Commons he was dictator.

Immediately after the General Election the Salisbury Cabinet met to consider its Irish policy and Lord Carnarvon at once tendered his resignation. The conclusion to be drawn is obvious. Compact or no compact, Lord Carnarvon had reason to believe that the

Cabinet were prepared to pursue a certain line of policy which it now appeared they had no intention of pursuing. The reason for the *volte face*, too, is plain. Tories plus Parnellites formed too narrow a majority of the House for Governmental purposes. The Irish were no longer of any use and they were abandoned.

Correspondence with Mr Gladstone continued and his letters were still cautious. He seemed to fear the soreness of certain Liberals over the Parnellite opposition at the polls, but he professed to be very willing to co-operate with the Tory Government in the matter of Home Rule and he stated that he had acquainted the Government with his disposition. Letters of December 19th, 22nd and 24th are all more or less to this effect. He harped on the word 'bribe.'

As a matter of fact, Mr Gladstone had approached the Cabinet through Mr Balfour, both personally and by letter, urging that it would be a calamity if this great question were to fall into the lines of Party conflict. The Cabinet seem to have treated Mr Gladstone's letter with scant respect. In spite of Lord Carnarvon's tendered resignation, Lord Salisbury was resolved to make no concession to Home Rule. Lord Carnarvon agreed not to resign until the opening of Parliament.

A statement in the Press inspired by Mr Herbert Gladstone to the effect that Mr Gladstone was prepared to concede an Irish Parliament in Dublin was declared by the latter to be 'inaccurate and not authentic'. But on December 26th he issued a memorandum to certain of his more reliable followers to the effect that he would support the Tories in a Home Rule policy which should satisfy him and the Irish Nationalists and that if he were called upon to form a Government the preparation of a scheme of duly guarded Home Rule would be an indispensable condition.

On December 29th I wrote to Gladstone, forwarding a memorandum from Parnell. On the last day of the year he sent me a memorandum marked 'Secret', in which he summarised the position between Parnell and himself. It amounted to this: Parnell wanted a definite pledge that there should be no more coercion before throwing the Tories out of power and putting the Liberals in. Gladstone, while realising the gravity of O' Brien's statistics in the Nineteenth Century as to the result of exceptional legislation, refused to give this pledge. He alluded philosophically to the probable course of events if the Address went through unamended. Mr Parnell wrote to me to the following effect embodying the points I was to pass on to Gladstone.

DEAR MRS O' SHEA, – In reply to your query it would be inexpedient that the Government ... But, in any case, we should move a series of separate amendments to the Address – one asking for a suspension of the support by the naval, military and constabulary forces of the Crown of ejectments, pending the consideration by Parliament of the proposed Land measure; another praying the Crown to remove Chief Justice May from the Bench; a third condemning the practice of jury packing, resorted to by the Crown in all the recent trials; a fourth asking her Majesty to fulfil the promise contained in the Speech of last year for the equalisation of the borough franchise in Ireland to that in England; a fifth condemning the proclamation of the meetings at Brookeboro and Cullohill; and a sixth protesting against the proclamation and additional police force sent to several of the counties.

This would be an assault along the whole line of English misgovernment in Ireland and should, in my opinion, be delivered before we allow the Address to leave the house. The first fortnight or so of the session would thus be occupied while the Government were making up their minds as to their proposed Land Bill.

At the meeting of the Party I think of proposing a resolution recommending the minority to pay more deference to the opinion of the majority than they did last session and urging all the Irish members to sit together in opposition.

Kindly let me know what you think of these proposals.

Yours truly,

CHARLES S. PARNELL.

These blanks were left in the letter as the phrases omitted were too confidential to be written. I learnt them and quoted them to Gladstone.

On January 9th, 1886, Gladstone wrote a reply in the usual vague terms. On the 24th he referred to what he had said before about communications from him to Parnell before the Tory Government had had its chance. As to Mr Jesse Collings's motion he was not yet resolved. But two days later he had apparently made up his mind that the motion would benefit the recently enfranchised agricultural labourers and please then representatives, for he announced his determination to support it.

On January 29th he wrote asking me to assure Parnell that should he become Prime Minister the objection to private negotiations would disappear.

To this letter I replied:–

Mr P. has not expressed any apprehension of the nature which has been reported to you.

Yesterday Mr Labouchere introduced the subject to him and stated that he had been requested by Mr Herbert Gladstone on your part to ask whether he (Mr P.) would have any objection to 'open communications' of the nature of those t took place with Lord Salisbury on the Redistribution Bill, if they should become necessary by and by.

Mr P. put off Mr Labouchere by saying that he would think about the matter.

If you should in future have any messages such as those which Mr L has represented himself as having been authorised to make to him during the last few days, he thinks it would be more prudent that they should be sent through myself or Lord R. Grosvenor, as Mr P. has not a high opinion of Mr L's discretion.

When the time comes he will be glad to learn from you through Lord R. Grosvenor or myself the method you think it best to adopt for the purpose of the full interchange of views you deem desirable and indispensable with regard to Irish autonomy.

It may interest you to learn that some days since Mr P. sent Mr Harrington to Ireland, with directions to overhaul the doings of the branches of the National League and with power to dissolve any that would not keep within bounds. The first result of this you will see in enclosed cutting.

K.O' S

From Lord Richard's reply of January 30th I gathered that Labouchere, as usual, had been romancing. Lord Richard seemed of opinion that there were more desirable Mercuries.

The difficulty with Mr Labouchere was that he had the habit of mixing his own opinions with those of the person to whom he spoke and delivering the mixture in public.

On January 21st Parliament met to transact business and the resignations of Lord Carnarvon and Sir W. Hart Dyke were announced. Notice was given of a new Coercion Act and on the 26th the Government was defeated by 331 to 252 votes – not, however, on an Irish amendment, but on the motion of Jesse Collings raising the question of 'three acres and a cow'.

CHAPTER XXIX

THE FIRST HOME RULE BILL

'Memories, images and precious thoughts
That shall not die and cannot be destroyed.' – WORDSWORTH

BEFORE FORMING HIS CABINET MR Gladstone enunciated the necessity for an examination whether it was practicable to establish a legislative body to sit in Dublin and to deal with Irish, as distinguished from Imperial affairs.

Five of the the members of his last Cabinet – Lords Hartington, Derby, Northbrook, Selborne and Carlingford – signified their absolute opposition to Home Rule Two – Mr Chamberlain and Mr Trevelyan agreed to the inquiry provisionally. Two – Sir Charles Duke and Mr Shaw Lefevre – had been defeated at the General Election. Seven – Lords Granville, Spencer, Kimberley, Ripon and Rosebery, Sir William Harcourt and Mr Childers – agreed absolutely. Four new men – Mr Morley, Mr Campbell-Bannerman, Mr Mundella and Lord Herschell – came into the Cabinet. Mr Morley became Irish Secretary. A scheme was drafted by Mr Gladstone and Mr Morley. It consisted of two Bills, a Home Rule Bill and a Land Bill. On the scheme being laid before the Cabinet Mr Chamberlain and Mr Trevelyan resigned.

On April 8th, 1886, the evening of the introduction of the Home Rule Bill, Mr Gladstone sent his private secretary down to Eltham with a letter to me asking me to telegraph one word, 'Yes', if he was to introduce the Bill that night. In this case he was to speak shortly after four o'clock. Mr Parnell had not given him the required answer earlier, as he had up to the last moment been trying to induce Mr Gladstone to give the Bill wider and more comprehensive clauses than the G.O.M would assent to. Now, however, he had said to me, as he started that evening for the House: 'This Bill will do as a beginning; they shall have more presently. If the Old Man wires to know if it is all right answer 'Yes'. Mr Gladstone had previously arranged with me that I should be at home waiting for his message in order that I might let him know that Parnell and the 'Party' were ready.

His messenger was so late that I simply snatched Gladstone's letter from him and, scribbling my 'Yes' on the enclosed Government form, sent my waiting servant flying to the telegraph office with it. After which I had time to join in the regrets of Mr Gladstone's secretary that his master had made it impossible for me to get up to the House in time for his introduction of the Bill. The secretary told me that he would have 'derived considerable interest' from the proceedings, but I felt much more keenly than that about this Bill that I had taken so often in its swaddling clothes from parent to foster parent and I was very much disappointed at not being present at its introduction to a larger life.

The debate on the first and second readings lasted sixteen days. It is to be remembered that in his attack on the Bill Mr Chamberlain did not oppose Home Rule, but only this particular scheme.

There was a Mrs Rae an elderly lady, who haunted the ladies' gallery of the House of Commons and whom I and Mr Parnell were not always successful in avoiding, she being most anxious to help Mr Parnell politically. So far as I can remember Mrs Rae had in this instance become possessed or involved in some most curious scheme, purporting to bear the authority of Mr Gladstone, in regard to measures affecting Ireland. On March18th he wrote saying that he did not know the lady and did not understand her scheme. He seemed to desire Parnell to co-operate with Mr Morley.

A great wish of Willie's was to be appointed Under-Secretary for Ireland. I had on various occasions made the suggestion to Mr Gladstone, but without successful issue. Gladstone had a perfect manner of refusing appointments when personally asked for them; it was always an apparent pain to him, nothing but the knowledge of his duty restrained him from interference and though I was not really anxious that Willie should receive this appointment I was willing to please him by asking for it and it might have excited suspicion if I had not asked. I must admit that Mr Gladstone never to my knowledge of him all those years made an appointment from motives of private fervour. Here once more, when he wrote regretting he couldn't poach on his colleagues' patronage preserves his manners were perfect.

On May 8th an urgent letter from Gladstone at Downing Street was delivered at my house. Mr Morley had lost track of Mr Parnell and wanted to know where he was. It was apparently the most natural thing in the world to ask me where was Parnell. A form of Government telegram was enclosed for my reply.

In view of the fact that Mr Gladstone and his colleagues were so pained, surprised and properly shocked, when Mr Parnell was publicly arraigned as my lover, the frantic way in which they applied to me, when they were unable to find him, was, afterwards, a source of considerable amusement to us both.

From the time of my first interview with Mr Gladstone onwards, no time was lost in 'failing to trace him here' before hurried application was made to me at *my* – and Parnell's – permanent address. I did not choose that the Irish Party should have his private address – nor did Parnell choose it – but I was most particular that the Government should know it. Governments – especially Liberal Governments – are before all things simple-minded and of childlike guilelessness.

I remember when on one occasion the Government desired to know Parnell's views on certain matters before elaborating a Bill shortly to go before the House, a special messenger was sent to Eltham with a letter. I had gone to the seaside with my children and my servants had standing orders that they knew nothing of Mr Parnell or of his whereabouts. So the non-plussed Governmental messenger meditated upon my doorstep for one moment only, then, armed with '*Mrs O' Shea's* address' at Hastings, came straight on to receive Mr Parnell's reply and safely deliver it within the stipulated time. But there can be no doubt of course, that Mr Gladstone's 'Poor fellow, poor fellow, what a terrible fall', subsequent to the hounding, at his word, of his gallant opponent to death, by the Irish sycophants, alluded to the breaking of the eleventh commandment of social life: 'Thou shalt not be found out' (publicly), rather to the seventh of orthodox Christianity.

On May 14th Gladstone wrote with regard to the rules laid down by the Government for the Home Rule debate. He complimented the Irish on their speeches.

On June 7th Mr Parnell spoke on the Home Rule Bill. It was the last night of the debate and he had carefully prepared his speech for that night. I give the substance of it herewith. He said:

'During the last five years I know that there have severe and drastic Coercion Bills, but it will require a more even severe and more drastic measure of coercion now. You will require all that you have had during the last five years and more besides. What has that coercion been? You have had during those five years – I don't say this to inflame passion – you have had during those five years the suspension of the Habeas Corpus Act; you have had a thousand of your Irish fellow-subjects held in prison without specific charge, many of them for long periods of time, some of them for twenty months without trial and without any intention of placing them upon trial (I think of all these thousand persons arrested under the Coercion Act of the late Mr Forster scarcely a dozen were put on their trial); you have had the Arms Act; you have had the suspension of trial by jury all during the last five years. You have authorised your police to enter the domicile of a citizen, of your fellow-subject in Ireland, at any hour of the day or night and search any part of this domicile, even the beds of the women, without warrant. You have fined the innocent for offences committed by the guilty; you have taken power to expel aliens from the country; you have revived the curfew law and the blood money of your Norman conquerors; you have gagged the Press and seized and suppressed newspapers; you have manufactured new crimes and offences and applied fresh penalties unknown to your law for these crimes and offences. All this you have done for five years and all this and much more you will have to do again.

'The provision in the Bill for excluding the Irish members from the Imperial Parliament has been very vehemently objected to and Mr Trevelyan has said that there is no half-way house between separation and the maintenance of law and order in Ireland by Imperial authority. I say, with just as much sincerity of belief and just as much experience as the right hon. gentleman, that in my judgment there is no half-way house between the concession of legislative autonomy to Ireland and the disenfranchisement of the country and her government as a Crown Colony. But I refuse to believe that these evil days must come. I am convinced there are a sufficient number of wise and just members in this House to cause it to disregard appeals made to passion and to choose the better way of founding peace and goodwill among nations; and when the numbers in the division lobby come to be told it will also be told, for the admiration of all future generations, that England and her Parliament, in this nineteenth century, were wise enough, brave enough and generous enough to close the strife of centuries and to give peace and prosperity to suffering Ireland.'

The rejection of the Bill by a full House – 343 against 313 votes – was immediately followed by the dissolution of Parliament. Thus in July, 1886, the Liberals went out in alliance with the Irish leader, only twelve months before, they had gone out *denouncing* with all his followers.

* * * * * * *

So ends the most important period of my negotiations with Gladstone. The subsequent course of them may be sketched briefly.

In July, 1886, Gladstone replied to certain suggestions of Parnell recommending perseverance with the Home Rule scheme, with the objection that he unable to carry the Gladstonian Party beyond a certain point.

There were times when Mr Gladstone became uneasy in regard to the possible consequences so many interviews with me. Also someone said once to him: 'Supposing Mrs O' Shea told Parnell you said so and so and it was more than you meant to say?' On June 15th, 1887, for example, he wrote asking with utmost politeness for a letter instead an interview.

However, on August 22 of the same year I find him from Hawarden thanking me for some gift (of game or fruit) and expressing hope of the future.

Gladstone now told me that he wished to meet Parnell in order to talk over the political situation and I suggested that a visit to Hawarden by Parnell would have a good effect politically Gladstone then asked Parnell to Hawarden to talk over the political situation, an invitation which Parnell did not answer at once, as he first wished to ascertain the tactics of the Conservative Party.

On August 30th, 1889, Mr Gladstone wrote to Parnell a most private letter, lamenting that he had not heard from him and his friends with reference to a visit to Hawarden. The fact was that since Parnell had received Gladstone's invitation the Tories had been making advances and had just proffered a Roman Catholic University for Ireland. Gladstone was right in supposing that here was the cause of Parnell's silence. He was not angry, but he threatened Parnell with the effect of this new proposal on Nonconformist and Presbyterian Liberals. In October the air was clearer, the Government's Irish University scheme had gone awry and Gladstone was jubilant. He wrote on the 16th renewing the invitation. With regard to the Home Rule Bill he was all for reserve, with regard to Parnell's action against the Times all for dispatch.

It was two months later, however (on December 19th), that Parnell, on his way to Liverpool, visited Gladstone at Hawarden. It was a short but agreeable visit and at dinner Mr Parnell sat next to Miss Gladstone. The conversation turned upon actors and acting and Miss Gladstone said, 'Who is the greatest actor you have ever seen, Mr Parnell?' 'Your father, undoubtedly!' he promptly returned, much to her delight.

As Parnell became moderate in politics Gladstone became more extreme I remember one evening in April or May, 1888, driving with Parnell to Morley's house in Elm Park Gardens where Parnell and Morley had a quiet conversation together.

I waited in the hansom cab a little way off the house for a considerable time and at last Parnell came out with an amused expression on his face. As we were driving home he said:

'We can never satisfy English politicians. They imprisoned me for causing agitation in Ireland and now they want agitation if not outrage. Morley said to me: 'The people must be made to wake up a bit; can't you do anything to stir them up? Then with a laugh: 'If they knew how easy it was for me to stir Ireland up and how confoundedly difficult I have found it to quiet her down again, they would be very careful before giving me such an invitation!' And, with the experience of the past to give force and conviction to his words, he had shown Mr Morley the extreme danger of Mr Gladstone's suggestions.

CHAPTER XXX

MR PARNELL IN DANGER — FOUNDING OF

THE NATIONAL LEAGUE

'He who for winds and clouds
Maketh a pathway free,
Through waste or hostile crowds
Can make a way for thee.' – PAUL GERHARDT.

O NE MORNING IN 1882, I saw in the morning papers a cable message announcing the death of Miss Fanny Parnell. Mr Parnell was at my house at the time, but asleep. After an all-night sitting I would never allow him to be roused until four in the afternoon, when he would have breakfast and chat with me until it was time to go to the House. On seeing the newspaper cable from America about his sister I thought it better to wake him and tell him of it, lest he should read it while I was away with my aunt. I knew that Fanny Parnell was his favourite sister and he had told me that she was the cleverest and most beautiful woman in his family. This I knew was high praise, as Willie had met Mrs Thomson – another of Parnell's sisters – and had told me that she was the most strikingly beautiful woman he had ever met.

I woke him and told him of his sister's death as gently as I could, but he was terribly shocked and I could not leave him at all that day. For a time he utterly broke down, but presently a cable arrived for him – sent on from London – saying that his sister's body was to be embalmed and brought to Ireland and his horror and indignation were extreme. He immediately wrote out a message for me to cable from London on his behalf, absolutely forbidding the embalmment of his sister's body and saying that she was to be buried in America.

The idea of death was at all times very painful to him, but that anyone should be embalmed and taken from one place to another after death was to him unspeakably awful. For this, amongst other reasons, I could not bear to have him taken to Ireland – to Glasnevin Cemetery – after his death. My desire was to have him near me and as he would have wished, to have taken care of his grave myself. But I gave way to the longing of the Ireland he had lived for and to the clamour of those who had helped to kill him. How they dealt with him alive is history now, but how they dealt with him in death is not so well known; and I give an extract from the message of a friend who had gone to see his grave a few short years after his death: 'Your husband's grave is the most desolate and neglected spot in the whole cemetery and I grieve to tell you of the painful impression it made upon me.'

I then sent over a servant, with some flowers and his report was even worse. Fragments of glass from the broken artificial placed there years before; trampled, neglected grass and little of that but weeds; and the bare untidy backings and wires of the wreaths I had been sending for the greeting of so many days marked only in the calendar of our love.

Poor Ireland – a child in her asking, a child in her receiving and so much a child in her forgetting.

When Mr Parnell first came to Eltham he told me that he had had, since his boyhood at school, a habit of sleep-walking whenever he was at all run down in health. When he was in America he used to lock the door of his room and put the key into a box with a spring lock that he had bought for the purpose. He feared he might wander about the hotel in his sleep. Also he warned me, when he first came, that he was subject to 'somnambulism', very much as a highly- strung child is and in these he would spring up panic stricken out of deep sleep and, without fully awaking, try to beat off the imaginary foe that pressed upon him. It was a species of nightmare; not apparently excited by any particular cause other than general want of tone. After a few years of careful dieting I succeeded in freeing him of these painful and most wearing attacks.

When the attacks came on I went into his room and held him until he became fully conscious, for I feared that he would hurt himself. They were followed by a profuse perspiration and deep sleep of several hours. He was terribly worried about these nightmares, but I assured him that it was only indigestion in a peculiar form. 'You really think so?' he• would reply and when I told him that they would pass off with careful dieting he was reassured and he followed my directions so implicitly as to• diet that he soon proved me right.

He became very much run down again after his sister's death, but recovered perfectly and had no recurrence of these attacks until some years after, when he suffered from a nervous breakdown brought on by overwork. Sir Henry Thompson treated him then and he quickly recovered.

Soon after I met Mr Parnell I sent to Worcester for some white roses in pots to keep in my hothouse in order to provide my exigeant lover with buttonholes. He loved white roses, he told me and would not be content with any other flower from me; nor would he wear a rose from my garden, as be said anyone could have those who asked me for them. So I had to keep a constantly blooming company of white roses in my conservatory to provide a buttonhole of ceremony on his speech days, or on other occasions when I wished him to look particularly well Sometimes we would drive out miles into the country. Keston Common was a favourite resort of ours and, as we rarely took a servant with us, we would either put up the horse I drove (Dictator, given to me by Mr Parnell) at some inn, or tie him to a tree while we wandered about or sat under the trees talking.

He would do his best to learn the names of the wild flowers he picked for me – with uncomfortably short stalks – but, beyond being at last able to name a dandelion or buttercup at sight, he did not shine in any branch of botany. 'What did you call this fine plant?' he would ask with a glimmer of fun in his eyes. 'It is not a plant you have, but a single flower branch and it is called a king-cup – picked much too short!' I would answer severely and he laughed as he tumbled his: trophies into my lap and insisted that the ferns ruthlessly dug and cut out with his pocket-knife would grow all right, in spite of their denuded roots, if I 'made them do it, in the greenhouse'!

When it was too wet to go out, or if he was not well, he used to amuse himself at home in my sitting-room practising shooting with an air-gun. He used a lighted candle for target and became so expert in putting out the light this way that it became too troublesome to light the candle so often and we substituted other targets.

Sometimes he would go to the farther end of my aunt's park, where there was a pond basin, dried up long before and many happy hours were spent there, shooting in turn, with his revolvers.

I remember on one Sunday afternoon my aunt's bailiff came down, having heard revolver shots, though the sound was deadened by the high banks. The bailiff was much perturbed by our Sunday sport, chiefly because it was Sunday. He did not dare press his opinion upon me as he knew my position in my aunt's household was impregnable, but he had always been jealous of my coming to Eltham, where he had served her for over forty years and he was now so plainly antagonistic that Mr Parnell, who did not particularly wish his presence with me talked about, rose to the occasion with the tact he could exert when he considered it worth while.

'Oh, is that you, Mr ----?' rising from an absorbed examination of his last bull's-eye. 'Mrs O' Shea was telling me when we started this match of your being such a good shot with a gun. Do have a shot with my revolver; see here, I've got a bull's-eye five times running against Mrs O' Shea's one. Now let us see what you can do.'

Mr ---- hesitated; he was a fine shot and had won prizes in his youth and was susceptible to flattery.

Mr Parnell said dryly: 'I don't suppose you have had so much practise as I lately, but ----.' The bailiff turned a wary eye on his wife, who was waiting for him at the gate of a rookery some way off and Mr Parnell smiled as he said: 'The lady will not see you', in such a gently sarcastic manner that Mr ---- was nettled and picking up the revolver shot so wildly that he missed the little target altogether.

I said: 'Mr ---- can shoot, really, Mr Parnell, as I told you, but he is nervous!' So Mr ---- went on, making shot after shot with varying success till Mrs ---- appeared on the scene dressed in her best and Sunday virtue, which was resplendent in Eltham. She gazed with pain upon Mr ----, who to appear at ease, entered into a discussion of revolver patterns with Mr Parnell. I talked cheerfully to her for a few moments and introduced Mr Parnell, which gratified her immensely and the tow went off happy, but so conscious of the enormity of having given countenance to such a desecration of the Sabbath, in Sunday shooting, that we knew we were safe from their perhaps inconvenient chatter.

Mr Parnell was always interested in cricket and I had a private pitch laid out for him at Eltham in a two acre field. As a young man he had been an enthusiast and the captain of his eleven. He never went to matches, however, after he entered Parliament.

He talked to me much about Avondale. He loved the place and was never tired of planning the alterations and improvements he meant to make in the old house when we could marry. He often went over to Ireland expressly to see how things were going there, but after 1880 he could never stay even a few days there in peace. The after-effects of the awful famine, in such terrible cases of poverty and woe as were brought to his notice the moment he arrived in his old home, made it impossible for him to remain there at all. No one man could deal charitably with all these poor people and live and as time went on Mr Parnell's visits became necessarily shorter, for the demands were so many and the poverty so great that he could not carry the burden and continue the political life necessary to their alleviation. He told me that he despaired of ever having a penny in his pocket when he took me there, as he always hoped to do.

He was very fond of the old woman he kept at Avondale in charge of the house and who attended to his few needs when he was there; and whenever he went there he would get me to go to go to Fortnum and Mason's to buy a pound of their 4s.-a-pound tea for the old dame, who much appreciated this delicious tea, though she of course stewed it into poison before drinking it.

This old servant of his had the most curious ideas on 'first aid to the injured' and when on one occasion Mr Parnell had his hand crushed in some machinery at his Arklow quarries, she dressed the injured fingers with cobwebs from the cellar walls. To my astonishment he asked for cobwebs at Eltham once, when he had cut his finger, to 'wrap it in'. My children, with delighted interest, produced cobwebs (and spiders) from the Cellar and I had the greatest difficulty in preventing a 'cure' so likely to produce blood-poisoning. He accepted the peasant lore of Ireland with the simplicity of a child and I still remember his doubtful 'Is that so?' when I told him it was most dangerous to put anything so dusty as a cobweb on an open wound. 'Susan Gaffney said cobwebs would *stop* the poison – they all do it', meaning the peasants.

On August 16th, 1882, he was presented with the freedom of the City of Dublin. He wished to avoid a public demonstration, but the Corporation insisted on making the most of the occasion.

MORRISON'S HOTEL, DUBLIN
Saturday, August 20, 1882.

MY OWN QUEENIE, – Your two letters have given me the greatest pleasure and I am so much obliged to Wifie for the trouble she has taken about the request I made to her.

The two D.'s (Dillon and Davitt) have quarrelled with me because I won't allow any further expenditure by the ladies and because I have made arrangements to make the payments myself for the future. They were in hopes of creating a party against me in the country by distributing the funds amongst their own creatures and are proportionately disappointed.

I hope to have everything settled by Tuesday evening so as to enable me to leave town then and after a week in the country propose to return to Wifie.

YOUR OWN HUSBAND

In October, 1882, was founded the National League, which was to fill the gap caused by the suppression of the Land League. A Convention had been called for the 17th of the month.

October 10, 1882

MY OWN QUEENIE, – I hope to be able to start for London on Thursday evening.

The doctor says it was an attack of dysenterical diarrhoea, but not of a severe character and very little fever. It is now quite over. He says my stomach must have been getting out of order for some time.

I hope Wifie has been taking good care of herself and that she has not been alarmed.

Her husband will go right back to her and will not return to Avondale for the shooting.

With ever so much love, my own Queenie,

YOUR LOVING HUSBAND.

Friday evening, October 14, 1882.

MY OWN DARLING WIFIE, – I have been so longing to be with you during all these dreary hours, still more dreary as they have been made by the knowledge that Wifie has been unhappy and anxious all the time. Her letters came to quite safely and were a great pleasure and I want some more.

On Tuesday or Wednesday, I forget which, I left my room for the first time and caught a slight cold, which threw me back somewhat, but I have more than regained my lost ground today and am to leave my room again tomorrow and if don't over-eat myself or catch cold again, shall go on right.

The Conference will most probably last two days, but I hope to be able to leave on Wednesday, or at latest on Thursday evening, to be with my Queenie until the end of the Session.

Do please write me a nice letter, my darling.

YOUR OWN HUSBAND.

October 17, 1882

WIFIE, – I have arrived all right and got through the first day of the Convention successfully.

You will be glad to hear that the telegrams which I missed were of no importance and I received them this morning unopened, as well as your also unopened.

With best love to my own Katie.

The Convention duly met, Parnell presiding and the National League was formed, with Home Rule and peasant proprietorship as the two main articles of its creed.

Sunday.

MY OWN DARLING WIFIE, – I have been so delighted to receive both your letters quite safely; you have no idea how much I long for a letter or a wire from you and how frightened and nervous I feel when, as sometimes happens, a whole day goes by without any news.

I was very much afraid that my little wife would not have approved of all my speech and so much relieved to find that you did not scold me.

Has there anything been done about the monument yet? I hope there will not be any hitch.

Am trying to get together a meeting of directors in Dublin for next Saturday, which I can take on my way back to you and which I trust may afford the desired relief. I have been doing a good deal of healthy and necessary work since my arrival here, out riding or driving in the open air all day long. I ride a horse called Tory, a splendid thoroughbred of my sister's, though he has now seen his best days. He goes just like an india-rubber ball. I have been very successful in that part of the business which I came over for that I have been able to attend to thus far; having already discovered several quarries on my own land, much nearer to the railway station than the one we are working on and for which we have to pay a heavy royalty. I have every confidence that one and all of them will be found suitable upon trial. Kerr is rather a duffer about anything except book-keeping. He ought to have found these out for himself long since, as I gave him the clue when leaving here last September.

My brother-in-law's funeral takes place tomorrow. I am going in a closed carriage and shall be careful not to expose myself or stand about in the churchyard.

I am certain of being able to finish up everything here so as to leave Ireland on Saturday or Sunday at the latest and shall soon have my only and best treasure in my arms again.

YOUR LOVING KING AND HUSBAND.

I shall be in Dublin on Tuesday evening and shall sleep at Morrison's that night, returning here next day.

From these quarries at Arklow Parnell supplied the Dublin Corporation with 'setts' for many of the streets in Dublin. These setts (granite, pavement kerbing) were not turned out quickly enough by his men at first, so he tried the experiment of giving the men a share in the profits and this he found answered well in keeping the supply up to the demand of the corporation.

Some of the polished granite work turned out by his men was beautiful and a heavy granite garden vase and a Celtic cross appeared in the London (Irish) Exhibition and also in the Cork Exhibition.

1882-83 was a very anxious time for me and the nervous tension caused by the violence in the political world and the continual threatenings of violence, intrigue and physical force, made privately to Parnell, against him and others, was so great that, by the end of '83, if I had not had my lover's health to care for I should myself have broken down altogether. As it was, there were days when the slightest sound or movement was an agony to me in the throes of neuralgia brought on by the overstrain of the nerves. But for his sake I concealed my misery of pain, as well as I could and in so doing won back a measure of health for myself, which would perhaps have been lost to me had I been able to give to my 'nerves'.

During this time I attended the sittings of the House as often as I was able, going up to town as soon as I could leave my aunt for the night, so that I might hear Parnell if he spoke and in any case drive home with him. We always drove home in a hansom cab, as we both loved the cool of the night or of the early morning air.

During these anxious days I did not let Parnell have one-half the threatening and other worrying letters he received. He brought me his letters and parcels from the House and from a London address he had, to be sorted out. I gave him those for his secretary's answering, any personal ones I thought he would wish to see and 'just as many 'threats' as I thought would make him a little careful of himself, for my sake. The bulk, of the 'warnings', threats of murder and invitations to murder I kept to myself, fearing that he would worry himself on my account and object to my continual 'shadowing' of him, which I considered his chief protection. He always carried a revolver in his pocket during this time and insisted on my being similarly provided when I drove home with him at night.

These precautions may appear fantastic in these later sober times, but they were very necessary during that time of lawlessness and unrest in Ireland, when the prophecy made by Parnell to me ere he finally decided to leave Kilmainham on the Treaty had become fact: 'If I turn to the Government I turn away from them – and then?'

The force of his personality was carrying him through the seething of the baffled hatred he would not use, but not without a danger so real and so acute that many a time I was tempted to throw his honour to the winds and implore from the Government the protection he would have died rather than ask for himself. But I held on to the end till the sheer force of his dauntless courage and proud will broke down the secret intrigue of spleen that, held by him back from England's governance, would have revenged itself upon the holding hand, had it dared.

There was a lonely part of the road between London and Eltham after going through Lee, over a common where, to the right, was a deep ditch and, beyond, the land of (the late) Mr Blenkiorn, breeder of racehorses. There were no houses near in those days and on moonlight nights we could see a longly way on each side of a rather desolate bit of country. The moon which gave light also gave shadows and more than once from some way off we saw the shadow of a man running behind the hedge on the way we had to pass. I always took the side of the hansom near the park, as I thought it would conceal to some degree the fact of Parnell's being there. I knew, too, that the fact of my being a woman was still some little protection, but I took the precaution of telling the driver to drive quickly and not stop for anyone at any lonely point in the road. Once, to my horror, when we were nearly over the common, I saw a man rise from the ditch and the glint of steel in the moonlight. The man driving saw it, too and, with a lurch threw us forward in the cab, he lashed his horse into a gallop. I could just see that the man threw up his arms as he staggered backwards into the ditch and a shot rang out; but nothing dreadful had happened after all. The man had obviously slipped as he sprang up the bank and, j throwing up his arms to recover his balance, his pistol had gone off – for neither of ours had been discharged. So this exciting drive had no more serious consequences than the rather heavy price of the cabman's putting up in the village till day brought him renewed confidence in the safety of the London road.

Sometimes after a late sitting Parnell and I would get some coffee at the early stalls for workmen on the way from London. In the early morning half-light, when the day was just beginning to break, we loved to watch drowsy London rubbing the sleep from her eyes, hastening her labouring sons upon their way to ease the later waking of their luxurious brothers. Parnell was always interested in manual labourers; he loved to watch them at work and he liked to talk to them of their work and of their homes. A man with a hammer or a pick-axe was almost an irresistible attraction to him and he would often get me to stand and watch the men engaged on a road or harbour work.

About this time (it was in 1883) Mr (afterwards Sir) Howard Vincent, head of the Detective Department of Scotland Yard, sent a note to the House of Commons asking Parnell to see him for a few minutes, as he had an important communication to make to him. Parnell was just going to speak, so he brought me the note up to the Ladies' Gallery and, hastily putting it into my hand, said: 'See to this for me.'

It was a morning sitting and I hurried off to Scotland Yard hoping to get back in time to hear Parnell speak and yet anxious to hear what the note meant. I was shown into Sir

Howard. Vincent's private room directly I arrived and he expressed great pleasure, as well as great surprise, at seeing me. I showed him his note to Parnell and asked him to what it referred. He answered that the 'officials' all considered the matter serious and that the Government were prepared to give Mr Parnell protection if he wished it.

I told him that Mr Parnell would, I was sure, not like that at all and, after a long conversation of no particular definiteness, Sir Howard said: 'I do think you believe in this particular threat against Mr Parnell, do you, Mrs O' Shea?'

I replied: 'Well, it does seem rather like a hoax to me. Would you mind letting me see the 'letter of warning'? He laughed and said: 'Not at all, but I've torn it up and flung it into the waste-paper basket.'

I promptly picked up the basket in question and turned it over on his table, saying: 'Let us piece it together.' He pretended to help me for a few moments, as I neatly put together various interesting documents and then, with a deprecating smile, swept them all together, saying: 'It is your game, Mrs O' Shea; you are too clever. Why didn't you send Mr Parnell round?' and we parted with laughing expressions of goodwill and amusement on his part that we had not been taken in.

The Government, of course, were bent on forcing protection on Parnell as a convenience to themselves and a means of ascertaining the extent of his influence over the Invincibles. The Government did not trust Parnell and they wished to frighten him into care of himself and thus weaken the trust of the Irish in him.

In 1882 or 1883, when Parnell and I were waiting at Brighton station to catch the train to London, we noticed that there was much crowding round the bookstall placards and much excitement among buyers of newspapers. Parnell did not wish to be recognised, as he was supposed at that time to be in Ireland; but hearing Gladstone's name mentioned by a passer-by, our curiosity got the better of our caution and we went to get a paper. Parnell, being so tall a man, could see over the heads of the crowd and reading the placard, turned back without getting a paper to tell me that the excitement was over the report of 'the assassination of Mr Parnell.' I then asked him to get into the train so that we should run no risk of his being known and managed to get through the crowd to buy a paper myself. How the repost arose we never knew, but at that time, when every post brought Parnell some threat of violence and my nerves were jarred and tense with daily fear for him, it took all my fortitude to answer his smile and joke at the unfounded report which left me sick and shaken.

CHAPTER XXXI

A WINTER OF MEMORIES

'Feeling is deep and still and the word that floats on the surface
Is as the tossing buoy, that betrays where the anchor is hidden.'
— LONGFELLOW

M R FORSTER MADE HIS NOTORIOUS attack upon Mr Parnell in February, 1883, accusing him of encouraging and conniving at murder, outrage and treachery. On his return home Parnell showed, as he would not deign to show in the House, a fierce joy in the false move of his enemies and the scorn and contempt of the lack of control which could lead a politician of Forster's experience into such a *faux pas* as this personal attack on him. Here, then, he had what he wanted; in this attack was the repudiation of those charges, made by the extremists' in Ireland and America, of pandering to the Government – made by them ever since he left Kilmainham on the Treaty – here was another cord to bind the Nationalist forces together without in any way repudiating that Treaty. Here was a fresh weapon given into his hand by an ex-Government official who could not govern his personal spleen by political intelligence.

'No', he said to me, when I asked him if he did not mean to answer Forster at all, 'I shall not answer. I shall let him hang himself with his own rope'.

But the Party would not have this and urged him so strongly that he did – not answer – but show his contempt of the whole thing and of the English politicians who had played their hand so badly. He said me before he started for the House: 'By the judgement of the Irish people only do I and will I stand or fall' and this he repeated in the House.

The astonishment of the House was unbounded. It had been prepared for anything but this scornful repudiation of the right of the English to judge him – for a downright denial of the charges made, for a skilful fencing with the arguments. The speech of Parnell was a challenge to war. Impassive as ever, betraying no slightest sign of emotion, he tore up the accusations and threw them scornfully in the face of his accuser.

'I assure the House', he said, 'that it is not my belief that anything I can say at this time will have the slightest effect on the public opinion of this House or upon the public opinion of the country. I have been accustomed during my political life to rely upon the public opinion of those whom I have desired to help and with whose aid I have worked for the cause of prosperity and freedom in Ireland and the utmost I desire to do in the very few words I shall address to the House is to make my position clear to the Irish people at home and abroad.

'I say it is impossible to stem the torrent of prejudice that has arisen out of the events of the past few days. I regret that the officials charged with the administration of this Act are unfit for their posts. I am sure the right hon. gentleman, the present Chief Secretary to the Lord Lieutenant, must admit that to the fullest extent and when he looks round on the right hon. member for Bradford, he must say: 'Why am I here while he is there?' Why was he (Mr Forster) deposed, he – the right hon. gentleman who has acquired experience in the administration of Ireland – who, according to his own account, knew everything, although he was almost invariably wrong? Why was he deposed and the right hon. gentleman (Mr Trevelyan), a 'prentice, although a very willing hand, put in his position? I feel that the Chief Secretary to the Lord Lieutenant must say with the Scriptures, 'I am not worthy to unloose his shoe latchet'. It would be far better to have the Act administered by the seasoned politician now in disgrace and retirement. Call him back to his post; send him to help Lord Spencer in the congenial work of the gallows in Ireland. Send him back to look after the secret inquisitions in Dublin Castle. Send him to distribute the taxes which an unfortunate and starving peasantry have to pay for crimes not committed by themselves. All this would be congenial work for the right hon. gentleman. We invite you to man your ranks and to send your ablest and best men to push forward the task of misgoverning and oppressing Ireland. For my part I am confident as to the future of Ireland. Although the horizon may be clouded, I believe our people will survive the present oppression, as they have survived many and worse misfortunes and although our progress may be slow, it will be sure. The time will come when this House and the people of this country will admit, once again, that they have been deceived and that they have been cheered by those who ought to be ashamed of themselves; that they have been led astray as to the right mode of governing a noble, a brave, a generous and an impulsive people; that they will reject their present leaders, who are conducting them into the terrible courses into which the Government appear determined to lead Ireland. I believe they will reject these guides and leaders with as much determination and just as much relief, as they rejected the services of the right hon. gentleman the member for Bradford.'

Some time afterwards, in an interview I had with him, Mr Gladstone referred to this declaration of Parnell's – that he would stand or fall only by the judgement of the Irish people.

'You know Mr Parnell's inmost feelings better than others; does this truly represent his mind, Mrs O' Shea?'

I answered, as I could truly do: 'Yes, Mr Gladstone, that is his only and absolute ideal. I may say Ireland's is the only voice he regards as having any authority over him in the whole world.'

'Yet Parnell is so much an Englishman in his coldness and reserve?'

'He is a paradox, Mr Gladstone, the enigma of genius herself, a volcano capped with snow. Englishman himself, at least he is descended from Englishmen, he hates England and the English and does not understand them; he loves Ireland and her people through and through, understands them absolutely and is in nature as apart and aloof from the Irish nature as you are yourself.'

The hard, flint-like eyes softened a little in the eagle face as the G.O.M. answered, with a little sigh: 'I have much sympathy with his ambitions for Ireland, Mrs O' Shea. His is a curious personality; you are right, I think – yes, a paradox indeed, but a wonderful man!'

At the end of June, 1883, Parnell went over to conduct Mr Healy's election at Monaghan (an Ulster stronghold), for which division he was returned a month after he had quitted Richmond Prison.

He immediately afterwards (on July 4th) attended the Cork banquet given in his honour. He wrote the following letter to me to allay the fears I had expressed in regard to certain political actions which he here repudiates and which had reached my ears from other sources:–

MORRISON'S HOTEL, DUBLIN,
Tuesday night.

When I received your note I at once determined to go over to you tomorrow morning and to give up my engagement to speak at the Cork banquet tomorrow night, as I knew my own was very much troubled about something and felt sure that I could comfort and reassure her. I have since been besieged the whole evening by entreaties and threats not to throw over Cork and it has been represented to me and with truth, that half the result of the Monaghan victory will be lost if I leave Cork to the Whigs and my enemies. I have been very much perplexed and dragged in different ways, but have at this hour (2 a.m.) made up my mind to ask my own Wifie to suspend her judgment for another twenty-four hours about whatever is tormenting her, to place some little confidence in her husband's honour and fidelity for that short time and to believe that he now swears to her and that he will same oath to her on Thursday evening, that whatever statement has been made about him which is calculated to lower him in wife's opinion in the slightest degree is a foul lie.

I can ask this of my own Wifie and that she will not withdraw her confidence and love from her own husband until he can return and defend himself.

I shall leave for Cork tomorrow morning's train at nine o' clock, speak at banquet and return by night mail the same day to Dublin and be in time to leave Dublin by mail train for London on Thursday morning. Let me know at Palace Chambers where I shall see you on Thursday evening.

Trust your husband and do not credit any slander of him.

AVONDALE RATHDRUM,
2 a.m., July 4, 1883.

MY DEAR MRS O' SHEA, – I seize a vacant moment to write you a few words, as it does not look as if Irish affairs would permit me to see you for some time longer. Perhaps even a week or ten days may pass by before I can see Eltham again. I also wish you to forward enclosed to Captain O' Shea, as I have not his address.

I have had several conversations with Fr. White, who is a very superior man and has impressed me very much.

I intend to make it my first business to look up West Clare and trust that Captain O' Shea may be able to meet me there.

With best regards, yours always sincerely,
C.S. PARNELL.

MORRISON'S HOTEL, DUBLIN,
Tuesday.

MY DEAREST WIFIE, – Your letters received and always give me the greatest happiness to read.

Please continue writing. I will make arrangements to have them kept out of sight here.

Shall see Captain O' Shea Wednesday evening or Thursday morning and do what I can. I fear his position in Clare is irretrievable.

With best love,
YOUR HUSBAND.

AVONDALE,

MY DEAR MRS O' SHEA, – Will you kindly direct, enclose and post enclosed.
   Many thanks for your letter, also for two from Captain O' Shea, which I will reply to shortly.
   Believe me, in haste, yours very truly,
   CHAS. S. PARNELL

Just before Christmas in 1883 I took a furnished house in Brighton for three months for my children. I had arranged to take a house in Second Avenue, which both Parnell and I liked, but Willie came down insisted on my taking a house facing the sea in Medina Terrace; so I (with difficulty) got out of my former agreement and certainly the house Willie chose was very much pleasanter, owing to its close proximity to the sea.

Willie undertook to stay here to be with the children while I went back to my aunt (coming myself to Brighton for one or two days in the week).

Willie asked Parnell to come and stay. He did so and Willie and he discussed the Local Government Bill at all hours, as Parnell wished to find out what the views of Mr Chamberlain and the Tories were – better ascertainable by Willie than others.

I went back to my aunt for Christmas Eve. It was bitterly cold and as the old lady never cared for festivities, she was soon glad to shut herself up in her warm house and 'forget in slumber the foolish junketings I permit in my domestics, my love.'

There was snow that Christmas, very deep at Eltham; and Parnell, who had joined me there, walked round the snowy paths of my aunt's place with me in the moonlight. Now and then he moved with me into the shadow of the trees as a few lads and men, with the inevitable cornet and trombone of a village 'band', plunged through the drifts on their short cut to the old house. There they sang Christmas carols to their hearts' content, knowing they were earning their yearly bonus, to be presented with a polite message of her 'distaste' for carol singing by 'Mrs Ben's' (as she was affectionately called in the village) man-servant the next morning.

Parnell and I enjoyed that pacing up and down the wide terrace in the snowy moonlight. The snow had drifted up against the old urns and the long, low balustrade that divided the north and south lawns; and the great shadows of the beech trees looked unfamiliar and mysterious – pierced here and there, where the blanket covering of snow had dropped off, but the cold glitter of moonlight on the whiteness.

Right away to the south lay the 'Chase', leading away to Chislehurst, wide, cold and lonely in the moonlight and I told Parnell that the cloud shadows that flitted over the glistening whiteness were the phantoms of the hunters of King John's time, who used to hunt over this ground, renewing their sport in the moonlight.

Parnell loved to hear these little imaginations and I loved to tell them to him for the sake of seeing the grave smile come and of hearing the naive 'Is that so?' of his appreciation.

We walked up and down in the moonlight till the carols died away and we heard the church clocks strike twelve. Then we stood together to listen to the Christmas bells sound clear and sharp from many villages on the frosty air, while Parnell again spoke to me of his belief that the soul after death resumed life in the planet under whose influence it was born. He spoke of his belief in a personal destiny and fate, against which it was useless for mortals to contend or fight and how he believed that certain souls had to meet and become one, till in death the second planet life parted them until the sheer longing for one another brought them together again in after ages. (On the day of Parnell's death, October 6, 1891, a new planet was discovered.)

I said, 'But it seems so lonely like that!' and he answered, 'It is lonely; that is why I am so afraid always of death and why I hope with every bit of me that we shall die together.'

The next day I went to Brighton to see the children for Christmas and in the New Year

Willie went to Ireland, returning to Brighton to stay with the children for a short time before they came home in February and he went to Lisbon.

The following telegrams and letters show the development of affairs during the course of this year:—

(Telegrams.)

Feb. 29, 1884
(Handed in at the House of Commons Office)
From Parnell.
To Mrs O' Shea, Eltham, Kent.

Thanks. Happy to accept your invitation to dinner this evening for seven o' clock.

May 30, 1884.
From Parnell, Avondale
To Mrs O' Shea, Eltham

Captain and I arrived safely
(Willie went to stay at Avondale for a couple of days. – K. P.)

May 31, 1884.
(Rathdrum Office.)
From Parnell to Mrs O' Shea

Captain leaves here tomorrow (Sunday) morning and leaves Kingstown tomorrow evening.

Dublin
Sept. 10.

Willie is looking very well indeed, in fact much better than I have ever seen him before.
I hope soon to be through pressing business here and in country and to be able to leave on Saturday
C.S.P.

Friday, Oct. 28, 1884.

MY DEAR MRS O' SHEA, – I shall be at Dover for a few days longer and afterwards propose visiting the Netherlands and returning through Paris. If I thought that Captain O' Shea would soon be in England I should wait for him, but if not should take my chance of meeting him in Paris on my return.

My stay in the Netherlands will not exceed three days, but I shall remain in Paris for at least a similar period. I say 'the Netherlands' because I don't yet know whether I shall have to go to Holland or Belgium or both. Kindly let me have a line or wire to former address.

Always yours,
CHAS. S. PARNELL.

I was ill at the time the following letters were written and Captain O' Shea was coming to Eltham a good deal.

ELTHAM, 1884.

Should have come sooner, but could not get away. There was an explosion of a bomb at the Home Office just before I left; it blew down a large piece of the front wall and did a great deal of damage, they say.

I will not go near the hotel tonight if I see a crowd there and will leave early in the morning and come down here to breakfast.

ELTHAM
Friday, 4 p.m.

I came down here late last night and was immensely relieved to hear that you were better.

I slept very comfortably here last night and had an excellent breakfast this morning, which Phyllis brought me.

Am now going up to London to settle the report of Labourers' Committee, which had not time to attend to yesterday and hope to be back about eleven o'clock.

Yours,
C.S.P.

ELTHAM

Do you think I had best wait here or go up to London and wait for a telegram from you?

We finished our committee yesterday, so if he[16] goes early, I could return perhaps early enough to see you this evening for a few minutes.

I felt very much relieved by your letter last night. However, it is evident you must take great care.

If you think I had best not wait, will you telegraph? Otherwise see me later, when I will wait.

Yours

Eltham

Many thanks for kind note.

I am going to London now and hope to return reasonably early, as the debate is not likely to last long. I do not feel the cold at all.

There ought to be no difficulty in my seeing you tomorrow and I will manage it.

I do not like your having a headache and you must really take care of yourself and not get up too soon.

Yours always.

I am obliged to go up early to attend Labourers' Committee, which meets at eleven today to consider its final report. Please send me telegram to House if you can, as I ought to be able to return early this evening.

Phyllis is looking after me first rate.

Yours.

Parnell was always unselfish and most considerate when I was ill and once when I was very weak after an illness of some duration he returned home to Eltham in broad daylight in a hansom-cab, triumphantly supporting one end of a large couch, the other end of which spread its upholstered length over the roof. This invalid's chair he, with the help of my maids, arranged in my sitting-room, adjusting its complicated 'rests' with earnest abstraction, after which he led the procession up to my room and in spite of my amused protests carried me down and placed me on the couch amid cushions and shawls and spent a happy evening in 'watching me' as I lay comfortably on my new possession.

In 1884 we ran down to Hastings for a few days in the middle of the Session, when my aunt's old friend came to stay with her and gave me freedom. Parnell delighted in these sudden 'run-away' visits to the sea when the House was in full swing of business and said they braced and freshened him up more than anything else could do. We stayed at the Queen's Hotel and Parnell revelled in the sudden freedom from politics – casting all thought and care from him as we walked by the sea and gave ourselves up to enjoyment of the fresh salt air.

He was hugely pleased, on going into a shop in Robertson Street for notepaper, to find some embossed with the monogram 'K.P.' in blue and gold. He declared it was a good omen and bought me more of it than I could use for many years. He also bought me a little red diary, after long and earnest efforts in selection. Red he did not like much, as he said it was the sanguinary hue of English oppression; but diaries can apparently only be bound in red, green or purple and purple was the colour of sorrow and green the most painful expression of all ill-luck!

This diary was to make up to me for my natural indignation at, nearly, his first act on returning to me from some absence. He had gone over to fire and caught sight of my diary, bound in green that I had inadvertently left on the mantelpiece. With an exclamation of horror he had thrown it into the fire, holding me back from the rescue I struggled to attempt and only replying to my indignant protests that he was sorry if the contents were really so valuable as I said, but anything between green cover was better burnt!

In these short visits to the seaside we always looked about for a house that Parnell could buy later on, but as he always kept a regretful eye upon Brighton, where it was inexpedient that we should be seen much together, we never really settled on one for purchase, though he rented one in Eastbourne with that idea, only to discover that a brother of his was living there. When we had a few hours to spare we had very happy times hunting round Sussex in the neighbourhood of Brighton (Brighton air did him so much good), hoping to find a suitable country house, but the train service was always a difficulty, except in the town itself.

CHAPTER XXXII

HORSES AND DOGS

Amid all the forms of life that surround us, not one,
excepting the dog, has made an alliance with us.'
− MAURICE MAETERLINCK

IN 1885 I HAD A new room built on to my house at Eltham, adjoining my sitting-room and leading into the greenhouse and thence to the garden. Parnell and I took the greatest interest in the building this room; he superintended every detail, saw that the cement was laid to the proper depth under the flooring and sent to Avondale for sufficient sweet-chestnut wood to have the room panelled half-way up and to make beautiful, heavy double-doors, window settings and the mantelpiece and fittings. It was a very comfortable and warm room when finished and, to celebrate its completion − it was to be Parnell's own study and workroom − I photographed him in it, sitting in his own special easy chair, surrounded by his assaying paraphernalia and holding his pestle and mortar. This was published years ago without permission or acknowledgement by one or other of two persons to whom I had given it, after my husband's death, as a very private and special memento of him. It hurt me much when I first knew of it − but people do these things.

Early in 1885 Parnell bought a new horse in Ireland which he arranged to bring to England and subsequently brought others over. The two letters which follow refer to these matters and were written to me in case the horses should be noticed arriving in Eltham and the fact reported to Captain O' Shea.

AVONDALE,
January 14, 1885.

MY OWN QUEENIE − A word to say that your promised letter has not yet reached me and I suppose it may turn up tomorrow. The parcel came safely to Dublin and the hamper here. Mary and I unpacked it with fear and trembling, lest there should have been no tea and sugar, as I had forgotten to say anything to you about them, but they were all right.

The new horse is very quiet and a very fine one; strong and short legs, with plenty of bone, a splendid fore-quarter and a good turn of speed. I suppose I may bring him back with me. The telegram

I sent you on Day of Convention was found late at night, posted in a letter box and was returned to bearer, who never said anything to me about it, otherwise you would have heard result about six o' clock.

With best love to my little wife,

YOUR KING.

MORRISONS HOTEL, DUBLIN.

February 3, 1885.

MY DEAR MRS O' SHEA, – I have sent two horses to London today (Euston) and should feel very much obliged if you would allow them to stand in your stables for a few days, until I can make other arrangements.

They will reach Euston about 1 p.m. tomorrow. Could you find two careful men to meet them? One saddle is gone with the horses, so another saddle would be necessary. They should be walked carefully through London, as one of them specially is very shy and unused to town.

I am going over to Liverpool tonight. I enclose order for the horses.

Yours very truly,

CHAS. S. PARNELL.

Parnell rented some stables fairly near my house for his horses and took much interest in their welfare. He was not a man who had very much knowledge of horses, but he was a fine horseman and on his hunter President, a beautiful horse of sixteen hands and a weight-carrier, he looked remarkably well. He took a scientific interest in the shoeing of the horses and to the great annoyance of his grooms, would constantly try new methods of shoeing in order to deaden the 'jar' of the contact of the road. This trial of new methods proved a boon to my horse Dictator – given me by Parnell – for the tenderness of his feet was completely cured when Parnell, dead against the conservative ideas of my stableman, insisted on his having leathers inserted between Dictator's foot and shoe.

This horse Dictator was a great pleasure to us, though he pulled rather badly. He was very fast and extraordinarily sure-footed, keeping his feet in the worst frost, even when driven on the slippery London paving in hard night frosts. He would trot away to London in much less time than Parnell could get there by any other means. Parnell did not drive well, leaving the reins slack upon the horse's back, so that he had no control over it in any emergency. My nervousness in this was so great that he very good-naturedly left all the driving to me, saying: 'Well, that's how the jarveys drive in Ireland!' in answer to my plaintive, 'I've never seen anyone drive like that.'

President was a very solid horse, in mind as well as in body and once when Parnell had ridden him up to New Cross in a frost President sat down violently and was so impressed with the safety of his position that he refused to get up again until Parnell – who was of immense muscular strength – with the help of a couple of stalwart policemen, literally lifted him to his feet.

Parnell then went into an adjacent saddler's shop to buy a 'rubber' to give President a rub down and, finding a rather original make of pocket-book on the counter with beautifully-sewn leather covers, became so immersed in the selection of one for me that at length an irate policeman looked in to order him to remove his horse at once, as it was causing 'an obstruction' Parnell, recalled to the problem of how to get President and himself to Westminster Bridge, where his servant was waiting to take the horse, proceeded to rub him down while considering the matter, thereby delighting the crowd of onlookers.

The policeman besought him to "get on the 'orse, sir and ride hoff", before the whole street got "'eld hup", but Parnell gently declined, as he knew that President had now no chance of keeping his feet on the ice-coated pavement. After fully considering the matter he found the chief thing was to get himself of the crowd as quickly as possible and, slipping a little comfort into the constable's hand, he ordered him to put the horse up at the nearest stables and drove off, ignoring all queries and protests.

He sent me a telegram from the House to assure me of his safe arrival, but forgot all about his waiting servant, who, after some hours, not daring to return home, telegraphed to me to know what he was to do, as his master had not arrived. The whole thing amused Parnell intensely, but unfortunately he had given the policeman the name of Prescott and, in absence of mind, sent his groom the next day to find and bring back the horse of 'Mr Stewart.' It was a most expensive trial of President's utility. The pocket-book I still use daily and prize very highly; it is as perfect, though much worn, as when he bought it, some twenty-six years ago.

After my old collie Elfie died, Parnell offered to get me another dog and, as I wanted an Irish wolf-hound, he and I went to see one that was advertised for sale. It was a magnificent animal, but we had much doubt as to its true breed and decided that Mr Parnell should not buy it.

He then suggested bringing me an Irish setter the next time he went to Ireland and, as the idea pleased me, he brought a half-grown setter given him by Mr Corbett, mp, who said this dog, Grouse, was the very best he had ever had. Grouse became at once the constant companion and pleasure of his master and myself. He was a beautiful dog and most faithful and affectionate. Mr Parnell would tease him by pretending to be jealous when Grouse lay at my feet with his head on my foot and when the dog rose with the dignity that always characterised him and went over to Parnell, resting his head on his knee and assuring him of his absolute devotion, I would in my turn despair having no dog to love me.

After a few moments of this game poor Grouse would sit exactly between us, looking from one to the other and whining at the impossibility of pleasing us both at once. Then Parnell would move to my side on the sofa so that Grouse could rest his chin on our clasped hands, to his great contentment. The dog always slept in Parnell's room and, in his last illness, when the doctors wished to have Grouse removed, Parnell would not allow it.

Mr Corbett was sad when he heard that Grouse had become a lady's pet as the old sportsman considered it a sin to 'spoil' a gun dog; but I think that if he had known the pleasure Grouse gave 'the Chief' he would have been glad that the dog should have exchanged the Wicklow mountains for the hated Saxon's home. Parnell took Grouse for the grouse-shooting one season and telegraphed to me that he had done very well, but he soon brought him back to me.

Another dog that Parnell brought home to me from Ireland was a mongrel Irish terrier that he had found wandering in the streets of Killaloe. He had been dreadfully savaged and was quite savage when handed over to me at Brighton with muzzle and chain on, but with kindness and good feeding he soon became as devoted to us as Grouse was and with him used thoroughly enjoy following Parnell when he rode over the Downs for his daily exercise.

After we went to Brighton Parnell would give the dogs a swim in the sea every day and Grouse's strong swimming was a great delight to his master. Pincher, the terrier, was the cause of much anxiety as he used to swim right out to sea – so far that we lost sight of his dark little head – and Parnell had very often to get a boat out and fetch the exhausted little beast back. This little dog lived for many years after his death (Grouse only two years), but he would never allow another man to touch him without trying to bite him. He was fond of Parnell but always on guard with other men, though quite good-tempered with women. Parnell used to say that Pincher must have been so badly treated by some man that he had learned distrust of all males. Many a time he came home from his rides with rueful amusement at the exaggerated value placed upon their legs by shepherds or labourers he had met on the Downs who had been bitten by Pincher with a careless indiscrimination that at last earned him a muzzle.

Parnell also brought to Eltham a very old setter, Ranger. He had been a splendid dog and now his limbs were too feeble to follow his faithful heart in his master's sport. So Mr Parnell took pity on him, asked Mr Corbett to let him have the dog for a lad who would care for his old age and Ranger came to us, spending the evening of his life in basking on the sunny lawn at Eltham, wagging a dignified tail of appreciation and greeting to those of us he met on his stiff walks about the place or dreaming his doggie dreams of the sport of the past, happy and cared for till he died.

* * * * * * *

The following letter was sent to *United Ireland* on April 11th, 1885, in regard to the proposed visit of the Prince of Wales to Ireland:–

You ask for my views regarding the visit of the Prince of Wales. In reply, I desire to say that if the usages of the Constitution existed in Ireland as they do in England there would, to my judgment, be no inconsistency in those who believe in the limited monarchy as the best form of government taking a suitable part in the reception of the Prince. But in view of the fact that the Constitution has never been administered in Ireland according to its spirit and precedents, that the Crown as wielded by Earl Spencer other Viceroys is despotic and unlimited to the last degree and that in its present instance the Royal personage is to be used by two English political parties in Ireland for the purpose of injuring and insulting the Irish Nationalist Party and of impeding if possible, their work, I fail to see upon what ground it can be claimed from any lover of constitutional government under a limited monarchy that the Prince is entitled to a reception from the independent and patriotic people of Ireland or to any recognition save from the garrison of officials and landowners and place-hunters who fatten upon the poverty and misfortunes of the country. Let me suggest a parallel. Would it be tolerated in England for a moment if the government, for their own party purposes, on the eve of a General Election, were, to use the Prince of Wales as an electioneering agent in any section of the country and were to send him upon a Royal progress in order to embarrass their political opponents? The breach of constitutional priviledge becomes still graver when we consider that it is the march of a nation which is now sought to be impeded – the fruition of a long struggle and of many sacrifices which the adventitious aid of this Royal visit is enlisted to injure. I have, however, every confidence that our people, having been suitably fore-warned, will not allow their hospitable nature and cordial disposition to carry them into any attitude which might betaken as one of condonation for the past or satisfaction for the present state of affairs.
CHARLES S. PARNELL.

This letter was written at Eltham and there was a laughing battle between us over the writing of it. I threatened to make him hang out 'Union Jacks' from every window of Avondale if he made things unpleasant for the Prince and he, in pretended horror, wrote the above and tossed it to me for the alterations, (which I, of course, did not make) that my 'English prejudices' demanded. But he seriously believed that this visit of the Prince to Ireland was timed by the advisers of his Royal Highness singular and malicious advertence to the state of the political situation and he commented most strongly upon the poverty of imagination and chivalry of great country such as England who could find no better use for her Prince than that of an electioneering agent

CHAPTER XXXII

CAPTAIN O' SHEA'S

PARLIAMENTARY DIFFICULTIES

'Anfanck bedenck das Ende' – GERMAN PROVERB.

CAPTAIN O' SHEA HAD MADE himself so thoroughly unpopular in the Irish party that when, in 1885, he desired their co-operation on his seeking re-election for County Clare none but Parnell was ready to help Him. From his first entry into the House, he had refused to sit with the body of the Irish Party and from his vantage point of the Ministerial benches kept up an undercurrent of sneering comment, or, still more galling, an appearance of deprecating amusement at the mannerisms, accents or garments of his colleagues, which was more irritating to them from its intangible air of tolerance.

With his own set in and out of the House, Willie was very popular. He was witty and his wit was a little cruel; a raconteur, his stories lost nothing in the telling and as a diner out he was much sought after. But his set did not include the then Irish Party. To Willie it would have been sacrilege to himself not to be at all times perfectly dressed and to dine out of evening clothes as bewildering as to dine in them would have been to the majority of those on the Irish benches.

To point out to Willie that most of these men were giving their services to their country at considerable loss to themselves and that more than one had been singled out and invited to enter the lists by Parnell solely because of some outstanding merit of cleverness, was to provoke the languid rejoinder that he could 'rejoice in, but could not sit with, unvarnished genius.'

Willie's intimacy with Mr Chamberlain was also a considerable factor against his position with the party and his persistent voicing of Mr Chamberlain's opinions provoked considerable distrust. 'Listen him then, with his "Chamberlain and I" and will tell me how much is "Chamberlain" and how much "I" in that cabal?' was how one of them voiced the discontent.

To give an instance of the feeling of some of the Irish members I may tell of one incident that certainly had its funny side also. Parnell came home one night, or rather early morning, while Willie was still member for Clare. After his supper and while placidly lighting a cigar, he observed with a slight smile, 'A man waiting in the Lobby tonight for Willie – to kill him.' 'To do what?', I exclaimed with horror. 'To kill him; it's alright; don't get excited! – he was much too drunk to be able to kill anyone; but I wish Willie would not annoy them all so much. From what I could make out Willie smiled at his pronunciation of "Misther Spaker, Sorr." Willie's smile is a bit of twister sometimes!'

And now Willie was keenly anxious to be returned again for Clare and was making it known to all that he did not intend to give the party pledge again.

I was anxious that Willie should remain in Parliament. Politics were a great interest to him and gave him little time to come down to Eltham. When he did so, the perpetual watchfulness and diplomacy I had to observe were extremely irksome to me. Years of neglect, varied by quarrels, had killed my love for him long before I met Parnell and since the February of 1882 I could not bear to be near him.

* * * * * * *

AVONDALE, RATHDRUM,
October 23, 1885.
MY DEAR MRS O' SHEA – Will you kindly enclose in envelope and direct and post enclosed?

The weather here has been very wet and cold, but I hope to get away soon and see you shortly on my return to London.

.Kind Regards to all.

Yours very truly, in haste,

CHAS. S. PARNELL.

The enclosure was the following private letter to me, sent thus to allay suspicion if they were seen at Eltham.

AVONDALE, RATHDRUM,
October 28, 1885.
MY OWN LITTLE WIFIE, – He (Captain O' Shea) arrived here this morning and left for the North, where he is to see one of the leaders and ascertain whether they will let him in. He then wants me to see Lord Richard Grosvenor, but I would much prefer not doing so, as it would probably very much come out.

If the Old Man (Gladstone) agrees to proposition the best plan will be for you to write and tell Willie that it is all right, so as to get me out of seeing Lord R.

I suppose you have been advised as to nature of proposition, so I need not detail it here.

When I arrived at Euston I found him (Captain O' Shea) on the platform before me, also T P and we all the went over together I asked the latter about the former's chances and he was positive he had none, pledge or not. O' Kelly on my arrival was of the same opinion and advised me strongly to let him go North or else make some provision for him outside politics. He called to see me next morning and told me he considered his chances very had, also that nothing would induce him to take pledge. I said very little and while we were talking over the situation O' Shea tapped at door. He said he would like consult O' K., so invited him in. The latter strongly advised him not to stand and while conversation was proceeding he informed O'K. he would not take pledge, when O'K. told him at once that it was not in the power of mortal man to get him in for any National constituency without it and that even I could not do it. He then decided to give it up and it was arranged he should stand for a constituency in the North which we do not intend to contest and where he will have a chance. The rest you know.

I hope to be able to cross Sunday, if not obliged to attend Galway Convention Monday, where the 'ring' is endeavouring to put in a man who is obnoxious to me.

I often wish that I had wings and an invisible suit so that I could fly across to you every evening after my day's' work is done. I hope my queen is driving out every day. Home Rule will draw either phaeton or buggy by himself if you give him his time and the more quiet exercise he the better, but Dictator goes too fast for him.

H. behaved very badly about Fermanagh, threatening and striking O' K. on Monday evening to intimidate him from going forward, but the latter squared up to him like a man and cowed him.

I shall go to Dublin to morrow morning by first train and shall be there all day and probably Saturday night.

YOUR OWN KING AND HUSBAND

On Parnell's writing to me that it really was practically impossible to get him returned again for County Clare, nor, without the pledge, for any other Irish seat under his control, I wrote to Willie and in return received a letter of bitter complaint accusing Parnell of ingratitude and treachery. Now already, in the use of these terms by Willie, certain persons – enemies of Parnell's policy – with that over-anxiety of the dishonourable to use the meanest weapons of attack in preference to those of nobler forging – professed to see the indications of a loathsome treaty between Parnell, Willie and myself. Willie was under the impression that he had been the chief negotiator of the Kilmainham Treaty and that he had, on another occasion, done Parnell signal political service in a certain negotiation with Mr Gladstone and thinking, as he did, that this was: so and having a very keen sense of his own importance, with far too much vanity to understand that he had become not merely unpopular but absolutely disliked in the party, he believed and fervently protested that Parnell was behaving with singular ingratitude and treachery to him in not more strongly supporting his candidature. That Parnell had and was pressing it so strongly as to jeopardise his own position he could not understand. His true reason for doing so – my desire – he did not know; nor did he know, what Parnell knew, that ugly rumour had already begun the campaign of brutality that, not daring to meet its foe in the open, wars with the dirty word, the filth flung at a woman's love and, with only the knowledge of its own motives 'and methods, the belief that where there is a wrong that wrong must surely be of the basest kind.

Parnell could not apply to Lord Richard Grosvenor himself – as was Willie's cool proposition – but on receipt of Parnell's letter, after some consideration, I went to see Lord Richard, point-blank told him that I most particularly wished Willie to continue in Parliament and asked him if there was any chance of getting him returned for one of the divisions of Liverpool. Lord Richard was very kind and though full of the business caused by the General Election, he devoted a whole morning to showing that I was asking, if not the impossible, at least the unreasonable thing of him. He said, 'And we don't even know what O' Shea's politics are!' 'You know Chamberlain's', I replied and in spite of a smile he sat down again to consider the matter afresh.

The upshot of this interview was that, on leaving Lord Richard, I wrote to Willie that Lord Richard Grosvenor had promised to use his influence for him for Liverpool and I give the interchange of telegrams that resulted:–

DUBLIN,
October 21st, 1885.

To O' SHEA, ELTHAM.
No use, am leaving for Birmingham tonight to see Chamberlain.
B.[17]

CREWE,
October 22nd, 1885.

To O' SHEA, ELTHAM.
Energetic action on Gladstone's part necessary; wrote you from Chamberlain's.
B.

DUBLIN
October 24th.

To O' SHEA, ELTHAM, BLACKHEATH.

He (Parnell) is at Morrison's. Fairest compromise offered me in North, but he declares himself, as usual, powerless.

B.

Thereupon I wrote to Gladstone and on 24th October he replied to the effect that the matter lay wholly within the province of Lord Richard Grosvenor, to whom he was forwarding my letter and one of Willie's of the same date. He might perhaps see Lord Richard and in any case would tell him, what he already knew, how sorry he would be if Willie was not elected for the new Parliament. To go beyond this would, as I should understand, lead to much inconvenience and confusion of duties.

THE SHELBOURNE HOTEL, DUBLIN,
Sunday, October 25th, 1885.

DEAR KATE, – I am going to Belfast tomorrow. I scarcely know why. However, one likes to see a game out.

I have kept my temper more or less well so far. Mr Chamberlain, with his knowledge of what I did at various times for Parnell, considers the latter – well, thinks very ill indeed of him. He (C.) and all my life friends say that if he had any feeling, any spark of honour, he would have told his party that he was under such a promise and such an obligation that my seat must be secured, or he would resign his leadership.

Lord Claude Hamilton was in the train in which I returned last night and pointed me out to the Orangemen at Portadown, so that it appears the murder is out and that my attempt at Mid Antrim will appear tomorrow morning.

My impression is that I shall be in London on Tuesday and that I was not wrong in fearing, ere I left it, that I was on a wild-goose chase.

No one can ever deal successfully with lying and treachery.

Your B.

Dickson was very civil, but, of course, wants S. Tyrone, for which they are starting O' Brien.

On October 29th Lord Richard telegraphed to me from Chester acknowledging the receipt of my letter late the previous night. He had hoped to be able to reply definitely that day, but was unable. He had not heard, as expected, that morning.

THE SHELBOURNE HOTEL, DUBLIN,
November 2, 1885.

DEAR KATE, – The doctor cannot yet tell me when I may hope to leave this wretched place. I am certainly recovering, but very slowly. He says the slightest cold would bring on a relapse which might be fatal. I shall stay a night at Chamberlain's on my way back.

Of course I knew nothing about your political movements and arrangements.

All I know is that I am not going to lie in ditch. I have been treated in blackguard fashion and I mean to hit back a stunner. I have everything ready; no drugs could make me sleep last night and I packed my shell with dynamite. It cannot hurt my friend (Chamberlain) and it will send a blackguard's reputation with his deluded countrymen into smithereens.

I have got your telegram. He won't be of high 'importance' soon.

I wonder the little girls have not written to me; no one cares a bit for me except my poor old mother.

I am very tired from writing a lot of letters.

Yours,

W. H. O'SHEA.

In spite of my letters and telegrams Willie was still indignant and unwilling to leave Ireland for an English constituency. He was ill and felt his disappointment the more keenly for this reason. After this last letter I saw Lord Richard Grosvenor again and on the result wired to Willie as follows:–

> November 4, 1885.
> To O'SHEA, MP
>
> Grosvenor says as you written declining he working another direction, but says if anything done must be done by him alone, so if you think any besides old place do communicate him first before any whisper gets out about it. Address twelve Upper Brook Street. We just going your mother.
> DICK.

> DUBLIN,
> November 4, 1885.
>
> To O'SHEA, ELTHAM, KENT.
>
> Letter mistaken. He (Parnell) first refused to perform promise respecting present place, pleading inability to cope with opposition of his own friends. He then offered compromise North, stating only minority 550, then to you 700. It is actually 2,000.
> WILLIE.

On receipt of a letter from me of the 4th November Willie began to waver in his determination to keep to Ireland and replied:–

> DUBLIN,
> November 5th, 1885.
>
> To O' SHEA, ELTHAM.
>
> What seat? Chamberlain thought nothing left England except forlorn hopes. Representatives of fishermen came today. Very sorry their friend (O' Shea) so perfidiously sacrificed.

On the 8th he wrote me as follows:–

> SHELBOURNE HOTEL, DUBLIN,
> November 8th, 1885.
>
> DEAR KATE, – I shall leave by the mail packet tomorrow night.
> I lunched today at Sir Richard Martin's; Lord Justice Barry and four or five other gentlemen there. There is much talk in Dublin about my affair. All agree that Parnell's conduct is loathsome, except a few who say he is a poor cur whipped by O' Brien and Healy. He has run away to England.
> As I have reason to believe, he may deny his having promised me to secure my reelection 'without trouble', I wrote him duplicate notes last night, one to Avondale, the other to Morrison's Hotel, which must effectually prevent his telling that lie through forgetfulness.
> Chief Justice Lawrence sent me a very kind message. I shall stay at Holyhead tomorrow night, as I am still very weak and easily tired.–
> Yours, W.H. O' SHEA.

I then wrote more fully to him and again urged Lord Richard to do his best for him in Liverpool. He replied by wire on the 9th, saying that he would write to Liverpool on Saturday. He had wired that day.

On November 13, the Parliamentary agent, Wyllie, wired me that he had informed their Liverpool correspondent and had wired Willie.

On the same date Willie telegraphed me from Chamberlain's that another man had been chosen and that he should return to London. By this time I was so determined that Willie should be returned for Liverpool that I threw all caution to the winds so far as Lord Richard and Gladstone were concerned and sent a peremptory message to Wyllie asking where the former was. He replied from London that Lord Richard was expected there that morning and on receiving my further message, Grosvenor replied with really natural irritation that he could not possibly tell what candidate had been settled on the previous day.

I then telegraphed to Willie on the morning of November 14:–

If you think it wise, tell your Liberal friends (Holt and others) privately that you have reason to know that Mr P. will stand unless you are accepted. I can get that put in Liverpool papers tonight if you telegraph him. Am to hear from Grosvenor this morning.

Willie replied that he was ill and had to come to London to see Montagu (afterwards Sir Samuel Montagu and Lord Swaythling) about some company affairs; he could return to Liverpool on Monday and thought Stephens would retire in his favour 'if Grosvenor put pressure on'. That evening I heard from Lord Grosvenor that the fulfillment of my wishes was possible but complicated and the following morning he telegraphed me that he had wired Liverpool fully as required that morning and would wire Gladstone as wished. The next day he sent another message to the effect that he was surprised to have received no news from Liverpool. Wyllie wired that he was doing his best and hoped that Willie would not contemplate going elsewhere. They did not know that Willie had returned to London. The latter wired me that he would return to Liverpool, but that he must have strong recommendations from Gladstone and Grosvenor to present to the Council the next day.

This caused me much thought and considerable annoyance. Determined as I was that Willie should be returned for Liverpool and (as a Liberal) no longer be in the Irish Party – to the great benefit of its leader – I did not wish to rouse the irritation of Mr Gladstone by too strong insistence on his intervention. He was in Scotland, of course, busied by the election and making speeches daily and I knew by this time far too much of men and matters to be guilty of the indiscretion of forcing the hand of the G.O.M. on a matter which was not essential, even though I most keenly desired it. Parnell was in Liverpool trying to ensure Willie's candidature without appearing to do so. I had not time to consult him and felt that, if it could be done at not too great a loss, we must get Gladstone's influence on the side of keeping Willie out of Ireland until the Home Rule Bill was passed. So I sent a carefully worded telegram to Gladstone and the next day received the reply that he must first know who was the other candidate and would consult Lord Richard.

So here I had another check and I grimly determined that I would make Lord Richard Grosvenor's life a burden to him until I had landed Willie safely on the Liberal benches.

From Willie I now heard that 'Chamberlain said' that if proper measures were adopted Willie was the best possible candidate, but Gladstone's and Grosvenor's recommendations were indispensable and. must be immediate. After a few moments' thought I deliberately telegraphed to Willie (now at Liverpool):

You will hear from Grosvenor and Gladstone before or at meeting. Important not to disclose P.'s (Parnell's) knowledge of your candidature until accepted by local Liberals, even then best allow P. himself announce his acceptance of your candidature.

DICK.

I then wired Lord Richard for an appointment. He distressfully replied that he had telegraphed to Liverpool as I desired; but this would not do; Gladstone's approval of Willie's candidature was also necessary, Grosvenor could obtain it and the G.O.M.'s weak 'consult Lord R.G.' had left this way open to me.

So I went to him and he was extremely kind, though he did say, 'We have our own troubles, Mrs O' Shea, in this election, don't harry us more than you can help! Yes, Gladstone shall telegraph, as it is your good pleasure. I am not at all sure that I approve of you in your political capacity; you are so terribly strenuous and determined! What! No, I will most certainly *not* go to Liverpool myself!' But before I left he promised me that he would go if I felt it was absolutely necessary and let him know the next day.

I had given him the following message, given me by Parnell before he left me for use in case of too much difficulty in getting the G.O.M. and Lord Richard to act on Willie's behalf:–

'If Liberal Party adopt O' Shea as candidate for Exchange Division of Liverpool and withdraw their candidate from either Kirkdale Division of Lancashire, whichever of these two it might be arranged that P. should stand for; the latter would secure the Liberal candidates the Irish vote in the other six Divisions of Liverpool and the Bootle Division of Lancashire; Scotland Division, of course, going to T. P. O' Connor.

'This arrangement would secure without doubt three out of the following four Liberal candidates: Smith, Southurst, Samuelson and Whitbread, candidates respectively for Abercrombie, Kirkdale and West Toxteth Division of Liverpool and Whitbread for Bootle Division of Lancashire, giving Liberal candidates fair chance of six divisions – otherwise Parnell, J. Redmond, A. O' Connor and J. Barry will be brought forward for four of former divisions.'

On my return home I was confronted with fresh work. Some time before Willie had asked me to come to his chambers to lunch and to meet Mr Samuel Montagu, with whom he was working some loan business (for the Spanish Government) on behalf of the latter's banking company. Willie wished me to meet Montagu as the latter was very desirous of getting into Parliament, Willie having told him that I often acted as private messenger between the Irish and Liberal Leaders. He was very anxious to ask me if I would try to secure him the Irish vote in the Whitechapel Division of London.

Willie was anxious to please Montagu, with whom he had much business in hand – owing to his having so complete a knowledge of Spain and the Spanish language. I had told him that he overrated my powers, but he pressed the point so earnestly that to please Willie I said I would do my best.

Now I had asked Parnell about getting the Irish vote for Mr Montagu and he had said he did not see what harm Montagu could do and it was just as well to get the Irishmen to support him as not. In the stress of Willie's business we had both forgotten him, however and now he plaintively telegraphed for news and should he see anyone. To him I replied that the Irishmen would vote for him, I was assured and wrote at once to Parnell to ask him to do what he could. The next morning Mr Montagu telegraphed to me with touching simplicity, thanking me for kind advocacy and stating that Willie had telegraphed him that he had nothing to fear. Yet, he pointed out, O' Connor had spoken absolutely against Gladstone and the Liberal Party. Possibly an exception might be made according to promise.

I felt that events were becoming almost too much for me, but sent him a message to say that his return was certain (as a matter of fact, I believed his opponent was obnoxious to all parties), wired to a London agent of Parnell's (under such name as he would know the message emanated from him) to beat up the Irishmen for Montagu; told Parnell I had done so and then set myself again to attend to Willie's candidature.

On the morning of the 20th Willie wired me:–

'If Grosvenor would come all might be put right',

and I forwarded this to Grosvenor so that he might redeem the promise he had made me the day before. He replied that he had wired Liverpool and would go down that night if still wanted, but that it was exceedingly inconvenient.

At the same time I had a telegram from Parnell, at Liverpool, to 'send W. a tip to be civil'. Willie was, I believe, incensing the Irishmen of Liverpool by; talking of Parnell's 'perfidy' again.

I went up to London and told Lord Richard that now he absolutely must go, as he had promised me he would. He said: 'Well, look here, Mrs O' Shea, it is an awkward position, but I'll go, as I said I would, but I want you to come with me.'

I looked quietly at Lord Richard and held to my self-control with all the force I possessed. Go with him to Liverpool to help by canvassing and by the influence of my personal charm, my husband by law to contest this seat, backed and aided in my efforts by the presence of my lover himself! Was Grosvenor mad? or was it possible that all this time that I had been in constant communication with him and Gladstone as the only intermediary they had known, between themselves and Parnell, he had imagined that I did this work from a sheer love of politics, from vanity, from any one thing in the world but the love of Parnell himself? Was this man a monk, a priest, an absolute child, to think these things could be? These thoughts raced through my head, but no! as I stared across at Grosvenor making little lines and figures on his blotting pad and not looking at me, I knew that this courteous gentleman knew full well; that he was a man of the world (no less than Gladstone, who was well aware I did not live with my husband and who had received so many letters from Parnell dated from my house), I knew that he was asking me not to press him into a false position.

I said: 'Parnell is in Liverpool working quietly for Willie'. He replied, still not looking at me: 'I was not sure'. I went on: 'I cannot personally work for Willie in Liverpool and', after a pause, 'I am more useful to him here'.

'Yes, you are more useful to him here, but – well, don't be too useful to him!'

'You will go down, Lord Richard?'

'Yes, I will go down and I will do my best – we owe you that – but frankly I do not want it known. It will be safe to tell him that.'

We arranged that in telegraphing to me that he would call Willie 'Jack' for better privacy and he asked me to drive round with him to fetch his things so that I could explain exactly how matters stood in Liverpool in time for him to catch the train.

On my return home I found a telegram from Willie saying:–

Offer finally rejected, would he retire man Scotland (division of Liverpool) in view of great services received in past and necessary in future?

I at once replied that such a scheme was impossible, that R. (Grosvenor) was going down and G. (Gladstone) would immediately send 'approval'. But Willie was off at a tangent and replied:–

Considerable Liberal majority Scotland. Liberals have handsomely left division for Irishmen; therefore nothing more suitable. He (Parnell) will not like doing it yet; only way to redeem his character.

To this I did not reply, thinking that the morning might produce saner vision all round. But that night; came:–

Awaiting your views. It will be disgraceful if Scotland not arranged. B.

Almost at the same time:–

Telegram just come authorising me state Mr Gladstone wishes me obtain seat. Stephens has issued address. They have done everything with eyes open, saying it will be best in the end.

B.

I replied:–

Issue your address for Exchange tonight. Stephens must retire if you are firm. Am sure Scotland impossible.

DICK.

The next day I received the following letter from him:–

ADELPHI HOTEL, LIVERPOOL,
November 19.

MY DICK, – To finish everything my stylographic pen won't mark and the pens here are the worst things in the inn.

One must always remember that it is the Whigs who manage things whenever Chamberlain and Schnadhorst are out of it, for it is they who subscribe to the organisation.

The Liberal candidates are a wretched lot – Sam Smith didn't attend the meeting this morning. Holt was with him until after twelve last night. At first he was warmly in favour of the arrangement, but afterwards said it would be bad for the party in Liverpool in the long run, that the howl would play the mischief, the howl of a Parnell treaty. I could plainly see that Parnell's candidature is looked upon as bogus. There is a move to withdraw Stephens by and by, so as to leave Parnell, if he means business, to fight the Tory candidate single-handed. How would this look if he were at the same time ordering his men to vote for the Tories in the other divisions? I suggested that Parnell might do exactly the same thing – retire himself as soon as Stephens had done so. I said there is a Liberal majority in Scotland Division, because I heard it stated with confidence several times. I cannot see why in any case Mr P. should not give me that seat, because it isn't more difficult than lying and it was a distinct bargain made by himself the night of the close division about Egypt. He said: 'If you vote with us against the Government I promise you your re-election without trouble or expense.' However, I suppose I may as well make up my mind to be out of it. I am not the bit the worse of coming here this time, but I have been taking the greatest care.

Some said some of the Dissenters would be as mad as the Whigs.

Your B.

On the 21st Willie telegraphed me first that he had had a long interview with Grosvenor and was to have another later. This was followed by:–

When speaking or writing about me essential (Parnell) should say advised them (electors) to support me on account great services rendered country.

B.

Later still: –

If the treachery (what Willie considered was Parnell's treachery) in Ireland had been acknowledged in September I could have had any suitable English seat. The regret of all classes and execrations against Stephens. Extraordinary.

B.

Lord Richard Grosvenor had returned to London. I had communicated with him the night before and he now wired that he had only received the telegram at eight that morning and had replied. He most particularly asked me to prevent Willie publishing the letter he wrote in regard to Willie's candidature. He now pressed this point and reassured me as to Willie's nomination.

At 1.30 p.m. that day Willie wired:—

O' Shea, Baily, Parnell and Stephens nominated. Hope Grosvenor will telegraph permitting me to publish letter he wrote with Chamberlain's and Bright's.

I had already told him he must not do this and now replied:—

Don't publish letter. Lord Richard's address: Arms Hotel, Crewe, tonight.

Now came a wail from poor Mr Montagu that at a large Irish meeting people were told to vote for his opponent. He had telegraphed to Liverpool.

I sent him a hopeful message, which was really all I could do for him then and, when a little later I received a message from Parnell saying 'Stephens will retire', I felt that for the moment Parnell must be allowed a little respite from my importunities.

The same evening I was much depressed at receiving from Grosvenor a message sent at Wrexham on his way to Crewe, saying that:

Jack had published his letter on the Saturday evening, had heard nothing since the morning. Parnell not nominated. He slept at Crewe Arms that night.

In publishing Lord Richard Grosvenor's letter, against my promise, Willie had done much mischief and I felt that in view of the way Grosvenor had put himself to an immensity of trouble to secure his candidature, Willie's action was more than inconsiderate.

On December 14th Lord Richard wrote me from the Liberal Central Office, 41 and 42 Parliament Street, to say that he had just that minute (5.30 p.m.) returned. Here was the letter — *no one* had seen it and to only one man (Billson) had he mentioned the fact contained in it. He was very sorry that his journey and efforts had produced no result, but he had tried his best and they had sat in conclave till 2 a.m. that morning. O' Shea should leave Liverpool that night and on no account meet Parnell there. As it had failed everything must be blotted out and forgotten. Stephens had no chance whatever — he made that safe before leaving — so no notice need be taken of him, but he would go to the poll.

He found it would be impossible now to find Captain O' Shea a seat, but vacancies were sure to occur before long, when he would not be forgotten where a suitable chance offered.

Mr Parnell worked harder than ever he had before to get Willie returned for Liverpool, but it was in vain. With all the weight of Parnell's influence upon the Irish vote in Liverpool, with all the support of Lord Richard Grosvenor and, through him, of Mr Gladstone, Willie was beaten by a few votes. The next day Parnell came back to me. I was suffering from a nervous breakdown owing to the sudden relaxing of the intense strain and work that I had been through, coupled with my bitter disappointment at Willie's defeat and Parnell nursed, soothed and comforted me as tenderly as a woman.

And now came the demand we expected from Willie. He could not bear to be out of Parliament, more than all he could not bear to be out of it by defeat and he went to Parnell in the House and insisted that his 'services in regard to the Kilmainham Treaty and also in acting between Chamberlain, Mr Gladstone and himself' deserved the recognition of Parnell's support in again trying for an Irish seat. Moreover, he declared that Parnell had long before solemnly promised him his support should the occasion arise, soon after their first meeting indeed.

Parnell pointed out that the situation was so utterly different that such a promise, even if made, was, by force of circumstances, most certainly cancelled, that his candidature for the only Irish seat available (Galway, vacant by the fact that Mr T.P. O' Connor, elected for both, had chosen Liverpool) would be met by the fiercest opposition and that he even doubted his (Parnell's) own power over the Irish Party being strong enough to bear the strain of such a nomination for Galway. Willie replied angrily that he was extremely popular in Ireland and that he would be very sorry to be on terms of popularity with such a 'rapscallion crew' as the party.

'Well, then, you need not be sorry, for you are very unpopular with them', Parnell replied, busily thinking.

Meanwhile Willie fumed and urged his point with the deadly, nagging persistency that I had so often known and given in to, in the old days, for the mere sake of hearing no more of a subject.

Presently Parnell said consideringly, 'And you will not take the pledge even' (the party pledge to sit, act and vote together) and Willie answered 'No, he would sit where he liked and vote as he pleased', to which Parnell could only reply: 'Then the thing is not worth discussing further' and left him.

But Willie would not leave it there. He *must* be in the House and there was only Galway available.

The party were worrying Parnell for a nomination and uneasy at the delay in his proposing a candidate. Parnell and I were much troubled. We feared that if Willie once contested an Irish seat again the foul insinuations of Callan and Co. would surely be used against him as being Parnell's nominee (see letter of January 15th, 1886, from Mr Parnell to me,) and these would necessarily be investigated by Willie and the truth sifted from the foul lie.

That this would lead to action that might endanger the triumph of the Home Rule Bill was fairly certain and the silence of years made of none effect at the very time when this silence was to be rewarded by Ireland's freedom. Over and over again had Parnell said: 'Once we get Home Rule through Ireland is safe and we may be happy in sight of all the world; but till then I fear these English hypocrites.' However, Willie would give me no peace. I must see Mr Gladstone, Lord Richard Grosvenor, Mr Parnell. It was nonsense to suppose that with all the 'wire-pulling' I had had to do, I now had not the small amount of influence he required to secure him a seat in Parliament. Mr Chamberlain fully supported him in this view, he said and considered Parnell shamelessly ungrateful for not proposing him for Galway. In the end he told me that he intended to go to Ireland, that he meant to stand for Galway and should get proposed by someone else if Parnell would not do it, adding that it was my 'duty' to see Parnell and tell him firmly that I would no longer be his 'cat's-paw' with Gladstone if he did not support Willie now.

Of course, without Parnell's advocacy Willie would have had no chance at all of being returned for any Irish constituency, but he would have had the opportunity of doing much mischief and there were at work against 'the Chief' certain hostile factions whose venom was all the more bitter for being hidden and, as they supposed, secret.

In going over the problem with me, weighing up the pros and cons, Parnell said:

'I can force Willie upon Galway, but it will be such a shock to my own men that they'll not be the same again. Or I can leave it alone and ... and ... will do almost as much mischief with him there. Queenie, you must see him again and tell him I'll propose him if only he will consent to take the party pledge. Tell him I cannot insult the others by proposing him without this.'

I did so, but it was no use. Willie was not well and would not even discuss the matter, merely reiterating his intention of going to Galway the moment he could get his shoe on (he suffered much from gout) and his disgust at the ingratitude of 'the man he had let out of prison', to say nothing of Gladstone's, Grosvenor's and my own ingratitude.

I went home and on Parnell's return I told him of my failure. He only nodded and, gazing into the fire, said quietly, 'It is no matter, Queenie, I was thinking this afternoon that we are giving ourselves much trouble about what really does not concern us. I'll run him for Galway and' with sudden fierceness 'I'll get him returned. I'll force him down their throats and he can never again claim that I have promised and not performed. It will cost me the confidence of the party, but that much he shall have and I shall be done with his talk of pledges.'

Then, after a pause, 'We won't mind, Queenie, if it leads to worry and fuss. If it were not for the Bill (Home Rule) I should be delighted and, after all, if the country (Ireland) wants Home Rule she'll get it sooner or later. Anyhow, what shall be shall be and I told T. P. tonight that I meant to propose Willie.' As I looked at him amazed, for I had had no idea that he had come to this decision, he laughed with the rare flash of humour that sometimes beset him at unlikely moments. 'You should have seen his face, my Queen; he looked as if I had dropped him into an ice-pit.'

Captain O' Shea was returned for Galway.

CHAPTER XXXIV

SEASIDE HOLIDAYS

'Green leaves afloating,
Castles of the foam,
Boats of mine aboating,
Where will all come home?' – STEVENSON.

IN MAY, 1886, I TOOK my children to the Queen's Hotel, Eastbourne, for a change and, after a few days spent in looking for lodgings, I settled them in St John's Road. Parnell enjoyed the bathing at Eastbourne greatly and was much distressed that the weakness of my heart prevented my joining him in his swims and that boating had most disastrous effects on me.

He was boyishly determined that I should at any rate join him in some way in his sea 'sports' and one warm May evening he insisted that if I went into the sea fully dressed it could not hurt me. I thought it would at any rate be most uncomfortable, but to please him I held tightly to his arm while we waded far out to sea till the waves came to my shoulder and threw me off my feet.

He held me tightly, laughing aloud as the ripple of waves and wind caught my hair and loosed it about my shoulders; and, as I grew cold and white, my wonderful lover carried me, with all the weight of my soaked clothing, back to the shore, kissing the wet hair that the wind twisted about his face and whispering the love that almost frightened me in its strength. Luckily the dusk of evening had come down upon us and I was able to get back to the house in my wet things, half-walking and half-carried by Parnell, without unduly shocking Eastbourne's conventions.

As I thought I should be able to be away from my aunt, with occasional flying visits to her, for about two months, Parnell had two of our horses brought down to Eastbourne. He had during that time to go to London and Ireland, but it was on the whole a peaceful little interlude in his strenuous political life and we were very happy. He rode his horse President in the morning and afterwards I drove him far out into the country around Eastbourne with Dictator in my phaeton.

We often drove out to Birling Gap – a favourite haunt of ours – and there we selected a site for the ideal house of our dreams; a place where one could hear nothing but the beating of the surf on the rocks below and the wild call of the seabirds. He loved that place, where we could be absolutely alone save for the coastguardsman along the cliff, who never intruded his interesting conversation, but who was always ready for a chat when we cared to hear his stories of the sea.

It was impossible to drive near the place, so we had to leave Dictator and the phaeton far off on the last bit possible to drive upon. Parnell had an easy method of 'hitching' a horse to something, in the firm faith that he would find it there on return a few hours later and this made me very uneasy where my far from patient Dictator was concerned. Parnell would settle the horse with a feed, in charge of his groom, well sheltered behind a hill and take a fantastic pleasure in observing the sulky gloom of the young man's face after an hour or so of this isolated meditation.

Parnell had a great love of seastorms and when there was a gale blowing from the west and rough weather assured, he loved to get me out to Birling Gap to listen to the roar of the sea and the screaming of the wind as it blew around us, nearly carrying us off our feet. He would tie his coat about me and hold me firmly against the wind as it tore about us and while we gazed out at the raging waves he would exclaim: 'Isn't this glorious, my Queen? Isn't it alive?'

Our coastguardsman friend always seemed somewhat pleased to see us, though undoubtedly he thought us odd in our amusements. I have often thought since that if we had built our house in that isolated loveliness, where the sound of the sea and moan of the wind were incessant, there would have been some truth in what was said afterwards as to our house in Walsingham Terrace, that it was so 'terribly dreary'.

On one occasion we drove to Pevensey and, passing the station on our return, a crowd from some local train came pouring out. Parnell asked me to pull up to let the crowd go by; but to his consternation this attracted the attention of some young men in the crowd, who at once recognised him and, waving their hats, cried 'Parnell, Parnell!' with that horrible emphasis on the 'nell' that is so prevalent. Parnell, lifting his hat, urged me in an agonised tone to drive on, but it was too late. The crowd clustered about us, insisting on shaking hands with him and throwing covertly interested glances at his companion. They would not let us go on till he had made a little impromptu speech on current affairs, after which we drove off amid cheers. Parnell never swore and 'Goodness gracious!' learned from his nurse in extreme youth, was the strongest expression he ever used, but the dull, quiet anger such a contretemps as this caused him would, I felt, have been relieved could he have acquired the habit of 'language'. This little incident at Pevensey would lead to newspaper paragraphs and it was hard we could not have a few days' quiet amusement without having it boomed through the country. However, a brilliant thought struck me. If we were to be bothered by paragraphs let them be our own! So we drew up by the wayside and concocted a paragraph which told an over-interested world that 'Mr Parnell had been staying at Hastings with his sister and on visiting Pevensey with her had', etc., etc. This, forwarded to the Press Association, left us in peace at Eastbourne to complete our little holiday.

Apropos of Parnell's 'Goodness gracious', he was at first quite unconscious of his use of the words and it was only on Willie's plaintive query as to why he did not d--n like other men, instead of using 'that foolish and vulgar expression', he became aware of it. He then admitted with some amusement that he liked the homely old expression and did not d--n merely because it never occurred to him to do so.

On the cliffs towards Beachy Head is a house that at that time was built but not quite finished. Parnell took me up to see it and suggested that it might be a charming seaside retreat for us, even though not the ideal we always had in our minds. This house then had a beautiful and wide outlook over the sea and I liked it so much that he arranged to take it on a three years' agreement directly it was finished. He wanted to have all the walls distempered instead of papered and we spent many hours over this and the selection of

the Minton tiles for the hall. The details of the house interested him greatly and one day
when the men working there had gone to dinner Parnell showed me how to lay the tiles
with so much energy that we had finished their work by the time the men returned. He
then insisted upon my writing 'Heatherbell Cottage' on a tile, which he proceeded to inlay
over the front door, earning the comment from the men working there that he seemed to
know as much about the 'job' as they did.

He then turned his attention to making a smooth lawn in our little garden, spending
hours pulling a roller up and down, while I sat on the steps writing from his dictation 'A
Proposed Constitution for the Irish and the English Peoples' – a production that excited
the greatest wrath in the minds of some of the Irish Party at a subsequent meeting. I do not
think that the English members of Parliament were ever made acquainted with the benefits
proposed for their consideration under this 'Constitution.'

This Constitution was more fun than anything else. Parnell undoubtedly put it before
certain members of the Irish Party instead of one drafted by his own hand. He told me
afterwards that they looked 'absolutely ill' when they saw my handwriting, so he would not
withdraw it in favour of his own till later.

I was sitting on the doorstep of our new house one day, idly watching Parnell
build a bank that was to be turfed over to keep us from prying eyes, when he stopped
suddenly and, leaning on his spade, said: 'I am a poet! And descended from the poet,
Thomas Parnell.'

'*Not* a poet', I answered gently, 'even though descended from one.'

'I *am* a poet myself; give me a pencil and paper.' And, throwing himself down beside me,
he wrote down the following verse proudly. 'It came to me while I was digging', he said as
he tossed it over to me, 'and it is a real poem and makes me a real poet. It's as good as any
of Tom Parnell's stuff!'

I was forced to confess that I agreed with him, as I do now, that it was and is, as good
as and better to me than, any of Thomas Parnell's stuff, or 'the stuff' of any poet who ever
graced the world with song. This is it:–

> 'The grass shall cease to grow,
> The river's stream to run,
> The stars shall ponder in their course,
> No more shall shine the sun;
> The moon shall never wane or grow,
> The tide shall cease to ebb and flow,
> Ere I shall cease to love you.'
> CHAS S. PARNELL.

One evening in 1886, on his return from town, Parnell told me about Mr O' Brien's Plan
of Campaign. He did not approve of it and said that he did not wish to have anything to do
with the working of it, saying: 'I shall let O' Brien run it by himself.'

Parnell was looking and feeling very ill at this time and when Mr O' Brien took upon
himself to call at my house to see him, entirely uninvited, Parnell was not really well enough
to see him. He was suffering from nervous breakdown, chiefly brought on by gastric trouble,
which in its turn was produced by overwork and the strain of political life. All through his
life Parnell was delicate. From 1880, when I first met him (and nursed him into health)
to 1891, when he died, it was only by incessant watchfulness and care that I was able to
maintain his health at all. It is certainly the fact that only his indomitable will and power
of mind rendered him capable of enduring the strain of his public life and of the feats of
strength that few men of far greater physique would have attempted.

It was in allusion to this illness at the time of the visit of Mr O' Brien that Parnell said in his speech at the Eighty Club (May 8, 1888): 'I was ill, dangerously ill; it was an illness from which I have not entirely recovered up to this day. I was so ill that I could not put pen to paper, or even read the newspaper. I knew nothing about the movement until weeks after it had started and even then I was so feeble that for several months – absolutely up to the meeting of Parliament – I was positively unable to take part in any public matter and was scarcely able to do so for months afterwards. But, if I had been in a position to advise, I candidly submit to you that I should have advised against it.'

Mr O' Brien called again to see Parnell during the time he was so ill and he left his room for the first time to go down to the sitting-room to see him. They had a long talk over the Plan of Campaign and other matters and the interview left Parnell so exhausted that he was very ill again for some days afterwards.

Long after he told me, 'All I got for getting up to see O' Brien was that he went about telling people that I was insane.'

Mr Parnell had been feeling low and depressed all through the summer of this year and towards the autumn I became very much worried about his lassitude and general feeling of illness. I tried different diets without effect and, thinking it might be better for him to go straight to bed after 'the House', I took a house in London for him and settled him there, but he could not bear the loneliness and came back to Eltham as usual after a few nights. In November he became worse and I insisted upon his consulting a doctor, suggesting Sir Henry Thompson, as I had heard he was very clever. I took him to London on the afternoon of November 6, in a closed carriage and he was feeling so weak and nervous that he asked me to go in and see Sir Henry first for him. His nerves had completely broken down and I felt terribly worried about him. He stayed in the waiting-room while I went into the consulting-room. Here Sir Henry hurried in from dinner, extremely irritable at being disturbed at such an unseemly hour for a 'Mr Charles Stewart', whom he did not know. 'Look, look, *look!* Look at the clock! What's the matter? I have a consultation in a few minutes!'

I was very glad that the door between the rooms was shut, as I felt that such a reception in his state of nerves would have caused Parnell to leave the house without waiting for an interview. I began to point out that 'my' patient could not, in such a low state, face such an ungenial reception. So he permitted me to explain a little about Mr Stewart's ill-health and as he was kindness itself, losing every trace of impatience, he helped Parnell into his room, where, after receiving a smile of assurance from Parnell and having seen the relief in his face, I left them together, feeling what an inestimable blessing it was to have placed Parnell's health in such a haven of security: in so far as human skill could aid it.

The knowledge, throughout the rest of Parnell's life, of being able to obtain Sir Henry Thompson's advice was a great comfort to this overwrought man.

Sir Henry Thompson warned me that it was most important for Mr Parnell's health that his feet should be kept very warm, as his circulation was bad. When his feet became cold it upset his digestion and this so disorganised his general health that he was then laid up for several days. I always insisted upon his frequently changing his shoes and socks when he was at home and gave him a little black bag containing a change whenever he was sure to be away for a few hours, as I found that the trouble of the frequent changing was amply compensated for in warm feet and therefore better health.

So curiously inquisitive were some of the Irish Party about its contents that the little bag with the change of socks and shoes became an obsession with them till one of them made the brilliant discovery that 'Parnell had boots and socks in it to save him from wet feet!' Parnell used to complain to me when he handed it over to me that I might see by the different-coloured socks that he had kept his promise of 'changing' in town, that —'s eyes seemed to be boring holes in the bag and he was really thinking it would be better to hang the other shoes and socks round his neck if he must take them about with him!

When Parnell had to go over to Ireland he desired his secretary, Mr Campbell, to bring his correspondence down to me at Eastbourne in order that I might deal with one or two matters on which he desired immediate intelligence telegraphed to him in our private code. He had long since registered the telegraphic address of 'Satellite' for me that he might be able to telegraph with more privacy and this arrangement had proved its usefulness many times in political and private matters. He had himself put together the code words we used and insisted on my learning them by heart, to obviate the risk of any misunderstanding in case of loss.

Most of the words used were taken from his assaying operations, though not all and were sent as from one engineer to another about work in hand. In the code Willie appeared as 'Tailings' and with Middlings, Crude, Gas, Overseer, Slag, Concentrate, Deposit and a few other such words for Gladstone, Chamberlain and other politicians, our code was an excellent working medium of private communication.

Before we took the house in Eastbourne we made a flying visit to Bognor, but this, though in those days a pretty, fresh, little place, was very difficult to get at and impossible from a politician's point of view. We went there on a gloriously stormy day and thoroughly enjoyed it. In our search for houses we even got as far as Selsey, but when, on our going into the house we had come to see, the caretaker carefully double-locked the door, Parnell turned with a horrified gesture to me and insisted upon leaving at once without going over the house at all. It was an omen of misfortune, he said and we could never be happy in such a house.

I have always thought that one of the greatest charms of Parnell's personality was the extraordinary simplicity of his outlook on ordinary life allied to the extremely subtle trend of his intellect.

A man of moods, he never permitted a mood to blind him to probable, or possible, issues in political matters. A keen judge of character, he summed up, mentally docketed and placed in the pigeonhole of memory, each and every man who came into his political vision and could thus at any time place, sort and direct any pawn of the Irish political game. Yet in things having no political significance his simplicity was almost absurd in its naiveté.

An amusing instance of what I mean occurred while we were at Eastbourne in '86. There was a boy I employed about the house at Eltham, who was growing too fast and looked as though he would be all the better for a little sea air. As I was taking my own servants down to Eastbourne I took this boy down also for a holiday, since it made little difference as to expense. This child was, I suppose, about fourteen years old and once as I sat at the window, sorting Parnell's letters and enjoying the morning air, I was suddenly struck with consternation to see my protégé, Jimmie, escorted up the road between two of Eastbourne's largest policemen. I said to Parnell, 'Look!' and, following the direction of my horrified forefinger, he gazed sadly out at Jimmie and replied, 'Throwing stones, I'll wager. *More* paragraphs, sweetheart! You shouldn't have boys about.'

But the large policeman insisted upon an interview with 'the gentleman', with 'Mr Stewart' and, on my having the whole party in to hear the worst, we were informed that poor Jimmie had been caught trying to 'change a £50 note at the grocer's shop!' Mr Stewart's 'cold gravity of expression changed to one of deprecating amusement as I glanced indignantly at him. 'I had no change, constable, so of course sent the boy to change the note', explained Parnell. 'Told 'em so', threw in Jimmie, now feeling fairly safe and the centre of interest. But Eastbourne policemen are far too unimaginative to believe that boys of Jimmie's age are to be sent for change for £50 notes and it was with the utmost difficulty we got rid of these stolid guardians of our pockets.

Parnell, after sending the boy for change, had temporarily forgotten the matter and no explanation could convince him that it was the obvious thing that the boy should be 'arrested' on trying to change so large a note. 'Jimmie's a nuisance, but anyone can see that he is honest', was his conclusion.

On one of our excursions, ostensibly to look for a house, but really as much as anything for the purpose of getting away for a few hours to the sea, we went to Herne Bay. This was a charming and lonely little place then; a cluster of houses set in green fields and a fresh sea dashing over the little pier. It was always on days when the wind was high that the longing for the sea came over us and thus we generally found the sea responding to our mood.

At this little village of Herne Bay the house we saw was unsuitable, but the day is a memory of salt wind and rough waves, followed by a picnic dinner at the little inn, where Parnell ordered a fowl to be roasted and was momentarily saddened by my refusal to eat that murdered bird, which had been so pleasantly finding its own dinner when he gave the order.

CHAPTER XXXV

LONDON REMEMBRANCES

'My true love hath my heart and I have his.'
– SIR PHILLIP SIDNEY.

ONCE WHEN PARNELL HAD TO go to Ireland by the morning mail, after a late sitting of the House, I went up to the St Pancras Hotel, where he had a room that night and made the waiter bring up a tray into the bedroom, with a cold bird, some tomatoes and materials for salad dressing, adding a bottle of still Moselle (Parnell always drank still Moselle by his doctor's, Sir Henry Thompson's, orders and no other wine). I knew he would be rushed to catch the train when he returned in the early morning and that he would miss the little meal I always had ready for him and this missing a meal was very bad for him.

When I had prepared the supper table to my liking I sat down by the open window and watched the flare of light in the sky and the wide panoramic view of mean streets and wide spaces I had from this window, of one of the rooms highest up in this high building; and the shrieks and oaths of men and women came up to me as they quarreled and the drunken brawls of some past semblance of humanity floated up to me till dawn brought peace to the city, as these poor dregs of life slunk back to their dens to seek the oblivion of sleep. I shall never forget the sights and sounds of that night, for never before had the horror of a great city's streets at night been so forcibly brought before me.

In the early dawn Parnell came and, seeing his supper there, sat down to eat it without question, as I had known he would. He ate in a preoccupied way as he thought over his speech and after telling of various points in it, suddenly said, 'Ah, I was really hungry; and you found some tomatoes. I'll make the salad if you'll eat some.' So he made a delicious salad and we feasted upon it before I left him to go down to Eltham by the early train and to give him time for a short rest before catching the mail train for Ireland.

'There is one great comfort about this', I used to say to myself, after two hours' walking up and down that most uncomfortable station, Waterloo Junction, 'and that is that he *always* comes at last.' I had often to comfort myself with that reflection as I waited about at various stations for Parnell.

When he had to be late I often went up to the House to fetch him out to dinner at a restaurant. He hated dining in the House and there were one or two points in the diet ordered him by Sir Henry Thompson that I insisted upon for him where he would not take the trouble to insist for himself. After dinner I would drive him nearly back to the House. There he got out and if he felt lonely at the idea of driving down to Eltham by himself as he sometimes did, or if he thought he would want to talk to me again before he came home (as he very often did!) I would promise to wait for him at some station, so that he could find me without observation. It would have been much more comfortable, of course, for me to have waited in a house or rooms somewhere, but people were so extraordinarily curious about Parnell that it would have been impossible so to get any peace unless we changed the address every week and this would have been decidedly too expensive. As it was, he was often followed to the station by a detective or some private busybody who could not realise that even a public man may possibly prefer to keep a little of his life to himself.

So very many hours I waited for him at various stations! The officials (at each and all) were most kind and considerate to the lonely lady who had to be driven, by sheer force of regulations, from one waiting-room to another as the lights were put out and who finally would take to a steady tramp up and down the station platform till at length (such a long length sometimes!) she was joined by her husband and almost lifted into the hansom cab they invariably drove of in.

When I felt that he really wanted me to wait I could not bear to go home and though Waterloo was the most uncomfortable station of all to keep vigil in I often chose it, as, owing to the early morning trains at the Junction, I could always be sure that it would not be altogether shut up.

I think the officials must have known who Parnell was, as I always had a free pass (from him) for all these lines, but they never intruded and, in spite of my pass, received and kept his telegrams for me (he often telegraphed from the little office near the House, in the name 'Preston') with perfect tact. The porters were very good to me also and many a scuttle of coal was recklessly emptied on a waiting-room fire after hours as 'reg'lations 'gainst keepin' on gas strong, but it will be fairly cheerful like with the firelight, m'am.' The railway men are a kindly race, for I rarely tipped; these men.

HOUSE OF COMMONS,
12.30.

I arrived here tonight.

I fear I may be detained till rather late tonight, so hope you will not wait up for me. I expect to return home about 3.30.

The above is a note, one of very many, sent down to me at Eltham, so that I should, if I wished, go to bed before Parnell came home. I did this only once or twice, as I fancied I heard him directly I closed my eyes and would go down, only to find a dreary blank of disappointment. So I made him agree to my staying in my sitting-room, where from the open window I could hear for miles the regular trotting of the cab horse bringing him home.

He only stipulated that I should not go out along the roads to meet him at night. In March, 1887, I thought my King was looking tired and worried. There had been various annoying happenings owing to new reports of his life at Eltham having been put about. I had had unpleasant letters from Willie and the latter and I were not now on speaking terms. With this and his hard work Parnell was looking fagged and worn. His health, always an anxiety to me, seemed to fail and the languor that grew upon him frightened me. I determined that he should be spared the long cold night-drive down to Eltham and suggested his having a house near the House of Commons to which he could return and get immediate rest after a night sitting. He had a little house at Brockley, which he had taken in the name of 'Clement Preston' and furnished and here he had a man and wife to look after him. I had never lived there, but used to drive over to see him for a short time when it was inexpedient that he should be at Eltham. He never liked this house and hated the way the people used to hang about to see him go in and out, 'Clement Preston' apparently being but a poor protection in keeping off curiosity as to Parnell's habits. He wearily said he did not want to live in London unless I would live there too, but, as I pointed out, that was impossible and I took a house in York Terrace, Regent's Park (furnished) for him. Here I installed him with two servants, who absolutely worshipped the ground he walked upon and, having placed various books about, books that he considered of pleasant relaxation, such as engineering and mining treatises, with a couple of Dickens' works that he had always been 'going to read' and a few technical journals, I went home haunted by his grave, considering eyes and his sad: 'You must not leave me here by myself; I don't want to be here without you!', hoping that after a day or two he would settle down and feel the benefit of getting more quickly to bed.

The house was charming, with, on one side, a lovely outlook over Regent's Park. It was very pretty and comfortable and I used to make flying visits to him, to sit with him while he ate his breakfast. For three weeks I congratulated myself on having been self-denying enough to earn him better rest, even at the cost to myself of not having him so much with me; then, on my return from my aunt, whose great age was now beginning to tell upon her, late one evening, I felt anxious and worried about my lover, even though my goodnight telegram was awaiting me. He always telegraphed 'goodnight' if he was away from me. I tried to shake the feeling off, but after dinner I found myself mechanically making up the fire in my sitting-room as I did when sitting up for Parnell after a late sitting of the House. I felt amused at my absentmindedness and sat down before the fire, thinking that I would take advantage of the beautiful blaze I had made. I sat there idly, thinking of Parnell, wondering what exactly he was doing at that moment and presently, hearing the servants go to bed and feeling disinclined for bed myself, I got a book.

I could not settle to reading and began to feel very lonely and to wish I were really waiting up for Parnell, as I used to. Perhaps the loneliness was too great to him also, I thought and the extra rest might not compensate for it. I thought of my aunt, of how very old she was, of her immense goodness to me ever since I had lived at Eltham and of what a great blank there would be when she died – her life seemed to be like a flame flickering in the wind now and it might go out any day. I got up to shake off my sad thoughts and, throwing open the window, leant out and listened to the wind in the trees.

I heard the clock strike two and listened, as I had always done, about this time, for the regular beat of the horse's hoofs that would bring my King home. I could hear nothing and my longing for his presence was so great that I called out under my breath, 'I wish you would come. I do wish you would come'. Then I think I became drowsy, for I started up from the window, suddenly hearing three o' clock ring out from the village and the steady trottrot of a horse in the distance.

I held my breath to listen, my heart beating with an eager joy. I could hear the beat of the hoofs round the corner into the village as they came from the Common, then lost as they went up the High Street and suddenly clearer with the jingle of the cab bells as they turned the top of the road and stopped. I knew now and opened the door quickly as my love came up the little sidewalk past the window, giving the familiar signal as he went up the two steps; and I was in his arms as he whispered, 'Oh, my love, you must not leave me alone again.'

CHAPTER XXXVI

THE PARNELL COMMISSION

'For none on earth so lone as he
Whose way of thought is high and free',
Beyond the mist, beyond the cloud,
Beyond the clamour of the crowd.'

I HAD LONG SINCE HAD a high paling put round my garden to screen the garden from the inquisitive eyes of persons who had, until this was done, the impertinence to lean over the short stone wall and railings; to watch Parnell as he went in and out. This new paling was seven feet high. On the carriage gates there was bronze ornamental work, thick and heavy. Once this was cut through by someone unknown and fell, the next time the gate was opened, upon the head of the groom, as he stooped to unbolt it.

This little 'accident' was no doubt intended for Mr Parnell's or for my benefit and the fact that the young man's arm was pushed against the gate, above his head, as he stooped to ease the bolt, doubtless saved him from a cracked skull. As it was, he was badly bruised and cut, some fifty pounds of bronze work falling partly upon him. After this he examined the work on the other gate and, finding that this also had been cut through, with the help of the gardener lifted it off before further damage was done.

This pointless and malignant spite might easily have had far more serious consequences, since my children were going out by these gates driving their ponies and it was quite by chance that they had called the groom to open the gates for them, for one or other of them generally played at being the 'footman' on these occasions. The police could not trace the perpetrators of the little pleasantry.

I then made a beautiful, thick rosehedge at one side of this garden and the roses grew and flourished to such an extent that it proved an effectual screen from the too pressing attention of persons, who had not, I suppose, very many interests of their own.

On the morning that the (so-called) Parnell letters appeared in the *Times* (March 7, 1887), they were cut out and pasted on the gate by a person or persons unknown; and here also the perspicacity of our local police failed to find the merrymaker.

On that day I did not give Parnell the *Times* opened as usual for his glance over the political reports while he breakfasted. He asked for it, but I wanted him to finish his breakfast first and replied: 'The *Times* is unusually stodgy; do eat your breakfast first.'

He said he *must* finish a bit of assaying he had left overnight, before going to London and would not have time for papers afterwards, so I told him of the letters and propped the *Times* against the teapot as usual.

He read the whole thing; meditatively buttering and eating his toast the while. I supplied him with marmalade and turned over the folded paper for him so that he could read more easily.

He made no remark at all till he had finished breakfast and carefully clipped the end off his cigar; then, with a smile, he tossed the paper at me, saying, '*Now* for that assaying I didn't finish! Wouldn't you hide your head with shame if your King were so stupid as that, my Queen? '

I helped him to set his chemicals right, urging on him that the thing was very serious and that he must attend to it; but he only replied: 'You think about it for me while I am finishing this. Now don't spoil this for me. It will do presently!' and I subsided with the *Times* while he worked at his crucibles and jotted down results – absolutely absorbed for more than two hours and only brought back to politics by my call of: 'You absolutely must start now.'

He had a wonderful little machine – a balance that gave the weight of almost infinitesimal parts of a grain – and this might be touched by no one but himself. He now reluctantly covered it with its glass case and lovingly padded it round with a cloth, lest a rough movement in the room should put it out of balance.

I said, 'Now, my King, you must attend to the *Times*. You must take an action against them.'

'No. Why should I?' struggling into his coat as I held it for him. 'I have never taken any notice of any newspapers, nor of anyone. Why should I now?'

However, he promised me he would consult the 'Party' about the letters and left assuring me that the English *Times* was a paper of no particular importance, after all.

He got home before I did that evening and I found him on my return weighing the infinitesimal specks of his morning's extraction of gold with the utmost accuracy. He gave me a smile and the fireflame of his welcoming eyes as usual, but murmured, 'Don't speak for one moment; I'll tell you the moment I have finished this' and I had to sit with as much patience as I could muster while he finished his calculations. Then, coming over to me in triumph, he informed my for once uninterested ears that he had now completed the extraction of something or other of a grain of the gold for my wedding ring.

On my firmly recalling his attention to the matter of the letters he said wearily – all the interest and buoyancy gone – 'They want me to fight it, but it will be a terrible nuisance, my Queenie; I have seen Lewis and he is going to see Russell – Sir Charles, you know – and then I am to see him again.'

He was very undecided about the necessity of taking the action against the *Times and* more than once pointed out to me that the opinion of that paper and its readers did not really interest him; but, on my refusing to accept this at all and urging that Ireland required that he should defend himself in this and that my view was that of the Irish Party, he promised to take the matter seriously, merely remarking with an amused cynicism that if Ireland wanted him to cudgel a clean bill of health out of England she would find work for all the blackthorns she grew.

Soon my absorbed study of the forged letters caught Parnell's interest, he shook off his apathy and joined my study of his handwriting of many years and those of the various possible (and impossible) imitators. Once he became interested he threw himself into it as wholeheartedly as he did into any other hobby. We spent hours in this study of calligraphy and made some interesting and amusing discoveries!

After a couple of interviews with Mr Lewis and Sir Charles Russell, Parnell one evening asked me if I would mind seeing Lewis, as he had expressed a wish to see me. I went therefore to Ely Place and had an interview with Mr (Sir George) Lewis. After we had talked over the situation he gave me tea and made an appointment for another interview in a few days' time. I put before him my various conclusions as to handwritings, one of which he considered might be useful.

We had frequent consultations after this and, as the time of the trial drew near, Lewis's offices and the passages leading to it, with the waiting rooms, were filled with the witnesses from Ireland concerned in the trial. The case did not worry Parnell much except that it took up so much of our all too little leisure time, which was so precious to us.

The following letters, written from Avondale during the anxious time preceding the trial, will serve to show how little the matter affected his ordinary interests.

August 30, 1887

MY OWN WIFIE, – I have been exceedingly anxious about you ever since I left. You seemed so very ill that it has been haunting me ever since that I ought to have stayed in London.

My own darling may write to me whenever she pleases.

I was so longing for a telegram all day yesterday, but not getting one came to the conclusion that you had not been able to go to London.

I have been round the place here, everything going on well. The new mine is improving, so I have been tempted to continue it for a short while longer.

It will not be necessary for me to remain here longer than a few days, so that whenever you are ready for me I can return.

YOUR OWN LOVING HUSBAND

I am very well indeed.

January 4, 1888

I finished will before going to bed on Monday and will execute it and send it north tomorrow. Am pretty sure to be able to return next Monday or Tuesday at latest.

MY OWN DARLING QUEENIE, – I got off all right yesterday morning, forgetting the lamp, however, until I was in train, when I decided upon telegraphing them from Chester to send it on at once, which I did. I am having the carpenter to fix a strong hook in the ceiling joist for it to hang upon and it will be a great improvement on the present state of affairs, as the consumption of candles is enormous, while giving very little light. They are undoubtedly the best and safest lamps out; in fact, absolutely safe.

One of the little lamps here was broken since, so I have suspended the other one also, as it was no use by itself.

The room will be very nice for a large suspended lamp; it is about 13 ½ feet high, by 24 feet by 20 feet.

I had only half an hour to wait at Kingstown for the train, which I spent in the waiting-room and a quarter of an hour at Bray.

The sea was rather rough, but not too rough for me. I studied the swinging of a lamp minutely during the passage and derived valuable lessons for the new ship (He studied the balance of the lamp for the 'new ship' he was inventing–the one he was always trying at Brighton).

Am going to Arklow in the morning. Everything going on here very well, notwithstanding which I have been advising and admonishing K. (Kerr, Mr Parnell's agent and bailiff) all day.

E. (Emily Dickinson, Parnell's sister) is here all by herself, mother being expected tonight.

Miss B. B. was very old, very ugly and very vulgar; in fact, E. says the worst sponge that ever got hold of my mother. She drank nothing but whisky and took it to bed with her.

There was dancing after theatricals till six in the morning (Mrs Delia Parnell was giving the theatricals and dance in the great new cattle-shed he had had built from his own plans, modelled on the plan of the new station at Brighton).

I am very anxious about my own love and so glad to get telegram today; expect letter tomorrow. Raining torrents all day.

YOUR OWN HUSBAND

A couple of weeks before the action came on Parnell came home in great amusement. Lewis had written asking him most particularly to call, as he had had a consultation with Sir Charles Russell and wished to report the result to Parnell. On Parnell's calling, thinking some new phase of the case had been evolved, Mr Lewis had 'hoped he would not be annoyed', but Sir Charles and he were rather worried about his (Parnell's) clothes and would he very much mind having a new frockcoat from Poole's for the trial! Parnell had great fun with me over that Poole coat and when it came home we tried it on with great ceremony, Parnell stroking its silk facings with pride and insisting upon a back view of it in the long mirror in my room.

Mr Lewis inspired me with the greatest confidence and his charmingly deferential manner fascinated me, while the keen brown eyes seemed to read the hidden secrets of the soul. He was always exquisitely dressed and, when I made some playful remark about Parnell's new coat, he told me in confidence that Parnell's Irish homespuns were a great trial to him – this with such earnestness that I tried to suppress my laughter, as I explained to him what a pleasure it was to me to be possessed of a man who was above clothes; not below them in slovenliness, but above them and unconscious of his coverings.

Very many years after this, long after my husband's death, this acquaintance with Sir George Lewis served me in good stead. Circumstances arose which rendered me very doubtful and uneasy in regard to the probity of my trustee and solicitor, who had charge of my whole income and the capital thereof. I had had no communication with Sir George Lewis for very many years; but then the happy thought struck me that he would advise me privately and disinterestedly. My son went to him on my behalf and it is entirely owing to the prompt action taken by Sir George that any part of my little income was saved to me.

My trustee had been speculating wildly and, among that of other clients, every penny of my small fortune had been misappropriated. Sir George compelled the repayment of what was possible by the discredited and ruined man and thus saved me by his kind and energetic intervention from absolute destitution. Apart from the very serious loss it entailed upon me, the downfall of my trustee, clever, good-looking and altogether charming, was a great blow to us all. He had been so much a friend and I and my son and daughters had trusted him so completely.

The result of the Parnell Commission is well known. I continued to see Mr Lewis regularly before the case came on and on one occasion he asked me if I would mind going to Wood's Hotel, close by Ely Place, to meet him on a matter that had to do with the case! This I did and being early, awaited him in the coffee room. When he came we had a long business talk about the case and he assured me that the issue was now completely secured. People were passing in and out as we talked and several I noticed passed very close to us and stared curiously at me before going out.

Suddenly, on observing this, I asked Mr Lewis why he had arranged our interview in this place instead of at his office as usual. He made some evasive reply about a client of his who occupied a very distinguished position – and he mentioned this personage by name – having an appointment at the office and disliking the fact of any other person being received during the same hour of his visit.

I pointed out to Mr Lewis that he was surely speaking at random, as the person he mentioned could not be left about at his office like a nobody while he talked to me at an hotel. At this he laughed and asked that I should be satisfied with his reply until he saw me again and with this I had to be content, though I was somewhat ruffled at his not offering a sufficient explanation of his odd place of appointment and I curtly refused to make another at the office for the following week.

Our interview had ostensibly been for the purpose of discussing certain letters I had given into his care at a former interview, but, as he afterwards told me, he had asked those persons, who had, I thought, stared at me in the hotel, if they could identify me with someone who had been impersonating me with the hope of better entangling Parnell and of preventing him from publicly protecting his honour for fear of dragging me into the case. The 'gentlemen from Ireland' who had had so good a look at me were forced to admit that they had never seen me before in their lives.

Shortly before the case came on I asked Mr Lewis if he would mind my going to see Mr Soames (solicitor for the *Times*). He answered, 'I do not see why you should not do so if you wish it' and to Parnell, who had just come in: 'It will be quite safe for her to see Soames'. 'Yes, of course, she knows best', answered Parnell and off I went, pursued by Mr Lewis's: 'You must come straight back here, Mrs O' Shea', as he put me into the waiting cab.

My waiting cab was always an acute irritation to Lewis. After his first greeting of me he invariably asked me if my cab was waiting. 'Yes, of course, how else should I get home?' 'You are not going to *drive* home!' with horror. 'No, but to the station.' 'Pay him off, my dear lady and I'll send for another when I have given you some tea', encouragingly. 'But I *like* this horse, he has such good legs.' Then dear Mr Lewis used to get intensely irritated and send someone flying to pay my cab to go away at once. I never dared at this stage to tell him that I always made a compact with the cabman that 'waiting did not count'.

On my arrival at Mr Soames's office he saw me at once without any pretence of being 'too busy'. In fact his office appeared almost deserted and he welcomed me as his 'cousin'. He took some time in arranging the exact collateral degree of our relationship, but beyond this our interview behind his closely shut glass-panelled door led to nothing. I was desirous of finding out which way his suspicions tended – as obviously he did not really think that Parnell had written the letters; he, on his part, was trying to find out why I had come.;

On the 1st of March, 1889, Pigott shot himself in Madrid. It was a painful affair and Parnell was sorry for the poor creature.

When Parnell attended the House for the first time after the result of the Parnell Commission was made known, I was not well and could not get to the Ladies' Gallery, as I had hoped to do, but long before he came I had had reports of the tremendous ovation he received; how every section of the House – Ministers, Opposition – all rose at his entry as one man, cheering themselves hoarse and shouting his name. I asked him afterwards if he had not felt very proud and happy then, but he only smiled and answered, 'They would all be at my throat in a week if they could!' I thought of that speech a little later on.

Soon after the death of Pigott, Mr Parnell met Mr and Mrs Gladstone at Mrs Sydney Buxton's (later Viscountess Buxton) 'at home'. Almost the only comment, when he got home was: 'That's over; thank goodness!'

On May 28th, 1889, Sir Charles and Lady Russell gave a reception in honour of the hero of the fight. Parnell hated these affairs, but, as I pointed out to him, it would be very sad if all those people assembled to meet him and he was not there. The reception was a time of adulation for him from first to last, I afterwards heard, but when Parnell came home and told me all about it he remarked: 'It was all very kind and just as troublesome as usual – or would have been had I not discovered a pretty little brown head with friendly eyes that looked as shy as I felt.'

I answered, 'Dear me, who was this charming lady? I should like to know!'

'That is just what she was, a charming little lady, an Irishwoman. You know, Queenie, you are the only Englishwoman I can bear! This was Katharine Tynan; you read some of her things to me' and he went on to speak of others at the reception, afterwards reverting to the pleasure he had felt in meeting Katharine Tynan, who he believed genuinely felt what all 'those others' were saying.

Presumably 'those others' were perfectly sincere in their appreciation of him, but Parnell, so English in his own nature, had a constitutional distrust of English people and curiously enough, he did not understand them well, while the Irish character was an open book to him. At a reception like this where the guests were, of course, mostly English, Parnell would retire behind his coldest, most aloof bulwark of exquisite courtesy and to use his own simile about Katharine Tynan: 'I felt as though a little friendly bird had made a song for me in an unfriendly land.' We often afterwards spoke of the 'little friendly bird' and, should Mrs Hinkson (Katharine Tynan) ever see this book, she will know that the 'Chief' appreciated both her loyalty and her song.

Directly the result of the Parnell Commission was made known Mr Parnell was elected a life member of the National Liberal Club; an election which afforded him a certain grave amusement at the time and a query later on, when the 'National Liberals' wished to depose him, as to whether a 'life member' can dare be so illogical as to continue life without the membership.

On the 8th March, 1889, he was entertained for the second time at the Eighty Club and a few days later at a great meeting at St. James's Hall. At both meetings the enthusiasm was so great that the whole body of people present rose en masse as he entered, cheering, waving handkerchiefs and shouting his name for some time before they allowed him to sit down.

Naturally these ovations of my hero gave me the greatest pride and joy, but he would never allow me to say much about them.

'You see, my dear, these people are not really pleased with me', he would say. 'They thought I had written those letters and now they are extolling their own sense of justice in cheering me because I did not write them. I might as wisely shout myself hoarse if a court of law decided that Gladstone had not told somebody to rob a bank!' And I would reply: 'Well, I love to hear and read about your being properly appreciated', only to get a reproving:

'You are an illogical woman. These people do not appreciate *me*, they only howl with joy because I have been found within the law. The English make a law and bow down and worship it till they find it obsolete – long after this is obvious to other nations – then they bravely make another and start afresh in the opposite direction. That's why I am glad Ireland has a religion; there is so little hope for a nation that worships laws.'

And when I persisted: 'But don't you feel a *little* excited and proud when they all cheer *you*, really *you*?' and the little flames showed in his eyes as he said:

'Yes, when it is *really* me, when I am in the midst of a peasant crowd in Ireland. Then I feel a little as I do when I see you smile across the street at me before we meet, but for these others it is then I know how I hate the English and it is then, if I begin to feel a little bit elated, I remember the howling of the mob I once saw chasing a man to lynch him years ago. Don't be too pleased with the clapping of these law-lovers, Queenie. I have a presentiment that you will hear them another way before long and I am exactly the same, either way!'

At the National Liberal Club, at which Sir Frank Lockwood presided, Mr Parnell and Lord Spencer shook hands for the first time. When Parnell rose to speak he received a perfect ovation. He said:

'There is only one way in which you can govern Ireland within the Constitution and that is by allowing her to govern herself in all those matters which cannot interfere with the greatness and wellbeing of the Empire of which she forms a part. I admit there is another way. That is a way that has not been tried yet. ... There is a way in which you might obtain at all events some present success in the government of Ireland. It is not Mr Balfour's bastard plan of a semi-constitutional, a semi-coercive method. You might find among yourselves some great Englishman or Scotchman, who would go over to Ireland – her Parliamentary representation having been taken away from her – and would do justice to her people notwithstanding the complaints of Irish landlordism. Such a man might be found who, on the one hand, would oppose a stern front to the inciters of revolution or outrage and on the other hand would check the exorbitant demands of the governing classes in that country and perhaps the result might be successful. But it would have to be a method outside the Constitution both on the one side and on the other. Your Irish Governor would have to have full power to check the evildoer; whether the evildoer were a lord or a peasant, whether the malefactor hailed from Westminster or New York, the power should be equally exercised and constantly maintained. In that way, perhaps, as I have said, you might govern Ireland for a season. That, in my judgment, from the first time when I entered political life, appeared to me to be the only alternative to the concession to Ireland of full power over her own domestic interests and her future. In one way only, I also saw, could the power and influence of a constitutional party be banded together within the limits of the law; by acting on those principles laid down by Lucas and Gavan Duffy in 1852, that they should hold themselves aloof from all English political parties and combinations, that they should refuse place and office for themselves or for their friends or their relations and that the Irish constituencies should refuse to return any member who was a traitor to those pledges.'

In July Parnell was presented with the freedom of the City of Edinburgh. In his speech of acknowledgment he said:

'In what way could Ireland, supposing she wished to injure you, be more powerful to effect injury to your Imperial interests than she is at present? If you concede to her people the power to work out their own future, to make themselves happy and prosperous, how do you make yourselves weaker to withstand wrongdoing against yourselves? Will not your physical capacity be the same as it is now? Will you not still have your troops in the country? Will you not still have all the power of the Empire? ... In what way do we make you weaker? In what way shall we be stronger to injure you? What soldiers shall we have? What armed policemen shall we have? What cannons shall we have? What single means shall we have, beyond the constitution, that we have not now, to work you injury?'

CHAPTER XXXVII

BRIGHTON HAUNTS

'We went as children joyous, or oprest,
In some absorbing care, or blest',
In nodding conversation – hand in hand.'
– (THE LOVER'S DIARY) HONORA SHEE.

MY AUNT APPEARED TO ME to be failing in health a good deal at the beginning of 1888 and though she sometimes seemed to be stronger and chatted with all her old interest in the things of the past, there were days when she was so quiet and drowsy that I feared to rouse her by talking. At other times she would like me to talk and read to her as usual, but was so languid and tired that a little smile and pressure of the hand I held was the only response she made. In April she had a slight attack of bronchitis and her doctor ordered her opium to ease her lungs. She much objected to all opiates, but her doctor's treatment seemed to ease her. She would not let me sleep in her house, as she thought, as usual, that it would 'disorganise the household', but I went now nearly every night across the park in the fragrant spring nights to inquire, under her maid's window, if Mrs 'Ben' was asleep. ,

The owls had nested for years in a great tree by my aunt's bedroom windows and I loved to watch them in the moonlight hawking for the food they had to supply in such abundance now to the screeching owlets in the nest. The old birds used to sit on Aunt Ben's window-sill and hoot and had done so, much to her pleasure, for the sixty or seventy years of her residence in the house; but now her maid shook her head sadly, as she leant out of the window to tell me of her mistress's condition, saying 'That's an omen, ma'am; the dear mistress must be going soon'. I answered irritably that the owls had hooted there since Mr Benjamin's time, as her mistress had often told her, but felt her 'time will show, ma'am', to be unanswerable.

On these May nights, if he was at home, Parnell would walk across the park with me and wait on a seat for me till I had obtained the latest bulletin.

One morning, very early, when her night had been restless, I made Mary Ann (my aunt's personal maid) come down and let me in. On going up to the great four post bed where the dear little old lady lay, looking as small and frail as a child, she put out one, now feeble, white hand and held mine. I told the maid she could go and rest a bit and I would call her if my aunt wanted her.

When she was gone, my aunt, who was breathing with difficulty, whispered as I bent down to kiss her hand: 'You do believe, do you not, my Swan?' I answered, 'Yes, auntie, of course I do believe, most firmly.' She said, 'I am glad. I wish you could come with me, my darling!' I sobbingly told her that I wished I could too.

I stayed by her side and smoothed her hand till she ceased to breathe and then waited by her as all her servants who had been with her for many years filed past the bed and took a last look at their stern, but just and much-loved mistress.

She left a great void in my life and the sensation I had sometimes felt so keenly hard I would now have given much to feel again. With this old lady died, so far as my acquaintance went, the last of the old courtesy of days when men might wear their gallantry without foolishness and women knew the value of their sex.

Through all the years in which I waited on my aunt I never heard her use a clipped word, or use a sentence not grammatically perfect and beautifully rounded off and although I sometimes felt impatient when chided for some swallowed pronunciation or ignored g's, I look back upon the years of my life spent in that old-world atmosphere as a very precious memory.

After my aunt's death Eltham became intolerable to me and I took a small country house near Mottingham till I could let my own house, Directly we left Eltham the pretty garden was devastated by relic-hunters, who pulled the place to pieces in obtaining mementoes of 'the house where Parnell had lived'.

The house at Mottingham was damp and we longed for the sea.

For various reasons we had been obliged to relinquish any idea of living in the little house we had finished, with so much pleasure at Eastbourne and at last we had removed the few things we had stored there and in 1887 had finally decided to take the end house of Walsingham Terrace (No. 10), Brighton. Shortly after my aunt's death we went to live there. The position was attractive to us: cornfields from one side of the house away up to Shoreham basin and harbour, a waste of hay at the back of the house, an excellent train service and a distance from Brighton proper to enable us avoid the crowd. While we were living there people used to walk and drive out to see 'Parnell's house', but this was not particularly annoying, as when he was at home we went out early, or late – anyhow at a time when the average person is kept at home by appetite. Personally, if it was not glaringly inconvenient, I was always rather proud and interested in the popular attention Parnell attracted wherever he went.

Here Parnell had the dining-room as his own sitting-room , where he kept the roll-top desk I had given him for all his papers and political work, while down in the basement there was a room in which he had a furnace fitted up and where we used to burn the crushed ore before assaying it. We spent so many hours down there and I sometimes feared the excessive heat must have been bad for him; but he did not think so and would become so absorbed in this work that I used to have the greatest difficulty in getting him out for the gallop on his horse President across the Downs, which did him much good.

I found at length the only way was to get his cap and whip and show them to the dogs. Immediately I did this they would begin to bark wildly and jump up at him to make him start for the run they loved so much. Parnell would then say reproachfully, 'Oh, Queenie, how can you deceive the poor dogs like that?' and I would answer that the only way to keep them believing in us was to go at once for that belated ride. Once started none of the party, dogs or horses, enjoyed it more than he.

In this house we had from the side windows of Parnell's and from my room in which he afterwards died, a view of the most wonderful sunsets I have ever seen in England.

Then the whole west was a veritable fairyland of gold and crimson and the harbour and Shoreham town, with the little country church of Aldrington against the setting of the Downs, were touched with a pearly mist of light that lifted them far out of the prosaic ugliness we knew by the blank light of midday. Parnell used to say to me as we walked away to the golden harbour, 'Is it really like this, my Queen, or as we see it at noon?' I could only reply that it was both that made life at once so interesting and so difficult.

Often in the following spring my King and I would drive out as far as the foot of the Downs near the training stables beyond Southwick and then, climbing to the crest of the hills, go for long walks, away over the Downs, walking or resting as we felt inclined, returning as night fell, to drive home.

One sunny morning, lengthening into a brighter day, I especially remember, when the southwest wind sent the flickering shadows across the Downs where its sea-scents mingled with the sweet pungency of the young herbage. As we walked along hand in hand we were gay in the glorious spring of the year, feeling that while love walked so closely with us youth could not lag too far behind and in the wide expanse of the South Downs, which appealed so much to both our natures, we forgot all care and trouble.

Very far away, standing clear against the skyline, there was a figure of a shepherd, his flock a little lower showed grey against the dull green distance. He stood motionless, as these lonely Down shepherds do. The tumbled heap by him, we said, was his dog. So we watched him some miles away for more than an hour. We wondered what he thought of and whether all this lonely loveliness meant anything to him, or if he would be glad to change his quiet life for the rush and hurry of a town.

Presently, from where we sat, at the highest point of the hills, we saw some horses going at full gallop over the training ground, the horses straining at the bit and seemingly glad to be alive. The dull thud of the hoofs came up to us to mingle with the incessant trilling of the skylarks and the bleating of the distant sheep. Now we turned seaward, overlooking Shoreham Harbour and watched the vessels going out to sea on voyages fraught with unknown possibilities.

In spite of the excessive beauty of the scene, in the region of thought it had a saddening effect on us; and, as the last gleams of sunlight fell across the sea, lightly touching the sails as they slipped out of the light into the wider darkness of the leaden waves, we turned and retraced our steps, I leaning on his arm as we went down to the valley again.

A favourite haunt of ours at Brighton was a little shop in Pool Valley altogether devoted to the sale of pebbles and crystals of various sorts, also of jet. Parnell did not like the jet, but was greatly interested in the pebbles and the polishing of them.

He spent much time after we had found this shop in watching the process of cutting crystals and polishing the pebbles. Onyx ball beads he selected in sizes with the greatest care and had a long chain of them made for me with a gold ball between each two onyx beads. To these he had added a locket composed of crystal and onyx and was much pleased with the result.

The chain, when finished, was a little heavy, but he had had such a happy time in selecting each bead and so carefully matching the markings that I wore it with a light heart till he noticed it was rubbing my neck and insisted upon my taking it off there and then for ever.

Another favourite haunt of ours was Smith's second-hand bookshop in Northstreet, where he would stand for an hour at a time poring over old books on mechanics, or mining, while I dug out 'bargains' amongst the poets of a bygone age and discussed books with the proprietor.

Parnell always tried to get a few days' shooting every year in Ireland on the grouse moors he hired at Anghavanagh and I had much pleasure in getting together hampers of provisions for him in London to take over with him, as the arrangements he had been used to before I met him were decidedly primitive and very trying to his health. I always found that a good supply of hams and tongues, with the very best tea that I could procure, a new spirit kettle (every year) and a goodly supply of rugs and blankets rendered him sufficiently comfortable and returned him to me without the acute attacks of indigestion that had formerly rendered these holidays among the mountains so little gain to him in health.

I had to insist upon his learning to make his own tea to save him from the 'stewed' tea made by his servant in Ireland and I found it better to label the tea I got for his personal use: 'For presents' and that which he might give away: 'For Mr Parnell's own use', as he said plaintively, 'They seem to like my tea best!'

He used to love these shooting expeditions, but would never stay more than a few days, as he could not bear to be away from me longer. I used to wish it were possible for me to go to Ireland with him in order that he might enjoy his shooting to the full, but that was impossible and he always declared that: 'Three or four days broke the back of that little shoot, anyhow!'

For many months Parnell tried to invent a vessel which would so cut through the water as to obviate any sensation of the motion of the waves. When he had done this the ship was to be built and I would be enabled to cross the Atlantic as comfortably as I now made the journey to Brighton! Incidentally this invention was also to make our fortunes. Although the building of the ship had to be indefinitely postponed, the models made and tested by Parnell were really wonderful. He had had no training in mechanics, nor did he know anything of shipbuilding or engineering, except such information as he obtained from the various books he read for amusement at rare intervals – but these models he made and tried off the under-deck of the Chain Pier at Brighton were extraordinarily ingenious.

I do not venture to record this on my own authority, for I know absolutely nothing of such matters, but the firm, who cast the copper 'floats' for him from his plans and continually altered and corrected the models after trials, came to the conclusion that Mr 'Smith' was on the verge of a very useful invention; though, to his annoyance, they would not dissociate the torpedo-like structure from Portsmouth and the Admiralty. I frequently took my children down to Brighton for a few days' change and on these occasions Mr Parnell would stay at a place near the Chain Pier and we would spend most of the day on the under-deck of the pierhead trying the 'invention'. Once a hobby like this got hold of him he could think of nothing else in his leisure time and this note is a specimen of many sent round from his hotel:–

Am making new float, which will sink five feet and shall have it ready to try tomorrow at 12.30. Will meet you on Chain Pier at that hour. Am anxious to make this trial before returning and we will take Hassocks and Burgess Hill in afternoon on way back to look at houses to let.

This new model we tried in all weathers and, as at last it seemed to answer perfectly, with the exception of its lack of speed, he said he would patent it and get someone who had more knowledge than he to overcome the speed difficulty. To my uninitiated mind the thing looked like a treble torpedo-boat. Had he lived I think he would have gone further into the matter, but, by the time this was finished, one thing after another occurred with such rapidity that it was perforce laid aside.

I remember one rough, stormy day when we had been much worried and were wondering whether the time of waiting we had imposed upon ourselves (that Ireland might not risk the leadership which seemed her only hope) till the way could be opened to our complete union before the world, was not to be too long for our endurance. It was a wild storm and Parnell had to hold me as we slowly beat our way to the pier head. The chains were up to prevent anyone going on to the lower deck, but Parnell lifted me over and we tried the 'float', though it was useless to do so, as the waves shattered the slight thing against the pier before Parnell could sink it to the required depth.

Then we stood looking out at the great waves – so near and shaking the whole pierhead in their surge. Parnell remarked that the old place could not last long and as I turned to get a fresh hold on him, for I could not stand against the wind and the motion of the sea sickened me, the blazing fires in his eyes leapt to mine and, crushing me roughly to himself, he picked me up and held me clear over the sea, saying, 'Oh, my wife, my wife, I believe I'll jump in with you and we shall be free for ever.'

Had I shown any fear I think he would have done it, but I only held him tight and said: 'As you will, my only love, but the children?' He turned then and carried me to the upper deck, hiding my eyes from the horrible roll and sucking of the sea beneath our feet.

In going through some old letters I have found this copy of one sent by my husband to Cecil Rhodes and think it is sufficiently interesting to publish, though it must stand alone, as the bulk of what was an extremely interesting interchange of views is lost. Parnell had taken considerable notice of Rhodes's tactics in South Africa and when he received a letter from Rhodes expressing the wish to see him he took an early opportunity of calling upon him informally at the Westminster Palace Hotel, in London.

DEAR SIR, – I am much obliged to you for your letter of the 19th inst., which confirms the very interesting account given me at Avondale last January by Mr McNeill as to his interviews and conversations with you on the subject of Home Rule for Ireland. I may say at once and frankly, that you have correctly judged the exclusion of the Irish members from Westminster to have been a defect in the Home Rule measure of 1886 and further, that this proposed exclusion may have given some colour to the accusation so freely made against the Bill that it had a separatist tendency.

I say this while strongly asserting and believing that the measure itself was accepted by the Irish people without any afterthought of the kind and with an earnest desire to work it out with the same spirit with which it was offered – a spirit of cordial goodwill and trust, a desire to let bygones be bygones and a determination to accept it as a final and satisfactory settlement of the longstanding dispute between Great Britain and Ireland.

I am very glad that you consider the measure of Home Rule to be granted to Ireland should be thoroughgoing and should give her complete control over her own affairs without reservation and I cordially agree with your opinion that there should be effective safeguards for the maintenance of Imperial unity. Your conclusion as to the only alternative for Home Rule is also entirely my own, for I have long felt that the continuance of the present semi-constitutional system is quite impracticable. But to return to the question of the retention of the Irish members at Westminster. My own views upon the points and probabilities of the future and the bearing of this subject upon the question of Imperial federation – my own feeling upon the measure is that if Mr Gladstone includes in his next Home Rule measure the provisions of such retention we should cheerfully concur with him and accept them with goodwill and good faith, with the intention of taking our share in the Imperial partnership. I believe also that in the event I state this will be the case and that the Irish people will cheerfully accept the duties and responsibilities assigned to them and will justly value the position given to them in the Imperial system. I am convinced that it would be the highest statesmanship on Mr Gladstone's part to devise a feasible plan for the continued presence of the Irish members here and from my observation of public events and opinions since 1885. I am sure that Mr Gladstone is fully alive to the importance of the matter and that there can be no doubt that the next measure of autonomy for Ireland will contain the provisions which you rightly deem of such moment.

It does not come so much within my province to express a full opinion upon the larger question of Imperial federation, but I agree with you that the continued Irish representation at Westminster immensely facilitates such a step, while the contrary provision in the Bill of 1886 would have been a bar. Undoubtedly this is a matter which should be dealt with in accordance largely with the opinion of the colonies themselves and if they should desire to share in the cost of Imperial matters, as undoubtedly they now do in the responsibility and should express a wish for representation at Westminster, I certainly think it should be accorded to them and that public opinion in these islands would unanimously concur in the necessary constitutional modifications.

I am, Dear sir, Yours truly,

CHAS. STEWART PARNELL

June 23, 1888

Nearly the whole of the Rhodes-Parnell correspondence was accidentally destroyed. This is unfortunate, as it was most interesting and gave Mr Rhodes's views very fully; but I do not remember it sufficiently well to care to comment upon it. It is so many years – over fifteen – since I last went through it. Mr Parnell had a very high opinion of Cecil Rhodes's 'statesmanship.'

CHAPTER XXXVIII

THE DIVORCE CASE

'Papel y tinta y poca justicia.'
('Paper, ink and a little justice')
– OLD SPANISH PROVERB.

IN NOVEMBER, 1890, PARNELL WAS served with a copy of the petition in the divorce case, O' Shea *v.* O' Shea and Parnell, by Wontner at Messrs. Lewis and Lewis's. I was served with the petition in the same month at 10 Walsingham Terrace, Brighton. Mr George Lewis and his confidential clerk came down and took some evidence for the case from me, but Parnell declined to instruct any solicitor from the first to last. He, however, accompanied me when I went to town to consult Sir Frank Lockwood, my counsel, a junior counsel being also present.

'The consultation broke up in peals of laughter', said one of the less important of the evening papers of the time. This was quite true, but it had no bearing on the case at all, for the laughter was caused by the extremely funny stories told us, in his own inimitable way, by Sir Frank Lockwood. The two or three times I saw him stand out in my memory as hours of brilliant wit and nonsense, that cheered and invigorated us far more than the advice we did not ask for could have done. Parnell would not fight the case and I could not fight it without him. The last time I saw Sir Frank Lockwood, the day before the case came on, he begged me to get Parnell to let him fight it. I was suffering acutely from neuralgic headache at the time, but I did my best to get Parnell to defend the case, though to no purpose.

We left Sir Frank Lockwood with a promise to telegraph to him by eight o' clock the next morning if we would go up and appear in Court at all, as he had to be there by ten o' clock.

We had to return to Brighton in the Pullman car, as we could not get a carriage to ourselves. It was crowded and Parnell was known; it was therefore very difficult to talk without being overheard. Parnell appeared absolutely unconscious of the eyes furtively watching him from behind every newspaper, or, indeed, openly in the carriage and he had the power of putting himself absolutely beyond and above self-consciousness. This is what rendered him so absolutely impervious to criticism. But to me, with a splitting headache, the gleam of so many eyes, seen through a mist of pain, had the most uncanny effect. They seemed like animals watching from their lair. Parnell gave me a cheerful little smile now and then and directly we got home he insisted upon my going to bed. There he fed me himself with the tiny amount I forced myself to take to please him and held the glass to my lips while I sipped the sparkling Moselle I had been ordered to take for the bad attacks of neuralgia.

After he had had his own dinner he came up and smoked by my bedside. I tried to persuade him to go up with me in the morning to the Court and make some fight in the case, but he said:—

'No, Queenie. What's the use? We want the divorce and, divorce or not, I shall always come where you are. I shall always come to my home every night whatever happens. Now I'm going to read you to sleep.'

He was always the most gentle and tender of nurses and would sit by my side for hours without moving when I was ill, reading or thinking. After a short sleep I lay awake wondering what it would be best to say to Lockwood in the morning. I had told him that anyhow I would go up; but, as my lover said, what would be the use of it? And whatever I could make of Captain O' Shea's desertion — or practical desertion — of me, I knew absolutely nothing of his private life and cared less. Our position would be worse if we were not enabled to marry, for we were inseparable while life lasted.

Then, after going over the pros and cons till my brain felt on fire, I said irritably, 'I don't believe you are listening to what I say!' He replied, 'I am not, beloved; here is the telegram all written out for you while you slept. We have been longing for this freedom all these years and now you are afraid!'

I broke down and cried, because I feared for him and for his work and he soothed me as one would a child as he told me that his lifework was Ireland's always, but that his heart and his soul were mine to keep for ever — since first he looked into my eyes that summer morning, ten years before. He continued:

'Queenie, put away all fear and regret for my public life. I have given and will give Ireland what is in me to give. That I have vowed to her, but my private life shall never belong to any country, but to one woman. There will be a howl, but it will be the howling of hypocrites; not altogether, for some of these Irish fools are genuine in their belief that forms and creeds can govern life and men; perhaps they are right so far as they can experience life. But I am not as they, for they are among the world's children. I am a man and I have told these children; what they want and they clamour for it. If they will let me, I will get it for them. But if they turn from me, my Queen, it matters not at all in the end. What the ultimate government of Ireland will be is settled and it will be so and what my share in the work has been and is to be, also. I do wish you would stop fretting about me. We know nothing of how or why, but only that we love one another and that through all the ages is the one fact that cannot be forgotten nor put aside by us.'

He spoke slowly, with many silences between sentence and sentence and presently I said: 'But, perhaps I have hurt your work.'

'No, you have not. I sometimes think that is why you came to me, for I was very ill then and you kept the life in me and the will to go on when I was very weary of it all; you have stood to me for comfort and strength and my very life. I have never been able to feel in the least sorry for having come into your life. It had to be and the bad times I have caused you and the stones that have been flung and that will be flung at you are all no matter, because to us there is no one else in all the world that matters at all — when you get to the bottom of things.'

Late next morning I awoke from the deep sleep of exhaustion to find him sitting by me superintending the arrangement of 'letters, tea and toast' and to my anxious query as to the time I was answered by his quiet laugh and 'I've done you this time, Queenie; I sent the telegram long ago and they must be enjoying themselves in Court by now!'

That was Saturday, November 15th and on Monday, the 17th, my Brighton solicitor brought me down a copy of the 'decree nisi'. We were very happy that evening and Parnell declared he would have the 'decree' framed. We made many plans for the future that evening of where we should go when the six months had passed and the decree made absolute. I even ventured to suggest that he might marry someone else once I was set completely free, but my lover was not amused and scolded me for suggesting such disgusting ideas.

Sir Frank Lockwood was terribly distressed about us and his inability to 'save Parnell for his country', but he was very kind to me and did all he could to help me in certain legal matters.

On November 26th there was a meeting of the Irish Party, which my King attended. The meeting was adjourned until December 1st. When my lover came home to me that evening I would not let him speak till he had changed his cold boots and socks; then he came over to me and took me into his arms, saying: 'I think we shall have to fight, Queenie. Can you bear it? I'm afraid it is going to be tough work.'

I said, 'Yes, if you can.' But I must confess that when I looked at the frail figure and white face that was so painfully delicate, whose only vitality seemed to lie in the deep, burning eyes, my heart misgave me, for I very much doubted if his health would stand any prolonged strain.

I burst out passionately, 'Why does it matter more now, they have all known for years?' and his rare, low laugh came out with genuine amusement as he replied, 'My sweetheart, they are afraid of shocking Mr Gladstone.'

'But Gladstone —' I began, bewildered.

'Just so, but we are public reprobates now, it just makes the difference. He is a "devout Churchman", they tell me'.

While Parnell sat down at work at his manifesto I deliberated for hours as to whether I ought to let him go on. Should I urge him to come abroad with me? – I knew he would come if I said I could not bear the public fight. I looked at him as he sat now absolutely absorbed in what he was writing and now looking across at me when he had something ready to be pinned together. He did not speak, only the smoulder in his eyes grew deeper as he wrote.

I loved him so much and I did so long to take him away from all the ingratitude and trouble – to some sunny land where we could forget the world and be forgotten. But then I knew that he would not forget; that he would come at my bidding, but that his desertion of Ireland would lie at his heart; that if he was to be happy he must fight to the end. I knew him too well to dare to take him away from the cause he had made his lifework; that even if it killed him I must let him fight – fight to the end – it was himself – the great self that I loved and that I would not spoil even through my love, though it might bring the end in death.

I looked up feeling that he was watching me and met the burning fireflame of his eyes steadily, through my tears, as he said, closing his hand over mine, 'I am feeling very ill, Queenie, but I think I shall win through. I shall never give in unless you make me and I want you to promise me that you will never make me less than the man you have known.' I promised it.

He was feeling very ill. November was always a bad month for his health and the cold and damp gave him rheumatism. His left arm pained him almost continuously all this winter. I used to rub it and his shoulder with firwood oil, in which he had great belief and pack his arm in wool, which seemed to be some relief.

On Saturday morning, November 29th, his manifesto appeared in all the papers.

War was now declared and the first battle was fought in Committee Room 15, where all the miserable treachery of Parnell's followers – and others – was exposed. The Grand Old Man had spoken and his mandate must be obeyed. Ever swift to take advantage of a political opportunity, he struck at the right moment, remorselessly, for he knew that without giving away the whole of his policy Parnell could not point to the hypocrisy of a religious scruple so suddenly afflicting a great statesman at the eleventh hour. For ten years Gladstone had known of the relations between Parnell and myself and had taken full advantage of the facility this intimacy offered him in keeping in touch with the Irish leader. For ten years. But that was a private knowledge. Now it was a public knowledge and an English statesman must always appear on the side of the angels.

So Mr Gladstone found his religion could at last be useful to his country. Parnell felt no resentment towards Gladstone. He merely said to me, with his; grave smile: 'That old Spider has nearly all my flies in his web' and, to my indignation against Gladstone he replied: 'You don't make allowances for statecraft. He has the Nonconformist conscience to consider and you know as well as I do that he always loathed me. But these fools, who throw me over at his bidding, make me a little sad.' And I thought of that old eagle face, with the cruel eyes, that always belied the smile he gave me and wondered no longer at the premonition of disaster that I had so often felt in his presence.

For the Irish Party I have never felt anything but pity – pity that they were not worthy of the man and the opportunity and seeing the punishment that the years have brought upon Ireland, that their craven hearts could not be loyal to her greatest son. I have wondered at the blindness of her mistress, England; wondered that England should still hold out the reward of Home Rule to Ireland, whose sons can fight even, it is said, their brothers, but who fight as children, unknowing and unmeaning, without the knowledge of a cause and without idea of loyalty.

How long the Irish Party had known of the relations between Parnell and myself need not be here discussed. Some years before certain members of the Party opened one of my letters to Parnell. I make no comment.

Parnell very seldom mentioned them. His outlook was so much wider than is generally understood and his comment on members of the Party was always, both before and after the split, calm, considerate and as being impersonal to himself.

He regarded the Catholic Church's attitude towards him as being the logical outcome of her profession. He was not, even in the last months, when the priests' veto to their people turned the fight against him in Ireland, bitter against them, even though I was. His strongest comment was:– 'They *have* to obey their bishops and *they* Rome – and that's why the whole system of their interference in politics is so infernal!'

Mr Gladstone sent the following letter to Mr Morley on November 24th:–

...While clinging to the hope of communication from Mr Parnell to whomsoever addressed, I thought it necessary, viewing the arrangements for the commencement of the Session tomorrow, to acquaint Mr McCarthy with the conclusion at which, after using all the means of observation and reflection in my power, I had myself arrived. It was that, notwithstanding the splendid services rendered by Mr Parnell to his country, his continuance at the present moment in the leadership would be productive of consequences disastrous in the highest degree to the cause of Ireland.

I think I may be warranted in asking you so far to expand the conclusion I have given above as to add that the continuance I speak of would not only place many hearty and effective friends of the Irish cause in a position of great embarrassment, but would render my retention of the leadership of the Liberal Party, based as it has been mainly upon the presentation of the Irish cause, almost a nullity.

Thus Mr Gladstone signed the death-warrant of Home Rule for Ireland.

As a matter of historical interest I give the full text of the manifesto issued by Mr Parnell to the Irish people:–

TO THE PEOPLE OF IRELAND

'The integrity and independence of a section of the Irish Parliamentary Party having been apparently sapped and destroyed by the wire-pullers of the English Liberal Party it has become necessary for me, as the leader of the Irish nation, to take counsel with you and having given you the knowledge which is in my possession, to ask your judgment upon a matter which now solely devolves upon you to decide.

'The letter of Mr Gladstone to Mr Morley, written for the purpose of influencing the decision of the Irish Party in the choice of their leader and claiming for the Liberal Party and their leaders the right of veto upon that choice is the immediate cause of this address to you, to remind you and your Parliamentary representatives that Ireland considers the independence of her party as her only safeguard within the Constitution and above and beyond all other considerations whatever. The threat in that letter, repeated so insolently on many English platforms and in numerous British newspapers, that unless Ireland concedes this right of veto to England she will indefinitely postpone her chances of obtaining Home Rule, compels me, while not for one moment admitting the slightest probability of such loss, to put before you information which until now, so far as my colleagues are concerned, has been solely in my possession and which will enable you to understand the measure of the loss with which you are threatened unless you consent to throw me to the English wolves now howling for my destruction.

'In November of last year, in response to a repeated and longstanding request, I visited Mr Gladstone at Hawarden and received the details of the intended proposals of himself and his colleagues of the late Liberal Cabinet with regard to Home Rule, in the event of the next General Election favouring the Liberal Party.

'It is unnecessary for me to do more at present than to direct your attention to certain points of these details, which will be generally recognised as embracing elements vital for your information and the formation of your judgment. These vital points of difficulty may be suitably arranged and considered under the following heads:–

(1) The retention of the Irish members in the Imperial Parliament.

(2) The settlement of the land or agrarian difficulty in Ireland.

(3) The control of the Irish constabulary.

(4) The appointment of the judiciary (including judges of the Supreme Court, County Court judges and resident magistrates).

'Upon the subject of the retention of the Irish members in the Imperial Parliament Mr Gladstone told me that the opinion and the unanimous opinion, of his colleagues and himself, recently arrived at after most mature consideration of alternative proposals, was that, in order to conciliate English public opinion it would be necessary to reduce the Irish representation from 103 to 32.

'Upon the settlement of the land it was held that this was one of the questions which must be regarded as questions reserved from the control of the Irish Legislature, but, at the same time, Mr Gladstone intimated that while he would renew his attempt to settle the matter by Imperial legislation on the lines of the Land Purchase Bill of 1886, he would not undertake to put any pressure upon his own side or insist upon their adopting his views – in other and shorter words, that the Irish Legislature was not to be given the power of solving the agrarian difficulty and that the Imperial Parliament would not.

'With regard to the control of the Irish constabulary it was stated by Mr Gladstone that, having regard to the necessity for conciliating English public opinion, he and his colleagues felt that it would be necessary to leave this force and the appointment of; its officers under the control of the Imperial authority for an indefinite period, while the funds for its maintenance, payment and equipment would be compulsorily provided out of Irish resources.

'The period of ten or twelve years was suggested as the limit of time during which the appointment of judges, resident magistrates, etc., should be retained in the hands of the Imperial authority.

I have now given a short account of what I gathered of Mr Gladstone's views and those of his colleagues during two hours' conversation at Hawarden – a conversation which, I am bound to admit, was mainly monopolised by Mr Gladstone – and pass to my own expressions of opinion upon these communications, which represent my views then and now.

'And, first, with regard to the retention of the Irish members, the position I have always adopted and then represented, is that, with the concession of full powers to the Irish Legislature equivalent to those enjoyed by a State of the American Union, the number and position of the members so retained would become a question of Imperial concern and not of pressing or immediate importance for the interests of Ireland. But that with the important and all engrossing subjects of agrarian reform, constabulary control and judiciary appointments left either under Imperial control or totally unprovided for, it would be the height of madness for any Irish leader to imitate Grattan's example and consent to disband the army which had cleared the way to victory.

'I further undertook to use every legitimate influence to reconcile Irish public opinion to a gradual coming into force of the new privileges and to the postponements necessary for English opinion with regard to constabulary control and judicial appointments, but strongly dissented from the proposed reduction of members during the interval of probation. I pointed to the absence of any suitable prospect of land settlement by either Parliament as constituting an overwhelming drag upon the prospects of permanent peace and prosperity in Ireland.

'At the conclusion of the interview I was informed that Mr Gladstone and all his colleagues were entirely agreed that, pending the General Election, silence should be absolutely preserved with regard to any points of difference on the question of the retention of the Irish members.

'I have dwelt at some length upon these subjects, but not, I think, disproportionately to their importance. Let me say, in addition, that, if and when full powers are conceded to Ireland over her own domestic affairs, the integrity, number and independence of the Irish Party will be a matter of no importance; but until this ideal is reached it is your duty and mine to hold fast every safeguard.

'I need not say that the questions – the vital and important questions – of the retention of the Irish members, on the one hand and the indefinite delay of full powers to the Irish Legislature on the other gave me great concern. The absence of any provision for the settlement of the agrarian question, of any policy on the part of the Liberal leaders, filled me with concern and apprehension. On the introduction of the Land Purchase Bill by the Government at the commencement of last Session, Mr Morley communicated with me as to the course to be adopted. Having regard to the avowed absence of any policy on the part of the Liberal leaders and party with regard to the matter of the land, I strongly advised Mr Morley against any direct challenge of the principle of State-aided land purchase and, finding that the fears and alarms of the English taxpayer to State aid by the hypothecation of grants for local purposes in Ireland as a counter-guarantee had been assuaged, that a hopeless struggle should not be maintained and that we should direct our sole efforts on the second reading of the Bill to the assertion of the principle of local control. In this I am bound to say Mr Morley entirely agreed with me, but he was at the same time much hampered – and expressed his sense of his position – in that direction by the attitude of the extreme section of his party, led by Mr Labouchere. And in a subsequent interview he impressed me with the necessity of meeting the second reading of the Bill with a direct negative and asked me to undertake the motion. I agreed to this, but only on the condition that I was not to attack the principle of the measure, but to confine myself to a criticism of its details. I think this was false strategy, but it was strategy, adopted out of regard to English prejudices and Radical peculiarities. I did the best that was possible under the circumstances and the several days' debate on the second reading contrasts favourably with Mr Labouchere's recent and abortive attempt to interpose a direct negative to the first reading of a similar Bill yesterday.

'Time went on. The Government allowed their attention to be distracted from the question of land purchase by the Bill for compensating English publicans and the agrarian difficulty in Ireland was again relegated to the future of another Session. Just before the commencement of this Session I was again favoured with another interview with Mr Morley. I impressed upon him the policy of the oblique method of procedure in reference to land purchase and the necessity and importance of providing for the question of local control and of a limitation in the application of the funds. He agreed with me and I offered to move, on the first reading of the Bill, an amendment in favour of this local control, advising that, if this were rejected, it might be left to the Radicals on the second reading to oppose the principle of the measure. This appeared to be a proper course and I left Mr Morley under the impression that this would fall to my duty.

'But in addition he made a remarkable proposal, referring to the probable approaching victory of the Liberal Party at the polls. He suggested some considerations as to the future of the Irish Party. He asked me whether I would be willing to assume the office of Chief Secretary to the Lord Lieutenant of Ireland, or to allow another member of my party to take the position. He also put before me the desirability of filling one of the law offices of the Crown in Ireland by a legal member of my party. I told him, amazed as I was at the proposal, that I could not agree to forfeit in any way the independence of the party or any of its members; that the Irish people had trusted me in this movement because they believed that the declaration I had made to them at Cork in 1880 was a true one and represented my convictions and that I would on no account depart from it. I considered that, after the declarations we had repeatedly made, the proposal of Mr Morley that we should allow ourselves to be absorbed into English politics was one based upon an entire misconception of our position with regard to the Irish constituencies and of the pledges which we had given.

'In conclusion he directed my attention to the Plan of Campaign estates. He said that it would be impossible for the Liberal Party, when they attained power, to do anything for these evicted tenants by direct action; that it would be also impossible for the Irish Parliament, under the powers conferred, to do anything for them and, flinging up his hands with a gesture of despair, he exclaimed: 'Having been to Tipperary, I do not know what to propose in regard to the matter.' I told him that this question was a limited one and that I did not see that he need allow himself to be hampered by its future consideration; that, being limited, funds would be available from America and elsewhere for the support of those tenants as long as might be necessary; that, of course, I understood it was a difficulty, but that it was a limited one and should not be allowed to interfere with the general interests of the country.

'I allude to this matter only because within the last few days a strong argument in many minds for my expulsion has been that, unless the Liberals come into power at the next General Election, the Plan of Campaign tenants will suffer. As I have shown, the Liberals propose to do nothing for the Plan of Campaign tenants by direct action when they do come into power; but I am entitled to ask that the existence of these tenants, whom I have supported in every way in the past and whom I shall continue to support in the future, shall not constitute a reason for my expulsion from Irish politics. I have repeatedly pledged myself to stand by these evicted tenants and that they shall not be allowed to suffer and I believe that the Irish people throughout the world will support me in this policy.

'Sixteen years ago I conceived the idea of an Irish Parliamentary Party, independent of all English parties. Ten years ago I was elected the leader of an independent Irish Parliamentary Party. During these ten years that party has remained independent and because of its independence it has forced upon the English people the necessity of granting Home Rule to Ireland. I believe that party will obtain Home Rule only provided it remains independent of any English party.

'I do not believe that any action of the Irish people in supporting me will endanger the Home Rule cause or postpone the establishment of an Irish Parliament; but even if the. danger with which we are threatened by the Liberal Party of today were to be realised, I believe that the Irish people throughout the world would agree with me that postponement would be preferable to a compromise of our national rights by the acceptance of a measure which would not realise the aspirations of our race.

* * * * * * *

On November 18th, 1890, there was a meeting of the National League in Dublin. On the same day the following paragraph appeared in the London letter of the *Freeman's Journal:* –

'I have direct authority for stating that Mr Parnell has not the remotest intention of abandoning either permanently or temporarily his position or his duties as leader of the Irish Parliamentary Party. This may be implicitly accepted as Mr Parnell's firm resolution and perhaps by learning it in time the Pigottist Press may be spared the humiliation of indulging in a prolonged outburst of useless vilification. In arriving at this determination, I need not say that Mr Parnell is actuated exclusively by a sense of his responsibility to the Irish people, by whose suffrages he holds his public position and who alone have the power or the right to influence his public action. The wild, unscrupulous and insincere shriekings of the Pigottists on the platform and in the Press can and will do nothing to alter Mr Parnell's resolve.'

Parnell wrote to me from London after the meeting in Committee Room 15.

MY OWN DARLING WIFIE, – I have received your letter through Phyllis and hope to return to Brighton tonight per last train and tell you all the news. Meanwhile I may say that I am exceedingly well, having had twelve hours' sleep last night.

The meeting adjourned today till tomorrow at 12 or 1 to consider an amendment moved by one of my side that Gladstone, Harcourt and Morley's views should be obtained as to their action on certain points in my manifesto.

YOUR OWN KING.

December 3, 1890.

The following letters speak for themselves:–

PARNELL to MR. WILLIAM REDMOND.

MY DEAR WILLIE, – Thanks very much for your kind letter, which is most consoling and encouraging. It did not require this fresh proof of your friendship to convince me that I have always justly relied upon you as one of the most single-minded and attached of my colleagues.–Yours very sincerely,

CHARLES S. PARNELL.

PARNELL to DR. KENNY.

MORRISON'S HOTEL, DUBLIN,

Saturday.

MY DEAR DOCTOR, – I shall be very much obliged if you can call over to see me this afternoon, as I am not feeling very well and oblige, yours very truly,

CHARLES S. PARNELL.

Don't mention that I am unwell to anybody, lest it should get into the newspapers. C. S. P.

To all his brothers and sisters and, most of all, to his mother, Parnell was most generous and affectionate and of that generosity and affectionate regard I have abundant proof.

One of the last letters he wrote was to his mother.

I am weary, dear mother, of these troubles, weary unto death; but it is all in a good cause. With health and the assistance of my friends I am confident of the result. The statements my enemies have so often made regarding my relations with you are on a par with the endless calumnies they shoot upon me from behind every bush. Let them pass. They will die of their own venom. It would indeed be dignifying them to notice their existence!

CHAPTER XXXIX

A KING AT BAY

'Vulneratus non victus.'

IN DECEMBER A VACANCY OCCURRED in Kilkenny and, on December 9th, my King started for Ireland and stayed with Dr Kenny for the night in Dublin. Of the great meeting in the Rotunda I give Miss Katharine Tynan's description, because of all the eyewitnesses' accounts of it that I have kept, none gives the true glimpse of Parnell as she does.

'It was nearly 8.80 when we heard the bands coming; then the windows were lit up by the lurid glare of thousands of torches in the street outside. There was a distant roaring like the sea. The great gathering within waited silently with expectation. Then the cheering began and we craned our necks and looked on eagerly and there was the tall, slender, distinguished figure of the Irish leader making its way across the platform. I don't think any words could do justice to his reception. The house rose at him; everywhere around there was a sea of passionate faces, loving, admiring, almost worshipping that silent, pale man. The cheering broke out again and again; there was no quelling it. Mr Parnell bowed from side to side, sweeping the assemblage with his eagle glance.

The people were fairly mad with excitement, I don't think anyone outside Ireland can understand what a charm Mr Parnell has for the Irish heart; that wonderful personality of his, his proud bearing, his handsome, strong face, the distinction of look which marks him more than anyone I have ever seen. All these are irresistible to the artistic Irish.

'I said to Dr. Kenny, who was standing by me, 'He is the only quiet man here.' 'Outwardly', said the keen medical man, emphatically. Looking again, one saw the dilated nostrils, the flashing eye, the passionate face; the leader was simply drinking in thirstily this immense love, which must have been more heartening than one can say after that bitter time in the English capital. Mr Parnell looked frail enough in body – perhaps the black frockcoat, buttoned so tightly across his chest, gave him that look of attenuation; but he also looked full of indomitable spirit and fire.

'For a time silence was not obtainable. Then Father Walter Hurley climbed on the table and stood with his arms extended. It was curious how the attitude silenced a crowd which could hear no words.

'When Mr Parnell came to speak, the passion within him found vent. It was a wonderful speech; not one word of it for oratorical effect, but every word charged with a pregnant message to the people who were listening to him and the millions who should read him. It was a long speech, lasting nearly an hour; but listened to with intense interest, punctuated by fierce cries against men whom this crisis has made odious, now and then marked in a pause by a deep drawn moan of delight. It was a great speech – simple, direct, suave – with no device and no artificiality. Mr Parnell said long ago, in a furious moment in the House of Commons, that he cared nothing for the opinion of the English people. One remembered it now, noting his passionate assurances to his own people, who loved him too well to ask him questions.'

During this meeting the anti-Parnellites took the opportunity to seize Parnell's paper, *United Ireland* and the offices. A witness's account of the incident contained in Mr Barry O' Brien's 'Life of Charles Stewart Parnell' appealed to me immensely, because this little affair was of intense interest to me and all, or nearly all, I could get out of Parnell himself on the subject was a soft laugh and, 'It was splendid fun. I wish I could burgle my own premises every day!'

Something like this appears to have happened. The anti-Parnellite garrison was strongly entrenched in the offices of the newspaper – doors and windows all barred. The streets were filled with a crowd of Parnellites crying death and destruction on the enemy and pouring in faster from the side streets. Men threading their way through the mass were distributing sticks and revolvers.

Parnell had been apprised of the event at the meeting and a pony-trap was waiting for him outside the Rotunda. He got into it with Dr. Kenny and they dashed off to the scene of action. At the sight of their Chief the crowd went wild; cheers for Parnell and curses for his enemies filled the air. At full gallop the pony-trap dashed through the mass of people (which gave way as if by magic) and was brought up before the offices with a jerk that sent the horse sprawling on the ground. Parnell jumped out of the trap, sprang up the steps and knocked loudly at the door of the offices. There was a dramatic moment of silence – the crowd hushed and expectant. Then Parnell quietly gave some orders to those nearest him. In a brief space they were off and back again with pickaxe and crowbar. Parnell wished to vault the area railings and attack the area door, but he was held back. So several of his followers dropped into the area, while Parnell himself attacked the front door with the crowbar. The door yielded and he and many others rushed into the house. A second party came from the area and the united force dashed upstairs. The rest was a Homeric struggle between garrison and besiegers, fought from staircase to staircase and story to story. At length the garrison was downed to the last man. A window of the second story was removed and Parnell came out to his people. He had lost his hat, his hair was tumbled, his face was quite white and his eyes were filled with the wild joy of the battle. His face and clothes were powdered with dust and plaster. For a moment again the crowd was silent; then it burst into a roar.

Parnell made a short speech, came down, got into the trap and drove to the railway station.

On the 11th, when he nominated Mr Vincent Scully, he stayed at Kilkenny. That day he wrote to me that he was feeling ill and his telegram of 'good night' was weary in tone. But the next day he wrote that he was feeling far better and his letter was very hopeful of success. He insisted on returning to me every Saturday, if it was in any way possible, during these months of fighting and going back to Ireland on the next evening, Sunday. I begged him to spare himself the fatigue of this constant journeying, but he could not rest away; so, in despair, I gave up the fight against my own desire to have him at home for even these few hours. This election lasted ten days. Polling took place on December 22 and that morning he telegraphed to me not to expect victory, so I knew he was sure of defeat long before the poll was declared. He returned to Dublin that night and addressed a meeting outside the National Club.

It was during one of these last meetings that someone in the crowd threw lime in the Chief's face. It has been said that the thing was a hoax and that the substance thrown was flour. It was not flour, but lime and had not Parnell shut his eyes in time he would undoubtedly have been blinded. As it was his eyes were not injured and but for a tiny scar on the outer edge of his right eye he was not hurt. I well remember the awful hours I passed pacing up and down my room at Brighton waiting, waiting for news after seeing the morning paper. He had telegraphed to me directly after the cowardly assault was made, but he could not send it himself as he could not leave his friends. The man to whom he gave the telegram for despatch boasted to his fellows that he had a message from Parnell and in the crowd and scuffle it was taken from him; so it was not until midday, when my own telegram of inquiry reached him, that Parnell knew that I had not received his and by the time his reassuring message arrived I was nearly out of my mind. The newspapers had made the very most of the affair and I thought my husband was blinded.

At the end of December Mr William O' Brien returned from America, but, as a warrant was out for his arrest, he could not return to Ireland. Much against his own wish Parnell went over to Boulogne to see him, as the Party were so anxious that he should go. He did not think that it would do any good and, feeling ill, he hated undertaking the extra fatigue. He felt, too, that he would have to fight 'all along the line' in Ireland and continued the war without cessation, although he went over to Boulogne several times to hear what Mr O' Brien had to say. He was, however, on good terms with O' Brien and suggested him as leader of the Party in the event of his own resignation. The suggestion did not prove acceptable to the Party.

Throughout this time he occasionally attended the sittings of the House and, on returning home one sad evening, he did not speak much after his first greeting. I felt that something had troubled him unusually, but forbore to worry him, knowing that he would tell me presently. After a while he turned to me and all he said was, 'O' Kelly has gone too.'

I did not answer in words, for my heart bled for him in this the only personal sorrow he had suffered in the disloyalty of his Party. Anger, scorn and contempt, yes! but this was the first and only blow to his affections. For the first time since that miserable and most cowardly exhibition of treachery in Committee Room 15 there was a little break in his voice. They had been friends for so long and had worked with each other in American and Irish politics so intimately. He had loved him and now O' Kelly had 'gone too'.

When Mr Gladstone gave the word and the insecure virtue of the country obeyed it, because it is a very shocking thing to be found out, the anti-Parnellites were extremely ingenious in inventing new forms of scurrility in connection with my supposed name. From one end of chivalrous Ireland to the other – urged on more especially by a certain emotional Irish member of Parliament – the name of Kitty O' Shea was sung and screamed, wrapped about with all the filth that foul minds, vivid imaginations and black hatred of the aloof, proud Chief could evolve, the Chief whom they could not hurt save through the woman he loved!

They hurt him now a little, it is true, but not very greatly. My husband said to me after the Kilkenny election, 'It would really have hurt, my Queen, if those devils had got hold of your real name, *my* Queenie, or even the 'Katie' or 'Dick' that your relations and Willie called you.' And then I was glad, so very glad that the gallant company of mudslingers had with one accord leapt to the conclusion that those who love me called me 'Kitty' because my name was Katharine. For me it was a little thing to bear for the man who loved me as never woman has been loved before and the only thing that I could not have borne would have been the thought that one of those who hated him had pierced the armour of his pride and touched his heart.

The conferences with Mr William O' Brien resulted in his finally sending him the following letter:–

My proposal now is:

(1) That you should suggest to Mr McCarthy to obtain an interview with Mr Gladstone at Hawarden and ask from him a Memorandum expressing the intentions of himself and his colleagues upon these views and details, as explained by the delegates in their interview with Mr Gladstone on December 5th.

(2) That Mr McCarthy should transfer this Memorandum to your custody and that if, after a consultation between yourself and myself, it should be found that its terms are satisfactory, I should forthwith announce my retirement from the chairmanship of the Party.

(3) That the terms of this Memorandum should not be disclosed to any other person until after the introduction of the Home Rule Bill and not then unless this Bill failed to carry out those terms; but that if the Bill were satisfactory I should be permitted to publish the Memorandum after the passing of the former into law. I would agree that instead of adopting the limit of two years as the period in which the constabulary should be disarmed and turned into a civil force and handed over to the Irish Executive, the term might be extended to five years; but I regard the fixing of some term of years for this in the Bill of the most vital importance. I also send you the enclosed copy of the clause of the Bill of 1886 relating to the Metropolitan Police and Constabulary. I do not think it necessary to insist upon the charge for the latter during the period of probation being paid out of the Imperial funds, as I do not wish to increase Mr Gladstone's difficulties.

P.S. – It should be noted that Gladstone can scarcely refuse to communicate with Mr McCarthy on these subjects, as in his letter to the delegates he stated that as soon as the question of the leadership of the Party was settled he would be in a position to open confidential communications again and he has publicly acknowledged Mr McCarthy's election as valid.

On the 4th of January, 1891, Mr O' Brien wrote, saying that he had given as much thought as he was able to the important proposal it contained. On a first reading of Parnell's letter O' Brian thought he saw a disposition to drop the objection to McCarthy as chairman. If so, the new proposal would seem to diminish the difficulties of conciliating English opinion. If not, the necessity which the Hawarden plan involved of employing McCarthy in a transaction so painful to himself personally would seem to O' Brien to raise a formidable obstacle to that form of securing the guarantees desired. He had long been trying to think of some other way and when they met in Boulogne on Tuesday, he hoped to be able to submit it with sufficient definiteness to enable them to thrash it out with some prospect of an immediate and satisfactory agreement. Those who were bent on thwarting peace at any price were building great hopes on delays or breakdowns of their Boulogne negotiations; but he was beginning to entertain some real hope that with promptness and good feeling on both sides they might still be able to hit upon some agreement that would relieve the country from an appalling prospect and that neither of them would have any reason to regret hereafter.

On January 5 Redmond telegraphed to Parnell that O' Brien had written to the latter the previous day and asking that nothing should prevent Parnell meeting 'us' on the morrow.

On January 9 O' Brien telegraphed that McCarthy and Sexton would be with him that day and that there were difficulties with Dillon.

Again, on the 18th, from Boulogne, he wired that indications were favourable; he presumed that there would be no objection to McCarthy's voice as to satisfactoriness of assurances if obtained.

Whereupon Parnell wired to Mr O' Brien from Limerick:–

While at all times willing to consult with McCarthy upon any points of special difficulty which may from time to time arise, I am obliged to ask that the terms of the Memorandum shall be adhered to, which provide that you and I shall be the sole and final judges.

On January 30th O' Brien wired that he had just received materials for final decision. It was most important that Parnell should see them at once. If Parnell could cross to Calais or anywhere else that night, O' Brien would meet him with Dillon.

On February 4th Parnell wrote to Dr. Kenny:–

I went to Calais on Monday night to see O' Brien. He had received the draft of a letter proposed to be written and purporting to meet my requirements, but I found it of an illusory character and think that I succeeded in showing him that it was so. He will endeavour to obtain the necessary amendments to the draft.

The next day he sent the following letter to Mr Gill: –

MY DEAR GILL (Mr Gill was an Irish member of no particular attachment who proved useful as tin intermediary), – I have carefully considered the position created by the information conveyed to me by you yesterday as to the new proposals and demands of the Liberal leaders and it appears to me to be a very grave one and to add materially to the difficulties attending a peaceable solution. You will remember that under the Memorandum of agreement arrived at between O' Brien and myself more than a month since at Boulogne it was provided that the judgment as to whether the intentions of Mr Gladstone were in accordance upon certain vital points with the views expressed in that agreement was to be given by myself and O' Brien, acting in conjunction and that I have since felt myself obliged to decline a proposal from O' Brien to add another person to our number for the performance of that duty. In addition, you are aware that last Tuesday I met O' Brien at Calais for the purpose of coming to a final decision with him as to the sufficiency of a draft Memorandum respecting the views of the Liberal leaders which he had obtained and which, although at first sight it appeared to him to be sufficient, after a consultation with me was found to require considerable alteration and modification in order to secure the necessary guarantees regarding the vital points in question.

You now inform me that a new condition is insisted upon for the continuance of further negotiations – viz., that the question of the sufficiency of the guarantee is decided upon by O' Brien, apart from me and in conjunction with I know not whom, that he is to see the draft of the proposed public statement and that he must bind himself to accept it as satisfactory before it is published, while I am not to be permitted to see it, to judge of its satisfactory character, or to have a voice in the grave and weighty decision which O' Brien and certain unknown persons were thus called upon to give on my behalf as well as his own. I desire to say that I fully recognise the candour which O' Brien has shown in this matter and the absence of any disposition on his part to depart either from the spirit or the letter of our agreement without my knowledge or consent. It is unnecessary for me to enlarge upon the humiliating and disgraceful position in which this fresh attempt at exaction on the part of the Liberal leaders would seem intended to place me. It suffices to say that neither my own self-respect – nor, I am confident, that of the Irish people –would permit me to occupy it for a single moment. Besides this consideration, I could not, with any regard for my public responsibility and declarations upon the vital points in reference to which assurances are required surrender into unknown hands, or even into the hands of O' Brien, my right as to the sufficiency of those assurances and guarantees. But within the last twenty hours information of a most startling character has reached me from a reliable source, which may render it necessary for me to widen my position in these negotiations. It will be remembered that during the Hawarden communication the one point of the form upon which the views of the Liberal leaders were not definitely and clearly conveyed to me was that regarding the question of the retention of the Irish members at Westminster. It was represented to me that the unanimous opinion was in favour of permanently retaining a reduced number, 34, as the symbol of Imperial unity, but not with a view of affording grounds, occasions, or pretexts for Imperial interference in Irish national concerns, it being held most properly that the permanent retention of a large number would afford such grounds.

But from the information recently conveyed to me, referred to above, it would appear that this decision has been reconsidered and that it is now most probable that the Irish members in their full strength will be permanently retained. This prospect, following so closely upon the orders of the Pall Mall Gazette that it must be so, is ominous and most alarming.

In 1886 the second reading of the Home Rule Bill, as I can prove by documentary evidence, was lost because the Liberal leaders declined till too late to agree to the retention of any Irish members in any shape or for any purpose. This resolve was formed because the Irish Party from 1880 to 1885 have proved their independence, courage and steadiness on many a hard-fought field and it was felt necessary to get rid of them at any cost. But the majority of the party of today having lost their independence and proved their devotion to the Liberal leaders, it is considered desirable to keep them permanently at Westminster for the purpose of English Radicalism and as a standing pretext for the exercise of the veto of the Imperial Parliament over the legislation of the Irish body.

I refrain at present from going further into the matter, but will conclude by saying that so long as the degrading condition referred to at the commencement of this letter is insisted upon by the Liberal leaders, I do not see how I can be a party to the further progress of the negotiations.–

My dear Gill, yours very truly,

CHAS. S. PARNELL.

Other letters to Mr Gill explain themselves:–

February 6, 1891.

MY DEAR GILL, – I have your letter of last night and note that you say that the first part of mine to you of yesterday is founded on a misunderstanding which you can remove. Although I cannot see where there is any room on my part for misunderstanding the information which you conveyed, I shall be very glad if it should turn out as you say and in that case, of course, the negotiations could be resumed. Will you, then, kindly write and explain what the misunderstanding was and how you think it can be removed, as I fear it may not be possible for me to see you at the House of Commons this evening?

Yours very truly,

CHAS. S. PARNELL.

February 7, 1891.

MY DEAR GILL, – I am writing O' Brien by this evening's post upon the subject of our conversation on Wednesday and for the present perhaps it would be better that the negotiations should be conducted by correspondence between himself and me. As regards your note just received, I am sorry that I cannot agree with you that it gives at all an accurate account of the information you then conveyed to me, although, while you expressly stated the conditions, new to me, of the Liberal leaders, I agree that you did not say that you spoke to me on behalf of them, or at their request, nor did I so intimate in my letter of Thursday.

Sincerely yours,

CHAS. S. PARNELL.

Parnell had always found Messrs. O' Brien and Dillon had a depressing effect upon him, as he said it was so hard to keep them to the difficulties of the moment, while they were so eagerly passing on to the troubles of tomorrow.

On 22nd April, 1891, Mr Frederick Kerley wrote from 10 Broad Court, Bow Street, W.C., to Mr Thomson, to say that he had succeeded that day in serving Mr Parnell with a copy of the Judge's Order, which Mr Thomson had handed to him on the evening of the 20th instant. He saw Mr Parnell at 7.5 p.m. pass through the barrier on to the Brighton platform at Victoria Station. He walked by his side and, addressing him, said, 'Mr Parnell, I believe? 'Parnell replied, 'Yes.' He said he was desired to hand him that paper, at the same time handing him the copy, when the following conversation ensued:

Parnell: 'What is it?'

Kerley: 'It is a Judge's Order.'

P.: 'Oh, it is the costs.'

K.: 'Yes, it is. That is a copy, this is the original and the signature of Mr Justice Butt' and Kerley showed the original to him.

P.: 'Oh, very well.'

K.: 'This is Mr Wontner's card, who is the solicitor in the matter.'

Mr Parnell took the card and said, 'Thank you.'

It had all been done very quietly. No one saw what was done and Parnell was not subjected to the slightest annoyance and he did not appear to be the least annoyed. Kerley did not enclose the original, as he was afraid to trust it through the post, but would hand it to Mr Thomson personally.

WONTNERS, 19 LUDGATE HILL, E.C.

Wired 10 a.m., 23 April, 1891.

Copy Order costs P. served personally last evening. Letter follows.

CHAPTER XL

CAPTAIN O' SHEA'S LETTERS

'Tis the talent of our English nation,
Still to be plotting some new reformation.'
– G. CHAPMAN.

21 OLD BROAD STREET, LONDON, E.G.,
March 31, 1882.

MY DICK, – I got your telegram and will do nothing till I hear again about the shares. I did not intend to attend the general meeting of the bank, but Sandeman came and brought me with him. It was very satisfactory.

A great intrigue last night. Walter, the proprietor of the Times, was to have told with Marriott. Finding the Government would have a better majority than was expected, he wrote a note at 11.15 to Marriott saying friends of whose judgment he had a high opinion thought it would be bad for the cause that he should tell Mr Winn, the Opposition Whip and Marriott then asked me to tell. I felt, of course, that the Government would never forgive me; still it might do well in Clare and they are a wretched lot, Gladstone and Co.

I suggested Peter Taylor, Sir Tollemache Sinclair, or Joe Cowen in the order named and after much difficulty I finally got off.

The Government were greatly elated by 39.

Rozenraad will not be managing director of the bank. He wants to teach me details, he says and propose me.

BOYSIE.

HOUSE OF COMMONS,
May 1, 1882.

MY DICK, – Lord Arthur Hill has given notice that he will ask Forster tomorrow whether there is any truth in the statement in the Times today.

I met Chamberlain at Euston and drove with him to the Board of Trade. I then attended a meeting of Shaw, Dickson, M. Henry and Co. and they propounded a scheme for arrears. I had an appointment with Chamberlain, who had meantime been at the Cabinet Council, in his room after questions. He said that for the moment he had absolutely nothing to say to me only to impress upon me that if a row ever occurred and an explanation was called for we were agreed that no negotiations had taken place between us, but only conversations. As to the answer Forster was to give tomorrow, I observed that Forster was a duffer if he couldn't get out of that much, that he had plenty of practice in answering questions, but Chamberlain replied he hadn't improved much.

I am to stay about here tonight, but I doubt the Government allowing Chamberlain to say much more to me at present. Gladstone will make his statement tomorrow at 9; I will try to run down to Eltham if possible in the afternoon, unless I hear you are taking the Chicks anywhere.

I am getting quite hopeless and the dates of payments are staring me in the face.

YOUR BOYSIE.

HOUSE of COMMONS,
July 20, 1882.

MY DICK, – Sir John Lubbock sat next me on one side and Miss Rathbone on the other. Sir John is very interesting. Cotes, the Whip, was there. He said there was much rumour at Brooks' about Forster's reentering the Cabinet. I should think this is impossible. It would finish the Government. I think Chamberlain would have known. On Monday night he told me he believed the rumour to be a d——d lie.

Afterwards went to Sir J. McKenna's. It was very funny indeed. The Boys, Healy, T.P. O' Connor. Chamberlain not in the House today. Tomorrow I dine with Sir William Hart Dyke (damnation on a volcano kind of life), Saturday to Alfred Cohen's till Monday.

I hear nothing about my people. I dare say I shall see you somewhere tomorrow if this Bill gets through. I constantly go to see if there is a telly.

YOUR BOYSIE.

HOUSE OF COMMONS,
Tuesday, August 1, 1882.

MY DICK, – Chamberlain must think me an ass, or Parnell a knave and I dare say both. I have twice telegraphed to Morrison's Hotel today and no answer. *

The Lords swear they will stick to their amendments. The Government will, on the other hand, stick to their Bill pure and simple and risk all by it.

If the Irish Vote comes over to assist them on Thursday. Chamberlain has just asked me whether I have had a telegram (12.30).

YOUR BOYSIE.

The memorial mentioned in the following letter was for the reprieve of a young man, Francis Hymer, who was condemned to death (and subsequently hanged) for shooting a man. There was no direct evidence against him and Captain O' Shea got much support in the effort for his reprieve. The young man was a small 'gentleman farmer' and a very distant connection of Captain O' Shea's.

SHELBOURNE HOTEL, DUBLIN,
August 26, 1882.

MY DICK, – I have been to the Viceregal Lodge with the memorial. Lord Spencer said that in so grave a matter and one in which such a momentous responsibility lies on him, it would not do to discuss the matter, but that the matter would be fully weighed, etc., etc., etc.

Yesterday I was for a long time with Trevelyan. It was funny to see his three boys playing cricket in the grounds of his lodge with constabulary sentinels at each corner. The lodges are charming places, but I have not been in the Under Secretary's. I tried to get a photograph of it yesterday, but I failed. I tellied (telegraphed) I thought it better to say nothing to Parnell. I see G.O.M. got back to town yesterday, but I dare say he smells a rat and will not see you yet awhile. I am very low about everything and your letter is dreadful and I don't know who Mitchell is.

It is dreadful work here and the weather is beastly. However, Lady Corrigan has sent a messenger to beg of me to come and dine this evening at Killney. The house is next to the Fitzgeralds'.

I am greatly afraid the G.O.M. will leave us in the lurch.

Mr Gray says he will have full revenge on the Government. They ought to let him out.

Great love to chicks.

YOUR BOYSIE.

DUBLIN,
August 31, 1882.

MY DICK, – I am longing to get home. No one knows I am writing, so say nothing in your letter about it to my people. Great numbers of inquiries, but Mr Parnell, although in next street, never sent. P for pig! Gout come in old place, not bad. Dearest love to chicks. Great many telegrams.

YOUR BOYSIE.

Am all right, but very helpless for present.

Sunday.

MY DICK, – My arm is getting much better of the sprain, but I cannot write much yet. I have had a better day today all round. A great many people are constantly calling and writing. I hear that Mr Parnell is gone to England. I merely say he never took the trouble to send a message or write a line. I saw your letter to Aunt Mary today and one from Gerard. I am quite satisfied with fish, especially as I don't want the gout to go to my arm. Nice note from Fawcett. Also from Harcourt. Nothing from Chamberlain. John Morley has been with me today for a couple of hours.

I hope to see Trevelyan tomorrow and it is still laborious.

I must write to chicks,

YOUR BOYSIE.

(Captain O' Shea had broken his arm, having been thrown out of a jaunting car in Dublin.)

NEWPORT HOUSE, NEWPORT, Co. MAYO,
September 29, 1882.

MY DICK, – Yes, I am afraid that the Grand Old Humbug is gammoning us. It is very handy of him to be able to put the claims on Lord Spencer's shoulders. Of course, Lord Spencer would not stand out one moment against the G. O. M.'s real wish.

I wrote to Mr P. about his conference, but he has of course not answered my letter. Perhaps it will be as well to wait to try and frighten G. O. M. (which I am afraid would now be a difficult job) till I have seen Parnell.

I have £100 coming due on October 17th, £300 on November 13th and £300 on December 3rd at the National Bank. I must go to Limerick immediately.

The enclosed from Ellard is rather humbug.

I hope to leave this on Tuesday. It is a fearful journey, because I cannot get on to a car from Claremorris to Tuam and I believe I must go to Dublin and thence down to Limerick, two days' journey. I am sorry we cannot manage the bank any longer. You see how it will be getting on. I think I told you about George Ds. being flush of stuff and my borrowing. I don't see any way out of it at all and believe the end is at hand.

YOUR BOYSIE.

SHELBOURNE HOTEL, DUBLIN,
October 17, 1882.

MY DICK,–I was at the Castle this morning and saw Trevelyan about various things and Parnell's complaints as to the unfair exercise of the Crimes Act in various places. He of course admitted me at once and was very civil. I then went to see the Assistant Inspector General of Constabulary.

As I wanted to see Jenkinson on a matter of extra police force in Limerick the Assistant Inspector General sent down my card by his messenger. A reply came up that Mr J. was engaged with the Inspector of Constabulary for Limerick. He kept me waiting an hour. In the meanwhile the Assistant Inspector General gave me the opinion of the heads of departments on Jenkinson. They call him 'His Majesty the Lion of Pride.' (He was in the Indian Service.) He knows nothing whatever of the country and assumes the command of everything, meddling and muddling all, but is an immense favourite with

251

Lord Spencer. They say at the Castle, however, that he can scarcely get Burke's place, it would be too glaring. The fact is nothing is too glaring.

I wonder if J. knows anything.

I wish you could get Matt (my nephew Sir Matthew Wood) to let me No. 1 Albert Mansions very cheap. I cannot understand why he lives in Jermyn Street.

Gout bad enough, wrist greatly swollen. Journeys deferred, should like to leave Friday morning so as to worry Parnell on Thursday if his convention goes in on Wednesday. Will go to see him by and by.

YOUR B.

SHELBOURNE HOTEL, DUBLIN,
October 17, 1882.

I forgot to say that Canon O' Brien of Athenry writes in Freeman that it was not the Archbishop of Tuam who forbade the priests to attend the meeting at Athenry, but his refusal to go was caused by Mr Watt Hain's not having placed before him the programme for approval.

Of course this is mere equivocation.

YOUR W.

On August 2 and 15, 1883, Chamberlain wrote to Willie with reference respectively to certain Bills and praised Parnell's perfect loyalty. On January 30 of the following year we find him giving Willie his opinions on the Irish Land question and doubting if much would be done until the Franchise question were settled. The next letter which comes to my hand is from Mr Childers and it also is about the land. He complains that what the Land Act concedes – an advance from the Treasury to the landlords – is very different from what the Irish want – an advance to the tenant himself. The obvious difference being that in the former case it was by no means certain that the tenant got the money. It is plain from these letters that Willie was in constant communication with Chamberlain, Gladstone and (directly and indirectly) with Trevelyan.

LIMERICK,
October 20, 1884,

MY DICK, – I am so absolutely done up that it is impossible to write much. It is very doubtful whether the game is worth the candle.

However, the Fenians have now shown such an extraordinary support that, as they themselves say, there will be murder in the Co. Clare if I am opposed.

It took me all my time with some of them to allow a vote of confidence in Parnell to be put to the meeting yesterday. It was a terribly wet day, but the 'flower of the flock' came from immense distances, although no public announcement was made. The attendance of some of my 'friends' rendered it impossible for the priests to be present, but they showed their feeling towards me by harbouring me directly the show was over and giving me an excellent dinner. Not that I have eaten 2 Ib. of meat since I left Dublin and I should have been in pieces in another three or four days. The thing, although it is doubtful whether worth doing at all, as you will be able to judge when I see you, has been very thoroughly done.

My absence has enabled my enemies to triumph at the Bank.

I leave tomorrow and dine with Father Healy at Bray, Lord Justice Barry, etc., etc. I shall try to rest absolutely on Wednesday and come over on Thursday.

YOUR BOYSIE.

There are various matters mentioned in a letter from Chamberlain of November 4, 1884, but it seems to have been written to let out his anger that the Irish had supported Lord Randolph Churchill in the House. But The O' Gorman Mahon received the benefit of a slap on the back for having 'voted straight.'

SHELBOURNE HOTEL,
Tuesday, December 15, 1884.

MY DICK, – Another 'Cousin' has turned up today who must be as old as Methuselah. Everyone said at any rate he must be dead.

It is provoking beyond expression. Maria expresses her intense dislike of these relations in several of her letters.

I am wonderfully popular in this country amongst all the respectable people and amongst the Fenians. What a man I should be to take up the 'Small Farmers' and Labourers' League'! In six months the present 'Boys' would be scuttling for their lives.

There is immense distress in the country – no employment for the labourers; the farmers, instead of working, reading United Ireland and shouting for Home Rule at meetings. Home Rule for them– meaning their farms for nothing. Credit being stopped everywhere, at the banks, by the wholesale firms and down to and by, the village shopkeepers. Crime is being reestablished. The other night near Derryneveigh (Captain O' Shea had some property at Derryneveigh – farms and grassland) a party fired into a house. The wife was giving her two little children supper; a bullet lodged in her leg.

I think that the Constabulary are beginning to feel the general disorganisation, wondering if something is really going to happen and they 'don't see' things.

There is an awful load of responsibility on anybody who, for private purposes, prevents things being settled.

Wait till the labourers learn their power and go in for the plunder.

YOUR B.

I was sitting with Taming today when the telegram arrived announcing that the Boys were out last night near Rathkeale, County Limerick, half killing a farmer who had paid rent.

A letter from Chamberlain, dated December 17th and addressed to 'Mr W.H. Duignan', is extremely interesting. Having recapitulated what his correspondent had told him of the latter's experiences in Ireland and of the persistence of Nationalist sentiment, Chamberlain went on to analyse the meaning of the word Nationalist and to lead up step by step to his proposal of a National Board for Ireland to sit at Dublin, which was afterwards shelved by Gladstone in favour of an Irish Parliament. It is plain from this letter that Chamberlain as a Radical was not a Home Ruler in the widest sense and even then refused to recognise Ireland as a separate people.

LONDON,
Wednesday, 1 A.M.

MY DICK, – I have just written to Mr Parnell to say that I shall be here at 12 o' clock and shall wait for him. I have a communication of the most urgent and important character from Chamberlain. The latter wanted me at twelve tomorrow, but it became too pressing and he asked me to come to his room at twelve tonight instead. It is too long to write, but telly and I can come to A. M. at any time during the afternoon and tell you all about it.

YOUR B.

Much more important than Reln.

Mr Parnell did not think it well to keep this appointment, as he distrusted proposals coming from this quarter as to Irish affairs.

LONDON,
January 9, 1885.

MY DICK, – Colonel Sandeman did not come until the 7.45 train. He returns to Hayling on Monday. I propose to go with him until Wednesday.

On Thursday I have the appointment with Chamberlain. But you see that Parnell is inveighing against the Land Courts and promising the dupes 'Liberty' in the immediate future, so he appears to have altogether shifted from commonsense again.

This is the Reign of Rant again and what is one to think of a fellow who acts thus in the midst of negotiation?

Tell Norah I shall come down early tomorrow to spend her birthday with you all.

YOUR B.

Nothing from Madrid.

1 ALBERT MANSIONS, LONDON, S.W.

MY DICK, – Just back from Heneage. Mr. Parnell has not come.

It is impossible to convey what Chamberlain told me today by letter and it is important you should know it directly. Sebag sends a postcard (to save 1/2d.), which I enclose.

I shall come down to Pope Street by the train reaching that station at 12.22. Please send the young ladies to meet me.

YOUR B.

The following note from Parnell explains why the appointment was not kept:–

Thursday.

MY DEAR O' SHEA, – I have been in bed for the last week with a bad cold and have only been able to get out today for the first time.

Will call back to see if you have returned about six or a quarter to six.

Yours truly,

CHAS. S. PARNELL.

1 ALBERT MANSIONS, LONDON, S.W.,
January 19, 1885.

MY DICK, – I have been feeling wretched all day, but I had to write the enclosed twice. I telegraphed to Mr Parnell to Avondale and Morrison's Hotel last night to telegraph back where to post a letter to him this evening, but he hasn't, so I have sent it to Morrison's Hotel on chance.

Please post the enclosed by the 10 o' clock post to Chamberlain. Seal with wax.

I wonder whether you are coming tomorrow.

Nothing from Madrid, but I doubt whether we could expect anything.

YOUR BOYSIE.

1 ALBERT MANSIONS, LONDON, S.W.,
Monday night, 1885.

MY DICK, – I think I must ask you to come up tomorrow. Broadbent thinks me very ill. As far as I can judge, he thinks my heart affected.

He has ordered an old-fashioned mustard poultice immediately to my foot. I suppose to try to get the gout thoroughly into it.

He says I am in a very low state.

If you can come put on the lightest clothes you have got and drive up. If you can bring the little girls I should be very glad.

I feel very ill. I went to the House this afternoon. Lord R. Churchill has laid down as one of his conditions to Lord Salisbury that Sir S. N. should not be Leader of the House of Commons, but Hicks-Beach.

He divided the House against an arrangement made at Lord S.'s suggestion and assented to by Sir S. Northcote. I don't think Lord S. will be able to form an administration.

Come if you can. Care killed the cat and may kill me this time.

Monday night.

MY DICK, – I had an hour with Card. Manning at his house this evening. He was very anxious to see me.

Tonight he writes to Rome that I informed him that only one member of the Cabinet, Lord Granville, opposes the nomination of Dr Walsh as Archbishop of Dublin, while several are active supporters of it and the rest.

He talked also a good deal about the self-government question and he was most charming, came downstairs and accompanied me to the door.

Yours, W.

(Telegram)

March 2, 1885.

FROM O' SHEA TO MRS. O' SHEA, ELTHAM, KENT.

Telegraph how are. If you see Gladstone today tell him how Grosvenor annoyed me about post offices. Here after two.

1 ALBERT MANSIONS, LONDON, S.W.

MY DICK, – I had better come and talk the thing over early tomorrow. I shall telly by what train I shall come to Pope Street.

Today Chamberlain promised me the Chief Secretaryship on the formation of the Government after the election.

He would, while holding his own office (probably Secretary of State for the Home Department), help me in the matter.

This is an enormous thing, giving you and the Chicks a very great position.

Have you seen the extract from United Ireland (Parnell's paper) in the evening papers? Of course, it will strike Chamberlain and Dilke as a piece of bad faith; and no doubt it is.

Yours, O' S.

HOUSE OF COMMONS LIBRARY,

March 17, 1885.

My DICK, – Montagu came here at 11 o' clock and I introduced him to Chamberlain.

Previously Chamberlain told me that much had occurred since yesterday and that if an arrangement could be made to get the Redistribution Bill and the Crimes Bill quickly into law the Government, who are not anxious to bring the Session to an end too quickly, might bring in Local Government Bills, including one for Ireland, on the basis of the proposals which I handed Chamberlain in January.

I have just seen Parnell but he appears to funk making a treaty. It is too bad, as it is a great chance, especially as it would probably allow of my being Chief Secretary in the next Parliament. He says he will think over it, but he is unable, or unwilling, to face difficulties.

Montagu told me not to write anything, but to consult a solicitor; so I shall go to Ashurst Morris and Co. tomorrow. In the meanwhile he will see Sebag and prevent anything being done tomorrow.

YOUR B.

Chamberlain has just asked me to postpone going for a day so as to let him know 'Parnell's mind'. He hasn't much, but I tellied tonight that I should be in Madrid by Friday.

MADRID,

April 2, 1885

MY DICK, – It was very stupid of the Direct Spanish to send the telly to Albert Mansions. I am very sorry to hear that your chest is still troubling you and I am afraid that as long as you have to cross the park in bad weather you cannot be safe. Anything is better than making yourself ill. Aunt is certainly very unreasonable.

I have been expecting a telegram from Bailey Hawkins all the morning to say that the arrangements are completed for the £200,000 deposits. It is very tiresome work and difficult, too, to keep the persons interested here quiet.

It was a lovely morning. I went to San Isidro to the Mass of the Knights of Malta. They looked very grand in their uniforms, some in white, others in black cloak according to their section of the order. Great red crosses embroidered on the white cloaks, white crosses on the black. There were fourteen of them. The church was hung with banners of the Order and the names of Ascalon and other great battles of the Crusades. The music very fine. There has been a very heavy shower since.

I see by the morning papers that Gayarre sang in the cathedral at Seville yesterday and that it was difficult to restrain the faithful from applauding him.

If Aunt accuses me of extravagance you can truthfully tell her that my sister's illness was an immense expense to me. This hotel is simply ruinous and I never have anything but 1s. 6d. wine. I must have a sitting-room to transact business.

YOUR B.

MADRID,
April 10, 1885.

MY DICK, – After an immense amount of trouble and negotiation the Prime Minister (of Spain) agreed to all that the London people required, even what I told you was unreasonable.

This was the night before last. But the Minister of the Colonies objects and there is a crisis in the Ministry. Canovas wishes to get rid of him; the question is whether Canovas, whose power has been greatly weakened, will have the courage to go to the King with the resignation of the Minister of the Colonies, or whether he will dread the King's possible answer:

'You may as well all resign and have done with it.' Martos seems to fear that Canovas will not have the pluck. Well, perhaps it does not matter much, because when I was at the Ministry yesterday the telegram announcing the attack of the Russians on Pendjeh arrived and was shown me. I expect to hear important news tonight and I do not stop working on account of the rumours of war. I have no doubt all would be right with regard to the caution money.

I am sure you did a dangerous thing in taking such a drive to fetch Bader. You see, he was sure not to come after all. From his letter I should think your lung quite as dangerous as Aunt's cold.

I see by the Standard of Wednesday, just come, that Mr Whiteside is dead – I have sent a telegram to Miss Whiteside.

You see I have done everything mortal could do about the Cuban business and it will be hard if after so much success one's efforts should be thrown away. Monpribat has just come up from Seville. It was chokeful for Holy Week, but the weather very bad. General Armas is very suspicious of Martos, but he was always a conspirator.

I think I shall telly tomorrow and get away, but I greatly fear Bank and great bother in London.

YOUR B.

HOUSE OF COMMONS,
Thursday night.

MY DICK, – There is to be a meeting of Cabinet Ministers at Spencer's house tomorrow at 11.

Chamberlain and Dilke think it certain that the Government will go out.

If Lord S. were alone he would perhaps give way, being really a weak creature, but, Lord Hartington being with him, they think he is sure to stand fast. These will take Lord Selborne and Lord Carlingford.

If the Whigs win, C. and D. would resign and Shaw Lefevre and Trevelyan would go.

Just called again to C.'s room.

YOUR B.

HOUSE OF COMMONS,
May 1, 1885.

MY DICK, – I have been expecting to hear all day from you. It appears that Gladstone is very strongly in favour of our solution and to Chamberlain's surprise Hartington did not reject the proposal offhand as was expected. The final determination was to take two or three days for reflection.

I wish Lord Spencer would go out. I suppose I told you that the Cardinal has power to assure Parnell and the Government of the full support of the Catholic Church in case of their taking up the Co. and Central Board Government Bill.

I am holding out against the bank, but only by the skin of my teeth and it cannot continue many hours.
YOUR B.

I hope if you are coming up tomorrow you will lunch at Albert Mansions – or if not send me the chicks and we would wait; that is if you had not been to see Mr Gladstone today, as I have no word. I have nothing to do tomorrow, or I could come down for the day? Breakfast with C. Sunday morning.

May 4, 1885.

MY DICK, – I have just returned from Dilke, who tells me that peace is certain, on the exact terms stated in the Daily News of Saturday.

I find a telegram from Ashurst Morris and Co., asking me to go to see them, so I have telegraphed in Hall's name that he has orders to open telegrams this morning and telegraph; but is sure I cannot be back in town until late. This is to gain another day.

It is impossible to go on. The Cuban business must take time. The reason I am anxious about the Local Self-Government Scheme is that if Chamberlain has power, which I think he will in the next Parliament, he will offer me the Chief Secretaryship, or the equivalent position if the name is abolished, if the boys will let me have it. Gladstone ought not to know this.

Please let me know by the first post whether I am to take tickets for the conjurer for Wednesday. Tomorrow I shall be all day on the Shannon Navigation Select Committee.

YOUR B.

HOUSE OF COMMONS, 4.30 P.M.
Friday, May 8, 1885.

MY DICK, – After questions I am going to bed. I am feeling very ill and worried.

As for tomorrow, I can do anything you like. I shall have to call on Chamberlain about eleven, as usual, but that will not take more than a quarter of an hour. He generally sees me twice a day now. The same on Sunday, unless he goes to Birmingham, which he tells me is unlikely this week; otherwise I could have come both days to Eltham, if more convenient.

Mr Parnell is very unsatisfactory. He told me last night, with a sort of wave of chivalry that I might convey to Chamberlain that he didn't hold them to the bargain; that they were free to compromise with their comrades if they chose. He does not much care for anything except the vague arid wild politics which have brought him so much money.

I do not see how the Ministry can sustain the shock of next week. Gladstone will be glad, I fancy, of the chance of private life. It will be interesting to see what he will do for us, or offer.

YOUR B.

1 ALBERT MANSIONS, LONDON, S.W.,
May 30, 1885. Friday night.

MY DICK, – Dilke on arrival sent for me. Nothing arrived at. Hartington was quite well when he arrived, but put out owing to the conversation at dinner. Walker was at table and whenever Lord Hartington appealed to him with regard to the speech to be delivered in the North for support against Dilke's arguments Walker would advise: 'I think you'd better say nothing at all about that.' So Lord H. was so ill the next morning that he could not go to Ulster.

Dilke, Lyulph Stanley and the Bishop of Bedford dined at Grays and there met Dr. Walsh. Lord Spencer was much annoyed by Stanley and the Bishop expressing themselves as pleased with Dr Walsh as Dilke did. Altogether he seems to lead Lord Spencer a life.

YOUR B.

1 ALBERT MANSIONS, LONDON, S.W.,
June 2, 1885.

MY DICK, – I have been waiting all day here and am just giving you up. I am to dine at the Sandemans and to go to Epsom with Colonel S., who entertains me in the tent of his corps tomorrow.

I was particularly anxious to see you; indeed, I do not know what to do without seeing you and it is impossible to write.

YOUR B.

Saturday, 2.15 P.M.

MY DICK, – If tomorrow I hope you will telly early so as to prepare the feast.

I have got a list shoe, but I find I can as yet play no tricks, so I have reverted to cotton wool.

I am greatly disgusted with Gladstone, Grosvenor and Co. You will see he has thoroughly done you as near as may be – no lease, no anything; the most trivial, dishonest hound and in such a fix. No wonder he is ill!

Chamberlain wants me on the 15th, as I am not able to go for a chat today. He sent to know.

I see by the papers Mr Parnell has arranged to go to Milltown on the 23rd or 24th or something.

I have had a very bad attack this time. I shall be glad of the books. I send back Lord M.

YOUR BOYSIE.

Chamberlain's letter to Willie, dated June 10th, was an interesting speculation on what would be the next Government and what would happen to coercion. The possibilities seemed to be: A Conservative Government (1) with Coercion; (2) with Randolph Churchill, a Liberal Government; (3) with Coercion; (4) with Chamberlain and Dilke; and the letter is good evidence of Chamberlain's determination to have nothing to do with a Coercion Act.

On June 26, 1885, Chamberlain sent Willie the following extract from *United Ireland:*–

MESSRS. CHAMBERLAIN AND DILKE'S VISIT TO IRELAND.

The recent speeches of Mr Chamberlain surpass in their cynical hypocrisy anything we have seen from even British statesmen. Base as we consider the conduct of Radical Ministers to have been in abetting the horrors which the Gladstone Government have carried out in Ireland, we never could have supposed they would have stooped to the arts which they are now attempting to practise in order to curry favour once more with the Irish people. We plainly tell Messrs. Chamberlain and Dilke that if they are wise they will keep out of Ireland altogether. We do not want them here. Let them stop at home and look after their own affairs. In plain English, this proposed tour of theirs is simply adding insult to injury. We regard it as a mere electoral manoeuvre. The truth is, so long as the House of Lords exists none but a Tory Government can pass an effective Home Rule scheme.

Chamberlain footed this quotation by invoking his 'Dear O' Shea' and with a number of exclamation marks.

JUNIOR ARMY AND NAVY CLUB,
ST. JAMES STREET, S.W.,
Tuesday.

MY DICK, – We are of opinion that the formula holds good, 'No rational beings who have had dealings with Mr Parnell would believe him on oath.'

We know that he has recently said that he is under no obligation or promise to me!!!!!

The marks are of admiration, not of surprise. He has not told the lie to my face, but the man who, after promising to assist in every way Mr Chamberlain's journey to Ireland, can let his paper the same week abuse him like a pickpocket, is not to be respected by Mr C. and I have already told the scoundrel what I think of him.

The worst of it is that one looks such a fool, getting Mr C. to write such a letter as that of Saturday to no purpose.

There was no knowledge of the result of tonight's up to the hour of starting for the House.

I am worried, if not out of my wits, out of my hair. The little left came out this morning after a sleepless night and I am balder than a coot is. Such fun.

I wonder whether I shall die soon, or if the day will come. Would I had understood it had come when I was asked to go to Kilmainham.

YOUR B.

JUNIOR ARMY AND NAVY CLUB,
ST. JAMES STREET, S.W.,
Wednesday.

I have seen today a great number of mp's of various parties, King Harman, Kerr, Orangemen, Sir W. Barttelot, Gregory and many other English Tories, Sir Lyon Playfair and a score of English and Scotch Tories. One and all spoke in astonishment and disgust of Parnell's conduct towards me.

None of them, of course, knew the absolute baseness of it.

But to all I replied: 'Poor devil, he is obliged to allow himself to be kicked to the right or the left and look pleasant. But he has the consolation of having been well paid for the pain – £40,000 the tribute of the priests and people of Ireland!'

The people of Ireland, hearing of the mortgages on Parnell's estates in Ireland, started a subscription to pay these off. The subscription list was headed by the Archbishop of Cashel, I believe and, in all, the priests and people of Ireland subscribed and collected £40,000, thus enabling Parnell to clear the estate from all debt.

June 23, 1885.

To O' SHEA, ELTHAM, KENT.

Ambassador has received telegram from Spanish Prime Minister saying I had better come, so if affairs arranged today shall leave Saturday.

1 ALBERT MANSIONS, S.W.,
December 22, 1885.

MY DICK, – My mother did not leave until eight. I took her home. She was in dreadful spirits and I am very anxious about her. She wishes to leave the hotel, but does not know where she would like to go.

I came back about half past eight and shortly afterwards a Fenian chief called. His friends wanted to see me, so I went with him and was introduced to some of the principal 'men'. They thoroughly understood that my political views and theirs are 'as the poles apart', but they say they will stick to me through thick and thin. I fancy that their admiration for me may be somewhat influenced by objection to certain members.

I have ascertained that Brady, Secretary to the National League, which has offices at Palace Chambers, Westminster, is to go to Galway on Wednesday. This looks like business. I believe he is at the best with T. P. O' Connor. The real boys say that the latter has taken a house in Grosvenor Street and that he will take in Irish members as lodgers!

YOUR B.

The real boys want Galway 'fought', but there have been many outrages in the neighbourhood and it would be difficult to identify oneself with the invasion.

Enclosed from 'Fenian Chief.'
TULLA, Co. CLARE,
December 28.

I saw the Colonel yesterday and gave him the copy to send to Fitzgerald.

I saw I. Malone today and showed him the original document.

He travelled with P.N.F. about a week ago and had a conversation with him upon the subject. P. N. F. is willing to do all he can, but wishes to have the movement commence here in Clare. Come to Limerick, giving timely notice, so that all may be prepared.

Bryan Clune will meet you in Limerick, where everything can be arranged.

All I can say is that if Bryan Clune stands for Galway it will be pretty hard to beat him and if at the last moment he yields to the request of his Clare friends and retires in favour of any person, that person will be rather safe.

When the friends were in trouble you gave them a helping hand and they don't forget it. We stand to the man that stood to a friend and a friend's friend. God save Ireland!

The following letter from Parnell to me at this time gives his view of the trend of affairs:–

AVONDALE,
January 15, 1886.

MY OWN LITTLE WIFIE, – I was unable to go to Dublin and so did not hear any news from McG. about the other election matter. However, Blake, whom I saw at Kingstown and who had seen Phillip Callan the other day, volunteered me the information that he was plotting to do all the mischief he could to members of the Party. Subsequently he told me that C. intended some of it for me and later on he asked me whether I had ever spoken to a lady in London about C. and turning him out and that C. had told him he had evidence that I had and this was why I would not agree to his candidature. The 'lady in London' is, of course, Mrs O' Shea and this is how her name is going to be introduced into the matter if the Court permits it.

Of course the point he will make is that I did not oppose him on account of his bad character and conduct, but because she wished me to and upon this peg will be sought to be hung other statements and questions. Is it not ingenious?

I hope my own darling has been taking care of herself and that her chest is much better; please telegraph me when you get this how you are, as I have been very anxious. I trust you drive every day.

I fear I shall not now be able to leave till Monday evening as there is some experimental work going on at Arklow, the result of which I want to see before I go and it will not be finished till Monday.

I have been all alone here, my sister having left on the Saturday before I arrived. I am longing for you every day and every night and would give worlds to have you here.

YOUR OWN LOVING KING.

Nothing will be done about any vacancies till I return.

Mr Chamberlain had referred in the House to a speech which Parnell was reported to have made in the Dublin Mansion House on September 1st, 1885 and Parnell had questioned the accuracy of the reference. On April 10th, 1886, Chamberlain sent Parnell a quotation from the report he had seen. It ran thus:–

We are told upon high authority that it is impossible for Ireland to obtain the right of self-government. I believe that if it be sought to make it impossible for our country to obtain the right of administering her own affairs that we will make all other things impossible for those who so seek. There shall be no legislation for England.

Mr Chamberlain accepted Mr Parnell's repudiation. Parnell replied to this letter on the 21st, stating that what he actually said was:–

I believe that if it be sought to make it impossible for our country to obtain the right of administering her own affairs that we shall make many things impossible for those who so seek.

On the 24th Chamberlain wrote refusing to see any difference in sense between the report and the fact as admitted. There was anyhow a threat.

Later on Lord Hartington made some reference in a speech at Glasgow to the effect of Parnell's influence in Willie's Galway election; he stated that until Parnell arrived on the scene Willie was not the popular candidate, but that Parnell's authority was sufficient to put down all opposition. Willie was very angry at this and on June 28th, 1886, he wrote to Lord Hartington expressing his annoyance. Lord Hartington took some time to reply and Chamberlain, prompted by Willie, nudged his memory. Finally, on August 25th, he wrote expressing astonishment that Willie was annoyed and repeating what he had said at Glasgow.

August 29, 1886.

DEAR LORD HARTINGTON, – My anxiety that you should be made aware of my political position was much greater than so small a matter justified and now that Chamberlain has spoken to you about it I am quite satisfied.

I did not like being picked out by you as having owed a seat in Parliament to Parnellite terrorism and I can assure you that the intimidation at Galway in February was against, not for, me. Until it was artificially created by Messrs. Healy and Biggar, I was, notwithstanding my so-called 'Whiggery', a popular candidate and Chamberlain had within the last day or two seen a letter in which one of the best judges of the feeling of the borough mentions that no one could have opposed me at the last election if I had only voted for the second reading of Mr Gladstone's Bill.

I remain, yours sincerely,

W. H. O' SHEA.

1 ALBERT MANSIONS,

Saturday morning, October 3, 1886.

DEAR KATE, – I have just returned and found your telegram which you sent on the 29th after my departure. I do not know where you are. Yours,

W. H. O' SHEA.

Towards the end of this year our relations became violently strained, as the following letters plainly show:–

Sunday, December.

DEAR WILLIE, – I am perfectly disgusted with your letter. It is really too sickening, after all I have done. The only person who has ever tarnished your honour has been yourself. I will call and hear what you wish to tell me, although I cannot see that any good can come of our meeting whilst you use such disgusting and ungrateful expressions about me.

K. O' SHEA.

1 ALBERT MANSIONS, S.W.,
December 12, 1886.

DEAR KATE, – I shrink from the possible eventualities of discussion with you, especially as today before our daughters.

As in former controversies, I beg of you to seek someone with a knowledge of the world for a ibelous.–Yours,

W. H. O' SHEA.

1 ALBERT MANSIONS, S.W.,
December 19, 1886.
[Private]

DEAR SIR, – It was stated in the Pall Mall Gazette yesterday that Mr Parnell was staying on a visit with me. The fact is that I have had no communication whatsoever with Mr Parnell since May. You have been deceived probably by some Parnellite, because there are dogs of his, I am told, who in return for the bones he throws them snap when they think it safe.

I have considerable cause of complaint regarding notices equally unfounded which have previously appeared in the Pall Mall Gazette and I should be glad to show you how you have been made the victim of your misplaced confidence.

I am leaving London on Tuesday morning, but I should be glad to call tomorrow if you would send me a telegram mentioning an hour. I have been thinking of speaking to Cardinal Manning on the subject, but I dare say it can be treated without intervention.–Yours faithfully,

W.H. O' SHEA.

W. STEAD, ESQ.,
Pall Mall Gazette Offices.

1 ALBERT MANSIONS, S.W.,
April 22, 1887.
MY DEAR SIR, – I have received your letter of this date. What I asked you to advise Mrs O' Shea about was this and only this:

That reports being wide and strong as to her relations with Mr Parnell it would, for her children's sake, be expedient that she should declare her renunciation of communication with him.

You have either given her this advice or you have not. However this may be, I understand that she refuses to recognise what I hold to be her duty to her children.

Please return the correspondence which I sent you in confidence and accept my apology for having sought to impose upon you a task which does not fall within the scope of professional duty.–Yours faithfully,

W. H. O' SHEA.

(To H. PYM, ESQ. WHO WAS AT THAT TIME MY SOLICITOR)

1 ALBERT MANSIONS, S.W.,
April 22, 1887.
MY DEAR SIR, – You say that kind favours have been shown to me by Mr Parnell and you convey that I am under obligations to him. The fact is the absolute reverse.

Mr Chamberlain (who knows everything connected with these things) wrote the truth on the subject in February, 1886. –Yours faithfully,

W. H. O' SHEA.

(To H. PYM, ESQ.)

In reply Mr Pym wrote on August 25th, returning all the letters and telegrams left with him for perusal. He maintained that the advice that he should give me was a matter which must be left to his own discretion, although he had been glad to receive from Willie any suggestions on his particular wishes. He trusted that by this time Gerard had returned home, as otherwise he foresaw his position with Mrs Wood might be very seriously compromised.

Writing from Paris on December 5th, 1888, en route for the Riviera, Chamberlain ibelousd with Willie over his difficulties with me about which Willie had been writing to him. He also referred to the Parnell Commission and seemed to think it was not very important one way or the other. He had some interesting things to say about the naiveté of the *Times* in dealing with Pigott and the reluctance of Parnell to go into the box.

My former husband, William Henry O' Shea, was, of course, a Catholic and descended from an old Catholic family and though by no means 'devout in the practice of his religion', the Catholic tradition was born and bred in him. The old religion was the only possible one to the various families of O' Shea; indeed, they were almost oblivious to the fact that there were others. Captain O' Shea, although considered by his family painfully lax as regards his religion, was in truth very proud of his family traditions in the old faith and of the fact that he was himself a Knight of St. Gregory and Count of the 'Holy Roman Empire', the ancient titles and orders of which he always used when in Catholic countries.

Thus, when he decided to take action against me and Mr Parnell, he instinctively turned to the head of the Catholic Church in England, Cardinal Manning. This, however, is not a Catholic country and these domestic disagreements are therefore adjusted in a simpler fashion.

The following extract from Captain O' Shea's diary under date of October 19th, 1889, explains his point of view on the matter:–

At 8.30 P.M. called on Cardinal Manning. Explained that while anxious to conform with the regulations of the Church, I saw no way outside applying for a divorce. He said he had been told of the scandal, but had dismissed it from his mind. He asked whether I had proof of actual infidelity. He read a paper on which I had transcribed copies of *Pall Mall* paragraph, May 14th, 1886; he expressed great sympathy and much grief. Finally he asked whether a separation deed could not be arranged. I said it would be useless. He begged me to give him time. To this I agreed.

The subsequent letters to Cardinal Manning are of interest:–

124 VICTORIA STREET, S.W.,
October 21, 1889.

YOUR EMINENCE, – I cannot write without thanking you once more for your great kindness on Saturday.– I remain, your grateful and faithful servant,

W. H. O' SHEA.

The same day Cardinal Manning replied expressing his sympathy.

124 VICTORIA STREET, S.W.,
November 26, 1889.

YOUR EMINENCE, – I have been waiting in England for a long time to the detriment of other interests. It is, therefore, imperative that my course of procedure should be determined. Personally I have everything to gain by the completest publicity and subject to my undeviating respect for the judgment of your Eminence, I am anxious to lose no further time in complying with the procedure ordered by the Church, so as to be placed in a position to proceed.

Hoping you will be able to receive me in order to give me your instructions, I remain, your Eminence, your most dutiful servant,

W. H. O' SHEA.

H.E. THE CARDINAL ARCHBISHOP.

The same day Cardinal Manning wrote throwing cold water on Willie's desire for a separation.

124 VICTORIA STREET, S.W.,
November 27, 1889.

YOUR EMINENCE, – I must have expressed myself very badly if I conveyed to your Eminence's mind that the short statement which I placed before you confidentially for your perusal was the whole of the evidence I possessed.

It was intended merely as a sketch of circumstances which might have given to your Eminence without trouble an idea of the state of affairs.

There has been no delay on my part.

I do not understand the drift of the pecuniary argument which somebody has apparently submitted to your Eminence, nor do I believe it has any foundation with regard to my children. Even if it had, there are other matters which deserve to be weighed at least as carefully. But if anybody has dared to refer to any such considerations as likely to affect myself I must protest in the most energetic terms. Your informant probably knows nothing about the subject, but he most certainly knows nothing about me and is incapable of forming any judgment as to my motives. I wish I could meet him face to face and he would not forget it; but should your Eminence object to give me the opportunity, it will only be just that you should convey to him my appreciation of his cowardly insult.

I have no wish to further engage Your Eminence's time and attention beyond what is officially necessary to direct me how to carry out the ordinance in such cases. – I remain, your Eminence, your faithful servant,

W. H. O' SHEA.

A note, dated January 3rd, 1891, in Captain O' Shea's diary contains a reference to the communication from the Cardinal, to which the foregoing letter was a reply:–

I was this day assured that Cardinal Manning says it was not Sir Charles Russell who guided him to the extraordinary expression of opinion in his letter of November 26th. My informant added that no doubt his Eminence spoke to R., who sent him Mr George Lewis!!!

On December 3rd, 1889, the Cardinal asked for further proof.

124 VICTORIA STREET, S.W.,
December 3, 1889.

YOUR EMINENCE, – I received your letter too late to wait on you this evening, but I hope to have the honour of being received by your Eminence at 8 P.M. tomorrow.

With the greatest respect, my object is to ascertain exactly from your Eminence as my Bishop the steps which the Church imposes on me under the circumstances and when and to whom, I am to submit officially the evidence which is to be transmitted to Rome. I have no right and I do not propose to trespass any further on your Eminence's time and kindness.–I remain, your Eminence, your faithful and obedient servant,

W.H. O' SHEA.

In his letter of December 4th the Cardinal details the course to be followed:–
(1) To collect all evidence in writing. (2) To lay it before the Bishop of the diocese and ask for trial. (3) The latter would give notice to the other party and would appoint a day for hearing. (4) Having given judgment, the case would go to Rome with full report of proceedings.

124 VICTORIA STREET, S.W.,
December 5, 1889.

YOUR EMINENCE, – I am much obliged for your letter of yesterday's date. Your Eminence had not explained the details of the proceedings required and I have today taken legal advice on the matter.

Your Eminence may take my word for it that the evidence will most conclusively prove my charge of adultery against Mrs O' Shea and Mr C.S. Parnell.

There are some points as to mode and date of hearing about which I must trouble you and unless I hear that the hour will be inconvenient I shall avail myself of your Eminence's permission and call tomorrow evening at eight.–I remain, your Eminence, your faithful and obedient servant,

W. H. O' SHEA.

124 VICTORIA STREET, S.W.,
December 13, 1889.

YOUR EMINENCE, – I have consulted my legal advisers with respect to the tribunal which your Eminence described to me at our interview of the 7th inst., as the Ecclesiastical Court which would decide and report to Rome on my charges against Mrs O' Shea and Mr C.S. Parnell. The Court would consist of your Eminence as President, of a Defensor Matrimoniorium, of a Chancellor and a Secretary. You added that I should be required to furnish beforehand in writing all the evidence against Mrs O' Shea and Mr Parnell; that you would afterwards fix a date for the hearing, citing all concerned and that the parties to the suit might be professionally represented.

It is my duty in the first place to reiterate my expression of the respect in which I hold your Eminence. We have treated together affairs of very great importance and in 1885, on the successful termination of one of them, you were kind enough to pay me a compliment so high that I ibelous it when I describe it as conveying that I had rendered a notable service to the Holy See.

It was about the same period that we had many conferences with reference to the scheme for local self-government in Ireland and your Eminence remembers the interview you had with Mr Parnell on the subject, of which you wrote the result to a member of the Ministry.

Although you afterwards refused to allow the letter to be published and thus saved him from exposure, your Eminence is aware that Mr Parnell, with the grossest personal and political treachery, denied that the proposal had ever had his sanction! It cannot, therefore, astonish your Eminence that I should hesitate to approach a tribunal before which a person, who is thus known to us both to be unworthy of credit, might make statements without the curb which, in an English court, having the right to administer an oath, the possibility of a prosecution for perjury would perhaps provide.

Your Eminence has found me loyal in all our dealings and at the same time frank and you will pardon me for recalling the outlines of our communication on the painful subject which we have been treating. In our first conversation you asked me to delay all action until you had spoken to ----. Your Eminence then promised it should be attended to immediately and two other names were mentioned, one of them that of the firm of Freshfield and Williams. I do not for a moment suggest that your Eminence was not at liberty to consult anybody else, but you wrote to me on the 26th ult. That you had on the 25th been fully informed on the matter. Your information cannot have been derived from ----, whom you had seen weeks before and it cannot have been assisted by Messrs. Freshfield and Williams, whom you had not seen at all. Your Eminence will, I trust, excuse me for expressing a regret that you should have made up your mind, even to the extent of giving advice, on the representation of an informant, whoever he may have been, respecting whom I have already sufficiently expressed my opinion.

Although you asked me never to speak to you about trouble, I must in closing this correspondence thank your Eminence for the time which you have spared me. – I remain, your Eminence, your most obedient servant,

W. H. O' SHEA.

His EMINENCE THE CARDINAL ARCHBISHOP OF WESTMINSTER.

The Cardinal's reply of December 15th is referred to in the following letter:–

124 VICTORIA STREET, S.W.,
December 17, 1889.

YOUR EMINENCE, – I should be sorry that your memory and mine should not be brought into accordance.

The three important points in my letter of the 18th inst. are:–

1st. – The expression of my regret that your Eminence should have made up your mind sufficiently to give advice without, at least, having conferred with Messrs. Freshfield and Williams.

That such a conference was contemplated is shown in our correspondence.

2nd. – My allusion to the negotiations respecting the opposition of Mr Gladstone's Government to the appointment of Dr. Walsh to the Archbishopric of Dublin, in which your Eminence was so deeply interested.

My recollection of everything connected with this matter is supported not only by that of the statesman whose support (which settled the business) I secured, but also by a correspondence between myself and an eminent prelate of the Church, who was carefully informed of every step that was taken.

3rd. – My statement as to the transactions with reference to the Irish Local Government scheme.

My recollection in this case is again in complete harmony with that of the statesman (Chamberlain) to whom I have just referred and who, in consequence of your Eminence's refusal to allow the publication of your letter, which would have exposed Mr Parnell's mendacity, afterwards (to my great regret at the time) refused your Eminence's invitation to an interview for the purpose of discussing another matter of great public importance. – I remain, Your Eminence, your most obedient servant,

W. H. O' SHEA.

These letters were, of course, given to me by my son and that quite recently – for this book, in fact. I do not know more about them, nor of the view the Roman Catholic Church took at the time, other than the general repudiation of divorce which it upholds.

It must be remembered that *I was on the other side* and knew nothing of these negotiations of Captain O' Shea with Cardinal Manning; also that I am not a Catholic.

In justice to the memory of Captain O' Shea I now publish the following letters, handed to me, with other of his father's letters, by my son, Gerard O' Shea:–

12 CHICHESTER TERRACE, BRIGHTON,
March 10, 1891.

HIS GRACE THE PRIMATE OF ALL IRELAND, ARMAGH.

YOUR GRACE, – My attention has been arrested by reports which I have recently read of public utterances in which Your Grace, when treating of the present position of affairs, has (alone of the Hierarchy, if I am rightly informed) glanced back at the road strewn with the torn fragments of a Papal Rescript, which at least up to a certain parting of the ways on December 3, 1890, was trodden by many who imagined themselves to be under ibelous guidance. If I have rightly interpreted the expression of your opinion, your Grace, viewing the situation in the light of experience, does not regard in perfect comfort everything that has been said or done of recent years, even in the high place of the Church in Ireland. Would that others were as clear-sighted and as frank! With the same opportunities of observing the evils which so surely attend even on the aiding and abetting of any play with the Ten Commandments, or with any of them, we actually find a Bishop who, after all that has occurred, goes out of his way, without any plausible reason, without any intelligible object, to break with a light heart and unbridled tongue the Commandment which forbids him to bear false witness against his neighbour.

On February 21st I addressed the following letter to His Grace the Archbishop of Tuam. My old acquaintance with that prelate and the urbanity of his manners forbid the very idea of any discourtesy on his part and having received no reply to my communication, I am driven to the conclusion that the good and prudent counsel which he no doubt proffered has been rejected by his own suffragan bishop:–

'12 CHICHESTER TERRACE, BRIGHTON,
'February 21, 1891.

'YOUR GRACE, – My attention has just been called to the following passage in a letter published by the Bishop of Galway on the 14th inst.:–

"In 1886, after having failed to foist Captain O' Shea upon a neighbouring county, the then leader had the effrontery of prostituting the Galway City constituency as a hush gift to O' Shea."

'In words which I forbear using in the case of a Bishop, Mr Chamberlain (who knows a good deal more about the Galway election of February, 1886, than Dr MacCormack) recently castigated Mr Timothy Healy for uttering this false and vile slander against me at the Kilkenny election.

'I write in the first instance to Your Grace because I am anxious, if possible, to avoid taking any action against a Bishop. But it is quite clear that the greatness and sanctity of Dr MacCormack's position render a libel promulgated by him all the more outrageous and damaging and his lordship must retract or defend his statement. – I have the honour to be, Your Grace, as ever, yours most faithfully,

'W.H. O' SHEA.

'HIS GRACE THE ARCHBISHOP or TUAM.'

Dr. MacCormack's libel on me is not only false, it is grotesquely false.

On the Saturday night before the election I spent several hours at the house of Dr Carr, then Bishop of Galway, now Archbishop of Melbourne. There were also present there the Archbishop of Tuam and Dr MacCormack, the present Bishop and the cause of this letter. The Archbishop was in the fullest sympathy with my candidature. When the next day a factitious opposition to it was developed by Messrs. Biggar and Healy, Dr Carr and his clergy, with commendable prudence, adopted an attitude of expectation and reserve. They did so, I was assured, with reluctance and the moment the course of events showed that the opposition was breaking down the Bishop wrote to me expressing his gratification that he and his clergy should find themselves in a position to accord me their hearty support.

In the meanwhile no clergyman had appeared at the meetings held by my opponents, with whom, indeed, there did not appear to be the slightest sympathy on the part of any respectable members of society, clerical or lay. This abstention, among other advantages, happily refutes beforehand any accusation of inconsistency against some gentlemen who are now red-hot for Mr Gladstone and his political colleagues. For Mr Biggar18 and Mr Healy reviled me at their meetings because I had been a supporter of a Government of which Mr Gladstone was Prime Minister and Lord Spencer Lord Lieutenant. They declared those politicians guilty of ibelou murder. Pointing towards Galway Gaol, they told their audiences that within its precincts Mr Gladstone and Lord Spencer had caused a man to be hanged of whose innocence they had absolute personal knowledge. They reviled me at their meetings because I had been a supporter of a Government of which Lord Spencer was Lord Lieutenant and Sir George (then Mr) Trevelyan Chief Secretary. They declared those politicians guilty of connivance with, if not the practice of, the unspeakable vice.

Such was the action of my opponents. What was mine? So likely was I to barter away my honour for a seat in Parliament that, having heard that on what purported to be good authority a report had been spread during the poll to the effect that I had taken the Parnellite pledge, I called on Dr Carr the next day and told his lordship that I did not see my way to retain a seat under any circumstances out of which unprincipled traducers might concoct an accusation of false pretence. It was only through personal regard for Dr Carr and at his urgent request that I finally agreed to leave the matter to the decision of Mr Chamberlain. To my regret Mr Chamberlain considered that, being bound by no statements except my own, I ought to continue to represent Galway. I did so for nearly four months and during that time I was in constant communication with Dr Carr and his clergy and lost no opportunity of endeavouring to carry out their suggestions and wishes. It is well known that in the meanwhile I had become very popular in the constituency and here again we have a test of my character. If I were such a man as Dr MacCormack insinuates – a man who would buy a seat in Parliament at the price of his honour – I need only have given a silent vote for Mr Gladstone's Home Rule Bill and my seat was as safe as any in Ireland.

There is another gross error in Dr. MacCormack's letter. He asserts that previously to the Galway election Mr Parnell had endeavoured to 'foist' me on a neighbouring county. Now, those who occupy responsible positions ought, when they choose to interfere in political matters, at least to take the trouble of making elementary references as to facts. This duty becomes all the more imperative when the character and conduct of an individual are mixed up in the political question. It is false that Mr Parnell made any effort to assist my candidature for Clare. It is true that he promised to do so, but he broke his word. Any inquiry in his immediate neighbourhood would have established the truth if Dr MacCormack had sought it and it was, besides, made clear in evidence before the Special Commission.

We Catholic gentlemen have good reason to complain of the ill-treatment to which we are subjected by some members of the Hierarchy and I venture to say that in no case has it been more undeserved than in mine.

I am, therefore, determined not to allow this ibelous letter of Dr. MacCormack's to pass unchallenged.–I remain, Your Grace, your most obedient servant,

W. H. O' SHEA.

124 VICTORIA STREET, LONDON, S.W.,
July 8th, 1891.

THE MOST REV. DR MACCORMACK, BISHOP OF GALWAY.

MY LORD, – I have the honour to acknowledge the receipt of your letter of May 30th withdrawing the libel on me which you published on February 13th. I regret the delay which has taken place, but (as perhaps you are aware) I had to transmit your Lordship's letter to Rome and await guidance therefrom. I accept the withdrawal and declare the incident in itself closed.

But I venture, solely upon public grounds, to avail myself of this opportunity to request your Lordship, under the fuller light which I am about to furnish, to reconsider the reasons which you inform me prompted you to defame me. Your Lordship will no doubt gladly receive the proof that these reasons afforded no justification whatever for the accusation which you publicly made and which, so far as I can ascertain, you have not yet publicly withdrawn.

Those reasons were five in number and I notice them in the order in which you have produced them in your letter of May 30th.

(1) Your Lordship was present in February, 1886, when I stated to His Grace the Archbishop of Melbourne (and to His Grace the Archbishop of Tuam) that Mr Parnell would support my candidature for Galway without my taking the pledge exacted from the members of his Party.

I was not a member of his Party and I had not the slightest intention of surrendering my independence and becoming a part of the mechanism of any political machine.

Your Lordship must most unfortunately have failed to notice the following correspondence which was published in December last throughout the Press of Great Britain and Ireland:−

'MR. T. HEALY AND CAPTAIN O'SHEA
'To the Editor of the Times:

SIR, − *Having been advised that I cannot deal with Mr Healy in the Law Courts, I must appeal direct to the public sense of decency and fairplay. I beg of you to help me by publishing the enclosed letters.−Your obedient servant,*
'(Signed) W. H. O'SHEA.
'December 27f

'KNOYLE HOUSE, SALISBURY,
'December 24, 1890.

'MY DEAR MR. O'SHEA, − *Under the circumstances I have no hesitation in writing to you to say that I, in my then position as Whip, did my best to promote your candidature as a Liberal and a supporter of Mr Gladstone in Mid Armagh and afterwards at Liverpool during the General Election of 1885.−I am, yours faithfully,*
'(Signed) STALBRIDGE.[19]

'HIGHBURY, MOOR GREEN, BIRMINGHAM,
'December 20, 1890.

'MY DEAR O'SHEA, − *I assume that you will take some notice of the brutal attack made upon you by Mr Healy the other day at Kilkenny, although, unless I am very much mistaken, you will have no legal remedy against him. His statements are entirely inconsistent with what I know of the General Election of 1885. According to my recollection, Parnell neglected at first to give you any assistance and did not, in fact would not do so, until he had seen letters from myself and another person pointing out that your services in the past as intermediary between himself and the Liberal Party had been of real advantage to both and that such services would continue to be equally necessary if it was desired to maintain any kind of friendly relations between the Irish Nationalists and the Liberal Party.*

'*As to Galway, I find that I wrote to you in January, 1886, to the same effect and you have now my full authority to publish the letter if you think it useful. I hope you will have no difficulty in getting permission to publish the letter from the other person to whom I have referred and this correspondence ought to afford sufficient evidence that no such complicity existed as your traducer has been base enough to insinuate.−I am, yours very truly,*
'(Signed) J. CHAMBERLAIN.'

The letter Mr Chamberlain refers to is:−

'[Private.]
40 PRINCE'S GARDENS, S.W.,
'January 22, 1886.

'MY DEAR O'SHEA, − *In the present condition of Irish affairs it is more than ever unfortunate that you have not found a seat. Is there any chance of your standing for one of those now vacant by double election in Ireland? Surely it must be to the interest of the Irish Party to keep open channels of communication with the Liberal leaders. If any possible cooperation is expected, it is clear that a great deal of preliminary talk must be held and at present I doubt if any Liberal leader is in direct or indirect communication with the Irish representatives. Certainly I find myself very much in the dark as to their intentions and wishes.*

'*Can you not get Mr Parnell's exequatur for one of the vacant seats? It is really the least he can do for you after all you have done for him.−Yours very truly,*
'(Signed) J. CHAMBERLAIN.'

(2) Your Lordship writes: 'If Mr Parnell exempted you from taking the election pledge for considerations bearing on party tactics, assuredly he would have intimated the grounds of exemption to his Parliamentary party or to some members of that body.'

Your Lordship must most unfortunately have failed to notice the following letter from Mr T. Harrington, which appeared in the *Freeman's Journal* of December 30, 1890:–

'To the Editor of the *Freeman*.
'43 O' CONNELL STREET, UPPER DUBLIN,
'December 29, 1890.

'DEAR SIR, – *The correspondence published in your columns this morning recalls the attack made upon Mr Parnell's leadership in 1886 by the same section of his followers who are at the bottom of the attack upon him today. Mr Parnell, during the Galway election in 1886, explained to his followers that he had only adopted Captain O' Shea as candidate for Galway at the special request of Mr Chamberlain, stating at the same time that under the circumstances he did not think he was justified in stating so publicly. Of course, the statement was received with incredulity by those who did not wish to be convinced and though the strongest confirmation was given to it immediately after the election, when Captain O' Shea followed Mr Chamberlain out of the House of Commons and refused to vote on the Home Rule Bill, yet there were men among Mr Parnell's followers who have been for years spreading calumny against him in connection with this election and by that calumny preparing the way for the desertion of the present day.*

'*Mr Parnell's vindication has at last come from the hands of his enemies.*

'*So, I believe, will his further vindication come yet.* – *Yours faithfully*',
(*Signed*) *T. HARRINGTON*.'

Although clad in the usual Parnellite bounce, the truth is apparent of this letter, written by a man who would willingly, if he could, tear my reputation to shreds. You cannot waive the fact away by declaring that you do not believe a word Mr Timothy Harrington says. Commonsense could not, in this instance, admit the plea for a moment, because every one knows that if they had had a chance of carrying a denial for four-and-twenty hours the spokesmen of the opposing faction would have gone to work with a will. But they were as quiet as little mice; the circumstance was known to too many; casehardened as they are against the veracities, they did not dare to utter a word of contradiction.

(3) Your Lordship writes: 'Mr Biggar undertook to supply the missing explanation to the people of Galway.'

Now, my lord, the time has come for plain speaking. No statement made by the late Mr Biggar could have affected my mind. To me the measure of his word was to be found in the accusations which again and again he fulminated against Mr Gladstone and Lord Spencer. The former he accused of murder, the latter of murder and connivance with the unspeakable vice. Your Lordship applies to the late Mr Biggar an honourable epithet. Unwittingly and owing to your ignorance of this man's life and character, you have wandered on very dangerous ground indeed. Critics have charged the Irish Hierarchy with over-circumspection in making up their minds last winter on a question of morality affecting a public man. Your Lordship has now most unfortunately appealed as against my honour to the language used by the late Mr Biggar. But he was (notoriously to the world, although unsuspected by your Lordship) a flagrant evil-liver...

You must have failed to observe a document (or if you saw it, your Lordship, charitable to all men except myself, did not heed its significance) which was published in the Press some time after his death and which threw a lurid glare upon his ways.

(4) I have no concern with any stuff which may have been said or shrieked at Galway or anywhere else by Mr William O' Brien.

And, finally –

(5) You write: 'When the Galway Election came to be reviewed in the light of the evidence given in the Divorce Court the duel challenge, etc., the case made by Mr Biggar seemed to me to be corroborated.'

Mr Justice Butt (who is very generally believed not to have entered upon the trial with any bias in my favour) expressed in his summing-up a distinct opinion on this very circumstance diametrically opposed to the impression which it conveyed to your Lordship's mind. I am not aware that your Lordship had an advantage over the judge and jury in coming to a right conclusion on the subject.

I add an extract from a letter which I had occasion some time ago to address to another member of the Hierarchy. The action which it discloses shows by itself how very unlikely it was that I should seek the representation of Galway by any ignoble bargain. But beyond all this, it is clear to any unprejudiced observer that if Mr Parnell could in the Divorce Court have shown the slightest ground for the plea of connivance in any shape or way, he would have proved it. He would then have won his case and if he had won it by any means whatsoever, he would without the shadow of a doubt have been left in undisputed possession of his leadership and of the loyalty to which, even after the adverse verdict, Mr Timothy Healy and Mr Justin McCarthy bound themselves in fulsome and degraded language at the Leinster Hall.

Captain O' Shea then proceeds to quote from his letter to the Archbishop of Armagh the passage beginning: 'On the Saturday night ...' and ending '... made clear in the evidence before the Special Commission.'

CHAPTER XLI

PARNELL AS I KNEW HIM

'If I must speake the schoole-master's language,
I will confess that character comes of the infinite moode, which
signifieth to ingrave or make a deep impression.'
– (CHARACTERS) OVERBURY.

WHEN I FIRST MET MR Parnell in 1880 he was unusually tall and very thin. His features were delicate with that pallid pearly tint of skin that was always peculiarly his. The shadows under his deep sombre eyes made them appear larger than they were and the eyes themselves were the most striking feature of his cold, handsome face. They were a deep brown, with no apparent unusualness about them except an odd compulsion and insistence in their direct gaze that, while giving the impression that he was looking through and beyond them, bent men unconsciously to his will. But when moved by strong feeling a thousand little fires seemed to burn and nicker in the sombre depths and his cold, inscrutable expression gave way to a storm of feeling that held one spellbound by its utter unexpectedness.

His hair was very dark brown, with a bronze glint on it in sunlight and grew very thickly on the back of the shapely head, thinning about the high forehead. His beard, moustache and eyebrows were a lighter brown. His features were very delicate, especially about the finecut nostrils; and the upper lip short, though the mouth was not particularly well shaped. His was a very handsome, aristocratic face, very cold, proud and reserved; almost all the photographs of him render the face too heavy and thicken the features.

He had an old-world courtliness of manner when speaking to women, a very quiet, very grave charm of consideration that appealed to them at once in its silent tribute to the delicacy of womanhood. I always thought his manner to women, whether equals or dependents, was perfect. In general society he was gracious without being familiar, courteous but reserved, interested yet aloof and of such an unconscious dignity that no one, man or woman, ever took a liberty with him.

In the society of men his characteristic reserve and 'aloofness' were much more strongly marked and even in the true friendship he had with at least two men he could more easily have died than have lifted the veil of reserve that hid his inmost feeling. I do not now allude to his feeling for myself, but to any strong motive of his heart – his love for Ireland and of her peasantry, his admiration that was almost worship of the great forces of nature – the seas and the winds, the wonders of the planet worlds and the marvels of science.

Yet I have known him expand and be thoroughly happy and even boyish, in the society of men he trusted. Immensely, even arrogantly, proud, he was still keenly sensitive and shy and he was never gratuitously offensive to anyone. In debate *his thrusts* were ever within the irony permitted to gentlemen at war, even if beyond that which could be congenial to the Speaker of the House or to a chairman of committee.

He was never petty in battle and all the abuse, hatred and execration showered upon him in public and in private, whether by the opponents of his political life or by the (self-elected) judges of his private life, caused no deviation in the policy that was his or on the path that he meant to tread. His policy was the outcome of long, silent deliberation, with every probable issue considered, every possible contingency allowed for and then followed up with quiet, unwearying persistency and determination. When he succeeded in forcing his will upon the House it was well, but he was not elated, passing on to the next point to be gained. When he failed, he had done his best; but 'the fates' willed otherwise than he and again he passed on to the next thing without perturbation. No one could flatter Parnell, neither could anyone humiliate him. 'What I am, I am, what I am not I cannot be', was his summing up of his own and of every other man's personality.

His cold, scientific way of sorting out and labelling his own Party at first made me hesitatingly complain, 'But, after all, they are human beings!' and his characteristic answer was 'In politics, as in war, there are no men, only weapons.'

In regard to 'Nationalisation', he declared that, while there must be growth, there could be no change and when I would point out in friendly malice that his 'nationalism' of one year need not necessarily be that of another and could very easily be less comprehensive, he would answer with smiling scorn, 'That only means that lack of judgment is righted by growth in understanding!'

Parnell went into nothing halfheartedly and was never content till he had grasped every detail of his subject. For this reason he gave up the study of astronomy, which had become of engrossing interest to him, for he said that astronomy is so enormous a subject that it would have demanded his whole time and energy to satisfy him. He was constitutionally lazy and absolutely loathed beginning anything, his delicate health having, no doubt, much to do with this inertia, of which he was very well aware. He always made me promise to 'worry' him into making a start on any important political work, meeting or appointment, when the proper time came and often I found this a very sad duty, for he was so absolutely happy when working at one of his many hobbies, or sitting quietly in his chair 'watching' me and talking or keeping silent as the mood possessed him, that it was misery to me to disturb him and send him off to do something that was not interesting to him. He used to comfort me by assuring me that it was only the 'beginnings' he hated and that he was all right when he was 'once started'.

He was extraordinarily modest about his own intellectual ability and decidedly underrated the wonderful powers of his mind, while he had the utmost admiration for 'brain', whether of friend or foe. Frequently he would say that that 'Grand Old Spider' (his private name for Mr Gladstone) was worth fighting because he was so amazingly clever. His own followers he picked with careful consideration of their usefulness to his policy and appreciated to the full the occasionally brilliant ability some of them showed. His mind, in politics at least, was analytical and he would sift and sort and mentally docket each member of the Irish Party, in company with the more prominent of the Liberal Party, till the whole assumed to him the aspect of an immense game, in which he could watch and direct most of the more important moves. The policy of the Conservatives he considered to be too obvious to require study.

In character Parnell was curiously complex. Just, tender and considerate, he was nevertheless incapable of forgiving an injury and most certainly he never forgot one. His code of honour forbade him to bring up a wrong of private life against a public man and he had the subtle love of truth that dares to use it as the shield of expediency.

Physically Parnell was so much afraid of pain and ill-health that he suffered in every little indisposition and hurt far more than others of less highly strung and sensitive temperament. He had such a horror of death that it was only by the exercise of the greatest self-control that he could endure the knowledge or sight of it; but his self-control was so perfect that never by word or deed did he betray the intense effort and real loathing he suffered when obliged to attend a funeral, or to be in any way brought into contact with death or the thought thereof. Whenever we passed, in our drive, a churchyard or cemetery he would turn his head away, or even ask me to take another road. The only exception to this very real horror of his was the little grave of our baby girl at Chislehurst, which he loved; but then he always said she did not die, she only went to sleep.

Oppression of the weak and helpless, or any act of cruelty, filled him with the deep hatred and indignation that had first led him to make the cause of his hapless country his own and he would spend hours in silent, concentrated thought, altogether oblivious of his surroundings, working out some point or way to lift a little of the burden of the wronged.

Parnell was very fond of animals and was their very good friend always, taking every care himself to see that his horses and dogs were properly looked after. During one of the last meetings he attended in Ireland he jumped off his car in the midst of a hostile crowd to rescue a terrier that was being kicked and run over by the mob.

His will was autocratic and once he had made up his mind to any course he would brook no interference, nor suffer anything to stand in his way. Yet, in his home life, he would come to no decision without seeking my approval and was absolutely unselfish and considerate. I have known him deadly white, with the still, cold passion that any deliberate thwarting of his will produced in him, sweep aside out of 'the Party' and out of all further recognition in any capacity a man who had done useful work and who, thus thrown out, might have been – and was – dangerous to Parnell's political policy in many ways. He had gone against Parnell's explicit instructions in a certain matter. I ventured to point out that this man might be dangerous as an enemy and he answered: 'While I am leader they (the Party) are my tools, or they go!' From his servants also he exacted prompt, unquestioning obedience always, but he was the most gentle and considerate of masters and they, as a rule, almost worshipped him.

He had much pride of family and family affection, but he was utterly undemonstrative and shy. Even when he nursed his brother John through a long and painful illness, caused by a railway accident in America when they were both very young men, the wall of reserve was never broken down and I do not think his family ever realised how strong his affection for them was.

Parnell was not in the least a well-read man. His genius was natural and unaided; he was a maker of history, not a reader of it. He took no interest in literature as such, but for works on subjects interesting to him – mining, mechanics, or engineering and (later) astronomy – he had an insatiable appetite and such a tremendous power of concentration that he absolutely absorbed knowledge where he chose. I have known him to argue some intricate and technical point of engineering with a man of thirty years' practical experience (in America and India), who at length admitted Parnell to be right and himself mistaken, though on this particular point Parnell's deductions were made from a two hours' study of the subject some three years or more before.

For pictures he cared not at all and music he absolutely disliked; though to amuse me he would sometimes 'sing', in a soft undertone and with much gravity, funny little nursery rhymes and snatches of the songs of his college days.

He certainly did not feel this with the working classes, with whom he would constantly converse and watch at work when we were out together. Agricultural labourers did not interest him so much, but he used to spend hours talking to mechanics of all classes, seamen, roadmenders, builders and any and every kind of artisan. To these he always talked in an easy, friendly way of their work, their wages and the conditions of labour and I never remarked that suspiciousness and reserve, characteristic of the English wageworker, in these men when Parnell talked with them. They seemed to accept him, not as one of themselves, but as an interesting and an interested 'labour leader', who had the unusual merit of wishing to hear their views instead of offering them his own.

Parnell was intensely superstitious, with all the superstition of the Irish peasant and in this he was unreasoning and unreasonable. This trait was evidently acquired in earliest childhood and had grown with his growth, for some of these superstitions are the heritage of ages in the Irish people and have their origin in some perfectly natural fear, or association, that has, generation by generation, by alteration of habit or circumstance, lost its force while retaining, or even adding to, its expression.

Parnell would agree perfectly that this was a fact, nevertheless to do so and so was 'unlucky' and there was the end of it – it must not be done. Certain combinations of numbers, of lights or circumstances, were 'omens' and must be carefully avoided. Evidently, as an intelligent child will, he had eagerly caught up and absorbed all and every suggestion offered him by the converse of his nurse and her associates and the impressions thus made were overlaid, but not erased, as he grew up isolated, by the very reticence of his nature, from his fellows. His dislike of the colour green, as being unlucky, he could not himself understand, for it is certainly not an Irish feeling, but it was there so decidedly that he would not sit in any room that had this colour in it, nor would he allow me to wear or use any of the magnificent silks or embroideries that were so often presented to him, if, as was generally the case, they had green in their composition.

Parnell had no religious conviction of creed and dogma, but he had an immense reverence, learnt, I think, from the Irish peasantry, for any genuine religious conviction. He personally believed in a vast and universal law of 'attraction', of which the elemental forces of Nature were part and the whole of which tended towards some unknown and unknowable, end, in immensely distant periods of time. The world, he considered, was but a small part of the unthinkably vast 'whole' through which the 'Spirit' (the soul) of man passed towards the fulfilment of its destiny in the completion of 'attraction.' Of a first 'Cause' and predestined 'End' he was convinced, though he believed their attributes to be unknown and unknowable.

As I have said before, he was not a man who read, or sought to acquire the opinions or knowledge of others, unless he had some peculiar interest in a subject. He considered and formed his own beliefs and opinions, holding them with the same quiet, convinced recognition of his right of judgment that he extended to the judgment of others.

Parnell's moral standard was a high one, if it is once conceded that as regards the marriage bond his honest conviction was that there is none where intense mutual attraction – commonly called love – does not exist, or where it ceases to exist. To Parnell's heart and conscience I was no more the wife of Captain O' Shea when he (Parnell) first met me than I was after Captain O' Shea had divorced me, ten years later. He took nothing from Captain O' Shea that the law of the land could give, or could dispossess him of, therefore he did him no wrong. I do not presume to say whether in this conviction he was right or wrong, but here I set down Parnell's point of view, with the happy knowledge that never for one moment have I regretted that I made his point of view my own in this as in all things else.

Parnell's political life was one single-minded ambition for the good of his country. He was no place or popularity hunter. Stung to the quick in early manhood by the awful suffering of the Irish peasantry and by the callous indifference of the English Government, he, with all the pure chivalry of youth, vowed himself to their service and, so far as in him lay, to the forcing of the governing country to a better fulfilment of her responsibilities. In the course of years the gaining of Home Rule for Ireland became for him the only solution of the problem. To this end he devoted all his energies and for this end men became as tools to him, to be used and thrown aside, so that he could carve out the liberation of Ireland from the great nation whom he declared could 'rule slaves as freemen, but who would only rule free men as slaves'.

Some have said that Parnell was avaricious. He was not. In small matters he was careful and on himself he spent the very smallest amount possible for his position. He indulged himself in no luxuries beyond the purchase of a few scientific books and instruments, on which indulgence he spent many moments of anxious deliberation lest he should need the money for political purposes. His own private income was spent in forwarding his political work, in the 'relief funds' of Ireland's many needs and on his estates in Ireland, where he did his utmost to promote industries that should prove to be of real benefit to the people. To his mother and other near relations he was always generous and to the many calls upon his charity *in Ireland* he was rarely unresponsive.

In temper Parnell was quiet, deep and bitter. He was so absolutely self-controlled that few knew of the volcanic force and fire that burned beneath his icy exterior.

In the presence of suffering he was gentle, unselfish and helpful. Indeed, I may say that at all times at home he was the most unselfish man I have ever met.

Of his moral courage all the world knows, yet no one, I think, but myself can know how absolute it was; how dauntless and unshaken, how absolutely and unconsciously heroic Parnell's courage was. Through good report, or ill report, in his public life, or in his private life, he never changed, never wavered. Hailed as his country's saviour, execrated as her betrayer, exalted as a conqueror, or judged and condemned by the self-elected court of English hypocrisy, he kept a serene heart and unembittered mind, treading the path he had chosen and doing the work he had made his own for Ireland's sake.

And there are those who can in no way understand that some few men are born who stand apart, by the very grandeur of Nature's plan – men of whom it is true to say that 'after making him the mould was broken' and of whom the average law can neither judge aright nor understand. In his childhood, in his boyhood and in his manhood Parnell was 'apart'. I was the one human being admitted into the inner sanctuaries of his soul, with all their intricate glooms and dazzling lights; mine was not the folly to judge, but the love to understand.

CHAPTER XLII

MARRIAGE, ILLNESS AND DEATH

'O gentle wind that bloweth south
To where my love repaireth,
Convey a kiss to his dear mouth
And tell me how he fareth.'
– OLD BALLAD.

'He that well and rightly considereth his own works will find little cause
to judge hardly of another'
– THOMAS A KEMPIS.

ON JUNE 24TH, 1891, MR Parnell drove over to Steyning to see that all the arrangements for our marriage at the registrar's office there on the next day were complete. Mr Edward Cripps, the registrar, had everything in order and it was arranged that we should come very early so as to baffle the newspaper correspondents, who had already been worrying Mr Cripps and who hung about our house at Brighton with an inconvenient pertinacity. We had given Mr Parnell's servant elaborate orders to await us, with Dictator in the phaeton, at a short distance from the house about eleven o' clock on the 25th and told him he would be required as a witness at our wedding. This little ruse gave us the early morning of the 25th clear, as the newspaper men soon had these instructions out of the discomfited young man, who had been told not to talk to reporters.

On June 25th I was awakened at daybreak by my lover's tapping at my door and calling to me: 'Get up, get up, it is time to be married!' Then a humming and excitement began through the house as the maids flew about to get us and breakfast ready 'in time', before two of them, Phyllis Bryson, my very dear personal maid – who had put off her own marriage for many years in order to remain with me – and my children's old nurse, drove off to catch the early train to Steyning, where they were to be witnesses of our marriage. Phyllis was so determined to put the finishing touches to me herself that she was at last hustled off by Parnell, who was in a nervous fear that everyone would be late but the newspaper men. Phyllis was fastening a posy at my breast when Parnell gently but firmly took it from her and replaced it with white roses he had got for me the day before. Seeing her look of disappointment he said: 'She must wear mine today, Phyllis, but she shall carry yours and you shall keep them in remembrance; now you must go!'

He drove the maids down the stairs and into the waiting cab, going himself to the stables some way from the house and returning in an amazingly short time with Dictator in the phaeton and with a ruffled-looking groom who appeared to have been sleeping in his livery – it was so badly put on. Parnell ordered him in to have a cup of tea and something to eat while he held the horse, nervously calling to me at my window to be quick and come down. Then, giving the groom an enormous 'buttonhole', with fierce orders not to dare to put it on till we were well on our way, Parnell escorted me out of the house and settled me in the phaeton with elaborate care.

As a rule Parnell never noticed what I wore. Clothes were always 'things' to him. 'Your things become you always' was the utmost compliment for a new gown I could ever extract from him; but that morning, as he climbed in beside me and I took the reins, he said: 'Queenie, you look lovely in that lace stuff and the beautiful hat with the roses! I am so proud of you!'

And I was proud of my King, of my wonderful lover, as we drove through that glorious June morning, past the fields of growing corn, by the hedges heavy with wild roses and 'traveller's joy', round the bend of the river at Lancing, past the ruined tower where we had so often watched the kestrels hover, over the bridge and up the street of pretty, old-world Bramber into Steyning and on to the consummation of our happiness.

Parnell hardly spoke at all during this drive. Only, soon after the start at six o' clock, he said, 'Listen' and while smiling, 'They are after us; let Dictator go!' as we heard the clattering of horses far behind. I let Dictator go and he – the fastest (driving) horse I have ever seen – skimmed over the nine miles in so gallant a mood that it seemed to us but a few minutes' journey.

Mr Cripps was in attendance and Mrs Cripps had very charmingly decorated the little room with flowers, so there was none of the dreariness usual with a registry marriage. As we waited for our witnesses to arrive – we had beaten the train! – my King looked at us both in the small mirror on the wall of the little room and, adjusting his white rose in his frockcoat, said joyously: 'It isn't every woman who makes so good a marriage as you are making, Queenie, is it? And to such a handsome fellow, too!', blowing kisses to me in the glass. Then the two maids arrived and the little ceremony that was to legalise our union of many years was quickly over.

On the return drive my husband pulled up the hood of the phaeton and, to my questioning look – for it was a hot morning – he answered solemnly, 'It's the right thing to do.' As we drove off, bowing and laughing our thanks to Mr Cripps and the others for their kind and enthusiastic felicitations, he said: 'How could I kiss you good wishes for our married life unless we were hooded up like this!'

Just as we drove out of Steyning we passed the newspaper men arriving at a gallop and we peered out doubtfully at them, fearing they would turn and come back after us. But I let Dictator have his head and, though they pulled up, they knew that pursuit was hopeless. My husband looked back round the hood of the phaeton and the groom called out delightedly, 'They've give up and gone on to Mr Cripps, sir.'

On our return to Walsingham Terrace we had to run the gauntlet between waiting Pressmen up the steps to the house, but at my husband's imperious: 'Stand back; let Mrs Parnell pass! Presently, presently; I'll see you presently!', they fell back and we hid ourselves in the house and sat down to our dainty little wedding breakfast. Parnell would not allow me to have a wedding cake, because he said he would not be able to bear seeing me eat *our* wedding cake without him and, as I knew, the very sight of a rich cake made him ill.

Meanwhile the reporters had taken a firm stand at the front door and were worrying the servants to exasperation. One, a lady reporter for an American newspaper, being more enterprising than the rest, got into the house adjoining ours, which I also rented at that time and came through the door of communication on the balcony into my bedroom. Here she was found by Phyllis and as my furious little maid was too small to turn the American lady out, she slipped out of the door and locked it, to prevent further intrusion.

Then she came down to us in the dining-room, found on the way that the cook had basely given in to bribery, having 'Just let one of the poor gentlemen stand in the hall' and gave up the battle in despair – saying, 'Will Mrs O' Shea see him, Mr ---- wants to know?'

'Phyllis!' exclaimed my husband in a horrified voice, '*what* do you mean? *Who* is Mrs O' Shea?'

Poor Phyllis gave one gasp at me and fled in confusion.

Then my King saw some of the newspaper people and eased their minds of their duty to their respective papers. The lady from America he utterly refused to see, as she had forced herself into my room, but, undaunted, she left vowing that she would cable a better 'interview' than any of them to her paper. They were kind enough to send it to me in due course and I must admit that even if not exactly accurate, it was distinctly 'bright'. It was an illustrated 'interview' and Parnell and I appeared seated together on a stout little sofa, he clad in a fur coat and I in a dangerously *decollete* garment, diaphanous in the extreme and apparently attached to me by large diamonds. My sedate Phyllis had become a stage 'grisette' of most frivolous demeanour and my poor bedroom – in fact, the most solid and ugly emanation of Early Victorian virtue I have ever had bequeathed to me – appeared to an interested American State as the 'very utmost' in fluffy viciousness that could be evolved in the united capitals of the *demi-mondaine*.

I showed this 'interview' to my husband, though rather doubtful if he would be amused by it; but he only said, staring sadly at it: 'I don't think that American lady can be a very nice person.'

After he had sent the reporters off, my King settled into his old coat again and subsided into his easy chair, smoking and quietly watching me. I told him he must give up that close scrutiny of me and that I did not stare at him till he grew shy.

'Why not?' he said. 'A cat may look at a king and surely a man may look at his wife!'

But I refused to stay indoors talking nonsense on so lovely a day and we wandered out together along the fields to Aldrington. Along there is a place where they make bricks. We stood to watch the men at work and Parnell talked to them till they went off to dinner. Parnell watched them away till they were out of sight and then said, 'Come on, Queenie, we'll make some bricks, too. I've learnt all about it in watching them!' So we very carefully made two bricks between us and put them with the others in the kiln to burn. I suggested marking our two bricks, so that we might know them when we returned, but when we looked in the kiln some hours later they all appeared alike.

Then we got down to the sea and sat down to watch it and rest. Far beyond the basin at Aldrington, near the mouth of Shoreham Harbour, we had the shore to ourselves and talked of the future, when Ireland had settled down and my King – king, indeed, in forcing reason upon that unreasonable land and wresting the justice of Home Rule from England – could abdicate; when we could go to find a better climate, so that his health might become all I wished. We talked of the summer visits we would make to Avondale and of the glorious days when he need never go away from me. Of the time when his hobbies could be pursued to the end, instead of broken off for political work. And we talked of Ireland, for Parnell loved her and what he loved I would not hate or thrust out from his thoughts, even on this day that God had made.

Yet, as we sat together, silent now, even though we spoke together still with the happiness that has no words, a storm came over the sea. It had been very hot all day and a thunderstorm was inevitable; but, as we sheltered under the breakwater, I wished that this one day might have been without a storm.

Reading my thoughts, he said: 'The storms and thunderings will never hurt us now, Queenie, my wife, for there is nothing in the wide world that can be greater than our love; there is nothing in all the world but you and I.' And I was comforted because I did not remember death.

The news of our marriage was in all the evening papers and already that night began the bombardment of telegrams and letters of congratulation and otherwise! The first telegram was to me, 'Mrs Parnell' and we opened it together with much interest and read its kind message from 'Six Irish Girls' with great pleasure. The others, the number of which ran into many hundreds, varied from the heartiest congratulation to the foulest abuse and were equally of no moment to my husband, as he made no attempt to open anything in the ever-growing heap of correspondence that for weeks I kept on a large tray in my sitting-room and which, by making a determined effort daily, I kept within bounds.

'Why do you have to open them all?' he asked me, looking at the heap with the indolent disgust that always characterised him at the sight of many letters.

'Well, I like reading the nice ones and I can't tell which they are till they're opened', I explained. 'Now here is one that looks the very epitome of all that is good and kind outside – thick, good paper, beautiful handwriting – and yet the inside is unprintable!'

Parnell held out his hand for it, but I would not give anything so dirty into his hand and tore it across for the wastepaper basket, giving him instead a dear little letter from a peasant woman in Ireland, who invoked more blessings upon our heads than Heaven could well spare us.

Little more than three months afterwards the telegrams and letters again poured into the house. This time they were messages of condolence and otherwise. And again their message fell upon unheeding ears, for the still, cold form lying in the proud tranquillity of death had taken with him all my sorrow and my joy; and as in that perfect happiness I had known no bitterness, for he was there, now again these words of venom, speaking gladness because he was dead, held no sting for me, for he was gone and with him took my heart.

The very many letters of true sympathy which reached me after my husband's death were put away in boxes and kept for me till I was well enough for my daughter to read them to me. Among these were many from clergymen of all denominations and of all ranks in the great army of God. As I lay with closed eyes listening to the message of these hearts I did not know I seemed to be back in the little church at Cressing and to hear my father's voice through the mists of remembrance, saying: 'And now abideth faith, hope, charity, these three; but the greatest of these is *Charity*...'

Among our many wedding presents was a charming little alabaster clock from my husband's sister, Emily Dickinson. It was a ship's 'wheel' and we were very gay over its coming, disputing as to which of us should henceforth be the 'man at the wheel'. Parnell's mother also was very sweet and kind to me, sending me several much prized letters. Other members of my husband's family also wrote very kindly to me and I can still see his tender smile at me as he saw my appreciation of his family's attitude.

The presents we liked best, after Mrs Dickinson's clock, were the little humble offerings of little value and much love sent by working men and women, by our servants and by others of far countries and near. Parcels arrived from the four quarters of the globe and many were beyond recognition on arrival, but the fragments were grateful to me as bearing a message of true homage to my King.

Of other feeling there was little among these wedding gifts, though one evening my eldest daughter, who was with me, remarked casually to me that she had confiscated a newly arrived 'registered' parcel addressed to me. 'Oh, but you must not', I exclaimed, 'I want them all!' But she answered gloomily that this parcel had contained a mouse and 'not at all the kind of mouse that anyone could have wanted for days past.' So I subsided without further interrogation.

Once when Parnell and I were staying at Bournemouth we became very fond of some old engravings hanging in our hotel sitting-room, illustrating 'The Dowie Dens of Yarrow' and now, through these fighting months in Ireland, we used this old ballad as a medium for private telegrams, as we could not be sure they would not fall into other hands. The idea took root when he first left me to attend what I feared would be a hostile meeting in Ireland. He had wired the political result to me, but had not said how he was feeling. I telegraphed to him: 'O, gentle wind that bloweth south' and promptly came the reply to me: 'He fareth well'.

All through these fighting months in Ireland he telegraphed to me always in the morning and also in the evening of every day he was away from me and whenever he could snatch a moment he wrote to me. He was in no way unhappy in this last fight and had only the insidious 'tiredness' that grew upon him with such deadly foreshadowing of the end we would not see given him a little respite, he could, he said, have enjoyed the stress and storm of battle. To bend these rebels in Ireland to his will became but a secondary driving force to that of gaining for Ireland the self-government to which he had pledged himself for her and I think it gave that zest and joy in hardness to the battle that all the great fighters of the world seem to have experienced.

I am not giving all his letters of this time; just a few of the little messages of my husband's love in these last days I must keep for my own heart to live upon; but the two or three that I give are sufficient to show the high, quiet spirit of the man who was said to be 'at bay'. Letters, I think, rather of a king, serene in his belief in the ultimate sanity of his people and of the justice of his cause.

BALLINA,
March 24, 1891.

The reception here yesterday was magnificent and the whole country for twenty five miles from here to the town of Sligo is solid for us and will vote 90 out of 100 for us, the priests being in our favour with one exception and the seceders being unable to hold a meeting anywhere. I am to keep in this friendly district and to hold meetings there and shall not go outside of it.

The town of Sligo and the district from there to Cliffony, is hostile, the priests being against us and I shall not go into it, but we have a good friendly minority even in this district, whom our agents will canvass privately. You will see the situation on the map.

Wire me to Ballina, every day, which will be my headquarters; also write particulars if any news.

BIG ROCK QUAKRIES, ARKLOW, Co. WICKLOW,
August 15, 1891.

MY OWN WIFIE, – Your telegram only received this evening, in consequence of my being at the mine.

I think you might fix the end of the year as the time you and I would guarantee the payment of the costs (of the divorce case). If Wontner accepts this or any modification of it which would give me, say, three months to pay, telegraph Pym as follows: 'No'. If he declines to accept, or you cannot come to any definite arrangement with Wontner by Tuesday at midday, telegraph Pym 'Yes'. I have written Pym advising him accordingly about the appeal and sending the lodgment money, but it would be better if possible that you should telegraph Pym on Monday afternoon. I trust to be able to cross on Tuesday morning or evening at latest. It is very fine here, but I have had no shooting and do not expect any, as I have to be in Dublin all day Monday arranging about new paper. – With best love,

YOUR OWN HUSBAND.

You should ask Wontner to telegraph you definitely as early as possible on Monday.

MORRISON'S HOTEL, DUBLIN,
September 1, 1891.

MY OWN WIFIE, – I have received Magurri's letter safely and hope to be able to leave here on Wednesday (tomorrow) evening, sleeping at Holyhead and visiting the place in Wales (we had an idea of renting a place in Wales) next morning on my way back to London.

MacDermott says he does not think I can get the loan from Hibernian Bank concluded within a fortnight, but will hasten matters as much as possible. The bank and their solicitors approve the security and proposal generally, but it will take a little time to make the searches and go through other formalities which lawyers always insist upon in such cases.

By tomorrow I expect to have done as much as I possibly can for the present in the matter of the new paper. It has been a very troublesome business, as a dispute has arisen between different sections of my own friends as to who shall have the largest share in the management of the new organ.

This dispute somewhat impedes progress and increases the difficulties. However, the matter is not so pressing, as the Freeman question is again postponed for another fortnight. I expect to make a satisfactory arrangement about my Freeman shares, under which I shall lose nothing by them. Kerr is making progress in getting up a small company to buy a steamer and I think he may succeed.

I have been very much bored, as I am obliged to remain in the hotel all day every day, waiting to see people who may call about the different undertakings. I wonder whether you have been driving at all and how the eyes are and how you have been doing. You have not written to tell me. – With much love,

MY OWN LITTLE WIFIE'S HUSBAND.

MORRISON'S HOTEL, DUBLIN,
Monday, September 7, 1891.

MY OWN WIFIE, – I have told Kerr that he cannot have any of the first thousand, so he is going to manage without it for the present, so you may reckon on that amount.

The bank was to have given me that sum today, but a hitch occurred on Saturday which I removed today and the board will meet tomorrow and ratify the advance.

YOUR OWN HUSBAND.

In great haste.

The trouble about the jealousies of would-be directors on the new board still continues and have postponed selection till next week – crossing tomorrow night.

On my husband's return home from Ireland in September, after having established the *Irish Daily Independent,* he was looking so worn out and ill that I was thoroughly alarmed about his health. He was very cheerful and happy while he was at home and I had much difficulty in keeping him quietly lying down to rest on the sofa. But, though he protested while following my wishes, I saw as I sat watching him while he slept that the tired, grey shadows were growing deeper upon his beautiful face and that in sleep he had that absolute stillness which one only finds in very healthy children or in the absolutely exhausted sleep of adults.

I tried to induce him to see Sir Henry Thompson in, town, but he would not consent – saying that he could not waste a moment of his little time at home and that, though he did feel tired, that was all.

'I am not ill', he said, 'only a little tired. Queenie, my wife, you do not *really* think I am ill, do you?'

Knowing the one weakness of his brave heart, his anger and terror at the idea of illness and of the far off death that might divide us, I answered only that I thought he was *too* tired, that nothing, not even Ireland, was worth it and I besought him now at last to give it all up and to hide away with me till a long rest, away from the turmoil and contention, had saved him from the tiredness that would, I feared, become real illness if he went on.

He lay watching me as I spoke and, after a long pause, he answered: 'I am in your hands, Queenie and you shall do with me what you will; but you promised.'

'You mean I promised that I would never make you less than—'

'Less than your King', he interrupted, 'and if I give in now I shall be less than that. I would rather die than give in now – give in to the howling of the English mob. But if you say it I will do it and you will never hear of it again from me, my love, my own wife.' And as I gazed down into the deep, smouldering eyes, where the little flames always leapt out to meet mine, I knew I could not say it, I knew that in the depths of those eyes was more than even my love could fathom, that in the martyrdom of our love was to be our reparation.

I sent him off bright and happy to the last meeting at Creggs. As he drove off to the station and Dictator rounded the corner of the house, he turned, as usual, to wave to me and raised the white rose in his buttonhole to his lips with an answering smile.

He sent me a telegram from London as he was starting from Euston Station, one from Holyhead and another from Dublin. For the Creggs meeting he stayed with Mr and Mrs Mahoney and his telegram from their house was cheerful, though he said he was not feeling very well.

In the few lines I had from him here I knew he was in much pain again from the rheumatism in his left arm. He always told me exactly how he was feeling, as he knew that unless he did this I would have suffered untold misery from apprehension while he was away. From Creggs he telegraphed that he was about to speak and it was 'terrible weather'. I thought with satisfaction that I had put a special change into a bag for him and he had promised not to be parted from it, so I knew he would find means of changing his things directly after the meeting. His 'good night' telegram did not reassure me; he was in bad pain from the rheumatism, but hoped to get it out with a Turkish bath on the way home.

He stayed in Dublin to see about the new paper which, though 'going' well, was a perpetual trouble to him owing to the petty jealousies of the staff. He crossed over from Ireland feeling very ill, with violent pains all over him; he was implored to go to bed and remain there for a few days till he felt better, before starting for England; but he only replied: 'No, I want to get home; I must go home!'

He telegraphed to me from Holyhead as usual and directly he got to London and before coming on to Brighton, he had a Turkish bath in London.

He seemed to me very weak when he got out of the buggy. I had sent a closed fly to meet him, as well as the buggy, but as a forlorn hope, for he would always be met by Dictator in the buggy at the station.

I helped him into the house and he sank into his own chair before the blazing fire I had made, in spite of the warm weather and said: 'Oh, my Wifie, it is good to be back. You may keep me a bit now!'

I was rather worried that he should have travelled immediately after a Turkish bath, but he said it had done him much good. I did not worry him then, but after he had eaten a fairly good dinner I told him that I wanted him to have Sir Henry Thompson down the next day. He laughed at the idea, but I was very much in earnest and he said he would see how he felt in the morning.

He told me that he had had to have his arm in a sling all the time he was away, but that he thought he had become so much worse because the change of clothes I had packed separately in a small bag (which he had promised not to be parted from) in case he had to speak in the rain, had been taken home in error by his host and he had had to sit in his wet things for some hours.

I was much vexed when I heard this, for I always made such a point of his not keeping on damp things and provided against it so carefully when starting him off.

He said: 'It is no matter, really, I think and I won't go away again till I'm really well this time. They were all so kind to me, but I was feeling so ill that I had to point out that breakfast was made for me, not I for breakfast, when I was expected to come down quickly for it. I do hate being away from home, especially when I feel ill.'

After dinner that night he sat before the fire trying to smoke a cigar, but he did not care for it as usual and presently threw it away half smoked. He wanted to 'feel' I was there, he said, so I sat by his feet on the rug and leant my head against his knee while he stroked my hair. I stopped his hand because I feared the pain might come on again and held it while he smiled assent to my suggestion that he should try to sleep a little. Grouse and Pincher, our setter and terrier, had to come close by us and, as they settled by his feet, he said: 'This is really a beautiful rest.'

He dozed now and then and I could see how wan and exhausted the still, clearcut face was and I vowed to myself that he should not again leave my care until his health was completely reestablished.

Presently he asked for his stick and wanted to go into the other room for a while, but he could not walk without my assistance, his legs were too weak to support him. I was terribly worried now, but did not let him see it and only said: 'Now you are up you must let me help you to bed, so that you can get all the rest you need – and you are not going to leave home again till you take me for a real honeymoon in a country where the sun is strong enough to get the cold out of your bones. We will get out of England this winter.' And he answered: 'So we will, Wifie, directly I get that mortgage through.'

Then, as we made our painful way up the stairs – for the last time – he laughed at the Irish setter, who was trying to help him lift the stick he used and said: 'Grouse thinks we are doing this for his own special benefit'. I undressed him and got him into bed and he said: 'Come and lie down as quickly as you can, Wifie', but I rubbed him with the firwood oil and packed his arm in the wool he so much believed in, before I lay down.

He dozed off, but woke shortly and could not sleep again. He asked me if I thought the champagne Dr. Kenny had made him take in Dublin had made him worse, but I reassured him, for he had been so exhausted he had required something and no doubt Dr. Kenny had known that it would do him good, although in a general way it was bad for him.

During the night I made him promise he would see a doctor in the morning. Presently he said: 'I would rather write to Thompson, as he understands me.' I said I would telegraph to him to come down, but this excited my husband, who said, 'No, the fee would be enormous at this distance.' I pointed out that his health was more precious than the quarries and sawmills at Arklow, on which he was just proposing to spend some hundreds of pounds, but he put me off with, 'We'll make it all right in the morning, Wifie.'

Finding he still did not sleep, I gently massaged his shoulders and arms with oil and wrapped him in wool again.

He talked a good deal, chiefly of the Irish peasantry, of their privations and sufferings, the deadly poverty and the prevalence of the very pain (rheumatism) from which he was suffering, in their case aggravated by the damp, insanitary cabins in which they lived. And he murmured under his breath: 'There are no means at hand for calculating the people who suffered in silence during those awful years of famine'. That was what J.H. Mohonagy said of the famine, from '79 to '80. And he went on: 'I wish I could do something for them – the Irish peasantry – they are worth helping. I have always wished it, but there is so much between – and they 'suffer in silence', Wifie.'

In the morning he felt better and was much happier about himself. He absolutely refused to let me send for Sir Henry Thompson and, sitting up in bed after a good breakfast, smoked a cigar while he wrote notes for a speech. During his last absence I had bought a large engraving of Lord Leighton's picture 'Wedded' and, seeing this hanging in the room, he made me bring it and put it up at the foot of the bed for him to see. He was very much amused at the muscular young couple in the picture and waving his cigar at it said: 'We are a fine pair, Wifie, hang us up where I can look at us.'

I had ready for him to sign an agreement to rent a house near Merstham, Surrey, that we had arranged to take so that he could get to London more quickly and have a change from the sea. It was a pretty little country house and he had taken great interest in it. I would not let him sign it now, or do any business, but he made me read the agreement over to him and said that part of our real 'honeymoon' should be spent there. He later insisted upon writing to his solicitor (his brother-in-law, Mr MacDermott) about a mortgage he was raising on his estate, as he wished to have the matter completed quickly. (It was not completed, owing to his death.)

On Sunday he was not so well, but insisted that what he had written to Sir Henry Thompson was enough, as he would answer at once. My persistence seemed to fret him so much that I desisted and told him that I had sent for a local doctor, as I could not bear to be without advice about the pain.

He was a good patient in one way, scrupulously following his doctor's directions, but in another a very difficult patient, as he was so very easily depressed about himself, all the fatalism that was natural to him tending to overcome his immense desire for health. A short talk with the doctor who saw him seemed to inspire him with confidence and he said he felt better.

That night (Sunday) he did not sleep and this worried him a great deal, as he had a superstition that if he did not sleep for two consecutive nights he would die. I tried at first to reason him out of this idea, but he said he had always 'felt' this and had never before failed to sleep. I besought him to let me telegraph for Sir Henry Thompson now, but he would not allow it and became so feverish at the idea that I did not press the point, though I determined to consult the doctor in attendance about this in the morning. Towards morning he became very feverish and it was difficult to keep his skin in the perspiration that he desired.

That morning Sir Henry Thompson telegraphed recommending me to call in Dr Willoughby Furner, but as Dr Jowers was already in attendance and my husband liked him, there was no reason to change. That day he was in much pain, afraid to move a finger because of it. He heard from Sir Henry Thompson and, after I read the letter to him, he said: 'You see, sweetheart, I was right; Thompson says just what Jowers does; there's no need to have him down.'

After my husband's death I received the following letters from Sir Henry Thompson:–

35 WIMPOLE STREET, W.,
October 7, 1891.

DEAR MRS PARNELL, – I am indeed shocked and distressed by the news which the afternoon journals announce here today.

So little did I think when I received the letter written by my old esteemed patient, dated October 3, that his end was so near.

With the feelings which this shock have aroused I cannot do otherwise than ask permission to express my sincere sympathy and condolence in the terrible and, I imagine, even to you who must have known more of his health than anyone else, this sudden affliction. The more so as I think you accompanied him once, if not more than once, in his visits to me in Wimpole Street. Of such expression of feeling towards you in this great trial you will at least find multitudes ready to join and may find some slight consolation in the knowledge that sympathy with you will be widely felt both here and in America.

Under present circumstances I cannot expect or wish to trouble you to communicate with me. But I should be deeply interested in knowing (for my private interest in him and in what befell him) what followed the communication I made to you, whether you had attendance (professional) on the spot before my letter arrived and what was said, or supposed, to have been the cause of the fatal result, or any details which some friend could send me.

With renewed assurance of my deep sympathy, – Believe me, yours truly,
HENRY THOMPSON.

I think I must have received one of his very last letters, if not his last.

35 WIMPOLE STREET, W.,
Saturday afternoon, October 10, 1891.

DEAR MRS. PARNELL, – I am very glad you have written me, if the doing so, or if the reply I may be able to send you, can in any way help to mitigate any one of the numerous and infinitely painful circumstances, or their influence, rather, on your mind just now.

Such inquiries as those which suggest themselves to you are so natural that it is impossible to repress them.

One never knows exactly what might have happened in any incident of life had some other course been taken. But whatever course may be supposed, it is useless to pursue it, since only one can ever be taken in this life, namely, that one which is chosen by the individual in every case.

In reference to that asked by you, I feel very strongly that the sad catastrophe was by no means the outcome of any one act – or omission to act – and is far more truly indicated in that passage in yours which describes him as saying to Dr Jowers, 'had he only been able to follow my advice during the last few months', etc. There is the gist of the matter! I doubt whether anything would have saved him when passing through London. A blow had been struck – not so heavy – apparently a light one; but his worn-out constitution, of late fearfully overtaxed by a spirit too strong for its bodily tenement, had no power to resist and gave way, wholly unable to make any fight for itself against the enemy. Hence what would in a fairly robust state of health have been only a temporary conflict with a mild attack of inflammation, developed into a severe form, overwhelming the vital force with great rapidity and rendering all medical aid powerless. I don't believe that any medicine, any treatment, could have enabled his weakened condition to resist successfully. He wanted no medicine to combat the complaint. He wanted physical force, increased vitality to keep the attack at bay. I have nothing to say of the prescription, except that it appears to me quite appropriate under the circumstances and these I have learnt from the public press. Dr Jowers is an experienced and most capable man and I think you may rest assured that he could scarcely have been in safer hands.

If I were to regret anything it would be that he had not found a spare half-hour to come and see me some time ago. Let me see then how his strength was and whether he could not be fortified a little for the wearing life he was leading. But then these are acts of prudence and foresight which very few ardent men of action ever find time to take. Nevertheless, it is then that advice is really efficient. It is in nine times out of ten sought too late; when it is indeed a matter of little consequence what prescription is written, or, indeed, who has written it, provided only that it does no mischief.

I should very much have liked to see him again at any time. After the first visit I always knew my patient and felt much interested in him, although I never showed any reference to the fact, preferring to follow his own lead in reference to name, a matter he refers to in the letter of the 3rd inst.

By the way, you know, of course, I received that letter only on Monday morning and lost not an instant in replying, telegraphing that I was doing so.

You ask me to return it – 'his last letter' – as I suspected. I cannot tell you how I was valuing it and that I intended to place it among my most treasured souvenirs, of which I have many. But I cannot refuse it to his suffering and heart-broken widow, if she desires me to return it and will do so. It consists only of a few professional words, a patient to his doctor – nothing more and it is addressed by yourself – as I believe. It is not here – I am writing at the club; but if you still ask me I cannot hesitate an instant and will send it to you.

Come and see me any time you are able, by and by. I will answer any inquiries you may wish to make. I am at home (only let me know a day beforehand, if you can) every morning from 9.30 to 12 – not after, except by quite special arrangement.

With sincere sympathy, believe me, dear Mrs Parnell, yours truly,

HENRY THOMPSON.

My husband was in great pain on the Monday and seemed to feel a sudden horror that he was being held down by some strong unseen power and asked my help – thank God, always *my* help – to fight against it. He tried to get out of bed, although he was too weak to stand and I had to gently force him back and cover him up, telling him how dangerous a chill would be. He said: 'Hold me tight then, yourself, till I can fight those others.' Then he seemed to doze for a few minutes and when he opened his eyes again it was to ask me to lie down beside him and put my hand in his, so that he could 'feel' I was there. I did so and he lay still, quite happy again and spoke of the 'sunny land' where we would go as soon as he was better. 'We will be so happy, Queenie; there are so many things happier than politics.'

He did not sleep that night and the next morning (Tuesday) he was very feverish, with a bright colour on his usually white face. I wanted to send the dogs from the room, because

I feared they would disturb him, but he opened his eyes and said: 'Not Grouse; let old Grouse stay, I like him there.'

His doctor said that for a day or two we could not look for much improvement. After his medicine that afternoon he lay quietly with his eyes closed, just smiling if I touched him. The doctor came in again, but there was no change and he left promising to call early the next morning. During the evening my husband seemed to doze and, listening intently, I heard him mutter 'the Conservative Party'.

Late in the evening he suddenly opened his eyes and said: 'Kiss me, sweet Wifie and I will try to sleep a little.' I lay down by his side and kissed the burning lips he pressed to mine for the last time. The fire of them, fierce beyond any I had ever felt, even in his most loving moods, startled me and as I slipped my hand from under his head he gave a little sigh and became unconscious. The doctor came at once, but no remedies prevailed against this sudden failure of the heart's action and my husband died without regaining consciousness, before his last kiss was cold on my lips.

There is little more to add. All that last night I sat by my husband watching and listening for the look and the word he would never give me again. All that night I whispered to him to speak to me and I fancied that he moved and that the fools who said he was dead did not really know. He had never failed to answer my every look and word before. His face was so peaceful; so well, all the tiredness had gone from it now. I would not open the door because I feared to disturb him – he had always liked us to be alone. And the rain and the wind swept about the house as though the whole world shared my desolation.

He did not make any 'dying speech', or refer in any way at the last to his 'Colleagues and the Irish people', as was at the time erroneously reported. I was too broken then and too indifferent to what any sensation lovers put about to contradict this story, but, as I am now giving to the world the absolutely true account of the Parnell whom I knew and loved, I am able to state that he was incapable of an affectation so complete. The last words Parnell spoke were given to the wife who had never failed him, to the love that was stronger than death – 'Kiss me, sweet Wifie and I will try to sleep a little'.

THE END

[1] These letters were really sent from London.
[2] Sent to Dublin to be posted.
[3] Myself.
[4] Captain O' Shea
[5] That Captain O' Shea had left Eltham for Madrid.
[6] To Captain O' Shea
[7] Captain O' Shea
[8] O' Brien, Barry. *The Life of Parnell*
[9] Captain O' Shea
[10] He was to have addressed a meeting at Naas.
[11] Possibility of arrest
[12] Miss O' Shea here refers to the house of the Comte de ----, to whom she was then engaged. Miss O' Shea called there, with her friend, to break of the engagement owing to her continuous ill-health. She died not very long afterwards.
[13] From Captain O' Shea re. 'Kilmainham Treaty.'
[14] The day of our little daughter's funeral
[15] Lord Morley: has stated that Granville voted for the scheme and Lord Eversley that all Peers voted against it.
[16] Captain O' Shea
[17] My pet name in our early married life for Willie was 'Boysie'.
[18] Biggar was never one of Parnell's bitterest enemies except in his very outspoken objections to the O' Shea's. Parnell much regretted Biggar's death and sent a wreath for the funeral to show; his friendly feeling for him. There was another and more virulent force at work in Galway.
[19] Formerly Lord Richard Grosvenor.